Colman J Mahony

1 December 2005

Cork's Poor Law Palace
Workhouse Life 1838–1890

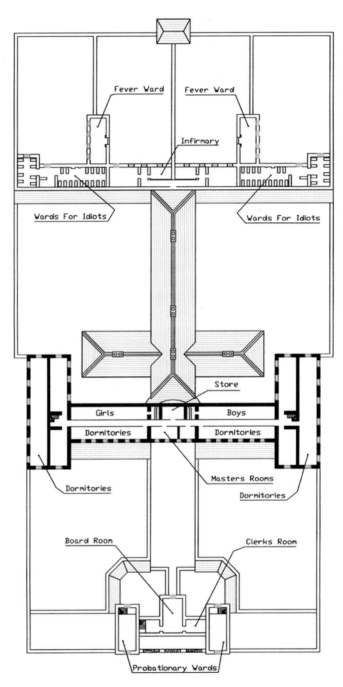

CORK WORKHOUSE FROM AN OFFICIAL PLAN OF 1843
Redrawn from the original in *British Parliamentary Paper 1843, Vol. X, [625] Report from Select Committee . . . to consider the state of the lunatic poor in Ireland . . .* Appendix R.1. page 132 (b)

Cork's Poor Law Palace
Workhouse Life 1838–1890

by

COLMAN O MAHONY

Rosmathún Press
2005

Published in 2005 by
Rosmathún Press
'Rosmathún', 7 Bellevue Terrace,
Monkstown, Co. Cork

British Library Cataloguing in Publication Data
A CIP catalogue record for this book is available
from the British Library

ISBN 0-9551326-0-6
978-0-9551326-0-5

Typeset by Tower Books, Ballincollig, Co. Cork
Printed by Inspire Design and Print, Skibbereen, Co. Cork
Cover Design Inspire Design and Print, Skibbereen, Co. Cork

Contents

	Acknowledgements	vi
	Abbreviations	viii
	Introduction	ix
1	Creation	1
2	Famine	27
3	Removal	73
4	School	98
5	Training	123
6	Work	145
7	Health I	173
8	Health II	205
9	Exiting	236
10	Ideology	272
	Conclusion	293
	Biographical Notes	297
	Appendix 1: Workhouse and hospital dietaries	299
	Appendix 2: Cork Mayors 1837-1891	307
	Appendix 3: John Arnott's entry in Cork Workhouse visitors' book, 6 April 1859	308
	Bibliography	311
	Index	327
	Pictorial Section	331

Acknowledgements

In compiling this book, I have received assistance and encouragement from many institutions and individuals.

The staffs of the Cork City and County Libraries were particularly helpful in providing access to a variety of books and nineteenth century newspapers. The staff of the Boole Library (UCC) were also most helpful and, in particular, I wish to acknowledge the assistance of the personnel in Special Collections (Q-1).

The Cork Archives Institute provided ready access to the records of the Cork Union board of guardians and other documentation. I wish to thank the archivist Brian McGee for granting permission to quote from these records. I also thank former archivist Patricia Mawe (nee Mc Carthy) and Michael Higgins for their assistance.

The staff of the National Archives of Ireland provided access to many sources including the Chief Secretary's Office Registered Papers, Poor Law Commissioners files and a variety of other material. I am grateful for their assistance. I wish to thank the Director of the National Archives for granting permission to refer to, and quote from documents held in the Archives.

Materials including pamphlets, parliamentary papers and reports were made available by the staff of the National Library. The library's director, Aongus Ó hAonghusa, was most helpful in locating specific items.

The British Library at Colindale was helpful in providing copies of nineteenth-century Cork newspapers.

Assistance has been received from many individuals including Kieran Burke, Liam Burke, Frank Heffernan, Pat Holohan, Brendan Mitchell, Owen O Donnell, Ed O Reilly, Ashlin Quinn, Frank Riordan and Martin Thompson.

I owe a large debt of gratitude to Dr Larry Geary who supervised the thesis on which this book is based. His patience and advice were invaluable during its compilation.

Tim Cadogan was most helpful with comments on a pre-publication draft. His thorough reading of the text ensured that points, which needed clarification, or elucidation, were addressed.

Pat Deasy of Tower Books was always helpful and professional and her experience and expertise were invaluable when deciding on presentation and format.

I owe a particularly special debt to my wife Eleanor whose interest and encouragement were invaluable at all stages of the work. Our children Cian, Caoimhe and Caoilte also provided valuable assistance; Caoilte gave further help with the dust jacket design.

In conclusion, I wish to thank *Puta,* who kept me company with her relentless purring, and *Kafka* (RIP), who was an eager and loyal companion on so many pleasant and relaxing rambles.

Finally, this book is humbly dedicated to Eleanor.

Abbreviations

CC	*Cork Constitution*
CE	*Cork Examiner*
CSORP	Chief Secretary's Office Registered Papers
CUL	*Letter Books of Cork Union Board of Guardians*
CUM	*Minute Books of Cork Union Board of Guardians*
NAI	National Archives of Ireland
PP	British Parliamentary Paper
SR	*Southern Reporter*

Introduction

In the popular mind workhouses are associated with humiliation, forced labour, poor conditions and other forms of degradation. It is commonly believed that inmates were deprived of their liberty, fed on poor quality food and forced to work on soul-destroying tasks such as oakum-picking and stone-breaking. It is also held that families were broken up and incarcerated in separate apartments never to meet again until, and unless, they left the institution. The associations with death and burial are perhaps the most enduring and it is commonly believed that all deceased workhouse inmates were routinely buried in a pauper's grave.

This popular perception of workhouses has been largely shaped by stereotypical images from writers of nineteenth century fiction. Charles Dickens's and Charles J. Kickham's depictions of workhouse life as cruel, harsh and dehumanising were in some part responsible for this image. National and local scandals such as those of the Andover workhouse in the 1840s and the Arnott inquiry into the Cork workhouse during 1859 also contributed to the popular view.[1] The negative images of the workhouse and the poor treatment of its inmates were constantly reinforced by regular newspaper reports of boards of guardians' meetings. The most harrowing image of the Irish workhouse comes from the famine period of the 1840s when the destitute, the diseased and the desperate were crammed into its wards and various auxiliary buildings in an often vain attempt to save lives. From that period also comes the image of the mass funerals, and the undignified, hasty and undocumented burials in pits and unmarked graves. Some poor law officials did not dispute these images and in 1863 Poor Law Inspector O Brien described the Cork

---

1 See Norman Longmate, *The Workhouse* (London, 1974), pp. 112-155, 194-220; Ian Anstruther, *The scandal of the Andover workhouse* (Gloucester, 1984 edition); John Arnott, *The investigation into the condition of the children in the Cork Workhouse, with an analysis of the evidence* (Cork, 1859); Terence Brodie, *The Report of Terence Brodie, Esq., M.D., Poor Law Inspector, to the Commissioners for Administering the Laws for the relief of the poor in Ireland, upon an investigation held into the condition of the children in the Cork Workhouse, and the sanitary state of the that institution, together with the minutes of evidence taken during said investigation* (Cork, 1859).

workhouse as 'a resort of misery or misfortune. It is the hospital for the lowest class; it is the home of the distressed; it is the last refuge of the idle, and thriftless, the broken down, the unfortunate. Towards it every-thing that is unlucky naturally gravitates'.[2]

A contrasting image of workhouse life had been put forward by other observers who argued that, in the institution, the poor were guaranteed regular meals, better sanitation and living conditions superior to what they could obtain outside.[3] Its roles as a maternity and general hospital for the poor and as a refuge for the aged, infirm and insane have also been cited in its favour. Again, it has been suggested that poor people entered the workhouse in the hope of being included in one of the emigration schemes to America or to the antipodes. In theory, adults were free to leave the workhouse at short notice, and, therefore, accord-ing to some observers, if hardships were being experienced these could be terminated by seeking a discharge. From the wealth of available evidence, material can be selected to support either opinion.

The early years of the Irish Poor Law had seen the transformation of institutional relief of the poor from the locally managed house of indus-try to the centrally controlled workhouse system.[4] The principal elements in the operation and management of the workhouse were the inmates, the guardians, the staff and the ratepayers, but all operations and deci-sions were overseen by the Poor Law Commissioners (later the Local Government Board). A copy of the transactions at each board of guardians' meeting was sent to the Dublin based Commissioners who questioned many resolutions and often forced the board to reverse hard-fought decisions. Others influencing life in the workhouse included contractors and suppliers of food, milk, fuel, clothing, footwear, bedding materials etc. Weather and seasons also affected the institution. The number of inmates usually decreased during the harvest when some left the house for casual work. The choice of food was also dictated by seasonal influences.

In compiling this study, I sought to establish if inmates of the Cork workhouse were subjected to a harsh vindictive regime or if they enjoyed a life of comparative security with regular meals and clean accommoda-tion. I hoped to disentangle the truth from the fiction and present a realistic and factual account of workhouse life. I examined activities such

2 *Cork Examiner*, 28 May 1863.
3 See David Roberts, 'How cruel was the Victorian Poor Law?', in *The Historical Journal*, Vol. 6, Feb. 1963, p. 101.
4 See Sir George Nicholls, *A history of the Irish Poor Law* (London, 1856, New York 1967 edition), pp. 222-302.

as education, industrial pursuits and health care, all of which had an influence on the daily lives of workhouse inmates.

The famine of the late 1840s and its impact on the workhouse occupies a central section of this book. During that period of hardship a constant battle was waged against food shortages, over crowding, sickness and disease. Battles were also waged in the board room where some guardians were satisfied to provide just enough sustenance to 'keep body and soul together'.[5] Alternative food sources were used to feed the inmates and additional premises had to be rented to cater for the huge number of applicants seeking workhouse relief.[6] The provision of hospital care is also examined. During its early years, the workhouse hospital was shunned by labouring poor, who were willing to suffer privation outside in preference to the 'stigma' of entering the institution. The ambivalent role of the guardians, who so often condoned poor conditions and sub-standard facilities, was not helpful. Nonetheless, in time, the reputation of the workhouse hospital grew as it came 'to resemble a public general hospital'[7], and it eventually became acceptable to a wide range of citizens.

Another chapter is devoted to the disruption caused by the settlement and removal laws, a topic that has been neglected by poor law historians. Under these laws, poor people who applied for workhouse relief in England or Scotland and who were subsequently identified as being Irish, or of Irish extraction, were promptly deported or 'removed' to an Irish port. Many of these unfortunate people had spent their entire lives in England or Scotland and some had no tangible links with Ireland. As Irish unions were not permitted to reciprocate by sending English paupers back to their homes, the one-sided legislation caused great resentment in Ireland. On occasions, proceedings at the Cork board of guardians' meetings were dominated by discussions relating to the admission of destitute paupers who had been unceremoniously discharged from ships at the Cork quays. The plight of the unfortunate deportees was not always the principal consideration and the guardians' main concern was often the extra expense involved in maintaining additional inmates in the workhouse.

---

5 *Cork Examiner* 14 June 1848.
6 Michelle O Mahony, *The impact of the Great Famine on the Cork Union Workhouse* (M.Phil. thesis, UCC, 2000). Her research is based principally on the extant records of the Cork Union board of guardians. Although the scope of the work is restricted by the absence of some minute books, the completed thesis does contain useful material, much of which is presented in a graphic and tabular format. As this present work goes to press, Michelle O Mahony's thesis has been published as *Famine in Cork city* (Cork, 2005).
7 Oliver MacDonagh, *Early Victorian Government 1830-1870* (London, 1977), p. 119.

On admission to the workhouse, applicants 'were compelled to submit to the grinding monotony of institutional routine; their hours of waking and sleeping, their diet, their clothing and their work were subjected to close control'.[8] In the Cork institution, adult inmates participated in a variety of work related activities, such as nursing, cooking, cleaning, baking, shoemaking and tailoring. An organised industrial department functioned during the 1850s but ceased to operate after a few years when the number of skilled able-bodied inmates declined. During that period also a capstan mill was used to produce flour for the workhouse bakery. This mill fulfilled the dual role of a production unit and a vehicle for punishing inmates by subjecting them to a repetitive and strenuous labour task.

In general, workhouse labour tasks *were* repetitive and unrewarding. Such was also the case with workhouse education, which was often casual and grudgingly provided. No real effort was made to make it interesting or relevant. Classrooms frequently served as holding-centres for detaining the unfortunate children during the daytime. Many of the guardians had little interest in improving the situation. They viewed the education of children as a luxury which was denied to many ratepayers. They adapted a dog-in-the-manger attitude and refused to take cognisance of recommendations from education officers. Thus, a flawed and unimaginative system of education was perpetrated.

In a few instances, such as when a Ladies Visiting Committee organised a system of industrial training for girls and when an apprentice training scheme was inaugurated for boys, the participating children derived real benefit. The reward for successful participation was employment away from the workhouse. The lot of workhouse inmates was also improved by a number of innovations such as the boarding out of infants and young children. As a result of this scheme, many young inmates were placed in good homes and adopted by families. Emigration schemes also allowed inmates leave the workhouse. In new surroundings the emigrants were released from the stigma of their workhouse identity and were free to start a new life.

A wealth of material, including the minute books and letter books of the Cork board of guardians, official documentation and reports, as well as full runs of local newspapers, has been used in compiling this study. A weekly record of the business transacted at the board of guardians' meetings is retained in the minute books. Although this material is irreplaceable, its brevity often restricts its value. Reports of the guardians'

---

8 Kathryn Morrison, The *Workhouse A study of Poor-Law Buildings in England* (Swindon, 1999), p.1.

meetings as published in the local newspapers, along with editorial comments and the views of correspondents have more than compensated for this shortcoming. At least two different Cork newspapers, with contrasting and often conflicting allegiances and viewpoints, are available for the period covered by this study. For the 1840s and much of the 1850s, full runs of at least three local newspapers are available.

The reports as published in the different newspapers are usually a faithful and matter-of-fact record of the business transacted and the motions passed. Unlike the often-stark records in the minute books, the newspapers consistently record the many and conflicting speeches and arguments which preceded the passing of particular resolutions, thus illuminating many areas of shadow. Frequently, spotlights are directed on all sides of a conflict, which allow us interpret the situation and make an informed evaluation of the issue. Dr Denis C. O Connor's memory of his period as medical officer in the Cork workhouse is a useful work.[9] The value of the book as a totally 'personal memoir' may be undermined because some of the content seems to have been written with the assistance of a newspaper cuttings file.

In the following pages, I have endeavoured to present a balanced account of the business and motives of the Cork board of guardians, as they related to the interests of the poor and workhouse inmates. The board members represented many different interests, including farming, business and ratepayers of various political creeds. Although the board's primary function was the delivery of poor relief, a conflict of interest among its members frequently interfered with its basic mission.

Applicants for workhouse relief included the aged and frail, the sick and diseased, the unemployed, the unemployable, deserted wives and children, unmarried mothers, prostitutes, abandoned children, and families who had become destitute. Applicants underwent a thorough and searching interrogation before admission was granted, so it is probable that the vast majority of inmates were deserving of the relief granted. Some guardians saw themselves as protectors of the poor and they did all in their power to ensure that the inmates were treated well and given adequate food. Others, who were principally interested in their own electoral constituency,[10] saw their roles as overseers of the workhouse and its management and they strove to keep expenditure to a minimum and thus protect the interests of the ratepayers. The conflicting interests often

---

9 Denis C. O Connor, *Seventeen years of workhouse life* (Dublin, 1861)

10 *Report from the Select Committee on Law of Rating (Ireland); together with the proceedings of the Committee, minutes of evidence and Appendix.* PP 1871, Vol. X, [423]. pp. 220.

resulted in lengthy disagreements at board meetings. Obstructing well-meaning proposals became a regular tactic. Those who sought to prevent or delay improvements in diet or conditions tabled counter-proposals or amendments. The behaviour of guardians and the style of business at these early meetings set the pattern for the future decades and the hapless workhouse inmates were the victims and sufferers in this political and often personal conflict.

1 Creation

The 1838 Act for the effectual relief of the destitute poor in Ireland (1&2 Victoriae, cap. 56) divided the country into 130 administrative units, or unions, which assumed responsibility for the welfare of poor and destitute individuals and families. Many writers have discussed the establishment of the Irish poor law system.[1] On a national level Poor Law Commissioners oversaw the administration of relief. Local administration was under the direct control of a board of guardians which was elected annually to represent the often conflicting interests and aspirations of themselves, their electors and the workhouse staff and inmates. The guardians appointed committees to monitor different aspects of the workhouse machine such as admissions, administration, education and expenditure. Reports from the committees were presented at the weekly meetings of the board of guardians. Reflecting the monotony of workhouse life, these reports were generally of a routine nature. Suggestions contained in the reports were frequently implemented without a discussion but proceedings were occasionally livened up by a heated debate.

Relief and assistance for the destitute was available in the union's workhouse, which was managed by a staff of officers under the charge of a workhouse master. Subordinate officers included a matron who had responsibility for the female departments, a storeman who took charge of purchasing and distributing food, clothing and other supplies, and medical officers who were responsible for the health and welfare of the workhouse inmates. The more routine business was carried out by minor officials and inmates assisted in departments such as the kitchens, laundries, stores, nurseries and hospital wards.

Matters relating to finance were a frequent cause of dissension amongst the guardians. All decisions, contracts, appointments and policy changes were closely monitored by the Poor Law Commissioners, who received a copy of the guardians' minutes and were also kept well

---

1 See for instance: Helen Burke, *The people and the Poor Law in nineteenth century Ireland* (West Sussex, 1987), pp. 24-50; Christine Kinealy, *This great calamity – The Irish Famine* (Dublin, 1994), pp. 13-30; R.B. McDowell, *The Irish Administration – 1801-1914* (London, 1964), pp. 175-180.

informed by their inspectors, and through correspondence from interested or devious guardians or observers. Within a short time of its foundation, the Irish poor law system became a well-regulated and highly efficient administrative machine.

During the spring of 1839 official documentation on the administration of the new poor law unions was circulated. Among the documents was an official order dated 3 April 1839, which declared the Cork Union.[2] The union included the city and its hinterland, an area of 265 square miles or 169,732 statute acres, and, according to the census of 1841, had a population of 163,492 persons. To facilitate the election of members to the new board of guardians, the city was divided into twelve electoral divisions and the county area had thirteen divisions. A total of 40 guardians were to be elected, with the two areas each returning 20 members. The board was to be completed by the nomination of 13 ex-officio guardians.[3]

The first elections took place in May 1839 and the following guardians were returned for the city wards:

Lee Ward: Edward England and James Minhear
St. Patrick's: William Fagan and Jer. E. Mc Carthy
Glanmire: Paul McSwiney and John Harley
Corn Market: Jer. J. Murphy and George Crawford
St. Finbarr's: William Crawford* and Samuel Lane*
Mansion House: Samuel Lane* and J. Stack Murphy
Exchange: Daniel Meagher and Thomas Lyons
Custom House: William Crawford* and John McDonnell
Blackrock: Michael Mahony
Bishopstown: Richard Gould
St. Mary's: Thomas Wyse
St. Ann's: Edward Hackett.
(W. Crawford* and S. Lane* were elected for two wards and it does not seem that alternative candidates were subsequently elected.)

In the county divisions, the elected guardians were:

Inniskenny: Charles Mathew and Daniel Lombard
Carrigaline: Colonel Thomas Burke and Christopher Lloyd
Monkstown: John Roberts and David Cagney
Cove: Samuel T.W. French, Thomas Robinson and William Cottrell

---

2 *Poor Law Commissioners Annual Report* (1840), pp. 48, 451. See also *Cork Constitution* (hereafter CC) 4 April 1839.

3 *Poor Law Commissioners Annual Report* (1839), pp. 24, 94; *Poor Law Commissioners Annual Report* (1842), Appendix E. No.9, p. 374, see also *Southern Reporter* (hereafter *SR*) 2 April, 11 April, 13 April, 18 April 1839; *CC* 14 April, 30 April 1839.

Ballincollig: Joshua Sullivan
Blarney: St. John Jeffreys
Inniscarra: Horace Townsend
Grenagh: Michael Murphy and William Low
Whitechurch: Joseph Hayes
Carrignavar: Thomas Shinnick
Rathcooney: Henry Morrogh
Kilquane: John Gleeson
Glanmire: Cornelius O Callaghan and John Cantillon.

Before the advent of the Irish poor laws, Cork's destitute poor were accommodated in an institution known as the house of industry, which stood on a site adjacent to the modern South Infirmary hospital. Under the 1838 Act this institution was to be superseded by a new workhouse. On 4 June, 47 of the new poor law guardians held their first meeting at which they elected William Crawford as chairman, Samuel Lane vice chairman and Joseph Hayes deputy vice chairman.[4] The day-to-day running of the house of industry remained under the control of the former governors for some further months.[5]

The Cork house of industry was retained as a refuge for the local poor and, by an order dated 15 February 1840 it was designated as the temporary workhouse for the Cork Union. A suitable location for a new workhouse was investigated but a number of sites, including one at Ballincollig, were rejected because of their distance from the city centre.[6] The Poor Law Commissioners also rejected the proposal to convert the house of industry because it would not provide adequate facilities for separating, or classifying, inmates by age and sex 'without which the Work-house would be open to imposition of every kind'.[7] Because of misgivings about the plan to construct a new workhouse,[8] a detailed survey of the house of industry was carried out and its unsuitability for conversion into a modern workhouse was confirmed.

Several locations were investigated and eventually a site on sloping ground between the Evergreen Road and the Passage Road was chosen.

---

4 *CC* 30 May, 6 June 1839; *SR* 30 May 1839; *Minute Books of Cork Board of Guardians* (hereafter, *CUM*) 4 June 1839; *SR* 4 June 1839. William Crawford died near Bristol on 6 April 1840.
5 *SR* 13 June 1839.
6 *CUM* 24 February 1840; *Poor Law Commissioners Annual Report* (1840), pp. 48, appendix D, pp. 308-10; *SR* 6 July, 18 April 1839.
7 *CC* 13 June 1839; *SR* 21 January, 9 February, 13 June, 13 July 1839; see also report on state of the workhouse in *CC* 4 May 1839.
8 *CC* 6 July, 9 July 1839; See also: Gerard O Brien, 'The New Irish Poor Law in pre-Famine Ireland: A case study', *Irish Economic and Social History*, Vol. XII (1985), pp. 36-40.

The owner, a Mr Foley, agreed to sell nine acres for £740 plus a yearly rent of £35. 1s. 6d. and the site was to have access from both roads.[9] Following criticism of this site, the Poor Law Commissioners organised a thorough inspection to ascertain 'the salubrity of the site, including thereon the quality of the water and the power of drainage'.[10] The water supply was found to be 'perfectly innocuous' and provisions for waste and sewage disposal were also deemed to be adequate.[11] Thereafter site preparation and structural work commenced at the new institution.

The recruitment of staff went ahead and in December 1839 David Barry of Cappoquin was elected workhouse master and Mrs Catherine Horgan was elected matron, at salaries of £80 and £60 respectively, plus residential accommodation, coal, candles and workhouse rations. A few weeks later Dr Denis C. O Connor was appointed workhouse medical officer.[12] Dr O Connor had been physician to the Cork General Dispensary for more than five years and had, in his own opinion, 'an intimate knowledge of the diseases and habits of the poor'. William Stoker Gardiner was appointed apothecary to the institution. Rev. William Hall, Rector of St. Nicholas', was appointed Protestant chaplain and Rev. George Sheehan, Catholic chaplain at salaries of £50 per annum each.[13]

9 PP 1844, Vol. XXX, [562], *Report on workhouse contracts*, pp. 56, 57; *Poor Law Commissioners Annual Report* (1841), Appendix E, No.13, pp. 208-9; See also *CUM* 21 November, 1839; Gerard O Brien, *The administration of the Poor Law in Ireland* (MA thesis, 1980), pp. 102-3. To secure a disputed right-of-way and to prevent intrusive building work, the Poor Law Commissioners also purchased an additional strip of land between their site and the Passage road.

10 *SR* 28 November 1839, 9 April 1840; *Poor Law Commissioners Annual Report* (1841); p. 122; PP 1844, Vol. XXX, [562] pp. 57 and 113; see also NAI, CSORP 1859 5550, Document No. 26 (I) Report by W. Voules of 22 July 1840; (II) Report by Denis Phelan of 27 July 1840.

11 The 32 feet deep well provided 4,540 gallons of water each day, which was used in all departments of the workhouse including the kitchen, washhouses, yards, water-cocks and hospital. A surprisingly small amount of just 270 gallons per day, on three days a week, was used to augment the supply from rain-water tanks in the hospital washhouse. *Poor Law Commissioners Annual Report* (1842), Appendix D. No.1, pp109-10. The entire system was inspected again in 1844 when it was falsely reported that the supply was contaminated with sewage, see: PP 1843, Vol. XLVI, [227]; *Return of No. of workhouses with unfit water and sewage* p.8; PP 1844, Vol. XXX, [562], *Report of the Commission for inquiring into the execution of the contracts for certain Union Workhouses in Ireland*, p. 57; PP1844, Vol. XXX, [568], *Appendix to the report of the Commissioners appointed to inquire into the execution of the contracts for certain Union Workhouses* in Ireland, pp. 18-20.

12 *CUM* 2 December, 23 December 1839, 10 February, 24 February 1840; *CC* 25 January 1840; *SR* 5 December, 24 December, 26 December 1839; 25 January, 11 February, 13 February 1840.

13 *CUM* 17 February, 29 February, 23 March 1840; *CC* 23 January 1840; *SR* 20 February, 26 March 1840.

Admission and Classification

At the meeting on 29 February 1840, when the House of Industry governors finally withdrew and handed over total control to the guardians, there were 1,401 inmates in the institution. This number was made up as follows:

MALES: 214 aged and infirm; 12 able-bodied; 63 boys above 13 years of age, and 97 boys under 13 years old, making a total of 386

FEMALES: 245 aged and infirm; 375 able-bodied women and girls over 13 years of age, and 197 girls under 13 years old, making a total of 817.

There were a further 198 children of both sexes under five years of age.[14] The small number of able-bodied men was an indication that the institution was resorted to by this class only in emergencies. When work was scarce, many families had to enter the workhouse but frequently the husband remained outside and searched for work. This was also necessary so as to retain the family's interest in their dwelling place and to ensure that it would not lose occupancy. Furthermore, if the husband did enter the workhouse, he would become tainted with the stigma of pauperism and thus damage his future prospects of acquiring employment. As it was contrary to regulations for family members to remain outside when others entered the workhouse, the wives registered either as widows or deserted when they sought admission. When the situation improved outside, the wife and children discharged themselves and rejoined the husband.

Prior to admission to the workhouse, paupers were cleansed and clothed in the institution's uniform, which consisted of a brown frieze suit for men, while the women's clothing included coarse linen undergarments, brown frieze petticoat and a short bed gown. To discourage theft, the clothes were 'made so distinctive as to be easily detected if seen outside doors'.[15] Because of a shortage of furniture, men were obliged to sleep three together in beds measuring five feet by three feet, and in the boys' department 97 inmates also slept three to a bed. As this arrangement was 'injurious to the health of the paupers and so revolting to the feelings' it was decided that no more than two adults or three youths under 13 years of age should be permitted to sleep in one bed, so new furniture was ordered.[16] In the female department women were sleeping

---

14 *CUM* 29 February 1840; *CC* 27 February, 3 March, 5 March 1840; *SR* 3 March 1840.
15 *CUM* 29 February 1840; *SR* 27 February, 3 March 1840; *CC* 29 February 1840.
16 *CC* 5 March 1840.

three or four to a bed and sometimes when young children accompanied them this brought the number in some beds to eight persons.[17] Rev. George Sheehan, the Catholic chaplain, addressed the situation, and with his assistance, the guardians managed to separate the women from their children, with promises that regular visiting times would be introduced. When the new arrangements were implemented in April 1840, 321 able-bodied women shared 164 beds, 51 nursing mothers with 49 infants had 56 beds, 145 girls under 13 years of age had 63 beds, and 72 children under five years shared 19 beds.[18] The guardians were pleased with the changes, which were calculated to provide 180 extra female sleeping places. Under the workhouse classification system inmates were placed in one of the following categories:

1. Males above the age of 15 years.
2. Boys above the age of 2 years, and under 15 years.
3. Females above the age of 15 years.
4. Girls above the age of 2 years, and under 15 years.
5. Children under 2 years of age.[19]

This new classification system took about three weeks to implement and part of the arrangements included vacating wards during daytime and using the day rooms instead. By its nature the classification system was inflexible and within weeks, a steady flow of applicants augmented the number of inmates by over 200, and crowding was again evident.[20] During the transition the guardians noticed some unacceptable intermingling of inmates, and when the chairman of the board found a group of 'good-looking boys' whitewashing the girls' ward he objected and insisted that women carry out the work. In the workhouse kitchen he noticed that women and men worked together. This was stopped immediately and instead, meals were carried to the entrance of the female wards in barrows and then distributed by women.[21] The new classification system did not separate prostitutes from other female inmates, and on a number of occasions it was found that attempts had been made to pressurise poor women into a life of prostitution.[22] The workhouse chaplains reported that 'immoral' women come into the house solely to tempt certain girls

---

17 *SR* 26 March 1840; see also *CUM* 20 December 1841 and 14 February 1842.
18 See table and report in *CUM* 13 April 1840 also *SR* 2 April 1840; *CC* 2 May 1840 provides details of accommodation at the start of May.
19 Thomas Aiskew Mooney, *Compendium of the Irish Poor Law; and general manual for Poor Law Guardians and their officers* (Dublin, 1887), Articles of workhouse rules, p. 284.
20 *SR* 28 May 1840.
21 *CUM* 13 April 1840; *SR* 16 June 1840.
22 *CC* 2 February 1841; *SR* 2 February 1841.

into a life of prostitution. They suggested that the 'deprived and virtuous' should be isolated so that the '*notoriously* immoral' could not influence innocent girls.[23] Though a committee was appointed to implement this suggestion, procuresses still came from brothels in the city to seduce attractive girls with offers of fine clothing and other goods.[24]

The guardians addressed many lapses of discipline which had been tolerated or overlooked by the house of industry governors. Workhouse tin-ware was regularly damaged by inmates who placed it on open fires to boil water or milk – this practice was forbidden by the guardians.[25] It was noticed that in the confusion surrounding the distribution of meals, some inmates managed to get two helpings and others got nothing. Another practice that caused concern was the casual manner in which inmates were allowed to leave the house in search of employment. To help stop these abuses it was suggested that each pauper would be given a number, which would be stamped on clothing or worn as a badge, and also embossed on their tin-ware.[26] They were to sit at the same place during each meal, and inmates leaving the house were to get an official pass. The guardians' resolve to discourage readmissions was rejected by the Poor Law Commissioners on the grounds that destitute people could not be deprived of workhouse relief or discouraged from seeking employment or assistance outside.[27]

In the months prior to the declaration of the Cork Union, the number of beggars arriving in the city increased from an acceptable trickle to a 'frightful and alarming nuisance'. The workhouse was seen as a magnet, for 'the Irish poor are so habituated to wretchedness – they know so little of the comforts of life, that the scantiest provision, which to an English-man would be starvation, will be luxury to them'.[28] Some sorry cases sought admission to the institution. During August 1839 Michael Toomy, 'a strong-built man, with a bad eye and a worse one, and a short leg and a shorter one' was admitted. A misfortunate woman with a breast disease also sought admission. Previously the Cork authorities had sent her to Dublin to reside with her brother. She failed to locate him and the Dublin board gave her 1s.8d. to help her return to Cork. After a three-week walk, the Cork board took no pity on her and, in turn, sent her

---

23 *CUM* 1 February 1841.
24 *Cork Examiner* (hereafter *CE)* 17 September, 22 September 1841.
25 *CUM* 25 May 1840.
26 *CUM* 21 February 1840.
27 *CUM* 30 March, 13 April, 28 May, 25 May, 15 June 1840; *SR* 18 June 1840; see also *SR* 27 February 1840.
28 *SR* 11 September 1838.

back to Dublin on the next steamer.[29] Frequently a large number of applicants sought admission on the same day. On 1 January 1840 of 84 applicants, just four were refused admission to the house. A week later 90 people applied and amongst those admitted were two Spanish sailors whose ship had sailed from Cove. At that time also, Mary Murphy, a 101-year-old woman came to the board room leaning on an 18 inch long walking stick 'so completely was she weighed down with age'. Only after her request that 'her stick, which had been her companion for about sixty years, should on her demise, be laid quietly alongside her in the coffin' was agreed to, did she enter the house. A short time later two prostitutes, one from Clonmel and her companion from Portsmouth, were admitted to the house.[30] In early 1840 about a quarter of the workhouse inmates were not residents of the Cork Union. Regardless of their residence, destitute applicants had to be accepted in any workhouse and they could not be forcibly ejected.[31] Many of the admissions were people 'who had seen better days' and their ranks included shoemakers, tailors, and weavers, deserted wives and deserted children. Among them were individuals who had previously left the house in search of work or had gone out seeking parents or 'run-away-husbands'. Also admitted were healthy young women and skilled workers 'who had out-worked their strength' or whose age prevented them from earning an adequate living.[32] The process of re-admission caused much annoyance to guardians who complained about the time wasted 'in the drudgery of wading through' the same cases, week after week. An increasing flow of unemployed tradesmen returning from England was also evident in the early 1840s.[33]

Dr O Connor criticised the admission of 'dying cases' who were sent in by relatives or friends so as to avoid burial expenses. This practice was not confined to the poor, and better-off people were known to hire cars and send sickly aged relatives to the workhouse. Dr O Connor expressed his fear that the reputation of the institution would be adversely affected by an increased death rate. The corpses of deceased inmates were useful for medical demonstrations but in December 1840 the guardians passed a resolution that it 'cannot sanction the giving up for anatomical purposes the bodies of such persons as shall occasionally die in this establishment'.[34] Little dignity, however, was attached to the workhouse

---

29 *SR* 17 August 1839.
30 *SR* 2 January, 9 January, 18 April 1840; *CC* 23 January 1840.
31 *SR* 25 February; 27 February 1840.
32 *SR* 11 May, 15 June 1841.
33 *SR* 7 September, 14 September 1841.
34 *CUM* 7 December 1840; *CC* 8 December 1840.

burials; cheap coffins were purchased and the 'miserable' caskets regularly disintegrated en-route to the graveyard with the result that corpses were carried along on a handful of loose boards. When local residents complained about the mode of conveying bodies, the guardians decided to use a hearse instead of workhouse inmates to transport the dead.[35] Because of the 'indecency and carelessness' with which the corpses were interred at St. Joseph's graveyard, its patron, Fr Theobald Mathew, was forced to send an official complaint to the guardians.[36]

The New Workhouse

The new workhouse was declared fit for the reception of paupers before the end of 1841 and its building work and materials were described as 'above average'.[37] The move to the new premises commenced on 23 December, but many of the inmates were reluctant to leave their familiar surroundings. A large number of the women were drunk and several had to be forcibly removed on stretchers. On arrival in the new complex, some of the men and women scaled the boundary wall and in the confusion 100 workhouse suits and 11½ pairs of blankets were stolen by decamping inmates.[38] Disorder reigned for some time, and windows and furniture were broken.[39] During a major riot in mid-January, about 500 women took over the institution. They broke windows, scaled walls and fought with the police. Poor quality potatoes were the principal cause of that disturbance which was quelled with some difficulty.[40] Many locks were broken and about 40 square feet of glass was demolished. Thirty-six women were expelled from the workhouse as a result of the disturbance.[41] Some guardians had sympathy for the female inmates who were forced to roam about the institution as they lacked a day room. They

35 *CUM* 3 May, 21 June, 12 July 1841; *SR* 28 June, 5 July 1842; *CC* 28 June 1842.
36 *CC* 2 December 1844.
37 PP 1844, Vol. XXX, [562], Report, pp. 55, 57; for details of the building costs etc., see also PP 1843, [275], *Return relative to erecting Poorhouses*, p. 14; PP 1847 vol. I.V, [157], *An account of the sum advanced . . . for building workhouses* p.4; PP 1844, Vol. XIV, [441], *Report from Select Committee on Union Workhouses (Ireland)*; see also PP 1843, Vol. XLVI, op. cit., pp. 78-9.
38 *CUM* 20 December, 27 December 1841; *CC* 28 December 1841; *CE* 24, 29 December 1841.
39 *SR* 11 January, 18 January 1842.
40 *CUM* 24 and 31 January 1842; *CC* 22 January, 25 January, 1 February 1842; *SR* 22, 25 January 1842 also *Poor Law Commissioners Annual Report* (1841), pp. 8-9.
41 A number of them were eventually readmitted to the workhouse. *SR* 8 February, 22 February 1842.

attempted to use the dining hall as a base because they had nowhere to sit and no employment to keep them occupied. Also, in the new complex inadequate arrangements were in force for separating prostitutes from the other female inmates.[42]

The grounds were unfinished and unsightly and:

> the entrance to the new Workhouse is . . . a long, narrow, bridle-road, barely of sufficient width to admit one of our "gingles", and that is in so infamous a state that the driver is compelled to dismount, wade ankle deep in mire, and lead his horse at the very slowest pace, in order to secure from dislocation the springs of his car, and the limbs of horse and passengers. This passage is of a straggling and most irregular formation, with not more than twenty feet of the same level, and so deep are the ruts, that both horse and guide often descend to their knees before they can find the centre of gravity. On the right, as you enter this passage, you find a low flat undulating, stretch of ground; – but the left is studded with deep precipitous earth-banks, mounds, pools of water, and long-exhausted lime stone quarries, all forming the margin of the road.[43]

Some male inmates were put to work on landscaping the site and roadway, and others were employed in washing yards, breaking stones and raising the height of the boundary wall from five to fourteen feet.[44] Following a private tour of the workhouse, in company with the Mayor of Cork, on 18 July 1842, the Marquis of Downshire criticised some aspects of the establishment.[45] Included on his list were the 'most shameful, most disgraceful, and most discreditable' toilets, inadequate ventilation and an inefficient sewerage system.[46]

Conditions in the New Workhouse

Early in the life of the new board of guardians, sub-committees, including a workhouse-committee, a finance-committee and an admission-committee, were appointed. When the new workhouse committee inspected the house it found that classification was unsatisfactory, discipline was lax and employment for inmates still remained

---

42 *CUM* 31 January 1842; *SR* 25 January, 2 February 1842.
43 *SR* 11 January 1842.
44 *CUM* 3, 10, 17, 24 January 1842; *Letter Books of Cork Union Board of Guardians* (hereafter *CUL*) 22 January 1842; *SR* 18 January, 25 January 1842.
45 The Marquis of Downshire was a landowner of extensive Irish property. It was not uncommon that visitors to Cork were taken on a tour of the workhouse.
46 *CUM* 18 July 1842; *SR* 19 July 1842.

an aspiration. In the wards 'the aged and infirm were classed with the young – the decayed artisan, and the reduced householder, with the common mendicant – the living with the dying – all was evidently a mass of confusion'.[47]

During his visit to the workhouse in the summer of 1842 the Marquis of Downshire was critical that the inmates were not employed and suggested that able-bodied females should be put into service outside the house. Able-bodied males were given tasks and some were busy levelling and paving yards. A request for 'two sets of men's harnesses' for manipulating trucks gives an insight into the workhouse master's opinion on how the unfortunate inmates should be treated.[48] The guardians rejected this opportunity to further humiliate the men and did not accede to the request. They were not generous to the workhouse boys and refused to sanction footwear for those engaged in breaking stones, even though 'their feet were wounded and bleeding'.[49] Other roles undertaken by inmates included those of wardmasters and mistresses, each having responsibility for three wards. Following the evening roll call these officers were locked into the wards with the inmates and released on the following morning, for which they were rewarded with an evening supper.[50] Paupers who acted as nurses in the workhouse hospital also received food and a small sum of money each week. As a cost-saving measure the allowance was withdrawn in July 1842. The nurses responded by discontinuing their service, which left young children and other patients without attention. When the women failed to respond to intimidation, they were put into the refractory wards, or confinement cells as a punishment. At around the same time a food allowance for school assistants was also withdrawn.[51]

For the vast majority of inmates, life in the workhouse consisted of idleness and boredom punctuated by meals, bedtime and gossip. The inmates made little effort to keep their own areas tidy and an inspector reported that all sorts of goods were hoarded in the wards. The beds and bedding were 'in a very unsatisfactory state – dirty and ragged and full of food and other things hid in them by the paupers – in one bed I found a tea pot – a chamber pot – some soap – some butter – a bundle of men's old clothing – a bundle of women's old clothing – a pair of shoes and a

---

47 *CUM* 25 April 1842, plus *SR* 5 April, 25 April 1842.
48 *SR* 19 July, 26 July 1842.
49 *CUM* 5 December 1842; *SR* 6 December 1842; *CC* 6 December 1842.
50 *SR* 3 May 1842.
51 *CUL* 3 August, 27 August 1842; *CC* 19 April, 12 July 1842; *SR* 14 July, 19 July, 30 August 1842.

lot of rags – In other beds I found food and articles of all kinds – especially rags and old clothing'.[52] Between September 1843 and September
1844, 104 tons of bedding straw were supplied to the workhouse. Nineteen tons were used in the hospital where the packing in each bed was
replaced with 24 lbs. of new straw each month, or more frequently, if the
doctors demanded a change.[53]

Fearing that they would interfere with the market or provoke opposition from local manufacturers, the guardians were reluctant to become
involved in the production of items to be sold outside the house. As a safe
alternative, workhouse labour was confined to commercially non-compet-
itive activities like stone-breaking, oakum-picking or spinning. An internal
report recommended that male inmates should manufacture workhouse
clothing. It was advocated that females could produce lace work or straw
bonnets, but the Poor Law Commissioners rejected a suggestion that any
profit from the venture could be given to the women on their leaving the
workhouse.[54] Although the Commissioners were aware of the difficulties
of providing employment, they advocated that any boy leaving the workhouse should do so 'imbued with habits of industry, and with his frame
braced and strengthened, and inured to laborious exertion, and with his
temper and mental faculties duly cultivated, and above all with a sense of
religious duty deeply impressed upon his mind'.[55]

In the period from its formation to 25 March 1842 the Cork Board of
Guardians expended just £16.9s.2d. on 'utensils and materials for
setting the poor to work'.[56] Not surprisingly, little was accomplished and
by mid 1844 the workhouse was being criticised as 'a horrid Bastille, the
dwelling-place of lethargic indolence and unbroken sloth – injurious to
the individual, destructive to the public. The citizens are compelled to
support, nay to perpetuate, a system of unproductive idleness in the very
heart of an active, bustling commercial community'. The inmates
became lazy and those leaving the house departed as they would 'an
ordinary jail, despised, helpless, oftentimes corrupted'.[57] Most of the
young male inmates had no work ethic and, although it was advocated
that they should be trained as agricultural labourers, just a few orphans

---

52 NAI, Poor Law Commissioners, Letters to James Burke 1844, 13 November
   1844.
53 *CUM* 28 October 1844; 25 October 1845. At that time the workhouse had 36
   beds for sick and aged inmates – about half were in the hospital and the remainder were in the infirm wards. *CE* 29 July 1844.
54 *SR* 29 September 1840.
55 *Poor Law Commissioners Annual Report* (1841), p. 10.
56 PP 1843, Vol. XLVI, [193], *Expenses of each Poor Law Union*, pp. 4, 10.
57 *SR* 26 June 1844.

worked with the house tradesmen. This work was reserved for orphan boys because it was feared that some parents would send their sons into the workhouse for training if others were eligible.[58] In an attempt to provide employment, a washhouse was constructed and clothing was washed and ironed by the pauper women.[59]

Discipline

The workhouse classification system had not been fully implemented by the end of 1842 and in some areas different categories were still grouped together. For example in the women's wards healthy and diseased prostitutes mixed with 'poor unfortunate but virtuous girls'.[60] An anonymous letter alleging that two women had attempted to seduce a ward master initiated a 'delicate investigation'. The matter was discussed at some length and one guardian said that he had no doubt that 'immorality and demoralisation prevailed to a frightful extent within the walls of the Cork Work House'. The allegation was strongly denied by officials such as Rev. G. Sheehan, Dr D.C. O Connor, P. Swiney, the current workhouse master, C. Horgan, the workhouse mistress, and George Carr, the storekeeper, none of whom had ever seen any evidence of immoral conduct. They were satisfied that it could 'not possibly be practised here, without being speedily detected and rigorously and justly punished'.[61] Though the ward master was 'honourably acquitted', not everyone was convinced that depravity could not be found in the Cork workhouse.[62] In June 1843 when two paupers were found to be pregnant, one claimed that an inmate had seduced her; the other said that a staff member was the

---

58 *CE* 3 July 1844; *SR* 2 July 1844; *CUM* 26 June 1843, 1 July, 15 July 1844; also *SR* 13 December 1842.

59 *CUM* 18 December 1843, 29 January, 11 March 1844, 5 April, 3 May, 9 August 1845; *SR* 31 October 1843, 23 January 1844.

60 *CUM* 30 January 1843; *SR* 22 November 1842; *CC* 6 September 1842. See also PP 1846, Vol. XI, *Medical Charities*, p. 277. Workhouse classification had three purposes, 'the provision of treatment according to the needs of each class; deterrence and discipline; and the prevention of 'moral' contagion arising from the mixing of men and women, adults and children, sane and insane and sick and healthy'. David Englander, *Poverty and Poor Law Reform in Britain: From Chadwick to Booth, 1834-1914* (Essex, 1998), p.32.

61 *CE* 17 November, 18 November 1842; *SR* 15 November, 22 November 1842. The signed denial was published in the local press and the Poor Law Commissioners were outraged that workhouse staff had engaged in this unofficial and unethical action. *CUL* 17 December 1842; *CUM* 21 November, 28 November, 19 December 1842.

62 *SR* 19 November 1842; *CE* 23 November, 30 November 1842.

father of her child.[63] Under questioning, one of them, a widow named Catherine Castles, claimed that Noble Rogers, an assistant in the boys' school, was the culprit. An investigation showed that poor classification was certainly interfering with discipline and 'it was all owing to the bad construction of the establishment by which the inmates could have such intercourse', and the master and matron were directed to prohibit further communication between male and female wards.[64]

Some months later the diverse group in the women's ward was composed of females ranging in age from 13 to 60 years, all of whom spent most of their time in the same room and yard.[65] The women spent much of the day lazing in corridors and passage-ways in the vicinity of the dining room with the nearby bread store being a particularly busy place of rendezvous. The male store workers had regular contact with female inmates as a result. Rev. Sheehan brought this to the attention of the guardians and, although he welcomed the developing friendships, he had concerns about 'alliances of a less honourable character'. As a consequence of the contacts at the store a number of marriages had taken place. Thomas Sullivan, a deputy storekeeper, had married an inmate named Mary Hogan, and James Crofts, a pauper assistant, had married another inmate named Spriggs. Sullivan had returned to the workhouse 43 hours after his wedding and Crofts, who was five years in the institution, had gone out of the house to marry at Shandon. When Rev. Sheehan made his report a liaison had just commenced between a deputy storekeeper and a young Catholic inmate named Twohy. The couple had left the house to spend some time together in the city; O Brien, the storeman, had returned but the girl remained out of the house.[66]

Rev. Sheehan attempted to discuss the matter with the individuals themselves but when this failed he made his report to the house committee. As all the men involved with the inmates were Protestants, a rational discussion on the issues became difficult when the priest's concerns were misinterpreted as stemming solely from religious motives. There may have been some truth in this because Thomas Sullivan had changed his religion from Catholic to Protestant some 18 years previously and Mary Hogan had become a Protestant just one month before her wedding.[67] Alfred Greer of the house committee accused Rev. Sheehan of 'patronising persons of immoral – nay, abominable characters' and said that

---

63   *CC* 27 June 1843; *SR* 27 June 1843.
64   *SR* 4 July 1843; *CE* 5 July 1843.
65   *CUM* 30 January 1843; *SR* 31 January 1843.
66   *SR* 2 July 1844; *CE* 3 July 1844; *CUM* 10 July 1843.
67   *CC* 2 July 1844.

immoral conduct resulted from paupers assembling together for Sunday Mass. He also implied that people who were guilty of crimes of a 'diabolical character' in the workhouse had been married in a hurry in the porter's lodge, and he specifically mentioned the former teacher James Reilly in this context. He also asked why charges had not been made against Michael Hayes and Mary Crowley 'who were discovered in a criminal situation in the dead-house of the establishment'.[68] The rhetoric continued for some time and it ended with a suggestion that the employment of storemen should be confined to boys under 15 years or men over the age of 60.[69]

Workhouse inmates were occasionally reprimanded for bad behaviour and sometimes they were expelled for breaches of the rules such as smoking, drunkenness, gambling, insubordination or theft.[70] For other offences solitary confinement was a regular punishment and in the former premises, an isolation ward had been reserved for 'ill conducted and quarrelsome women'.[71] In the official list of workhouse regulations a clear distinction is made between disorderly and refractory offences. Disorderly offences were less severe and included the use of obscene and profane language, making noise when silence was ordered, refusing to work, feigning sickness, gambling, or misbehaving at public worship. A repeat of any of these offences within seven days was deemed a refractory offence, as also were wilfully damaging or wasting property or materials, drunkenness, any sort of indecency, disobeying the master or matron, or bringing liquor or tobacco into the workhouse. For disorderly behaviour, paupers were obliged to perform an hour's extra work on two days and they also had to forgo any milk or buttermilk with their meals during that period. As a sentence for refractory behaviour, paupers could be put into solitary confinement for up to 24 hours.[72]

One misfortunate woman who was placed in solitary confinement had just two weeks remaining before she was due to give birth. Following a

---

68 *CC* 6 July, 9 July, 13 July 1844; *SR* 9 July 1844.
69 *CE* 10 July, also 15 July 1844; see also Gerard O Brien, Workhouse Management in pre-famine Ireland, *Proceedings of the Royal Irish Academy*, Vol. 86c. (1986), p 128.
70 *CUM* 14 September, 19 October 1840, 22 February, 5 June, 12 June, 21 June 1841; *SR* 8 September 1840.
71 *CUM* 8 February 1841.
72 *Poor Law Commissioners Annual Report* (1844), pp. 332-4; *CUM* 15 June, 22 June 1840; In January 1841 Sarah Hardiman and Catherine Donovan were confined to the blackhole for coming back to the workhouse in a state of drunkenness, and a Mrs Heard was also confined for bringing snuff into the house with the intention of selling it, *CUM* 25 January 1841.

riot in the house Mary Forrest had called the master some improper names and said "may the Devil transport you, you clown of a rascal". She was confined in a cell which had no furniture, seating, straw or blankets. As a result of her ordeal she gave birth to a stillborn baby. The master defended his treatment of the woman by pointing out that she was a 'most riotous and disorderly person and grossly abusive to him in her language; and her conduct was so bad that he was obliged to put her into the only place of solitary confinement the House offered, namely, one of the Idiot Wards, which certainly was without a bed or furniture of any sort'.[73] The house committee concluded that a place of punishment was necessary, and set about organising the acquisition of furniture. It was decided that women would not be placed in the blackhole (a dark punishment cell) until a doctor or apothecary's opinion on their state of health had been received.[74]

By the start of 1843 prostitutes in the workhouse were confined to wards of their own. Diseased women were kept in the lock, or venereal hospital, which had up to four women in each bed. At the start of February 1843 there were twenty-two prostitutes aged between 17 and 32 years in the penitentiary ward and a few weeks later the place was 'crowded to suffocation' with forty-four women. This overcrowding was attributed to camp followers who had arrived in the city during a recent military influx. Many were 'lying ill, in a most filthy manner on straw pallets without bedsteads, in a room not half sufficient for that number'.[75] When it was discovered that the women were able to converse with men outside, the ward windows were boarded up. During a subsequent disturbance the women broke tables and other furniture and demolished 99 panes of glass. Some of them were put on a diet of bread and water for twenty-four hours and others were expelled from the workhouse. Four men who had also misconducted themselves by 'inviting the paupers to refractory and outrageous conduct' and by playing cards and lighting 'lucifer matches' were also removed.[76]

The police were again called to the workhouse in July 1844 to quell a riot among 100 able-bodied women. Stones were thrown at staff and on this occasion, 500 windows were broken before the ringleaders were

---

73 *SR* 14 February 1843; *CE* 15 February 1843.

74 *CUM* 13 February, 20 March 1843; *CC* 16 February 1843; *Poor Law Commissioners Annual Report* (1844), p. 334.

75 *CUM* 30 January, 13 March 1843; *SR* 3 January 1844; *CC* 23 January 1844; see also Report on inspection of Cork workhouse, 13 November 1844, in NAI, Poor Law Commissioners, *Letters to James Burke*, 1844.

76 The four men were named as John Flynn, Timothy Callaghan, John Leary and Michael Sheehan. *CUM* 20 March 1843; *SR* 21 March 1843; *CC* 21 March 1843.

arrested. The disturbance resulted from an order that the women should surrender their shawls while they were in the house during summer months.[77] The arrested women appeared at the next Douglas petty sessions and several workhouse staff and inmates were present to give evidence. One of the accused was acquitted and others received sentences in the House of Correction, but before the proceedings terminated, they attacked the pauper witnesses and tore their clothing.[78] At the East Riding Sessions on 26 September a further group of women was tried for riot and unlawful assembly at the workhouse. Some were acquitted but Emma Sylva, Ellen Bailey, Johanna Reily, Hannah Goulding and Mary Murphy were each sentenced to three months' imprisonment.[79] During 1845 a dozen new punishment cells were constructed for refractory paupers. They measured three feet wide by seven feet long, had an entrance door at one end and a narrow window on the opposite wall.[80]

Diet

Outside the workhouse, most poor people survived on a basic diet of potatoes. This was noted in an internal guardians' report which observed that 'in this country it is impossible to go lower in providing for human subsistence than the food used by the people outside, unless, as happens sometimes during periods of famine, recourse is had to the very weeds of the fields, or of the sea shore. It is therefore evident the diet in an Irish workhouse cannot be of an inferior description'. The report recommended that workhouse inmates should be provided with three daily meals because it was customary for their peers outside to eat a breakfast, dinner and small supper.[81] For dietary purposes workhouse inmates were divided into the following classes:

1. Able-bodied working males.
2. Able-bodied working females.
3. Aged and infirm persons of either sex, and adult persons of either sex, above fifteen years of age, but not working.
4. Boys and girls above nine and under fifteen years of age.

77 *CUM* 15 July, 22 July, 29 July 1844; *CC* 23 July 1844; *CE* 24 July 1844; *SR* 23 July 1844.
78 *CC* 30 July 1844; *SR* 30 July 1844, also 17 September 1844.
79 *CC* 26 September 1844; SR 26 September 1844.
80 *CUM* 20 September 1845; *SR* 22 September, 9 October, 9 December, 20 December 1845; *CC* 23 September, 23 December 1845.
81 *CUM* 29 February 1840.

5.   Children above five and under nine years of age.
6.   Children above two and under five years of age.
7.   Infants under two years of age.[82]

Although hospital discipline was generally strict and inflexible, almost half of the workhouse inmates had contrived to have themselves transferred from the general wards, which had a staple diet of oatmeal porridge, to infirm wards where a superior diet of bread was provided. This finding, with its inherent implication that severe restrictions on personal freedom offered little deterrent to the poor, was interpreted by Assistant Poor Law Commissioner William Voules as an indication that confinement, discipline, restrictive rules and labour tasks offered little deterrent to the general poor who sought admission. Choosing to ignore the probability that the poor sought workhouse relief only when no other option was available, Voules insisted that quality and quantity of food were key-factors in attracting or deterring workhouse applicants. In his opinion two meals a day were 'amply sufficient' and he claimed that by providing three meals, living standards in the Cork workhouse would be raised above those of the general industrious poor.[83] Costs would also be affected. In the house of industry it had cost just over 2½d. per day to feed a pauper but as the proposed changes would raise this to almost 3½d., the expense of running the institution with 2,000 inmates would increase by over £3,000 per annum.

Assistant Commissioner Voules also feared that if the Cork workhouse provided a 'superior description of living' it would put pressure on other unions to imitate the standard. He believed that a uniform system was important, otherwise paupers would be attracted to Cork. He urged the guardians to 'abandon this third meal', for in the workhouse the poor would have the benefit of warm comfortable clothing and cleanliness, which, in his opinion, were more important. The guardians were divided on the issue of workhouse diet and in subsequent discussions a variety of views were expressed. Some favoured an alternating menu of stirabout, potatoes, broth and milk with meat twice a week.[84] Others were conscious that as Cork was the first workhouse to be declared in Ireland it had a responsibility to provide a worthwhile example to the rest of the country. The former house of industry master Mr Pearse recounted that many of the inmates found it difficult to adjust to two meals a day so they saved a portion of their dinner to eat as a bedtime supper. Dr O

---

82 T.A. Mooney, *Compendium of the Irish Poor Law* (Dublin, 1887), pp. 285-6.
83 *Poor Law Commissioners Annual Report* (1840), pp. 67-9; *SR* 12 March, 19 March 1840.
84 *CUM* 9 March 1840.

Connor said that if the inmates were provided only with vegetables, three meals would be necessary, but, if meat was included, two meals would be adequate. On three days each week the dinner porridge was enriched by the addition of eight beef-heads to the boiling mixture. A workhouse committee suggested that this should be increased to 16 beef-heads, which would raise the dinner cost by about 1d. for each 20 paupers. For breakfast the inmates received 6 ounces of meal and a pint of milk which cost about 1½d; the committee recommended that ½ lb. bread should be substituted for the meal as no extra cost would result. With these changes and the addition of ¼ lb. of bread and ½ pint of milk for supper it was estimated that the daily cost of feeding each pauper would increase to almost 3½d.[85]

Dining arrangements left a lot to be desired. Assistant Commissioner Voules reported that he was shocked by the facilities in Cork's work-house which 'was more like a gypsy encampment than anything else. The paupers were squatted here and there in groups, eating like uncivilised Indians, there was no place where they could partake of their meals like Christians'.[86] Following much discussion on the diet and dining arrange-ments,[87] it was agreed to monitor the menu over a period of months until an agreed scale was arrived at. [88]

Six months later, in the autumn of 1840 the guardians received a complaint that workhouse schoolboys were throwing bread over the insti-tution's boundary wall to friends on the other side. Though the boys' behaviour was most likely mere high spirits, some guardians said it proved that the inmates were too well fed. As a result, bread allowances for able-bodied men and boys were reduced from 12 ounces to 8 ounces and a review of allowances was again set in motion.[89] A well-balanced discussion was effectively banished by skilful use of clichés and emotive arguments. Mr French expressed his concern for the hard-pressed ratepayers – why, he asked, should inmates get a diet superior to farmers and others who contributed to their upkeep. Instead of bread and milk he advocated that the inmates should get potatoes and oatmeal porridge. This view was supported by Assistant Commissioner Voules, who still believed that the prospect of good food was attracting inmates to Irish

85 *CUM* 29 February 1840; *SR* 27 February 1840; *CC* 5 March 1840.
86 *SR* 19 March 1840.
87 *CUM* 16 March 1840.
88 *SR* 18 April 1840. It was later established that as the workhouse boiler had malfunctioned bread had been issued to inmates instead of potatoes. *SR* 23 April 1840.
89 *SR* 29 September 1840.

workhouses. Those opposed to changing the diet were outvoted, and a new daily food allowance of 6 lbs. of potatoes and two pints of milk for each pauper was sanctioned by fourteen votes to eleven.[90] The *Southern Reporter* was not impressed with the decision and said that instead of decreasing the food 'to the very minimum quantity that will sustain life', workhouse salaries should have been reduced as a cost saving measure.[91] It lamented that increased hospital costs on hitherto healthy inmates would soon negate any savings. Though the workhouse did not purport to be a luxurious institution, observers warned that 'it should not be converted into a place of pains and penalties for the unfortunate beings whose misfortunes in life reduce them to the necessity of seeking susten-ance within its always dreary and comfortless walls'.[92] The emotive tactics used to swing the votes at this meeting were to become a well-rehearsed scenario, and similar scenes were to be re-enacted on countless occasions in the future.

The introduction of the new diet created uproar and several hundred inmates, the majority of whom were women, rejected the food. Attempts to quell the row failed, and potatoes, which were sampled at the board-room, were found to be cold, wet and slimy. Nonetheless, the new dietary allowances were maintained for a while.[93] A softening of attitudes was evident at the end of November 1840 when the guardians resolved that, in the event of Her Majesty giving birth to a son and heir to the throne, 'on that joyous occasion a substantial meat dinner be given to the pauper inmates of the house'. Not everyone was happy with the resolu-tion, and one ratepayer complained that the guardians were very charitable and generous 'when they can do so at other people's expense'.[94] In the event the monarch gave birth to a daughter and the meat dinner was deferred until Christmas when each pauper got pota-toes and pork, with cabbage from the workhouse garden.[95] Just before Christmas the following daily dietary scale was introduced:[96]

---

90 *CUM* 26 October 1840; *SR* 27 October 1840.
91 *SR* 29 October 1840.
92 *SR* 10 November 1840.
93 *SR* 3 November, 19 November 1840. At around this time also the guardians were experimenting with timber-soled shoes for the workhouse inmates, and £10 had been allocated towards the experiment, with the footwear costing 2s. 8d. for male, and 2s. 2d. for female shoes. *CUM* 2 December, 7 December, 14 December 1840; *SR* 3 November 1840.
94 *CUM* 23 November 1840; *CC* 26 November 1840.
95 *CUM* 21 December 1840; *CC* 1 December, 22 December 1840.
96 *CUM* 4 January, 1840. At the start of January, alterations were made and the dinner bread allowance for children was substituted with 3 lbs. of potatoes and a pint of fresh milk.

	BREAD	MILK
Able-bodied men	1¾ lbs.	2 pints
Able-bodied women	1½ lbs.	2 pints
School boys	1¾ lbs.	2 pints
School girls	1½ lbs.	2 pints
Nurses	1½ lbs.	2 pints
Infants	½ lb.	½ pint
Children of both sexes under 5 years	1 lb.	2 pints
Servants and Persons attending hospital	1½ lbs.	2 pints
Aged and infirm males	1½ lbs.	2 pints
Aged and infirm females	1½ lbs.	2 pints

(*Source*: *CUM* 7 December, 14 December 1840)

Writing to the Poor Law Commissioners on 6 February 1841, Assistant Commissioner Voules explained that the Cork guardians had tried a 'great variety of dietaries' in the workhouse. As a result he was optimistic that 'a regular and permanent dietary' would soon be introduced which would reduce the 1s.5d. per week expended on feeding each pauper.[97] The Commissioners were not unduly impressed for in their 1841 annual report they noted that the Cork dietary 'although it has been very frequently changed still seems to us open to objection'.[98] In September 1841 a major review again took place. The diet at that time consisted of 8 ounces of oatmeal stirabout and a pint of milk for breakfast and 3¼ lbs. of potatoes plus ¾ pint of milk for dinner. Mr Meagher suggested that the allowance of stirabout be dispensed with as its preparation resulted in daily disruption, particularly on Sunday when it interfered with religious services in the house. The stirabout diet was degrading and depressing and had 'half skeletonised the paupers'; by replacing it with bread, the expense of using large amounts of coal for cooking and the wear and tear on furnaces and equipment could be avoided he argued. Again, warnings about 'pampering the paupers' and attracting poor people from other areas were heard. A vote on the issue was taken and by 18 votes to 10 the diet was changed to 12 ounces of bread and a pint of milk for breakfast and 3½ lbs. of potatoes and a pint of milk for dinner.[99] The Poor Law Commissioners intervened to advise the guardians that the paupers' diet should 'by no means exceed the ordinary mode of living of the labouring class'.[100]

97 *Poor Law Commissioners Annual Report* (1841), Appendix D., 1841, p.141.
98 *Poor Law Commissioners Annual Report* (1841), p.8; see also dietary scale in *CUL* 3 June 1841.
99 *SR* 7 September 1841; *CC* 5 October, 4 November 1840.
100 *CUL* 16 September 1841; *CC* 21 September 1841. For a discussion on the Cork workhouse diet, see Gerard O Brien, *New Poor Law in Ireland*, pp. 45-48; Gerard

The bread supplied to the workhouse was of poor quality and the committee warned that 'it would be necessary for the board to have a dentist employed to provide sets of strong teeth for the poor old creatures who were obliged to eat it'.[101] During summer 1842 potatoes became scarce and it was suggested that the inmates should be fed on rice so as to leave any potatoes in the market for the poor. The idea was rejected because it would necessitate the sending of large sums of money out of the country and it was decided to give the inmates bread instead of potatoes for one month.[102] The prospect of baking bread in the workhouse was discussed but Commissioner Voules did not favour this because the various operations such as purchasing wheat, grinding it into flour, preparing the dough and baking the bread presented too many opportunities for fraud and theft. Some speakers said that the manufacture of bread would provide useful employment for inmates but ultimately the suggestion was rejected.[103] The bread was checked as it arrived at the workhouse and frequently it was found to be undercooked or underweight; a large percentage of the potatoes was also found to be bad.[104] A full review of the workhouse food was undertaken and on the proposal of Farmar Lloyd a new diet, which would cost an average of 1s.0½d. per pauper per week, was agreed. The new allowances were as follows:

	BREAKFAST	DINNER	SUPPER
Under two years of age	¼ lb. bread ½ pint milk	¼ lb. bread ½ pint milk	
2 to 5 years	3 oz. oatmeal ½ pint milk	6 oz. bread ½ pint porridge	4 oz. bread
5 to 13 years	5 oz. oatmeal ½ pint milk	8 oz. bread ½ pint porridge	4 oz. bread
Over 13 years old or infirm	7 oz. oatmeal ½ pint milk	10 oz. bread 1 pint porridge	6 oz. bread
All able-bodied over 13 years	8 oz. oatmeal ½ pint milk	12 oz. bread 1 pint porridge	

The porridge, which was to be issued instead of milk, was to be made to a recipe of one gallon of water, 6oz. meat boiled to a jelly and 8 oz.

---

100 (cont.) O Brien, Workhouse Management, *Proceedings of RIA* (1986), pp. 117-21; Gerard O Brien, *Poor Law* . . . (thesis, 1980), pp. 141-50.
101 *SR* 26 April 1842.
102 *SR* 31 May, 7 June 1842; *CC* 7 June 1842.
103 *SR* 28 June 1842. It is interesting to note that at that time the general diet of Cork's poor consisted of bread and not potatoes.
104 *SR* 26 April 1842.

oatmeal for every four persons.[105] A sample of the porridge was described as 'a very unpalatable and mawkish compound, of an indescribable colour, and appeared to have scarcely the taste of meat, or any other nutritious substance'. Another description likened it to 'the fluid mixture of flour and water used by paper hangers, called paste'.[106]

When the Marquis of Downshire visited the workhouse he also criticised attempts to reduce the workhouse diet, for, in his opinion, the guardians had a duty to 'make the condition of the poor people as comfortable and as healthy as they can consistent with the proper and judicious regulations of such an establishment'.[107] Nonetheless, the new spartan diet remained in force for some months. In September 1842, when conditions outside the workhouse had improved, Mr. Fagan suggested that allowances should be reviewed and possibly improved, though 'it need not be better than would keep paupers in health'.[108] He did not accept that the porridge, or 'hogs' wash', was suitable food for the inmates, twenty-one of whom blamed the diet for making them ill. The board voted to change the menu and in October a potato-based diet was re-introduced.[109]

Politics

The move to the new workhouse premises coincided with a perceptible change in the attitudes of some guardians and distinct factions began to emerge and form at that time. The Conservative *Cork Constitution* was pleased with the success of certain parties at the 1842 Cork Union election and sent 'forth a shout of triumph at the result of the election for Poor Law Guardians, and thus, at once proclaimed the opinion of its party that the Board Room of the Work House is a fitting arena for political warfare'.[110] The election had been fought on party lines and as a result some hard-working guardians such as the city's Mayor and Mr Harley had lost their seats. The *Southern Reporter* analysed the new board and divided the participants into six factions:

1.   Those who favoured charging the cost of paupers to Cork city ratepayers, as opposed to a general union charge.

---

105 *CUM* 4 July 1842; *SR* 5 July 1842; see also *CUL* 7 June, 16 June 1842; *Poor Law Commissioners Annual Report*, 1842, pp. 24-27.
106 *SR* 19 July, 30 August 1842.
107 See *CUM* 18 July 1842.
108 *CC* 6 September, 13 September 1842; *SR* 6 September 1842.
109 *CUM* 3 October 1842; *CC* 4 October 1842; *SR* 4 October 1842.
110 *SR* 2 April 1842.

2. Those who were opposed to this.
3. Those who sought to create the greatest amount of confusion and thereby frustrate the system.
4. Those who wanted to give the system a fair trial and alter it as required.
5. Those who wished to give the inmates good wholesome food.
6. Those who strove to reduce the inmates' food to the lowest possible level.

During its first three years, the Cork Union had functioned without recourse to party political issues but, lamented the *Reporter*, it was about to become 'a fearful, discordant and rancorous political debating club'.[111] The *Cork Examiner* was also dismayed at the developments, which had transformed the boardroom into 'a mere arena for political sparring'.[112]

Under the prevailing system the vote of every ratepayer was important and it was in the interest of parties to ensure that the voting ability of their supporters was not undermined in any way. Only those who had paid their rates were entitled to vote and because of an error in one rate-collector's records, a number of Conservative voters had not been permitted to participate in the Cork Union elections. Though an investigation showed that the omissions were accidental, the incident provided some guardians with an opportunity to question the entire rating system so the business of the new board soon turned to political matters. The Union's credit rating was poor, as it owed about £16,000 to the government for building works, its local account was overdrawn by almost £9,500 and the bank had threatened that future cheques would not be honoured unless money was deposited in the account.[113] Poor rates were the principal source of union funding but their collection commenced only when the guardians agreed on a new figure. Once the revised rates were agreed, the books were signed and the process of gathering funds commenced. On this occasion, as a majority of the guardians would not agree to sign the books and thereby authorise the new rate, the collection had been abandoned. Disagreement about the rate itself was not the cause of the postponement – the real reason was that when the books were signed, defaulting ratepayers faced exclusion from voting in forthcoming elections. Failure to pay on time could have been caused by an accidental oversight or a lack of the necessary funds but, nonetheless, exclusion was the result. This situation prevailed until

---

111 See *CUM* 4 April 1842; *SR* 5 April 1842.
112 *CE* 6 April, 1842; see also Gerard O Brien, 'The establishment of Poor Law Unions in Ireland, 1838-43', *Irish Historical Studies*, Vol. XXIII, No. 90 (November, 1982), pp. 108, 110, 112, 115.
113 *SR* 7 April, 14 April, 19 April, 7 May, 17 May 1842.

a new rate was made and the books were again presented for signing.

Newspaper editorials and comments on Poor Law elections became increasingly hostile and partisan during the 1840s. The nationalist *Cork Examiner* and *Southern Reporter* newspapers advised readers to vote for Liberal candidates and the opposing *Cork Constitution* urged its readers to vote for Conservatives. In March 1844 the *Southern Reporter* lamented that the Tories had obtained a majority on the board. Similar trends were evident in other areas of public life and 'religion and party are mixed up with everything. The food of the paupers is even regulated by political bias. You will find the advocate of the horse potato, and the stinted allowance, of one political creed, and the supporter of more nutritious food, of another'.[114] The *Cork Examiner* also expressed disgust at the changing emphasis for, said the newspaper, the Conservatives

> have carried their unseemly hatred within the sacred precincts of a board-room, and have made the discomfort and semi-starvation of the wretched, crushed-down paupers the source of brutal joy, and the means of political annoyance to their antagonists outside the work-house. Every question of dietary – of nutrition for helpless infants, and indulgence for worn-out old age – has been battled over with a zeal worthy of a good cause, fierceness which did more honour to their powers of hating, than to their pretended humanity.[115]

Conclusion

The general pattern of life in the Cork workhouse and the behaviour of its guardians were cast during these early years. Constructive discussions on matters of importance to the lives of inmates or the management of the workhouse were often ruined by arguments about political or religious issues. Some guardians were concerned principally with saving money – or, more correctly, about not spending money. This manifested itself most noticeably during discussions about food for the inmates. Some guardians had a fixation about the most suitable and economic diet; others had their own 'nostrums' for feeding the inmates.[116] The workhouse food supply was often dictated by prevailing market conditions; for instance, during short-term seasonal potato scarcities, bread or porridge was commonly substituted as the principal food.[117] If the authorities had been consistent in recording and evaluating the various

---

114 *SR* 12 March 1844.
115 *CE* 13 March 1844.
116 *SR* 14 March 1843 also 23 May 1844.
117 *SR* 8 June 1842; *CUM* 14 August 1843.

dietary changes, a worthwhile and valuable source of reference could have evolved. Skilful monitoring and record keeping could have proven beneficial, or indeed invaluable, in times of scarcity, and most particularly during the subsequent Famine years.

2 Famine

In the mid 1840s the combined influences of the potato failure and the resulting food shortage precipitated a sequence of tragic events in the history of Irish poor law administration. Following the initial signs of disease, attempts were made to salvage some potatoes. When this failed, imported Indian corn (maize) was adopted as an alternative food source. Because of the scale of the disaster, members of the rural population were enticed into Cork City in an often-fruitless search for work or assistance. Initially, relief schemes were able to accommodate many of the applicants but as the demand increased, the hungry poor were forced to seek alternative assistance along with people who were sick or unable to work. Faced with the prospect of total destitution these unfortunate people had little alternative but to apply for workhouse relief. For a short time during 1846 the Cork guardians provided a form of outdoor relief. This venture was short-lived, and in response to a growing volume of applicants, additional accommodation was rented and temporary buildings were constructed. By the start of 1847 when the workhouse was catering for a huge mass of inmates, alterations were made to the diet, cheaper food was purchased and smaller quantities issued. Soon, overcrowded wards of unhealthy and hungry inmates threatened the health of the establishment. An outbreak of fever, which commenced at the end of 1846, escalated out of control and forced the closure of the workhouse to new applicants. Deaths increased alarmingly and workhouse officials were among the stricken.

The Potato Failure

Following the initial reports about losses to the potato crop on Ireland's east coast, discussions on the progress of the blight and the damage to local supplies became a frequent topic at meetings of Cork's board of guardians. By early September 1845 the disease was visible in potato fields near the city and calls were made to prohibit the export of cereals.[1]

As a result of the scarcity, the quality of the potatoes being supplied to

---

1 *CUM* 7 July 1845; *CE* 10 September, 12 September, 15 September 1845.

the Cork workhouse deteriorated and signs of blight were frequently visible. Contractors were finding it increasingly difficult to honour their commitments to supply the house. The inmates were provided with poor quality meals and the workhouse authorities responded by issuing larger quantities to compensate for the amount of bad food the paupers left on their dishes.[2]

Discussions on the progress of the disease at guardians' meetings elicited depressing reports and warnings that preparations should be made for the worst possible scenario. The quality of the potatoes being fed to the inmates continued to deteriorate and many were 'not fit for pigs, much less human beings'.[3] Dr O Connor was apprehensive about the situation and feared that the house was an easy target for unscrupulous dealers.[4] At a guardians' meeting in November 1845 the house committee reported that able-bodied inmates were receiving 6 ounces of bread for supper, the aged and infirm were getting an extra pound of potatoes for dinner and children were receiving a similar amount for breakfast. Assistant Poor Law Commissioner Burke spoke in favour of providing stirabout instead of potatoes for some meals, as it was a 'much healthier and cleaner description of food'. The guardians agreed to the Commissioner's suggestion and they also decided to experiment with kiln-drying damaged potatoes for conversion into biscuits.[5] This was in line with a government commission's suggestion that sound parts of diseased potatoes should be salvaged and used for making bread. These endeavours were a waste of time because the diseased potatoes soon 'melted into a slimy, decaying mass'.[6]

As experiments at restoring bad potatoes were unsuccessful the extraction of farina (starch) from damaged potatoes was attempted in the workhouse. The extract, which is high in carbohydrates, was used as an additive to flour and other foods.[7] As it was estimated that 3½ lbs. of

---

2 *CUM* 13, 20, October, 3 November, 15 December, 29 December 1845; *SR* 14 October 1845.
3 *CE* 5 November 1845.
4 *SR* 4 November 1845.
5 *CUM* 1 November 1845; *CE* 5 November 1845; *CC* 18 November 1845.
6 Thomas P. O Neill, 'The organisation and administration of relief, 1845 – 1852', in R. Dudley Edwards and T. Desmond Williams (eds.), *The Great Famine – Studies in Irish History* (New York, 1957), pp. 210-11; Cecil Woodham-Smith, *The Great Hunger: Ireland 1845-9* (London, 1962), p. 47; J. Donnelly, Jr., 'Famine and government response, 1845-6', in W. E. Vaughan (ed.), *A new history of Ireland* (London, 1989), Vol. 5, pp. 274-5.
7 *CUM* 20 October, 17 November, 1 December, 8 December 1845; *SR* 25 November 1845; This process is still used to extract starch for use as a thickener in foods such as puddings, custard, sauces, soups etc. *The New Encyclopaedia Britannica*, 15th, Edition (Chicago, 1989), Vol. 19, p. 347.

farina could be extracted from one hundredweight of potatoes, two machines were utilised for this process. The result was also disappointing and the absence of skilled supervisory staff was blamed. The poor quality and rapid deterioration of the potatoes supplied to the workhouse made it necessary to purchase additional quantities at the Cork market. These also were of low quality and the workhouse storeman was frequently unable to source a worthwhile supply.[8]

As the year came to an end, it became increasingly difficult to get a reliable supply, even on contract.[9] Because of the additional costs involved in purchasing greater quantities of potatoes, the expense of maintaining a pauper in the workhouse increased from 1s. 6d. to 1s. 10d. per week during December 1845.[10] Even though adequate evidence was available from many sources, the guardians could not agree on the extent of damage to the potato crop. Ever vigilant to the danger of letting their guard slip, some of the guardians refused to introduce any emergency measures which could be interpreted as an indication of generosity, or indeed humanity. In general, they turned a blind eye to the portents of the developing disaster. Although Thomas Sarsfield acknowledged that there would be 'a great deal of misery and wretchedness' in some parts of County Cork, he chose to believe that 'there was no fear of a general famine'. Others took a more realistic view, and in their opinion the true extent of disease had not yet been revealed.[11] The procrastinators were given solace by the editorial line of the *Cork Constitution*, which was content to state that although 'particular districts have suffered, chiefly through the ignorance or the indocility of the people, the general opinion is that providence, has spared us an abundance of our wants'.[12]

There was a temporary improvement in the quality of potatoes delivered to the workhouse at the start of 1846, and the guardians sanctioned a reduction from 4½ to 3½ lbs. per day for inmates. In an effort to ensure that only first class produce was supplied, the guardians insisted that all potatoes were graded and washed and that bad ones were returned to suppliers. Contractors refused to have their potatoes subjected to this process and during the second week of January 1846

---

8 *SR* 21 October, 18 November, 9 December, 16 December 1845; *CE* 22 October 1845.

9 *SR* 25 November 1845. A similar situation prevailed in the Midleton workhouse. Catherine M. Cotter, *From pauperism to prosperity* . . . (M. Phil., thesis, UCC, 1999), p. 48.

10 *SR* 4 December 1845; see also *12th Poor Law Commissioners Annual Report* (1846), vol. XIX, [704], Appendix B, No. 26, p. 170.

11 *CC* 2 December 1845; *SR* 4 December 1845. The authorities in Dublin Castle also suspected that exaggerated reports on the potato loss were being made. See J. Donnelly, Jr., 'Famine and government response 1845-6', pp. 276-7.

12 *CC* 16 December 1845.

some workhouse paupers had no breakfast as a result. Because potatoes were unavailable, it became necessary to feed some inmates with bread. From the previous year's price of between 3½d. and 4d. a weight (a weight was a stone and a half, or 21 lbs. of potatoes), the cost of potatoes increased to about 7d. in January 1846 and by mid-March they were selling in Cork markets at between 9½d. and 11d per weight. The number of bad potatoes in every purchase meant that the true price was in fact much higher.[13]

Potatoes delivered to Cork Market – and price per weight of 21 lbs.

Week ending 24 March 1841 to Week ending 24 March 1846

	CART LOADS	WHITE POTATOES	MINION POTATOES
24 March 1841	821	3½d to 4½d	5d to 6d
24 March 1842	506	4d to 5d	6d to 7d
24 March 1843	682	2½d to 3d	3½d to 4½d
24 March 1844	1018	3½d to 5d	5d to 5½d
24 March 1845	820	3d to 4½d	5d to 5½d
24 March 1846	476	7½d to 9d	9d to 11d

Source: *CC* 16 April 1846; See also PP 1846, Vol. XXXVII, [110] (p. 2) for prices of potatoes sold at Cork city markets in the period 1840 to 1846.

By the middle of January 1846, the guardians acknowledged that they should source a food other than potatoes so as not to 'drain the market upon the poor'.[14] It was customary to review the workhouse diet at the first meeting of each month and the house committee recommended that the inmates should be fed on oatmeal. Roger Mc Sweeny was contracted to supply the workhouse with 30 tons of oatmeal at £14. 9s. 6d. per ton, and an oatmeal breakfast was to be supplied to inmates after 1 February. This would reduce the weekly consumption of potatoes from 2,000 to 1,500 weights.[15]

---

13 *CC* 14 January, 19 August, 16 September 1845, 6 January, 17 March 1846; *SR* 8 January, 13 January, 22 January 1846; *CE* 16 February 1846; see also *Return of the price of potatoes*, PP 1846 Vol. XXXVI, [453], p. 13. It is interesting to note that even in this period of acute shortage, potatoes were being shipped from Cork to England as late as 25 March 1846. *CC* 26 March 1846; See also PP 1846, Vol., XXXVII, [28], *Copy of report of Dr. Playfair and Mr Lindley on the potato crop . . .*; PP 1846, Vol. XXXVII, [33], *Report of the Commissioners of Inquiry into . . . the failure of the potato crop*; PP 1846, Vol. XXXVII, [120], *Abstracts of the most serious representations made by the several Medical Superintendents of Public Institutions . . .*; PP 1846, Vol. XXXVII, [171], *Instructions to Committees of Relief Districts . . . in reference to the apprehended scarcity.*
14 *CC* 20 January 1846.
15 *CUM* 19 January, 26 January 1846; *SR* 27 January 1846, *CC* 3 February 1846.

As the number of inmates in the workhouse continued to increase during the spring of 1846 the *Cork Constitution* lamented that

> the accounts from the Work House are worse and worse. Every week adds to the number of applicants to the Board and of patients in the Hospital. Two Thousand Five Hundred paupers in the House not intended for 2000! Of these, 717 in hospital, 57 in the Fever Hospital, with 28 Lunatics! Where is it to end? And with the price of potatoes rising and the quantity diminishing, how are those poor who have hitherto continued to maintain themselves outside, to command food sufficient for the support of life?[16]

Accommodation

The guardians agreed that the number of inmates was excessive but this was justified because many would have starved if left to fend for themselves outside the house. Also, many of the new arrivals were young children or old, feeble and sick adults. To cater for the influx, some workshops and dormitories were converted into sheds.[17] Because of the overcrowding, beds were occupied by up to three inmates and in the nursery ward some beds accommodated six or seven persons. The Poor Law Commissioners were uneasy about the developments and they advised the guardians to discuss the situation with their medical officer. Dr O Connor was particularly concerned about the number of sick people entering the house. He was apprehensive that the overcrowding would facilitate the spread of sickness and disease. He emphasised that additional accommodation was essential and suggested that the city's blind asylum, which was located at the former house of industry building, would be suitable for housing the additional inmates. He had established that if the workhouse was reorganised, the institution's capacity could be increased to a maximum of 2731 places by 'heaping and squeezing the paupers together'. Following some discussion on the matter, the union clerk was directed to seek the Poor Law Commissioners' approval for taking an additional building, under the condition that the premises would be declared part of the Cork workhouse. The blind asylum was inspected and its trustees offered part of the premises at £60

---

16 *CUM* 2 March 1846; *CC* 3 March 1846.
17 *CUM* 23 February 1846; *CC* 17 February, 7 March 1846. A description of the workhouse in 1846 tells us that 'it consists of a great oblong central building, flanked by wings, with double fronting gables, – a gate house, wherin the Guardians hold their meetings, and, to the rear, an Infirmary, yards, linnies, etc'. J. Windele, *Historical and Descriptive notices of the city of Cork and its vicinity; Gougaun-Barra, Glengariff, and Killarney* (Cork, 1846 edition), p. 169.

per year, or if it were taken for three years, the rent would be £50. The Commissioners were in favour of taking the additional accommodation and Commissioner Burke suggested that it should be for the exclusive use of females. He was satisfied that the existing workhouse staff could be deployed to manage the new departments and that the only new employee required would be a gatekeeper.[18]

As usual, the guardians could not come to a majority agreement, and Richard Dowden warned that, as the 'Parliament of the Poor', the board had a responsibility to take the premises and reduce hardship. Another guardian, William Fagan, spoke of the danger overcrowding posed to the community at large and, in desperation, urged the board 'in the name of God, take the building'.[19] It was subsequently decided to rent the asylum for just one year and to provide a house to accommodate its 24 displaced inmates. The blind asylum was declared a ward of the work-house from 25 March 1846 and a number of workhouse inmates, including aged and infirm females, were transferred to this premises which became known as 'the lower house'.[20] To help cope with the increasing number of patients in the workhouse hospital the Poor Law Commissioners sanctioned the appointment of Dr John Popham as an assistant physician at a salary of £50 per annum.[21] From the original figure of 2,000 inmates, the number in the workhouse and its auxiliary had increased to almost 3,000 in April 1846.

At the start of April 1846 the medical officers protested to the guardians that the hospital wards contained 224 more patients than they had been designed to house. The infirm ward had 585 inmates, of whom 121 never left their beds and another 117 were confined to the ward. A further 582 aged and infirm inmates were scattered throughout the workhouse. To help care for the increasing number of patients, able-bodied women inmates were deployed as nurses. Other women who worked in the wash-room and laundry, were given an extra 4 ounces of bread each day to sustain them at their chores.[22] The institution had 263 infants and children under five years of age, most of whom were orphans or foundlings and many were suffering from measles or scarlatina. As these unfortunate children were fed on skimmed milk, which frequently turned to curds and whey after boiling, the visiting committee

---

18 *CE* 25 March 1846; *CUM* 9 March 1846; NAI, Poor Law Commissioners, Letters to James Burke, 1846, 7 March, and 12 March 1846.
19 *CC* 24 March 1846; *SR* 3 March, 7 March, 10 March, 24 March 1846.
20 *CUM* 30 March, 6 April 1846; *CC* 31 March 1846; *CE* 25 March, 29 April 1846; *SR* 2 June 1846.
21 *CUM* 9 March, 23 March 1846; *SR* 24 March 1846; *CUL* 20 March 1846. Dr John Popham retired from the workhouse in 1874. *CE* 3 April 1874.
22 *CUM* 18 May 1845.

recommended that new milk should be provided instead.[23] The number of fever patients was also increasing and each week over a dozen new victims were admitted, with many surviving just a few hours. It was frequently found that fever cases had earlier been discharged from the city's fever hospital and returned to dire poverty in their homes.[24]

Dr O Connor was fearful that a fever epidemic would occur in the workhouse because of the prevalence of the disease:

> Fever patients were in most instances removed to the general Fever hospital, but owing to the crowded state of that house they had to be turned out when convalescent, and after prowling about for a while they came to the workhouse, in a deplorable state. Last week an unfortunate man was discharged from the fever hospital, and after roving about the streets for a few days, he attempted to crawl to the workhouse, but fell on the road. He was removed to the house, and after ineffectual attempts to sustain him with wine, he expired.[25]

The medical officers were apprehensive that the 'dangerously crowded' state of the workhouse would lead to severe problems during the coming warm weather. During March 1846 the city's Mayor alerted the Chief Secretary to the situation and warned that as the workhouse was crowded and the fever hospital was inadequate for the amount of sickness in the city, up to 20,000 people were on the verge of 'absolute destitution'.[26] The city's other hospitals and public charities were unable to cope with the demands of the destitute poor. Following a meeting of Cork medical representatives at the start of March, Dr D. B. Bullen also contacted the authorities in the hope of prompting government intervention.[27]

Fever Hospital

At the end of 1845 Cork's fever hospital was under pressure from an unusually large number of applicants. To make room for extra patients its convalescent rooms were converted to a sick ward and because of the demands for accommodation, some 'half cured' convalescents were, irresponsibly, obliged to leave the institution.[28] Dr O Connor, the workhouse

---

23 *CUM* 13 July 1846.
24 *CC* 25 April 1846; *SR* 7 April 1846.
25 *CC* 24 March 1846.
26 *SR* 7 April 1846; PP, 1846, Vol. XXXVII, [201], *Scarcity Commission – the weekly reports of the Scarcity Commission, showing the progress of disease in potatoes, the complaints which have been made, and the applications for relief, in the course of the month of March 1846.* p. 9.
27 Dr D. B. Bullen to Chief Secretary, 7 March 1846, NAI, CSORP 1847 H4520.
28 *SR* 6 December, 9 December 1845.

physician, was concerned about the situation and he suggested to the guardians that a new fever unit should be constructed in the workhouse grounds to isolate fever cases from the general body of inmates. Although this would necessitate extra work, the doctor was willing to assume the duties purely in the interest of the inmates. His concern was given little credence and board members choose to ignore the seriousness of the situation. Many guardians were happy with the existing arrangement whereby the workhouse paid 1s. per week for each fever patient it referred to the city fever hospital. In January 1846 the Cork Union paid £14.15s. for patients cared for in that institution and some of the guardians considered this expenditure more than adequate.[29]

In February 1846, when the city's 140 bed fever hospital was packed with 155 patients, some of them sleeping two to a bed, and the workhouse had another 60 fever cases, 40 under 8 years of age, the guardians reconsidered the situation and voted in favour of building a 100 bed fever unit in the workhouse grounds.[30] Work had just begun on the project when a dispute about its location brought operations to a halt. The position of the proposed hospital at the front of the workhouse was rejected by some guardians and observers as being too close to the main building and too near the main road. One guardian said this site would be inappropriate because 'nervous people might be injured by the fear arising from passing such a building'. The ploy succeeded! The project ceased and the possibility of acquiring an alternative site was investigated but ultimately rejected.[31]

During the summer of 1846 the Cork City relief committee organised a variety of employment projects such as road works, stonebreaking and whitewashing schemes. Although many people did receive employment, a great number of others, including unemployed tradesmen, sought inclusion in the work groups.[32] By mid June the relief committee had about 1,200 men employed on its schemes but it was alleged that at least one third of them preferred to idle and did very little work – in reality, they were probably too exhausted to actively participate.[33] Many of the

---

29 *CUM* 2 February 1846; *CC* 6 January, 27 January 1846; *SR* 8 January, 27 January, 7 February 1846.

30 *CUM* 9 February, 16 February, 23 February 1846; *CC* 10 February, 24 February 1846; *CE* 11 February, 18 February 1846; *SR* 12 February 1846; *12th Annual Report of Poor Law Commissioners* (1846) Appendix B, No. 22, pp. 164, 167.

31 *CUM* 13 April, 27 April, 4 May, 18 May 1846; *CC* 14 April, 30 April, 5 May 1846; *SR* 16 April, 28 April, 5 May, 9 May, 19 May, 23 June, 30 June, 14 July, 21 July 1846.

32 *CC* 9 May, 11 May 1846.

33 *CC* 18 June, 9 July 1846; *CE* 8 July 1846; also PP 1847, Vol., LVI, [51], *Return of the several places in Ireland where depots of provisions have been established since the 1st day of January 1846. . . .*

rejected workers made their way to the workhouse and during the next few weeks large numbers of unskilled labourers continued to apply for relief. At the workhouse, they were questioned by the admission board, which consisted of a group of guardians, with responsible for screening new entrants. Commenting on the high level of general admissions, Thomas Sarsfield said that many were admitted by generous, but misguided guardians. Voicing the sentiments of his tight-fisted colleagues, he observed that if the generous guardians 'stayed away a few weeks, and left the business of admission to the hard hearted, the rate-payers would be saved a great deal of money'.[34] The *Cork Examiner* was not in favour of scaling down the relief works which offered poor labourers their only source of income. The newspaper was apprehensive that great hardship would occur after the harvest. With foreboding, it predicted that 'the evil day is approaching with swift pace. It is almost at hand'.[35]

Workhouse Relief

Unemployed labourers continued to call at the workhouse for assistance. On 20 September 1846 the workhouse master, acting on impulse distributed breakfast stirabout, which had not been eaten by inmates, to the hungry applicants. Although he was aware that this was contrary to workhouse regulations, he issued 22 lbs. of bread to other people outside the house. About 80 'quiet, well disposed, civil and thankful men', applied for food on the following day. The inmates donated a portion of their stirabout and milk and the master was able to give each applicant a small breakfast. The idea of giving applicants a breakfast, which would have to be consumed on the premises, was sanctioned by the guardians who did not believe that the gesture amounted to providing outdoor relief.[36] To ensure that the breakfast was eaten on the premises, participants were permitted to enter in the period up to 10 a.m. and were detained until 2 p.m. This also ensured that applicants were not able to locate employment. The number of people assembling at the workhouse increased rapidly and on Monday 29 September, from an 'army of clamouring men, women and children', 1,438 were

---

34 *CC* 7 July, 14 July, 28 August 1846; *SR* 14 July 1846.
35 *CE* 14 August, 17 August 1846.
36 *CUM* 21 September 1846; *CE* 23 September 1846 The policy of providing relief in the form of food to poor applicants who applied to the workhouse had been endorsed at a public meeting in Cork in February 1846. It was envisaged that applicants would receive a meal, which would have to be consumed on the workhouse premises. *SR* 26 February 1846.

provided with a breakfast.[37] The scene was described by the *Cork Constitution*, which used the opportunity to question the venture. The yard outside the workhouse

> had every appearance of a fair green. Hundreds of men, women and children were to be seen in all directions, with a dense crowd around the door, through which egress and ingress was with difficulty attained. Some few of the women were at work, sewing with their needles, but the overwhelming majority were listlessly gazing about them, sitting down, lying in the sun, or walking about. It was evident that all those people could not be in distress, and the guardians seemed to think so too, but the difficulty now was, to check a system of outdoor-relief to the really destitute, which was evidently abused. On this fearful number of names having been read out by the clerk, one of the guardians stated that he had been met that day coming to the workhouse and parties had asked him – "how could he, a Cork Guardian, tolerate such a fraud as that, for numbers of women and children were being fed at the workhouse, whose husbands were known to be in good employment?" Another guardian said the vast number of these were from the country.[38]

Donations from inmates were no longer adequate to feed the applicants, so milk and other foods had to be purchased for the daily breakfast. The response to the provision of a daily meal at the workhouse was certainly indicative of the level of misery in the city and its neighbourhood. In the two-week period to 5 October almost 16,000 meals had been provided at a cost of just less than 2d. each. The Poor Law Commissioners reacted strongly against this expenditure and pointed out to the guardians that there was no provision for this type of assistance under the Poor Relief Act. They also questioned the financial burden it would impose on the ratepayers. The Commissioners were apprehensive that such relief, which had already been adopted by the Fermoy guardians, some boards in Kilkenny and Tipperary, and was being considered by the Macroom board, would lead to a slackening of the workhouse relief system and indeed the workhouse test.[39] In conclusion, they warned that the assistance provided by the Cork guardians 'is fraught with a probability of evil consequences to the moral and social

---

37 *SR* 29 September 1846; *CC* 22 September 1846; *CUM* 28 September 1846; D. O Connor, *Seventeen Years of workhouse life* (Dublin, 1861), pp. 28-9.
38 *CC* 29 September 1846.
39 For an account of the relief given at the Cashel Workhouse during the autumn of 1846 see Eamonn Lonergan, *A Workhouse story: A history of St. Patrick's hospital, Cashel, 1842-1992* (Clonmel, 1992), pp. 24-26.

conditions of the labouring classes'.[40] The guardians discussed the matter at length on 5 October but, in spite of attempts to retain the scheme, goodwill had been undermined. Influenced by reports, many unsubstantiated, that most of the recipients were from outside the city and that some were subsequently seen demanding relief from other agencies, it was agreed 'that the system of giving breakfasts at the door, being contrary to law, cease, and that all means of providing additional accommodation in the house be taken, and that applicants be admitted in the usual way'.[41]

To avoid hostilities from disappointed applicants, a force of dragoons was stationed at the workhouse when the crowds assembled on the following morning. One pauper, en-route to the workhouse with three children, lamented that 'to our great mortification the two sides of the road were lined with police and infantry – muskets with screwed bayonets and knapsacks filled with powder, and ball, ready prepared to slaughter us, hungry victims'.[42] In the event, no disturbance took place, and a rare show of spontaneous philanthropy by the Cork guardians was brought to a sudden and unsavoury end. Some board members later claimed, without providing reliable examples, that many of the recipients either sold their food or fed it to pigs and they cited this episode as a reason for postponing the introduction of outdoor relief in the Cork Union.[43]

Some observers were disappointed that the Cork guardians had given in so easily and were of the opinion that 'as a *temporary* expedient, the relief afforded by the Cork Board and their imitators could not be wrong'.[44] The *Cork Constitution* was confident that there was plenty of employment available for labourers who were willing to work. The food provided at the workhouse was merely encouraging them to idle and

> no sensible man, we presume, will dispute the propriety of the reso-
> lution adopted by the Poor Law Guardians on Monday. However
> benevolent the motive which suggested the administration of outdoor
> relief, such relief could not have continued without entailing evils
> that the Guardians did not contemplate, and imposing burdens
> which the Union could not have sustained. There has long been an

---

40 *CUM* 5 October 1846; *CUL* 30 September, 5 October 1846; See also *13th Poor Law Commissioners Annual Report* (1847), pp. 24, 38; NAI, Poor Law Commissioners, Letters to Joseph Burke 1846, 25 September, 26 September, 1 October, 3 October, 7 October, 10 October 1846.

41 *SR* 6 October 1846; *CC* 6 October 1846; see also Helen Burke, *People and the Poor law* (West Sussex, 1987), pp. 126-7.

42 *CC* 8 October 1846; *CE* 7 October, 9 October 1846.

43 See for instance *CC* 12 April, 26 April 1849.

44 *SR* 8 October, 15 October 1846.

outcry against the influx of paupers from the rural districts; but could ingenuity devise a measure more calculated to stimulate the influx than that so judiciously abandoned?[45]

Once the prospect of getting a meal at the workhouse disappeared, the number of applicants seeking admission increased rapidly and in the second week of October 1846, 461 people were admitted to the house.[46] For the first time in its history, the number of inmates in the Cork workhouse and its auxiliaries exceeded 3,000 individuals. Further accommodation was urgently required and the master warned that the 'lives of the inmates are in immediate danger owing to the atmosphere which they are compelled to breathe being necessarily vitiated by the density of the mass of persons who are unavoidably stowed into its dormitories'.[47] As the year advanced, the number of admissions climbed steadily and during some weeks in excess of 600 applicants entered the house. With winter looming, the number increased steadily and by November, in excess of 4,000 people depended on workhouse relief.[48] The guardians were finding it 'utterly impossible to investigate the claims of such crowds of applicants upon one day besides attending to the unusually large heavy duties which they are exclusively called upon to discharge'.[49] The medical officers were apprehensive about sanitation and health as a consequence of the overcrowding. In some wards up to seven people slept in a bed. Dr O Connor said that if the situation continued it would be necessary just to feed and shelter the paupers during the daytime, and to discharge them from the house to find beds for the night.[50] As the guardians had only just terminated their short-lived initiative, O Connor's observation went unnoticed.

The Poor Law Commissioners took a more clinical approach and asked the guardians to review the list of inmates and expel as many as necessary to bring the number down to the limit set by the workhouse medical officers. They warned the guardians 'however distressing it may be to their feelings', not to endanger the health of the workhouse by

---

45 *CC* 10 October 1846.
46 *SR* 20 October 1846.
47 *CUM* 2 November 1846.
48 *SR* 13 October, 10 November 1846; The huge demand for workhouse relief was common in most of the country's poor law unions. See, C. Kinealy, 'The role of the Poor Law', in C. Póirtéir, *Great Irish Famine* (Cork, 1995), pp. 110-112; see also G. L. Bernstein, 'Liberals, the Great Famine and the role of the state', *Irish Historical Studies*, Vol. XXIX, No. 116 (1995), pp. 513-536; Peter Gray, *Famine, Land, Politics*, pp. 227-283; James S. Donnelly, Jr., *The Great Irish Potato Famine*, pp. 41-100, for an assessment of the government's response to the Famine.
49 *CUL* 20 November 1846.
50 *CUM* 2 November 1846; *SR* 3 November 1846.

admitting too many applicants.[51] Priority should be given to Cork Union residents and 'such destitute poor persons as by reason of old age, infirmity, or defect, may be unable to support themselves, and destitute children; and that the relief of the destitute able bodied poor is regarded as a secondary claim upon the Guardians, if there is not accommodation in a Workhouse for the relief of all applicants'.

This advice found ready support among some guardians who were ever eager to expel surplus inmates and 'drones'. Others threatened to resign if the instructions were put into effect. With some justification, Mr Jennings described the Commissioners' directive as 'the most heartless document that had ever emanated from a public body'.[52] During the previous few days the guardians had arranged to rent another part of the old house of industry, which was being used as a store. It was decided to prepare this for the immediate reception of paupers; thus the prospect of dismissing inmates was avoided, or postponed.[53] The *Southern Reporter* was not content to let the matter of expelling paupers rest, and in an editorial it took the Poor Law Commissioners to task, by referring to previous correspondence, which decreed that

> once a pauper is admitted, his destitution is acknowledged, and he cannot be forcibly ejected. . . . This is the law, and it is a law founded on justice and humanity. We say it is the law unless the Commissioners have lately promulgated an order to the contrary – for their ensealed orders have the force of law. We are not aware of their having done so. In fact it is against the spirit of the relief Act, which only recognises destitution as the test of relief, and eschews altogether the law of settlement.[54]

On 23 November the board of guardians discussed the usurpation of its workhouse space by non-Cork Union paupers. Although the accuracy of the Poor Law Commissioners' directive was questioned, some guardians were anxious to commence the discharge of the strangers and a division on the issue was only avoided after a long debate. Instead, it was decided to seek the Commissioners' advise on how 'to forward the strange paupers to their respective unions, and measures taken to have them received in their own workhouses'.[55] In a chastened reply, the Commissioners admitted that they were unable to advise on what basis

---

51 *CUL* 7 November, 21 November 1846.
52 *SR* 10 November 1846.
53 *CUM* 26 October, 2 November, 23 November 1846; *SR* 27 October, 3 November, 17 November 1846; *CC* 27 October, 3 November, 10 November 1846. The guardians handed this premises back to the owner, Mr. Ball, at the end of 1851. *CUM* 3 December 1851.
54 *SR* 10 November 1846.
55 *CUM* 23 November 1846; *SR* 24 November 1846.

people could be transferred from one union to another or on how inmates could be discharged and referred to another union. As the law stood, Irish poor law unions had no authority to remove paupers to another union and, in any case, guardians could not be compelled to receive such paupers.[56] The Commissioners were forced to conclude that 'if such a system and transference of paupers could be in any way affected at Cork, the same course would be adopted by other Unions in self defence and the Commissioners fear that the difficulties of the present emergency would be thereby much aggravated and no consider-able advantage attained perhaps by any particular Union'.[57] The delay in implementing the Commissioners' directive certainly preserved some unfortunate inmates from hardship, uncertainty and possible death.

Now that additional accommodation had been located, the medical officers were confident that the workhouse itself could accommodate 3,000 inmates, and the additional buildings 1,050 'with comparative safety to health, but not without interference with the comfort, neatness and order which have heretofore prevailed'. A number of sheds under construction at the workhouse would accommodate a further 300 people. Thus, the total number of places available would be 4,350, 'the utmost number which these buildings may be allowed to contain, with any security for health'.[58]

As the cost of providing food for the huge number of workhouse inmates was increasing rapidly, the guardians decided to establish a bakery on the premises.[59] At the end of October 1846 a baker was employed at a salary of 30s. per week; he was provided with eight pauper assistants who received extra rations as a reward for their labour.[60] New ovens were installed near the dining hall at a cost of £60 and the bakery was ready for operation early in November. During initial trials 800 loaves were produced and it was established that a mixture of one-way flour[61] and Indian meal provided an economical type of bread. The master was confident that under the baker's supervision, the inmates could produce an adequate supply of bread for the house. His calculations showed that by baking the bread in the workhouse, a saving of up to £2,000 per annum could be realised. This

---

56 *CUM* 30 November 1846; *SR* 1 December 1846; *CC* 1 December 1846.
57 *CUL* 28 November 1846.
58 *CUM* 19 October, 23 November 1846; *CUL* 21 November 1846; *SR* 24 November 1846.
59 *CUL* 30 September, 12 October 1846; *CUM* 11 May, 18 May 1846.
60 *CUM* 16 November 1846.
61 One-way flour was produced by grinding Indian corn (or other corn) on a single pass between the grinding stones; a finer or more palatable product resulted when corn was first ground to remove the bitter outer shell, or sieved to remove impurities before a second run through the mill.

optimism was justified when the initial returns realised a weekly saving of almost £70.[62]

The expense of maintaining an inmate in the Cork workhouse, at almost 2s.6d. per week, was the highest in the country and contrasted with just 1s.7d. in Bandon, and 1s.7½d. at Fermoy and Kinsale. Some guardians said that the large expenditure in the Cork workhouse made it attractive to paupers and thus caused the number of inmates to rise. The expenditure of 2s.6d. was based on the average cost of all inmates in the establishment. About one quarter were under medical care. For instance, on 21 November 1846, there were 4,250 inmates in the workhouse of whom 1,040 were on the medical officers' list, and of this number, 310 were in hospital.[63] The daily diet of able bodied inmates consisted of ¾ lbs. bread, 1½ pints of milk and ½ lbs. of meal. The cost of this fare amounted to just 2s.0½d. per week. In contrast, the average cost of a hospital inmate was about 3s.2d. As a cost saving measure, it was decided to remove milk from the menu and substitute soup. The recipe for the workhouse soup was: '100 gallons of water, 24 lbs. of soup meat or 4 cow's heads, salt and pepper as required, vegetables – say 4s.6d. worth to the 100 gallons, 56 lbs. of oatmeal. The quantities served to each to be the same as the milk now issued'.[64] The guardians were optimistic that this change and the production of bread would mean a significant reduction in costs.[65]

Paupers from outside the city continued to stream into Cork during the autumn and winter of 1846-7. Most of them failed to locate employment and many settled in the lanes and alleys with poor families where they merely added to the already overcrowded households; others slept in the streets or under doorways in appalling weather conditions. Fr. Mathew described them as 'living images of death, animated skeletons', and many succumbed to sickness, starvation and death.[66] The city's relief depots were selling food at below cost price and soup depots had been established throughout the city. By December 1846 many thousands were depending on these outlets, or on begging for their

---

62 *CUM* 14 September, 21 September 1846; *SR* 15 September, 22 October, 10 November, 12 November 1846; *CC* 15 September, 29 September, 13 October, 27 October, 10 November 1846; *CF* 28 November 1846. Commercial establishments in Cork were not favourably disposed towards the new workhouse bakery.

63 *SR* 17 November, 24 November 1846.

64 *CUM* 23 November 1846; *SR* 1 December 1846.

65 *SR* 17 November, 24 November 1846; *CC* 27 October 1846. As a gesture towards cost saving, it was decided to withhold the traditional meat dinner on Christmas day. Instead, the inmates celebrated with a double allowance of meat in their soup. *CUM* 21 December 1846; *SR* 22 December 1846.

66 See PP 1846, Vol. XI, [694], Part 1, *Medical Charities*, pp. 663 and 734.

survival.[67] Others, many 'too ill to work and ashamed to beg', sought admission to the workhouse, and within weeks the institution was 'crowded to suffocation'. The hospital in particular was filled beyond capacity with up to four patients sharing beds.[68] Because of demands on space, male patients had no dayroom and were frequently obliged to spend time outside the building. No provision was made for adverse weather and on 30 November the men remained in the open air during a snowstorm![69] The medical officers' previous optimism changed and they warned that 'one of two evils must arise – either diseases of an infectious character will be generated . . . or, on the other hand dangerous attacks of pulmonary disease must be expected to occur from the free ventilation necessary when too large a number of human beings are congregated together'.[70] Within weeks the doctors recorded that

> we request to state that fever has made its appearance in the house, but as yet without extending to any alarming degree. To add to the difficulties of our position, several of our nurse-tenders have been attacked with illness from over fatigue, and one of the most valuable of them after ten years of faithful service has fallen a sacrifice to a conscientious feeling of duty.[71]

Because many of the new arrivals were sick, the medical officers were apprehensive about the future health of the inmates. Expansion was again necessary and the Poor Law Commissioners approved the acquisition of an old barracks at Barrack Street to house the excess numbers in the workhouse.[72]

---

67 By December there were up to '5,000 half starved, wretched beings, from the country begging in the streets of Cork'. Fr T. Mathew to Charles Trevalyan, *Relief of the Distress in Ireland, Correspondence . . . (Board of Works Series)*, PP 1847, Vol. L, [746], p. 403; John O Rourke, History *of the Great Famine* (Dublin, 1875), p. 368; Transactions *of Society of Friends* (Dublin, 1852), p. 181; J. S. Donnelly, Jr., *Land and People* (London, 1975), pp. 86-7; *SR* 27 October 1847; *CE* 16 December 1847.

68 *CC* 29 October 1846; *CE* 4 November, 23 November 1846; *SR* 22 December 1846; John O Rourke, *Famine*, pp. 369, 476; Overcrowding of workhouse hospitals was not uncommon – see, for instance, evidence of Dr Henry Maunsell re Castlerea workhouse hospital and evidence of Dr Denis Phelan re Skibbereen workhouse hospital; PP 1849 Vol. XV, [356], *Select Committee on Poor Laws* (Ireland); pp. 121-2 and 139-40.

69 *SR* 1 December 1846.

70 *CUM* 2 November 1846.

71 *CE* 23 December 1846.

72 *CUL* 26 December 1846; *SR* 22 December, 29 December 1846; *CE* 30 December 1846; *CC* 22, 29 December 1846. The Fermoy workhouse was also overcrowded at this time. See E. Garner, *To die by inches* (Fermoy, 1986), p. 63; J. S. Donnelly, Jr., *Land and People*, p. 94.

On the morning of 3 February 1847 the workhouse was subjected to a display of desperation by a group of labourers who congregated outside its gate. When the van carrying 560 lbs. of bread for the inmates of the lower house left the premises, the labourers blocked the roadway and stole its contents. On the following day about 600 labourers carrying spades, shovels and other tools demolished the outer gate of the workhouse.[73] Most dispersed when the police arrived, but some of their number who remained failed to ransack the workhouse van, which was accompanied by a large group of inmates who 'resisted the oppressors stoutly, and thus secured their "daily bread"'. Subsequently, a force of police accompanied the workhouse van on its journey to the lower house.[74]

The limit of 4,350 inmates was not adhered to and by January 1847 this figure was exceeded by 1,000 inmates. With the exception of corridors, every available space in the workhouse was filled with bodies. Many paupers slept on straw on the bare ground, and in the dayrooms, beds were suspended from the ceilings during the day and lowered for occupation at night.[75] The workhouse chapel had been floored and accommodated between 500 and 600 people, and the schoolrooms had been adapted for sleeping purposes.[76] Because the Cork city fever hospital was unable to accommodate extra patients, the workhouse medical officers appropriated two detached wards for these cases, 'yet even this necessary step has been attended with the unavoidable evil of encroaching largely on the space into which the other classes are crowded'.[77] The doctors wanted more sheds for day room accommodation; if these were provided, the existing day rooms could be converted into dormitories and ventilated during the day.[78] That the number in the workhouse had increased by 900 in a fortnight concerned Dr O Connor and in mid-January he spoke on the necessity of getting a further building outside the house, to accommodate a selected group of inmates – possibly the boys. George Laurance had a more definite view on the problem of overcrowding and he felt that 'it was every bit as humane to let people starve, or act on their own resources outside, as to bring them to certain death by infection and plague'. Dr O Connor agreed that the house was dangerously overcrowded. 'On Sunday night when he went through it at

---

73 Not the city gate as stated in J. S. Donnelly, Jr., *Land and People*, p. 90, and Graham Davis, 'The historiography of the Irish Famine', in P. O Sullivan (ed.) *The meaning of the Famine* (London, 2000), p. 29.
74 *SR* 4 February, 6 February 1847; *CC* 6 February, 9 February 1847.
75 D. O Connor, *Seventeen years of workhouse life*, p. 29.
76 *CUM* 11 January, 18 January 1847; *CC* 19 January 1847; *SR* 19 January, 26 January 1847.
77 *CUM* 15 February 1847.
78 *SR* 19 January 1847; *CC* 19 January 1847.

ten o'clock, he found the inmates huddled together sleeping, head and feet, and he could scarcely walk without treading on them'. He later wrote that

> the overcrowding of the wards at this time was fearful. At night it was impossible to walk around them without treading on some one. The children slept soundly, though tossed about in the utmost disorder, while the aged spent the night sitting in bed, suffering from bodily infirmity, or ruminating on their misfortunes. The appearance of the last day's arrivals was still more painful. They were huddled on a layer of straw in the rags which they brought with them, with a covering of a few blankets, utterly disproportioned to their number. The absence of all discipline amongst these unhappy people added to the confusion. They roved about the house like wild creatures that had suddenly lost their liberty, defying all restraint, the necessity for which they could not comprehend. I am bound to say that the majority of them were in the lowest state of civilisation. They were the poorest inhabitants of the poorest districts. . . [they] were a degraded race, an encumbrance to society, and a source of weakness to the empire.[79]

Food and Diet

Conflict frequently occurred between guardians and members of the workhouse staff. Differences in attitude towards the treatment meted out to inmates were a recurring cause of disagreement. In few areas was this more evident than in matters relating to workhouse dietary allowances where the medical officers' advice and expertise were regularly contradicted by guardians whose sole objective was to cut down on expenditure. This conflict also highlighted the differing attitudes of individual guardians towards their role as 'guardians of the poor'. By the spring of 1847 the average weekly cost of maintaining workhouse and hospital inmates was about 2s.6d. and with over 5,000 inmates in the house some guardians were apprehensive about the overall expenditure and its impact on the ratepayers.

Thomas Sarsfield argued that the treatment prescribed for the 'lowest class of paupers' was extravagant because it exceeded what these people could receive in their own homes. Continuing with this logic, he said that as patients could not afford wine in their own homes, it should not be provided for medicinal purposes in the workhouse hospital. In a tirade against extravagance, he said that the purchase, in one week, of 345 chickens to make broth for sick patients was a waste of money. He also

---

79 D. O Connor, *Seventeen Years of workhouse life*, pp. 29-30.

claimed that it was 'sheer nonsense' to issue new milk to young children; this was damaging to their health, he said, and it should be replaced with skimmed milk. Dr John Popham explained that the coarse food normally issued in the workhouse was not suitable for hospital patients or for some children. New milk was given to infants under two years of age because most of them were orphans and to others because their mother's milk had dried up. Some hospital patients received wine as a stimulant but chicken broth was prescribed for many of the fever victims. It had been found that when convalescent patients were returned to the workhouse wards the change to a diet of porridge and hominy caused intestinal problems, and many of them died. During their first week in the convalescent wards the patients were given a cup of broth each day. On the following week they received four ounces of mutton chop daily. Thereafter, they were returned to the workhouse diet, but in a minority of cases mutton was provided for a further few days.[80]

Workhouse daily food allowance and costs – May 1847

		COST/ WEEK
Able bodied	¾ lbs.bread, ½ pint milk, ½ lb. oatmeal, 1 pint soup	1s.9½d.
5-13 yr olds	1 lb. Bread, ½ pint milk, 5 ounces oatmeal, ¾ pint soup	1s.11d.
2-5 yr olds	1 ⅛ lbs. bread, 1 pint milk, ½ lb. Oatmeal	1s.8d.
Under 2 yrs	1 lb. Bread, 1 pint milk, ⅛ lb. Oatmeal	1s.3d.
Aged & Infirm	1 lb. Bread, ½ pint milk, ½ lb. Oatmeal, 1 pint soup	2s.

(*Source: CUM* 10 May 1847; *SR* 11 May 1847)

Dr O Connor attributed the hospital's high expenditure to the guardians' policy of refusing entry to the workhouse to all but seriously ill paupers. This increased the medical officers' workload and endangered the lives of patients. In a direct criticism of the policy and the policymakers, Dr O Connor caustically observed that 'the Doctors did not fly away from the danger, but were risking their own lives, and it was not fair to say that the deaths in the House had any reference to the treatment practised there'. Thomas Sarsfield rose to the bait and retorted that 'it was the duty of Dr O Connor to attend to the house, for he was as it were in the capacity of a soldier, and should in the discharge of his duty, go to the cannon's mouth. It was not however the duty of the Guardians

---

80 The cost of feeding the workhouse inmates for the six months to 25 March 1847 was £14,588. This included an expenditure of £127.8s.11d. for chickens, £165 for wine, £486 for meat and £67.18s.9d. for soup meat. *SR* 14 June 1847. See also *SR* 15 July 1847 for a discussion on the value of wine in treating fever patients.

to go there at the present moment'.[81] The medical officers' efforts were fully supported by Alfred Greer who, although believing that healthy inmates 'should be fed on the lowest description of diet that could keep the animal functions in a proper state', recommended that medical opinion and experience should be respected when the health of hospital patients was an issue.[82]

At the start of May 1847 the house committee was directed to examine the workhouse dietary scale. Within a week the committee presented its findings, and a new menu which it believed could save the ratepayers up to £4,000 per annum. Among its recommendations was a proposal that allowances of meal, tea and sugar supplied to house officers should be replaced with small cash payments. A cheaper bread recipe comprised of one part second flour and three parts wheaten flour was introduced. The cost of allowances, which included small amounts of meat, to the 90 nurses employed in the workhouse totalled £13.10s. per week. The committee was satisfied that the nursing duties could be efficiently undertaken by a staff of 25, which would reduce costs to £3.1s.5d. per week.[83]

Workhouse Dietary scale as revised by House Committee – May 1847

DAILY ALLOW-ANCES	QUARTS OF HOMINY	POUNDS OF BREAD	PINTS OF PORRIDGE	PINTS OF MILK	COST/ WEEK
Able bodied	1	¾	1		1s.5½d.
5-13 yrs	¾	½	½		1s.0¼d.
2-5 yrs	½	½	½		10½d.
Under 2 years		½		½	8¾d.
Aged & infirm	1	¾	1		1s.5½d.

The recipes for hominy and porridge were as follows: 'The hominy for 100 paupers – 3½ lbs. each – 25 gallons water, 19 lbs. of rice, 19 lbs. of Indian Meal. The meal first boiled for two hours, the rice then to be added, and all boiled together for two hours longer, stirred one way, and to remain together for one hour more without fire, then taken up for use. Cost for each pauper ⁴/₅ of a penny. Porridge for 100 paupers – 13 gallons water and salt, 7 lbs. Indian meal – boiled for three hours'.

(*Source*: *CUM* 10 May 1847. This is the table as recorded in the guardians' minute book. The published table lists the cost of the 5-13 year olds' allowance as 1s. 3¼d. *CC* 11 May 1847; *CE* 12 May 1847; *SR* 11 May 1847)

---

81 *CC* 13 April 1847. The guardians no longer met in the workhouse. See p. 60 below.
82 *CUM* 12 April, 3 May 1847; *CC* 3 March, 6 April 1847; *CE* 14 April 1847; *SR* 30 March, 13 April 1847.
83 *CUM* 3 May, 10 May 1847; *SR* 11 May 1847; *CE* 12 May 1847.

The workhouse inmates did not welcome the new dietary allowances. When these were introduced during May about 300 women rioted. They damaged property, emptied milk churns and destroyed the food allocated for 200 inmates. The police were called to quell the riot and an additional 258 lbs. of bread had to be distributed to replace the damaged food.[84] The workhouse chaplains were not in favour of the revised allowances. They were concerned that the health of the inmates, and in particular the children, would suffer irreparable damage. For breakfast the children received four ounces of hominy made from equal portions of rice and Indian meal. Their dinner consisted of eight ounces of coarse bread and three noggins of mash (or porridge), extracted from a mixture of water, salt and 7 lbs. of Indian meal which had been boiled up to produce 100 rations. (On occasions the workhouse master added extra rice to thicken the hominy but when this was discovered, he was cautioned and warned that his behaviour would lead to dismissal.) The medical officers addressed the board on the matter and expressed strong reservations about the allowances which they feared were insufficient to preserve health, and were 'likely to engender immediate disease' in the children. The Poor Law Commissioners were also concerned about the dietary reductions and the assistant commissioner described the children's allowances as 'rather scanty'.[85] In an editorial comment, the *Cork Examiner* expressed the view that few of the workhouse inmates were receiving a sufficient amount of food to preserve their health. As this was being perpetuated in the name of the ratepayers, the newspaper asked: 'is it *their wish* that the wretched inmates of the Work-house, whose only sin is poverty, whose only crime is destitution, should be *deliberately and systematically starved to death?*'[86]

The resulting discussion provoked the usual arguments and rhetoric from guardians and one of them said that in the workhouse, paupers should get 'just enough to keep them alive and no more'. The medical officers were directed to compile an alternative dietary scale and this was presented at the next board meeting.[87] Though their allowances were 'as economical as is consistent with safety to human life', the medical officers warned the guardians that if the inmates, and particularly the children, were not treated well they would develop into 'useless cripples and be always on the hands of the Board'.

---

84 *CUM* 17 May 1847.
85 *CUM* 10 May, 24 May, 31 May 1847; *CUL* 21 May 1847; *CC* 18 May, 25 May 1847; *SR* 11 May, 18 May, 25 May 1847.
86 *CE* 26 May 1847.
87 *CUM* 24 May 1847.

Workhouse food allowances as recommended by Medical Officers – June 1847

		COST/ WEEK
Able bodied	Breakfast: 4 oz. rice and 4 oz. Indian meal stirabout, Dinner: 12 oz. brown bread and 1 pint of porridge.	1s.6¼d.
5-13 yr olds	Breakfast: 2½ oz. rice and 2½ oz. Indian meal stirabout, ½ pint of milk Dinner: 10 oz. bread and 1 pint porridge Supper: 4 oz. bread	1s.2d.
2-5 yr olds	Breakfast: 1 oz. rice and 1 oz. Indian meal stirabout, ½ pint milk Dinner: 6 oz. bread and ½ pint milk Supper: 4 oz. bread	1s.8d.
Under 2 yrs	½ lb. household bread and 1 pint of milk daily	10½d.
Aged & Infirm No. 1 diet (not in hospital)	Breakfast: 4 oz. rice and 4 oz. Indian meal stirabout ½ pint milk Dinner: 12 oz. brown bread and 1 pint milk	
Aged & Infirm No. 2 diet	Breakfast: 8 oz. Household bread and ¾ pint milk Dinner: 3 oz. Household bread and ¾ pint milk Dinner: 12 oz. brown bread and 1 pint milk Supper: One pint of sweetened gruel	

Note: The porridge to be made of oatmeal at a rate of 1½ ounces to a pint of water.

(*Source*: *CUM* 31 May 1847; *CE* 2 June 1847, *SR* 1 June 1847)

The suggested dietary modifications, although minor, provoked outrage from some guardians who refused to acknowledge that death could result from an inadequate diet. Mr Sheehy was opposed to the revisions, which would improve conditions for inmates, many of whom he dismissed as 'idle, useless drones'. The occupants of the women's wards were, he said, 'in a good measure composed of unfortunate creatures [prostitutes] who were occasionally issuing from the house on their nefarious dealings, and then returned to deposit their spurious offspring'.[88]

Criticisms of the changes suggested by the house committee were not confined to matters relating to food. Large areas of the workhouse were inadequately lit and in some hospital wards a 'solitary rushlight or farthing candle' was the sole source of light for up to 80 inmates. In some wards 'the dying [were] not being allowed a light to enable them to convey a drink to their parched mouths', and frequently the last rites

---

88 *CC* 1 June 1847; *CE* 2 June 1887; *SR* 1 June 1847; *CUM* 31 May, 9 June 16 June, 23 June 1847.

were administered in the dark. The ward staff were also poorly treated. The hospital's 63 unpaid assistant nurses were constantly confronted with sickness and disease. Their duties included washing and dressing new arrivals who suffered from a variety of contagious diseases. For this self-sacrifice they were rewarded with an extra allowance of tea and a small quantity of meat with their dinner. As a cost-saving measure, the guardians withdrew these allowances in June 1847. When the medical officers and some guardians sought their re-introduction, it was reasoned that such a precedent would be used as a 'wedge' by inmates who would utilise it 'to alter the entire dietary of the house'. Nonetheless, common sense prevailed and it was agreed to re-introduce the allowances for the nursing staff.[89] Undeterred, some guardians accused the nurses of drinking port wine which was intended for patients, and fearing that they would also partake of the mutton chops, it was decided to reduce the number ordered. A decision to deploy inmates to vegetable cultivation was abandoned only when it was discovered that there were too few able bodied inmates available to make the project viable.[90]

Some minor alterations were made to the dietary scales during the next twelve months. For instance, in February 1848, the infants were granted an additional four ounces of bread each day.[91] By June 1848 the allowances were as follows:

Food allowances – Summer 1848

CLASS	
1. Adults 15 yrs and over	Breakfast: a quart of stirabout made from 3 oz. oatmeal and 3 oz. Indian meal, plus ½ pint of boiling milk Dinner: ¾ lb. coarse brown bread and 1 pint of porridge containing 1 oz. rice and ¾ oz. Oatmeal
2. Nine to 15-yr-old children	As class 1, plus a supper of 4oz. brown bread which can be eaten dry, or with a canteen of pump water
3. Five to 9-yr-old children	Breakfast: 1½ pints of stirabout and ½ pint milk Dinner: as Class 1
4. Two to 5-yr-old children	Breakfast: 1 pint of stirabout and ½ pint milk Dinner: 8 oz. white bread and ½ pint milk Supper: 4 oz. Bread

89 *CC* 17 June, 24 June 1847; *CE* 18 June 1847; *SR* 17 June, 24 June 1847.
90 *CUM* 16 June, 30 June 1847.
91 *SR* 24 February 1848; see also *CUM* 20 September 1847.

5. Infants under 2 years	12 oz. White bread and 1 pint milk daily
6. Aged and Infirm	Breakfast: One quart of stirabout and ½ pint milk
	Dinner: 12 oz. brown bread and ½ pint milk

(*Source: CE* 14 June 1848; *SR* 17 June 1848)

By the summer of 1848 the cost of maintaining able-bodied work-house inmates had been reduced to 10½d. per week or 1½d. per day. This, said the *Cork Examiner*, 'is nothing more nor less than a starvation diet, so arranged as to thin the house in two ways – by death and repulsion. The inmates are quietly starved out, and the poor are as effectually kept out. This ensures a thin house and a low rate'. As a consequence of this policy many deserving poor shunned the work-house and looked upon it as 'the threshold to the grave – the entrance to the tomb. There, old age is extinguished – manly strength is withered up – female beauty is changed in ghastliness – childhood is blighted, as a flower by a harsh wind'.[92] One visitor reported that the workhouse bread was of poor quality and resembled 'a compound of discoloured husks and saturated sawdust'. A gloomy atmosphere pervaded the wards and the inmates were introverted and morose. In the dining hall 'great order and decorum prevailed, each unfortunate creature appearing more intent on discussing the contents of his canteen, together with his 12 oz. of bread, than otherwise employing himself'. In conclusion, the disgusted visitor testified that '*the inmates, of every age and class, are not sufficiently fed*'.[93]

As a response to such criticism, a committee was appointed in June 1848 to report on the dietary scale. Within a couple of weeks its findings were presented to the board. The changes it advocated included an additional ½ lb. of bread per day for able-bodied inmates; it also suggested that on two or three days each week, the inmates should get a helping of soup made from coarse beef or cows' heads. In common with many other Irish workhouses, the inmates of the Cork institution were suffering from an outbreak of scurvy. As an antidote it was suggested that cabbage, or some other vegetable, should be included in the porridge supplied to the inmates.[94] The usual display of intransigence and ill-will

---

92 *CE* 14 June 1848.
93 *CE* 28 June 1848.
94 *CE* 16 June, 23 June 1848; *SR* 29 June, 6 July 1848; see also, E. M. Crawford, *Food and Famine*, p. 71; E. M. Crawford, 'Scurvy in Ireland during the Great Irish Famine', *Social History of Medicine*, 1988, p. 295; E. Margaret Crawford, 'Migrant Maladies: Unseen Lethal Baggage', in E. Margaret Crawford (ed.), *The Hungry Stream, Essays on Emigration and Famine* (Belfast, 1997) pp. 143-45; E. M. Crawford, 'Subsistence crises and Famines in Ireland: A Nutritionist's view', in E. M. Crawford (ed.), *Famine the Irish experience 900-1900; Subsistence Crises and*

surfaced during the reading of the report at the guardians' meeting and Mr Sheehy sought to postpone any discussion on its content because he detected no want in the 'plump cheeks and ruddy countenances' of the inmates. Because of an input from the workhouse medical officers, who had previously recommended chops, chicken and wine for inmates, Thomas Sarsfield suggested that the new dietary report be received '*cum grano salis*'.[95] Criticising those who sought to reject or limit improved conditions for workhouse inmates, Mr Uniacke provocatively suggested that it would 'be more merciful to shoot them – to kill them by platoons'. The improvements were eventually agreed by twenty votes to sixteen and, following an evaluation by the Poor Law Commissioners, the new allowances were sanctioned in mid-July 1848.[96]

Sickness and Disease

Dr. O Connor was most apprehensive about the fever cases which were to be found almost everywhere in the house. In January 1847 only a few cases were malignant, but he envisaged that this would change. Fearing that an escalation of disease would spread to the city, the medical officers warned the guardians that 'driven to the fearful alternative of famine without the walls, and pestilence within, we cannot but consider the latter evil of overwhelming importance to the whole community'.[97] The Poor Law Commissioners were having misgivings about the sheds being constructed at the workhouse

> as they regard with apprehension the crowding together in a limited area, so large a number of persons as the workhouse will be able to contain when these buildings are finished. The Commissioners however do not doubt that the guardians, bearing in mind the serious responsibilities of such a large establishment, will be particularly scrupulous in constantly consulting with their medical officers respecting the number of admissions and the general sanitary arrangements of the workhouse.[98]

---

94 (*cont.*) *Famines in Ireland* (Edinburgh, 1989), pp. 208-9; C. Woodham Smith, *Great Hunger*, p. 194; For a discussion on the deficiency disease pellagra, see E. Margaret Crawford, 'Indian meal and pellagra in nineteenth century Ireland', in J. M. Goldstrom and L. A. Clarkson, *Irish Population, Economy and Society, Essays in honour of the late K. H. Connell* (London, 1981), pp. 151-161.

95 *CC* 6 July 1848.

96 *SR* 29 June, 6 July, 13 July, 29 July 1848; *CE* 7 July 1848; *CC* 22 June, 6 July, 13 July 1848.

97 *SR* 19 January 1847; *CUM* 15 February 1847.

98 NAI, Poor Law Commissioners, Letters to Joseph Burke 1847, No. 2139 of 21 January 1847, also NAI, Poor Law Commissioners, Letters to Joseph Burke 1846, 9 February, 15 February, 16 February, 23 February 1846.

Overcrowded wards, inadequate facilities for personal hygiene, the absence of fresh clothing and bedding – many inmates were sleeping on bare straw strewn on the ground – and the almost indiscriminate admission of new arrivals were a recipe for disaster. Fr. Maguire, the assistant chaplain, later recounted that in the workhouse it was difficult to get a bed 'that did not contain three fever patients; one holding only two was rare; and in the impoverished condition of their blood the spectacle presented by their bodies was indescribable. On one occasion I saw a man taking his breakfast in bed with a corpse next to him – there was no time to remove the body – and at another time when I had to sit on the ground to hear confession I found that my coat was covering the face of a corpse'.[99] The prevalent famine fevers – typhus fever and relapsing fever – were conveyed by lice. As Sir William P. Mac Arthur tells us 'the lack of cleanliness, the unchanged clothing and the crowding together, provided conditions ideal for lice to multiply and spread rapidly'.[100] The overcrowded sleeping and hospital wards, dining areas, corridors, and in fact most parts of the Cork workhouse were ideal for breeding and spreading the disease-carrying lice. The inmates who were deployed to sort and wash the workhouse clothing were particularly vulnerable and 'not one woman who washed escaped infection, and many of them died from fever'.[101] The danger of admitting extra inmates into overcrowded wards was obvious; some, it was believed, entered the workhouse 'for the sake of the coffin, and the bit of bread they would get when dying'.[102] Following

---

99 *CE* 20 October 1896.
100 Sir Wm. P. MacArthur, 'Medical History of the Famine', in R. Dudley Edwards and T. Desmond Williams, *The Great Famine – Studies in Irish history 1845-52* (New York, 1957, edition), pp. 271-2, see also pp. 265-6; L. Geary, "The late Disastrous epidemic'; Medical Relief and the Great Famine', in *'Fearful Realities': New Perspectives on the Famine* (Dublin, 1996), pp. 50-51; Laurence M. Geary, 'What people died of during the Famine', in C. Ó Gráda (ed.), *Famine 150* (Dublin, 1997), pp. 102-5; L. Geary, 'Famine, Fever and the Bloody Flux', in C. Póirtéir, *Great Irish Famine*, pp. 75-6; E. M. Crawford; 'Typhus in nineteenth century Ireland', in Malcolm and Jones (eds.), *Medicine, Disease and the state in Ireland, 1650–1940* (Cork, 1999), pp. 123-5; E. M. Crawford, 'Migrant Maladies: Unseen lethal baggage', in E. M. Crawford (ed.), *The hungry stream* (Belfast, 1997), pp. 141-2; V. A. Harden, 'Typhus, Epidemic', in *Cambridge History of Disease* (1993), pp. 1080-1; R. Dirks, 'Famine and Disease', in *Cambridge History of Disease*, p. 161; C. Woodham Smith, *Great Hunger* (1962), pp. 188-90; S. H. Cousens, 'Regional Death Rate in Ireland during the Great Famine, from 1846-1851', in *Population Studies*, vol. XIV (1960), pp. 56-7; E. M. Crawford and L.A. Clarkson, *Feast and Famine*, etc (Oxford, 2001), pp. 152-4; Joel Mokyr and Cormac Ó Gráda, 'What do people die of during famines: The Great Irish Famine in comparative perspective', in *European Review of Economic History*, Vol. 6 (2002), p. 354.
101 *SR* 9 December 1847.
102 *SR* 21 January 1847.

the example of the Skibbereen, Bandon and Macroom workhouses, the Cork guardians intervened to prevent the spread of disease. The workhouse master was instructed to limit the number of admissions to the amount of discharges on any day.[103]

The effective closure of the workhouse was discussed at public meetings in the city during January and February. Fr. Mathew's suggestion that the emergency merited a repetition of the guardians' short-lived venture into supplying food to non-resident poor was not implemented.[104] It was acknowledged that when the sheds in the workhouse grounds were ready, about 1,500 extra applicants could be accommodated, but the possibility of acquiring another premises was also explored. Although some guardians were opposed to taking additional accommodation because they anticipated that this would encourage country paupers, it was agreed that the police barracks at Elizabeth Fort in Barrack Street should be sought as an auxiliary workhouse. The Lord Lieutenant acceded to the request on condition that the police were re-housed in suitable premises.[105] Only when the police began their evacuation was it realised that the barracks was not extensive enough to serve as an auxiliary workhouse, and it was decided to use the premises as a temporary hospital instead.[106]

Before the end of January 1847 fever cases were to be found in almost every part of the workhouse with the number and severity of the stricken accelerating uncontrollably. Some were transferred to the city's fever hospital, but that institution was also under pressure for accommodation and an official lamented that the guardians 'have swamped us with their patients'.[107] The workhouse medical officers were unrepentant. With just 45 beds in the convalescent wards, they had inadequate accommodation for sick inmates and did not have the staff or the time to closely monitor the progress of illness.[108] Five of the patients sent from the workhouse

---

103 *CUM* 18 January 1847; *SR* 19 January, 9 February 1847; *CC* 12 January, 19 January, 9 February 1847; NAI, CSORP 1847 H1930. According to Dr Denis O Connor, the correct procedure had not been adhered to when the motion to close the workhouse was put forward. D. O Connor, *Seventeen Years of workhouse life*, p. 33.

104 Letter of 5 February 1847, Fr. Mathew to Sir R. Routh; *Correspondence from January to March 1847, Board of Works Series, [Second part]*. (London, 1847) Vol. LII [797], p. 103.

105 NAI, Poor Law Commissioners, Letters to James Burke 1847, No. 2139 of 28 January 1847, No. 2938 of 6 February 1847, No. 5774 of 11 February 1847; SR 26 January, 6 February, 9 February 1847; CC 9 February 1847.

106 *CC* 6 March, 9 March 1847; *SR* 9 March 1847.

107 *CC* 21 January 1847; see *CUL* 23 January 1847.

108 *CUM* 11 January 1847; *See Census of Ireland for the year 1851*, part V, Table of Deaths, Vol. I, PP 1856, vol. XXIX, [2087-1], p. 300.

died in one week in January and Dr Popham complained that the work-house hospital was 'so crowded that every day the lives of the physicians were endangered by going into an atmosphere impregnated by malaria'.[109] Ominously, the guardians gave the workhouse master permission to purchase 500 yards of calico shrouding.[110]

The medical officers' efforts at isolating fever cases were not successful and following a rapid and unprecedented increase in the number of deaths, the weekly totals escalated alarmingly at the end of January 1847.[111] The highest casualty rate was among young boys in the work-house, and 'the yards and play grounds, where they used to assemble for amusement, were at present completely deserted, and there was not a single child to be seen'.[112] As Dr O Connor later recounted, children in the workhouse at that time 'went out of life like bubbles bursting on a stream'.[113]

Because the number of deaths in the workhouse was so 'alarmingly great' during the first week of February, the Central Board of Health in Dublin sent Dr Richard Stephens to Cork to investigate and compile a report on the situation.[114] Dr Stephens was instructed 'to inquire and report to this Board on the character of the Disease at present prevalent there; the ages of the patients who have died within the week previous . . . the state of the House as to ventilation, and the Diet and Drink for the Sick; the number of cubic feet allowed to each inmate in the sick and healthy Wards; and generally as to the cause of the mortality or the means most likely to arrest its future progress'.[115]

Dr Stephens held an inquiry at the workhouse on 16 February and questioned officials in some detail on matters relating to sanitation and hygiene. A synopsis of the evidence showed that

- Almost 500 inmates retained their own ragged clothing.
- Linen was changed only every three weeks.
- Towels were scarce and inmates washed irregularly.
- The workhouse diet consisted principally of bread and porridge.
- The workhouse bread was served 'piping hot' from the ovens.
- Inmates ate their meals while sitting or squatting on the floor.
- Porridge was served in tin dishes called quarts from which three children

---

109 *CC* 12 January 1847; this was a common belief among doctors at that time.
110 *CUM* 25 January 1847.
111 See *Transactions of the Central Relief Committee of the Society of Friends during the Famine in Ireland in 1846 and 1847* (Dublin, 1852), p. 181. See also Laurence M. Geary, *Medicine and Charity in Ireland 1718-1851* (Dublin, 2004), p. 186.
112 *CE* 17 February 1847.
113 D. O Connor, *Seventeen Years of workhouse life*, p. 48.
114 *CUM* 15 February 1847; *CUL* 13 February 1847; *CE* 17 February 1847; *SR* 16 February 1847; NAI, CSORP 1847 H2981.
115 NAI, CSORP 1847 H1704.

dined together, thus ensuring that none got an equal share and increasing the risks of infection.
- In the fever wards two adults or up to four children occupied each bed.
- Many staff members, including teachers and ward personnel, contracted disease.[116]

Dr Stephens compiled a report on the workhouse and this was dispatched to the Central Board of Health in Dublin on 17 February 1847, along with statistical material on the incidence and consequences of disease. In the report, Dr Stephens attributed the high death rate in the workhouse to the 'debilitated or dying condition' of the people being admitted, to overcrowding and to the unsanitary state of its various wards.[117] This was corroborated in a report from Assistant Commissioner Joseph Burke, which used evidence from Drs O Connor and Popham to show that contagious fever was spreading through the workhouse.[118]

The report from Dr Stephens and the correspondence it generated, provides us with a valuable record of conditions in the workhouse at the time of his visit. The workhouse itself was in a 'completely chaotic state' and he was critical that people were permitted to visit friends and relations and endanger their own health and that of the inmates, by bringing with them 'the seeds of contagion'.[119] There can be no doubt that some of the visitors contracted illness in the workhouse, as diseases such as smallpox, dysentery, measles and fever were to be found in its wards. The boys' school had been converted into a dormitory and in an apartment measuring 45 feet by 30 feet, 102 boys slept in 24 beds; the female school was used as a nursery for children and their mothers. The general hall served as a dormitory and about 600 five to thirteen year old girls slept there in 130 beds. The five to nine age group slept together in groups of five children and up to four of the thirteen year olds shared beds. Many other examples of dangerous overcrowding were evident; for instance, in a ward housing children in the care of their parents, 72 persons occupied 21 beds, and in another ward 17 beds accommodated 17 women and 37 children.

From the evidence presented by Dr Stephens, the Central Board of Health attributed the high level of mortality in the Cork workhouse to overcrowding and want of ventilation in the wards, and to a lesser extent

---

116 *CUM* 8 March, 22 March, 9 April 1847; *CC* 23 February, 27 February 1847; *SR* 18 February, 23 February, 20 April 1847.
117 *CUL* 17 February 1847; PP 1847, Vol. LV, [257], *Report into the state of Workhouses in Cork etc.*; NAI, CSORP 1847 H5471.
118 NAI, CSORP 1847 H4338 – Report of 15 February 1847 from Assistant Commissioner J. Burke.
119 PP 1847, Vol. LV, [257], *Report into state of workhouses*, p. 5.

to the condition of the poor on entering the house. The board analysed the 91 deaths in the institution during the last week of January and found that just three people had died within a week of admission. A further 21 inmates died after three weeks and 28 others had been residents for over six months. This led the board to conclude that the new arrivals were reasonably healthy but that the health of inmates was endangered by a period of residence in the house. As a result of Dr Stephens's inquiry, the Cork guardians agreed to improve ventilation in the wards and to install perforated zinc vents on doors and windows.[120] Also, to avoid serving very fresh bread, arrangements were made to have it baked one day before serving. The Poor Law Commissioners asked the guardians to reduce the number of workhouse inmates by refusing to admit new applicants. They also instructed the guardians to return the dining hall and school rooms to their intended uses and they ordered their inspector, Joseph Burke, to ensure that the changes were fully implemented.[121] The guardians were left with little choice, and they passed a motion in favour of giving the medical officers the authority to decide on how many new inmates could be admitted each week.[122]

The outcome of Dr Stephens's inquiry failed to impress Dr O Connor and he later wrote that when the Poor Law Commissioners were concerned about conditions in the workhouse

> they sent gentlemen from Dublin, who paced the wards, measured their height and breadth, and having reduced all to cubic feet, went away. Much good was always expected from these visits, but I am not sure that any arose. One of these gentlemen made a notable discovery that the deaths in the workhouse were caused principally from the inmates eating hot bread; and the board having promised to correct this evil, he went away very happy. In every tragedy there is mixed up a little of the comic, and never more truly than on this occasion . . .[123]

Although the Cork board of guardians had resolved not to increase the number of inmates in the workhouse, many still sought admission. On 17 February there were about 50 starving paupers in the entrance hall when William Fagan, one of the guardians, came on the scene. He 'found some of them fainting and in convulsions from starvation . . .

120 NAI, CSORP 1847 H5471, NAI, CSORP 1847 H1959, minutes of Central Board of Health 20 February 1847; *CUM* 22 February 1847.
121 NAI, Poor Law Commissioners, Letters to James Burke 1847, Letter No. 5347 of 27 February and 9 March 1847; NAI, CSORP 1847 H4338, letter from Poor Law Commissioners to Central Board of Health 27 February 1847.
122 *CUM* 22 February 1847; *CC* 23 February, 2 March, 30 March 1847; *SR* 23 February, 2 March 1847; NAI, CSORP 1847 H4338.
123 D. O Connor, *Seventeen Years of workhouse life*, p. 33.

Most of these human beings, these British subjects – had not tasted food for two days, and the miserable children were clinging to their fainting mothers and screaming from the pains of starvation'. The applicants were given a little wine to revive them while Fagan returned to the boardroom to plead on their behalf. The guardians refused to admit them to the house but directed that they be given some food and sent on their way. This scene was witnessed by Dr. O Connor who saw them being 'sent away, to die in some obscure place where there will be no record of their deaths with which to shock the sensitive. The appalling sight which shocked this humane gentleman is a matter of daily occurrence'. Fagan recounted this episode at the next meeting of the Cork Soup Committee, of which he was a member, and it was agreed to provide gratuitous relief to destitute applicants during one hour each evening.[124] A certain amount of food was reserved for country applicants. The Mayor was satisfied that these recipients were deserving, for

> The ordeal to which these unfortunate beings are subjected is anything but attractive, and their endurance of it is the best test of want, for, first, they are exposed to a tremendous pressure, attended with a danger of personal injury; – next, they are immured for four hours in an enclosed yard, crowded with pens, where they can scarcely move; and finally they receive a portion of food, just sufficient to support life! As a test of destitution, this mode of relief is, therefore, far better than the distribution of soup by tickets.[125]

Each day at the Barrack Street soup kitchen, about 900 people were given a free quart of hominy made from rice and oatmeal. Over 300 gallons of meat soup were also distributed to ticket holders. At the Old Market Place kitchen, 2,500 people received hominy rations and 1,000 others were fed at Harpur's Lane. The free rations were distributed at around the same time in each depot and, to ensure that there was no duplication, recipients were confined on the premises for up to four hours. Soup and bread were distributed by other agencies and by private individuals. In total, about 9,000 people survived on free or reduced price food each day.[126] This was insufficient for the demand and it was estimated that at least 20,000 quarts of soup would have to be distributed each day, to give 'even a modicum of relief' to all those requiring

---

124 *CE* 17 February 1847; *CC* 20, 27 February, 2 March 1847; *SR* 18 February 1847.
125 *CC* 4 March 1847.
126 *CC* 14 April, 17 April, 19 April 1847; see also PP 1847 Vol. VI (2), [737-11], *Colonisation Report*; Evidence of Fr. Theobald Mathew, p. 243.

assistance. Because of the shortfall, 'any, especially the patient, silent victims of famine, are left to perish'.[127]

The Board of Health's directive on reducing overcrowding was a positive contribution towards improving the standard of health and hygiene in the workhouse. Its criticism of the workhouse bread was probably justified. Its quality was unreliable and inconsistent, and shortly after Dr Stephens's visit, 3,400 lbs. of good bread was ordered from the city because the produce of the workhouse bakery was unfit for use in the hospital.[128] Cork was not the only institution to attract official attention, and investigations were undertaken into conditions in other Irish workhouses during the Famine years.[129]

The general hygiene of the Cork workhouse, which was haphazard under normal conditions, was severely tested during this period of overcrowding. The primitive system of sewage disposal was still in operation. 'The most offensive material which accumulates in the wards during the night, and from the cess pits when opened by contractors' was added to the large heaps of manure and excrement every day. The stench pervading the entire complex became almost unbearable when the heaps were disturbed and loaded in carts for removal by manure dealers who paid for the waste. The workhouse sewerage system remained in this 'most defective state' for some time, and following a thorough inspection, clogged pipes were found in numerous locations.[130]

---

127 Letter of 15 February 1847, Edward Hackett to Mr. Redington, *Correspondence from January to March 1847, Commissariat series* [Second part] (London, 1847), Vol. LII [797], p. 15.

128 *CUM* 1 March 1847, also 29 March, 19 April 1847. In May 1847 the guardians directed that the workhouse bread be baked in the proportion of one part second flour and three parts wheaten meal. *CUM* 10 May 1847.

129 See for instance the following reports: PP 1847, Vol. LV, [257], *A copy of a report made to the Board of Health in Dublin, by the Medical Officers sent to inquire into the state of the workhouses in Cork, Bantry and Lurgan*: PP 1846, Vol. XXXVI, [294], *Copy of memorandum on the alleged neglect of sick paupers in the hospital of the Fermoy Union workhouse . . .;* PP 1850, Vol. L, [382], *A copy of a report made to the Board of Guardians of Castlebar Union, on the 20th of April . . .;* PP 1850, Vol. L, [461], *A copy of a report . . . with reference to the condition of Castlebar Union Workhouse;* PP 1850, Vol. L, [259], *A copy of a report addressed to the Poor Law Commissioners of Ireland, by Mr. Inspector Bourke, with reference to the condition of Kilrush Union;* PP 1851, Vol. XLIX, [442], *Copy of a letter addressed by the Poor Law Commissioners for Ireland, appointed Doctors Hughes and Hill as Inspectors, under the Act 10 and 11 Vict. C. 90 for inquiring into the causes of the mortality in certain Unions in the County of Clare.*

130 *CUM* 1 March, 7 July 1847; *CUL* 25 June 1847; *SR* 10 June, 15 June 1848. Renovation works at a cost of about £600 were undertaken under the supervision of experts from the Wide Street Board and the improvements were completed in mid 1849. *CE* 9 June, 16 June 1848, 22 June 1849; *SR* 13 July, 10 August, 19 October 1848; 21 June 1849; *CC* 13 July 1848. For information on workhouse sewerage systems, see also evidence of Dr Henry Maunsell, PP 1849 [356], pp. 124-8.

Under the provisions of the Temporary Fever Act (*9 Vict., Cap 6.*) boards of guardians were empowered to acquire additional premises for use as auxiliary wards. As we have seen, the workhouse itself was crowded, and when the number of deaths increased alarmingly in February and March 1847, it was observed that, instead of a house of refuge, it was assuming the role of a 'lazar house of death and woe'.[131] Applicants were no longer being admitted to the city fever hospital and in response to the unrelenting demands for accommodation, it was decided to reserve the North Infirmary for the exclusive use of fever cases.[132] By the second week of March, the Infirmary had 70 new fever patients and the board of guardians had already commenced using Elizabeth Fort at Barrack Street as an additional hospital ward for workhouse applicants.[133] Before the end of March there were 96 fever patients in the North Infirmary, and 202 in the city fever hospital. Because of the lack of convalescent wards, premature discharges, which helped spread disease, were again being made from the hospitals. Dr O Connor observed that 'fever was moving through the streets. The people labouring under it were not aware of it, and they reeled through the streets with sickness until they fell, being unable to walk'.[134] There was concern that fever was spreading beyond its pauper base and Dr Bullen noted 'a great increase in diseases of a malignant and deadly form amongst the better classes, especially typhus fever'.[135]

Before mid-March several well known citizens, including William Beamish, Mr Smyth, moral governor of the lunatic asylum, and George Laurance, the industrialist and poor law guardian, had died from fever. Among the others who contracted the disease were the workhouse schoolmaster, the fever hospital apothecary and the house surgeon of the North Infirmary.[136] Although the workhouse itself had no proper fever wards, 279 of its patients were under treatment for fever in mid April. During the previous couple of months many hospital staff had been stricken with the disease and three wardmasters, a wardmistress and a

---

131 *CC* 2 March 1847; *SR* 2 March 1847.
132 *Annual Report of North Infirmary* (Cork, 1849), p. 4.
133 *CUM* 1 March, 8 March 1847; *CUL* 24 February, 6 March, 13 April, 21 April, 1 May 1847; *CC* 9 March, 13 March 1847; *SR* 9 March, 13 March 1847; NAI, CSORP 1847 H3321; NAI, CSORP 1847 H3575; NAI, CSORP 1847 H3820; NAI, CSORP 1847 H3908; NAI, CSORP 1847 H4600.
134 *CC* 23 March, 25 March 1847.
135 *CC* 6 March 16 March 1847; D. O Connor, *Seventeen Years of workhouse life*, p. 40. For a discussion on the high mortality rates from fever, among better-off citizens, see – Sir Wm. P. MacArthur, 'Medical History of Famine', pp. 280-81; L. M. Geary, 'What people died of', p. 103; E. M. Crawford, Migrant Maladies, pp. 142-4; C. Ó Gráda, *Black '47 and beyond, The Great Irish Famine in history, economy and memory* (N.J. 1999), pp. 94-5; *Census of Ireland 1851*, part V, Table of Deaths, Vol. 1, Dublin, PP 1856, Vol. XXIX, [2087 –1], p. 302.
136 *SR* 18 February 23 February 25 February, 9 March 1847; *CC* 23 March 1847.

tailor had died.[137] Following the weekly inspection of applicants seeking admission to the workhouse on 18 March, a number of guardians and officials became ill. The stricken included Richard Dowden, Dan Daly, Thomas Jennings, the workhouse clerk Robert J. O Shaughnessy, the storekeeper George Carr and the assistant chaplain Rev Augustine Maguire.[138] In response to the danger, the guardians abandoned the workhouse boardroom. From 23 March, the city's Corn Exchange became the venue for their weekly meetings.[139]

With the exception of regular inspections by members of the house committee, few of the guardians went to the workhouse and the task of admitting paupers was undertaken by the master. The assistant commissioner was not satisfied with this arrangement and he requested that at least three guardians carry out the duty of interviewing and admitting applicants. There were no volunteers and Thomas Sarsfield said that under the circumstances it would be difficult to force anyone to return to the board room. Speaking of his own situation, he said that 'he had a duty to the public, but he also had a duty to his family to perform, which was a paramount duty, and if there was no means of admitting paupers without going to the workhouse, he certainly would not go there'. The system of confining paupers to the probationary ward prior to admission to the body of the workhouse had broken down, and most of them retained their own clothing. When the master confirmed that people with dysentery and fever were being admitted directly to the house, the guardians directed that further applicants would have to be inspected by the medical officers.[140] Admissions declined during the next few weeks, but when 21 applicants were admitted in one week in mid-April, the master reported that most of these hapless people had been left at the workhouse gate in a dying state.[141]

Fever continued to spread through the city during the spring of 1847 but, because of limited accommodation, patients were refused admission when they went to the hospitals.[142] Some returned to their homes and spread disease, but occasionally, such was the fear of infection, that their

---

137 NAI, Poor Law Commissioners, Letters to James Burke 1847, 7 May 1847.

138 During the illness of R.J. O Shaughnessy, his brother Mark S. O Shaughnessy carried out the duties of workhouse clerk. *CUM* 7 July 1847; *CUL* 27 February, 11 March 1847.

139 *CUM* 22 March 1847; *SR* 23 March, 25 March 1847. Twelve months were to elapse before they resumed meeting at the workhouse. The Bandon board of guardians took a similar action and they also deserted their boardroom and met at the town's courthouse. *CC* 1 April 1847.

140 *SR* 30 March 1847; *CC* 30 March 1847.

141 *SR* 6 April, 13 April 1847.

142 PP 1847, Vol. VI, [737-11], *Report on Colonization, etc.*, Evidence of Fr T. Mathew, p. 243; PP 1856, Vol. XXIX [2087-1], *Census of Ireland for the year 1851*: Part V, Table of deaths, Vol. 1, p. 301.

houses were closed up to prevent them regaining access. Others, particularly strangers from the country, who were treated with suspicion and intolerance by many guardians, were turned out of lodging houses when they became ill; thereafter, they wandered through the city and eventually 'perished miserably in the streets and alleys'.[143] The board of health suggested the construction of sheds in the workhouse grounds, to accommodate the rapidly increasing number of fever patients, but the former St Patrick's Orphan Asylum at Cat Fort was modified as a temporary hospital to accommodate 150 fever victims.[144] This hospital opened on 19 April, and within a few days, over 100 patients were 'cleanly and comfortably' accommodated there.[145] Before the end of June there were 100 patients in the city fever hospital; Cat Fort gave accommodation to 121 patients, Barrack Street housed 250 and the North Infirmary had a further 160 fever victims.[146] The guardians' policy of curtailing admissions to the workhouse enabled them vacate the lower house at the Blind Asylum in June when the inmates were removed to the main building. The vacated premises were subsequently retained as a hospital ward for fever cases from all the Cork hospitals.[147]

Some guardians believed that country paupers should fend for themselves and motivated by a desire to save money, they heartlessly sought to have them expelled from the workhouse. They advocated that the master should give inmates a 'friendly whisper' that rations would be provided to those who wished to depart to their home places.[148] On a more sinister level, a movement to exclude country vagrants from the city itself was gathering pace outside the workhouse. Under the aegis of the Cork board of health, a group of tough 'and if possible well-disciplined men' was employed as constables, to intimidate vagrants and prevent them from entering the city.[149] Adopting what Fr. Mathew described as a 'very unchristian and inhuman line of conduct', a ruthless policy was implemented and 'if these poor starving creatures are caught imploring food, they are seized upon, dragged to an open market, where they are confined without food until next morning, when they are placed under

143 PP 1847 [737-11], Evidence of Fr. Mathew, op. cit., p. 243; *Census of Ireland 1851*, part V, Table of Deaths, Vol. 1, Dublin 1856, Vol. XXIX, p. 301.

144 *CC* 13 March, 23 March 1847; *SR* 23 March, 25 March, 8 May 1847.

145 *CUM* 29 March, 19 April, 26 April 1847; *SR* 20 April, 24 April 1847; *CC* 17 April, 20 April, 24 April, 27 April, 29 April 1847; see *also Distress (Ireland), Treasury Minutes, 3rd Report, Appendix A, List of orders from Board of Health (*10, March 1847) Vol. XVII [836], p. 9; PP 1847, Vol. XLIX (16), [397], *Return of the number of workhouses, inmates etc.*, pp. 2 and 6.

146 *CC* 24 June 1847; NAI, CSORP 1847 H6255; NAI, CSORP 1847 H6876.

147 *CUM* 16 June, 23 June 1847; *CC* 17 June, 1 July, 8 July 1847.

148 *SR* 31 July 1847.

149 NAI, CSORP 1847 H5804.

the care of Constables, and sent five or six miles from the city, and then left to perish'.[150] To its shame, the Cork board of guardians allied itself with this inhumane policy. It published a handbill advising strangers in search of relief that, on detection, they would be seized and driven out of the city. Some guardians believed that in time, nature would take its course, and, as fever raged in the workhouse, one of the guardians, Dr Lyons, callously observed that 'death was balancing all things now, and would soon sweep away all the country paupers in the house'.[151] The women who washed the clothing and bedding were still facing danger and, as a reward for their selfless, but probably misguided, dedication, they were given an extra allowance of 4 ounces of bread each day.[152]

During the summer of 1847 fever or dysentery accounted for the majority of workhouse deaths, and eventually 'every nurse in the house took the disease'.[153] Dysentery attacks the intestines and bowels and people suffering an intestinal upset, for instance from unsuitable food, are predisposed to infection.[154] As the weeks passed, fever deaths decreased and dysentery became the principal killer by mid-June. At the start of July 65 fever cases and 124 dysentery cases were being treated in the workhouse and, in one week, the deaths from the diseases were eight and eleven respectively. Two weeks later there were 71 fever and 120 dysentery cases in the house and during the previous seven days there was one death from fever and 15 from dysentery. Between April and November 1847, the Cork hospitals treated 6,580 patients, of whom 522 died.[155]

Deaths in temporary hospitals up to August 1847

HOSPITAL	OPENING DATE	DEATHS
Cat Fort	19 April	98
North Infirmary	28 April	110
Barrack Street	24 April	161
North Sheds	30 May	48

(*Source: CC* 2 September, 4 September 1847)

150 NAI, CSORP 1847 H6843; PP 1847 [737-11], op. cit., pp. 243-4.
151 *CUM* 3 May 1847; *SR* 27 April, 1 May, 4 May 1847.
152 *Cork Union – FM1 Cork Workhouse Visiting Committee Book* (Cork Archives), 8 December 1847; 14 February 1848.
153 *CC 8* May 1849; see also, *Census of Ireland 1851*, Table of deaths, p. 251.
154 Sir Wm. P. MacArthur, 'Medical History of the famine', p. 269; L. M. Geary, 'What people died of', pp. 106-7; L. Geary, 'Famine, Fever and the Bloody Flux', in C. Póirtéir, *Great Irish Famine*, pp. 76-7.
155 *CC*15 July, 22 July, 9 November 1847; see also *Annual Report of Cork Fever Hospital for 1847* (Cork, 1848), pp. 3 and 5.

By the spring of 1848 the number of fever and dysentery cases had balanced out. Between 1 February and 2 March 177 fever patients and 156 dysentery victims had been treated in Cork's hospitals; in total, there were 123 deaths during that period.[156] In the Barrack Street hospital 63 fever patients and 68 dysentery cases of an 'exceedingly aggravated nature' were receiving treatment at the start of March.[157] Patients from some outlying hospitals were brought to Barrack Street when local institutions closed during the spring of 1848.[158] The number and severity of cases decreased during the summer and autumn and, although some officials were anxious that it should be available in case cholera reached Cork, the guardians spoke of closing the Barrack Street hospital.[159] A committee of seven guardians was selected to manage the hospital, and Doctor Jeffrey was appointed physician at 5s. per day. At the end of November the patients included 40 fever and 13 dysentery cases plus four smallpox victims.[160] The city was then experiencing a major smallpox outbreak and children suffering from the disease were frequently encountered on its streets. In January 1849 over 40 smallpox cases were being treated at the Barrack Street hospital and, because of the increased duties, the salary of the apothecary was raised to £70 per annum. The guardians recruited a number of officials to help stem the progress of the disease. Six vaccinators were appointed to the rural, and two to the city divisions. The latter officials were A.F. Roche and Surgeon Townsend. The vaccinators were paid 1s. for each of the first 200 vaccinations and 6d. for subsequent treatments.[161] At the end of February 1849 the 228 patients under treatment at Barrack Street consisted of 188 fever, 17 dysentery and 23 smallpox patients, and during the previous week there were five deaths from smallpox, one from dysentery and four from fever.[162] When cholera arrived in the city a few weeks later, the Barrack Street hospital assumed the role of principal receptacle for victims of the disease.[163]

---

156 *CC* 7 March 1848.
157 *CC* 24 February, 2 March, 16 March 1848; *SR* 4 March, 25 March 1848.
158 NAI, CSORP 1848 H2479; NAI, CSORP 1848 H3586; NAI, CSORP 1848 H4270.
159 *SR* 16 September, 28 September 1848; *CC* 14 September, 16 September, 21 September, 23 September, 28 September, 5 October 1848. The board of guardians severed its connection with the Barrack Street hospital when it handed over possession to the Corporation in February 1858. *CUM* 10 February 1858.
160 *CC* 12 October, 19 October, 26 October, 30 November 1848; *SR* 14 October, 19 October, 26 October, 9 November, 30 November, 7 December 1848.
161 *SR* 25 January, 22 February 1849; *CC* 22 February 1849.
162 *CC* 1 March 1849.
163 Up to the end of November 1849, 2529 cases were treated at Barrack Street hospital; the 444 deaths at the hospital included smallpox, measles, scarlatina, fever, dysentery and cholera victims. *Report of the Commissioners of Health, Ireland, on the epidemics of 1846 to 1850.* (Dublin, 1852), PP 1852-3, Vol. XLI, p. 10.

Cholera

Early in March 1849 cholera appeared in Cork's lanes and at 7am on Monday 9 April four cases were detected in an overcrowded male ward of the workhouse. These victims were able-bodied men from the country and all died within eight hours of contracting the disease. Dr O Connor concluded that their rapid demise resulted from 'exposure to cold, and their being unused to the confined air of the workhouse'. During the next two days another twenty cases occurred of which six proved fatal. To facilitate early detection of the disease, two men were appointed to inspect the dormitories and alert the medical officers to new cases which were immediately removed to hospital.[164] This system was refined within a few days and instead, a 'confidential' named Denis Mulqueeny visited each ward four times during the night and reported any changes to the resident surgeon. In anticipation of an escalation of disease, four children's wards were set aside for cholera patients and the children were moved to the auxiliary premises. The medical officers recommended that bread of a quality similar to that used in the hospital should be supplied to all inmates, that workhouse labour should be reserved for the fittest inmates, and then only after a good breakfast had been supplied.[165] As another precaution, they directed that instead of Indian meal, which had been associated with stomach problems since its general distribution a couple of years earlier, oatmeal should be used in the workhouse hominy. They also banned the use of vegetables from the workhouse table during the continuance of the disease.[166] On the advice of the medical officers extra staff were employed and six new biers were acquired for transporting cholera victims.[167]

During its initial outbreak the disease attacked far more males than females. The guardians discussed the phenomenon and concluded that in general the females were healthier and less emaciated than the male inmates – probably because they had sought workhouse relief at an earlier stage and left their husbands outside to search for work. The women's wards were kept in a greater state of cleanliness but within a fortnight cases occurred in the female side of the house.[168] Within a week of the outbreak the number of cases in the workhouse exceeded

---

164 *SR* 6 March 1849; *CUM* 11 April 1849; *Province of Munster* (hereafter *POM*) 14 April 1849.

165 *CUM* 11 April, 18 April 1849; *CC* 17 April 1849; *SR* 12 April 1849.

166 *CC* 19 April 1849; *SR* 19 April 1849.

167 *CUM* 2 May 1849; *POM* 21 April 1849.

168 *CC* 3 May, 10 May 1849; *SR* 17 April, 21 April 1849.

100 and the death rate at 38 was more than one in three.[169] Some of the fatalities had been admitted to the workhouse hospital in a state of collapse but the majority were inmates who had been transferred from internal wards.[170]

Though an increase in discharges from the house was noticed when the first cases occurred, the number of applications climbed during the next few weeks as inhabitants of the city lanes sought to escape the cholera. The workhouse could not accept all the applicants and every night its entrance was crowded with poor people sleeping under walls, in doors and in gateways.[171] Following a report from their inspector, Dr Phelan, the Poor Law Commissioners issued a sealed order at the start of April limiting the number of workhouse inmates to 6,300.[172] The provision of outdoor relief was discussed but rejected by the guardians because they feared this would attract applicants from country areas; instead, the board advertised for a store to house additional inmates.[173] The Poor Law Commissioners disagreed with the decision to acquire a building which would, in all probability, be 'ill adapted' for conversion to an auxiliary workhouse. Instead they advocated outdoor relief for 361 aged and infirm inmates whose accommodation could then be utilised by deserving applicants. The guardians refused to introduce outdoor relief in the Cork Union as they feared that it would become impossible to control. As a compromise the city's Mayor advocated that able-bodied labourers seeking employment should be provided with a daily meal at the workhouse, but again this was not entertained by the guardians.[174]

A new nursery block was then under construction at the workhouse and the contractor was instructed to prepare two rooms for emergency accommodation. The guardians went ahead with their plan to get additional accommodation and they rented a store at Douglas Street, which was capable of accommodating 400 people. The nursery block, with accommodation for 400 inmates, was soon ready for occupation and

---

169 *CUM* 18 April 1849; *SR* 19 April 1849.

170 The guardians and their families feared the disease so again it was decided to abandon the workhouse boardroom and meet at the city's Corn Exchange. The Poor Law Commissioners intervened and after a couple of meetings, they insisted that the guardians return to the workhouse. They reasoned that if the workhouse was dangerous it was unfair to expect the poor to enter the institution. *CUM* 24 April, 2 May 1849; *CC* 3 May 1849; *SR* 26 April, 3 May 1849.

171 *SR* 10 April, 24 April, 24 May, 26 May 1849.

172 *SR* 12 April 1849.

173 *CC* 12 April 1849. Some guardians believed that outdoor relief recipients would merely sell the food.

174 *SR* 17 April 1849, *CC* 19 April 1849; *CUM* 18 April 1849.

along with the Douglas Street store, it enabled the workhouse and its various auxiliaries to house over 7,000 inmates.[175]

By the start of May 1849 over 400 cases of cholera and 180 fatalities had occurred among the inmates of the workhouse and its auxiliaries.[176] At the lower auxiliary house, used as a fever hospital since June 1847, cholera of a 'very malignant character' spread rapidly. In the majority of cases, those attacked had already been ill at the workhouse. Two paid nurses were employed to care for the stricken and six female inmates were recruited to help.[177] Dr Popham reported to the board that 'the ravages of the cholera in the workhouse was very remarkable. The disease rushed through a ward attacking those in the last stages of other diseases, and terminating their existence, while all the healthy patients escaped'. On the physicians' advice it was agreed that inmates should be permitted to walk in the fresh air for an hour each day.[178] Staff were also affected by the disease, so temporary assistants and additional nurses were employed to carry out duties in the wards and hospital. To compensate for the extra workload, Dr Townsend's salary was increased to £5 per week and Dr Wycherly was recruited as a temporary assistant physician. In spite of reservations by the Poor Law Commissioners, the salaries of the workhouse chaplains and physicians were increased for the duration of the epidemic.[179] Burial of the dead was carried out at night and the seven men involved at this work were given an extra pound of bread for their trouble.[180] On one occasion, two gravediggers disinterred the body of a coloured man and removed his gold earrings and some clothing before re burying the corpse. A couple of days later one of the men, James Houlahan, was drowned in the South Channel. His companion had been found in a state of intoxication and was taken to hospital 'where the vigorous application of the stomach pump alone saved his life'.[181]

Having raged for about eight weeks, the cholera epidemic subsided at the start of June, by which time it had struck about 600 inmates and caused over 200 fatalities in the workhouse and another 200 deaths in the Barrack Street auxiliary house.[182] The workhouse physicians were

---

175 *SR* 19 April, 26 April, 21 June 1849. The Douglas Street premises was given up at the end of September. *CUM* 19 September 1849.
176 *SR* 3 May 1849; *CC* 28 April, 1 May, 3 May 1849.
177 *CUM* 2 May 1849.
178 *SR* 8 May 1849; *CC* 8 May 1849.
179 *SR* 21 June, 5 July 1849. Dr. Wycherly retired from the workhouse in January 1877. During his years in the institution he never took a week's holidays.
180 *CUM* 21 March 1849.
181 *CE* 3 October 1849.
182 *SR* 31 May, 12 June 1849; *CE* 8 June 1849. In the city itself there were 3176 cases of cholera and 1329 deaths. *Report of the Commissioners of Health, Ireland, on the epidemics of 1846 to 1850.* (Dublin, 1852), PP 1852-3, Vol. XLI, pp. 10 and 36.

relieved that considering the large number of inmates 'debilitated by sickness and distress', the number of fatalities had not been higher. For this, they credited recent dietary improvements and acknowledged that as the children in particular had benefited from the changes, the new dietary scale should be retained.[183]

At that time the true nature of cholera was not clearly understood. The helplessness of the workhouse authorities is underlined in a resolution passed by the guardians on 20 June 1849:

> the members of this Board feel the hand of the Lord has dealt lightly with them, and those under their care in the late visitation of cholera. In this they acknowledge his Divine goodness and forbearance, and desire to return to Almighty God their most humble and hearthy thanks.[184]

Cork Workhouse deaths 1849

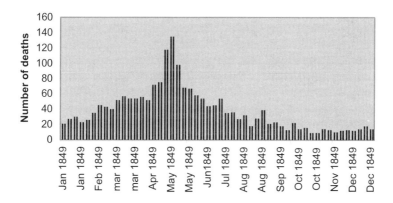

Chart showing increase in workhouse deaths during the 1849 cholera outbreak. From a norm of about 20 deaths per week the fatalities increased to 135 in mid-May. Thereafter, the deaths gradually decreased.

(Source: Cork Union board of guardians records.)

Deaths and burials

During the closing months of 1846 deaths in the workhouse accelerated rapidly. From a weekly total of sixteen at the start of November, the

---

183 *CC* 7 June 1849; *SR* 7 June 1849; *CUM* 13 June, 11 July 1849; *CUL* 7 July 1849.
184 *CUM* 20 June 1849; *SR* 21 June 1849.

number increased to 42 in the last week of the month; by the end of December, the weekly total had reached 62. Up to that time the bodies were buried without charge at St. Joseph's graveyard, which was situated just a few hundred yards from the institution. Deceased poor from other parts of the city were also buried in this graveyard. Because of the accelerating death rate, Fr. Theobald Mathew, the custodian of the graveyard, was forced to take decisive action to ensure that the cemetery was not overcrowded with corpses from the workhouse. In December, he advised the guardians that in the interest of public health, he would not allow any more workhouse paupers to be buried in the graveyard.[185] The board promptly advertised for a site on which to establish a workhouse graveyard. In mid-January 1847 a five-acre site offered by George Carr, the workhouse storeman, was accepted by the guardians.[186] The land was located at Moneygourney beside the main road from Carrigaline to Cork and the inspecting committee found that the site 'has an abundance of surface and depth of soil and is very eligibly situated, the distance from the back gate of the workhouse is less than three miles'.[187]

The workhouse burials continued at Fr. Mathew's graveyard during January 1847, but, obviously aware that the guardians had located a site of their own, he 'positively refused' to permit any more burials after the first week of February.[188] There were about 100 bodies in the workhouse mortuary when the embargo was issued. When the guardians met on 8 February the situation demanded an immediate resolution. Assistant Commissioner Burke drew their attention to an official directive that prevented them from using a site that did not adjoin the workhouse, thus ruling out the Moneygourney site. A special committee was appointed to investigate but in the meantime, the workhouse master arranged to bury the accumulating corpses at St. John's graveyard off Douglas Street. Only 28 bodies were buried before local residents 'became alarmed and excited and assembled in large numbers to oppose the interment'.[189] With corpses piling up in the mortuary and no one willing to provide a last resting-place, the guardians had no

---

185 PP 1847, Vol. VI, [737-11], *Report of the Select Committee of the House of Lords on colonization from Ireland together with minutes of evidence*; evidence of Rev. T. Mathew, p. 245.

186 George Carr was elected master of the workhouse in January 1849. He left Cork to become master of Liverpool workhouse in February 1852.

187 *CUM* 18 January 1847; *CUL* 30 January, 10 February 1847; *SR* 19 January 1847.

188 *CUM* 8 February 1847.

189 *SR* 9 February, 11 February, 16 February 1847; *CC* 16 February 1847. At that time dissected bodies from Cork's medical schools were interred at St. John's graveyard. NAI, CSORP 1850 H8298.

alternative but to ignore the official regulation and utilise the land at Moneygourney.[190]

The new workhouse graveyard was in constant use during the period of unusually high mortality at the start of 1847. Captain Broughton, the Inspecting Officer for County Cork, reported that when he passed along the road near the graveyard, he 'observed two men burying coffins as fast as they could place them alongside each other, and met a cart containing eight others, on its way to the same field, from the Cork Union Workhouse'.[191] Rumours about the mode of burial began to circulate and it was alleged that some of the paupers were given a coffinless burial and that on occasions up to four corpses were packed into a single casket.[192] Residents in the area complained, and on their behalf Rev. Ryan, PP, of Carrigaline presented a lengthy memorial to the guardians in which it was alleged that coffins were substandard and that they were buried in a 'quarry hole' under a shallow covering of loose earth. The clergyman reported that a doctor had told him that 'from the manner in which they were interred a nervous person would be likely to get fever if he saw one of the funerals'. To avoid controversy, Fr. Ryan suggested that the graves should be excavated during the daytime and that burials take place early on the following morning.[193]

As a result of complaints, the guardians had the graveyard inspected and Mr Greer reported that the site was well maintained and that corpses were buried at the required depth. He foresaw no problem with the decomposing corpses, for 'they were not the remains of pampered well-fed individuals, but of poor worn-out creatures. The bodies interred from the house were mere skeletons'. In addition to the workhouse dead, paupers from the city and many of those who died in the hospitals were also buried at Carr's Hill, or Carr's Hole, as the site became known.[194] When the chairman of the board of guardians visited the cemetery he said that it resembled 'a large deal yard from the number of coffins waiting for interment'.[195]

---

190 *CUM* 15 February, 1 March, 23 June 1847; *CUL* 10 February, 12 February, 13 February 1847; see also NAI, Poor Law Commissioners, Letters to James Burke 1847, No 3474 of 20 February 1847; NAI, CSORP 1847 H4338, Report from Asst. J. Burke to Poor Law Commissioners, 15 February, 1847. The problem of disposing of the large number of corpses was not unique to the Cork workhouse. See Jack Johnson, *The workhouses of the north west* (1996), pp. 37-39, 66, 93.

191 *Accounts and Papers (1847), Vol. LII; Correspondence from Jan to March 1847, re relief; Board of Work series [Second part]*, London 1847, Vol. LII, [797], p. 251.

192 *CUM* 1 March 1847; *CC* 9 March 1847.

193 *CUM* 8 March, 18 March 1847, see also *CUM* 22 March 1847 for a report on the burial ground; *SR* 9 March 1847.

194 *SR* 16 March, 16 September 1847.

195 *SR* 11 May 1847.

Because of the volume of burials, paupers were not interred in individual graves. Instead, long trenches were excavated and coffins were deposited in these each day. At the close of the day a temporary wall of loose stones was constructed to seal the trench from disturbance by dogs or other animals. On the following day the stones were removed and burials continued. Only when the trench was completely filled with coffins was it permanently sealed with earth. The inadequate temporary sealing of the graves led to numerous complaints about foul odours and allegations that dogs had stolen body parts.[196] In an attempt to secure the area, a fence was constructed around the graveyard and a workhouse wardmaster was deployed to supervise burials.[197]

During the summer of 1847 George Carr was prosecuted for creating a nuisance at the Carr's Hill graveyard and the case was heard at the Douglas petty sessions on 10 July. It was alleged that the bodies were not buried deeply enough and that they were sometimes disturbed by dogs. Witnesses claimed that foul smells were common in the area and on the road near the graveyard. Evidence on Carr's behalf showed that pits were excavated to receive only the number of coffins delivered in any given day and that large quantities of lime were used to cover the top and sides of the coffins. A maximum of 20 coffins was placed in each of the pits which, it was claimed, were properly sealed with earth to ensure that foul odours could not escape.[198] The Douglas magistrates were unable to give a verdict and they referred the case to a higher court.

In the meantime, a memorial against the graveyard was signed by 136 objectors and forwarded to the Poor Law Commissioners. The case against Carr was heard at the Cork county court on 7 August and he was found guilty of creating a nuisance, of placing in excess of 2,000 bodies in the graveyard and of exposing some without sufficient covering.[199] As a result, the board of guardians was unable to carry out burials and, again, bodies began to accumulate at the workhouse.[200] At the end of August the workhouse mortuary contained 40 corpses. Some had been awaiting burial for a fortnight and were 'emitting a most offensive and intolerable effluvia, notwithstanding the measures which are taken to

---

196 *SR* 17 June 1847; *CC* 29 May 1847.
197 *CUM* 16 June, 23 June, 30 June 1847. From the opening of the graveyard on 11 February to 23 June 1847, 2,216 paupers from the workhouse were buried at the Carr's Hill site. *SR* 24 June 1847; *CC* 24 June 1847. In the period January to June 1847, 2,882 people died in the workhouse. *CC* 15 July 1847.
198 *CUL* 5 July, 15 September 1847; *SR* 13 July 1847; *CC* 3 July, 13 July, 10 July 1847. The burial area at that time was 40 feet by 192 feet, and it was situated about 40 yards from the main road.
199 *CUL* 11 August, 27 September 1847; *SR* 22 July, 10 August 1847; *CC* 8 July, 10 August 1847; *CE* 9 August 1847.
200 *SR* 12 August, 26 August 1847; *CC* 12 August, 14 August, 19 August 1847.

neutralise it. Decomposition has set in and unless the nuisance be at once removed the consequences may be fearful'.[201] An alternative site could not be located and burials recommenced at Carr's Hill within a few days. Because the graveyard was some miles from the workhouse, many complaints were made by members of the public about transporting the bodies along the main road. The vice-chairman of the guardians remarked that the site would be ideal if it were possible to transport the dead by balloons![202] Other interested parties were also endeavouring to have burials discontinued and a section of the board of guardians was attempting to force George Carr to reduce the cost of the burials from the agreed 2s.6d. to 2s. or even 1s.6d.[203] Dissatisfaction about the method of burial and a dispute about the title to the land and its use as a graveyard lasted for some time, but burials continued and these were usually carried out at night.[204]

Conclusion

During the famine years the Cork board of guardians made a determined effort to contribute towards alleviating suffering and hardship. When potatoes were no longer available for feeding the workhouse inmates, little time was lost in introducing an alternative food supply. When the workhouse was unable to accommodate all the applicants seeking relief, arrangements were made to increase its capacity by building sheds or renting temporary accommodation. Most of the guardians were sincerely interested in providing accommodation and consequently, every available space was assigned to sick, starving or dying applicants.

However, because of a determination to avoid introducing outdoor relief in the Cork Union, some guardians viewed the rented accommodation as a purely temporary expedient and they were satisfied that contrary to providing outdoor relief, this commitment to grant assistance would end at the conclusion of the rental period. Their opposition to outdoor relief was almost paranoid, as they feared that its introduction

201 *SR* 2 September 1847; *CE* 3 September 1847; *CC* 2 September 1847.
202 *SR* 9 September, 16 September 1847; *CC* 9 September, 16 September, 23 September 1847.
203 *SR* 23 September, 30 September, 7 October, 14 October, 21 October, 28 October 1847.
204 *CUL* 4 October, 26 October 1847; *CUL*–(Inward letters), 4 September, 1 October 18 October 1847; *SR* 11 November 1847; 25 March, 20 April, 26 August, 2 September, 16 September, 23 September 1848; *CC* 26 August, 2 September, 9 September, 23 September, 5 October 1848; NAI, CSORP 1847 H10907; See also Daniel Hegarty and Brian Hickey, 'The Famine graveyard on Carr's Hill near Cork', *Journal of Cork Historical and Archaeological Society*, Vol. 101 (1996), pp. 9-14.

would open a floodgate, which would possibly never again be closed. By supporting the acquisition of indoor workhouse accommodation, they ensured that relief was available. Thus it did not become necessary to grant outdoor relief in the Cork Union during the famine.[205] This faction also anticipated that the practice of separating family members in the workhouse would discourage many applicants and thus prevent excessive expenditure.

Many unfortunate people certainly benefited from the food and accommodation offered by the Cork guardians. However, the almost uncontrolled expansion of the workhouse population endangered lives, including those of staff and guardians. The limited food was distributed as widely as possible but the allowances were far from generous and certainly did not encourage robust health. Periodic reductions in the allowances, whether designed to cut down on expenditure or make the available food go as far as possible, left the inmates with little more than a 'starvation diet'. Disease and sickness soon took their toll. Death and overcrowding necessitated the closure of the workhouse to further admissions when disease and sickness were at their highest levels. The medical staff worked long hours which endangered their own health. Their efforts on behalf of the poor inmates certainly provided some comfort, but their limited understanding of infectious diseases restricted their effectiveness and, as Cormac Ó Gráda notes, 'medical treatment is unlikely to have saved many lives during the famine'.[206]

The high death rate in the workhouse made it necessary for the Board of Guardians to acquire a burial site for its own use. As well as facing isolation in the workhouse, separation from the general population was accentuated by the prospect of a burial in the exclusive company of fellow paupers. Rejection of the paupers in life thus continued even after their death. Many victims of hardship were assigned to an anonymous grave at the paupers' cemetery. This graveyard continued in use for the life of the workhouse but the reputation it earned during the Famine overshadows all other memories and is the dominant theme in the folklore of the workhouse and the famine period.

---

205 I cannot find evidence to support the claim that the Cork guardians provided outdoor relief in 1847; see Michelle O Mahony, *The impact of the Great Famine on the Cork Union Workhouse* (M. Phil. Thesis, 2000), p. 34.
206 C. Ó Gráda, *Black '47 and beyond*, p. 96.

3 Removal

Although united with England, Wales and Scotland under the Act of Union, Irish people were treated as foreigners under the laws of settlement and removal. Less than twenty years after the Union, which united the two islands under common legislation, special provisions were introduced to legalise the removal of Irish and Scottish poor from England. On the other hand, English, Welsh and Scottish people were free to claim workhouse relief in Ireland without the penalty of removal.[1]

The Settlement Act of 1662 which gave local townships in England responsibility for poor law administration was designed to ensure that each English and Welsh subject had a parish of settlement.[2] Derived settlements were designed to keep families together – wives assumed their husband's settlement and children their parents'. Acquired settlements were earned from a number of situations, including serving an apprenticeship, completing a year's uninterrupted contracted service to one master, or renting property that had an annual rental of £10 or more. In reality the majority of settlements were derived in one of four ways – through a parent, through a husband, through a contracted year of service or through an apprenticeship.[3]

Migration was common and sections of the workforce were regularly on the move in search of specialised or seasonal employment. Poor migrants, and particularly married men with families, constituted a threat to local poor relief resources. Those who were legitimately settled in a parish were given priority for employment, so in times of hardship the non-settled suffered the most. In effect 'pauper settlement' related above all to the rights of the poor to poor relief in their own parish. The settlement laws allowed a parish to protect its resources by removing

1 PP 1855, Vol. XIII, [308], *Poor Removal*; p.25; *CUM* 4 June, 11 June, 25 June 1862.
2 *13&14 Charles II, Cap. 12, An Act for the better relief of the poor in this Kingdom*; J. S. Taylor, 'A different kind of Speenhamland', *Journal of British Studies* (1991), p.186; People had only one legal settlement, which was either derived or acquired.; K. D. M. Snell, 'Settlement, Poor law and the rural historian', *Rural History* (1992), pp. 146, 147.
3 J. S. Taylor, 'Speenhamland', *British Studies* (1991), p. 186 -7; Ross Cranston, *Legal foundations of the welfare state* (London, 1985), pp. 22-26.

poor interlopers to their own place of settlement, which was obliged to provide for them when they became destitute.[4] The laws permitted any parish to remove poor relief applicants and it was also legal to remove people who were not currently destitute but who were 'likely to become chargeable'.[5] Forced removals were common.[6]

An Act of 1795 also linked settlement with poor relief and people who had become destitute and were in need of poor relief could be removed to their parish of settlement, as could unmarried pregnant women and disorderly people.[7] The arrangement worked both ways. Parishes could expel alien poor relief claimants, and in turn, they could be subjected to supporting their own poor who had been expelled and returned from another parish. Costs were considered, and in situations of short-term hardship, relief would have been granted, but if the cost of removal was cheaper the parish authorities would have chosen this option.[8]

The Settlement laws and Ireland

The law of settlement became part of the everyday life of the English labouring classes. As no comparable Act operated in Ireland the native Irish artisans and labourers were not similarly conditioned. Those going to England in search of employment were often subjected to the rigours of the Act and it has been suggested that some parish officers used the laws of settlement to regulate migration.[9] Sojourners were often

---

4 N. Landau, 'The laws of Settlement and the surveillance of immigrants', *Continuity and Change* (1988) p. 412; K. D. M. Snell, 'Pauper settlement and the rights of poor relief in England and Wales', *Continuity and Change* (1991), p. 377, 378; K. D. M. Snell, 'Settlement', *Rural History* (1992), p. 146, 151; M. E. Rose, 'Settlement, Removal and the new Poor Law', in D. Fraser, The *New Poor Law in the nineteenth century* (London, 1976), p. 25.

5 K. D. M. Snell, 'Settlement', *Rural History* (1992), p. 146; N. Landau, 'The *Eighteenth century context of Laws of Settlement*', *Continuity and Change* (1991), p. 429; N. Landau, 'Settlement', *Continuity and Change* (1988), p. 399.

6 J. S. Taylor, 'The Impact of Pauper Settlement 1691-1834', *Past and Present* (1976), No.73, p. 60; K. D. M. Snell, 'Settlement', *Rural History* (1991), p. 393.

7 K. D. M. Snell, 'Settlement', *Rural History* (1991), p. 392-3; see also G. Cole and R. Postgate, *The Common People* 1746-1946 (London, 1976, edition) p. 127; George R. Boyer, An *Economic History of English poor law 1750-1850* (New York, 1990), p. 244; P. Gregg, *A Social and Economic History of Britain: 1760-1972* (London, 1973 edition), p. 31.

8 J. S. Taylor, 'Speenhamland', *Journal of British Studies* (1991), pp. 192, 187.

9 N. Landau, 'Settlement', *Continuity and Change* (1988), p. 400. Native English workers did not always welcome Irish labourers. See Sarah Barber, 'Irish migrant agricultural labourers in nineteenth century Lincolnshire', *Saothar*, No. 8, 1982, pp. 10-12. The problems encountered by Irish migrant workers in England are explored in depth by David Fitzpatrick in "A peculiar tramping people': 'The Irish in Britain, 1801-70', in W. E. Vaughan, *New history of Ireland* (1989), pp. 623-657.

welcome, particularly when local economies required skilled workers.[10] Unskilled Irish labourers were also important in agriculture. Because of the costs involved in sending them home, the Irish posed a problem for parish officers and, in general, they were treated as casual poor with no settlement and relieved in the parish in which they applied.[11]

In 1819 two Acts of parliament empowered the authorities to transport back to Ireland any Irish poor who had become a charge on local parishes in England.[12] Cork, Waterford Dublin, Newry and Belfast were subsequently defined as ports to which Irish poor could most suitably be removed. Within months people were being formally removed to Ireland when they became chargeable to a parish.[13] In October 1819 three families numbering five adults and 15 children, 14 of whom had been born in England, were seized by the authorities as they had become 'actually chargeable' and shipped from Carlisle to Belfast where they found refuge in the house of industry.[14] Some correspondence about the matter was generated and it was alleged that many Irish families went to Carlisle with the objective of living off its parochial relief. During 1820, 870 adults and 258 children were passed to Ireland through the port of Bristol.[15]

Between 1824 and 1831, 38,969 Irish poor were shipped through Liverpool to Irish ports.[16] Because of the number of people involved in transporting the poor to ports the scheme cost far more than had been anticipated. The poor from some counties had to be transported over a number of days which necessitated a large expenditure on food, accommodation, carriage and supervising personnel. The 1828 select committee on Irish and Scottish vagrants reported that the cost of removing a single adult from London to Liverpool amounted to

---

10 J. S. Taylor, 'Speenhamland', *British Studies* (1991), p. 188, 201-2; Roger Swift, 'The historiography of the Irish in nineteenth century Britain', in P. O Sullivan (ed.), *The Irish World wide* (London, 1992), p. 55; F. Neal, *Black '47 Britain and the Famine Irish* (London, 1998), pp. 31-33; Jeffery G. Williamson, 'The impact of the Irish on British labour markets during the Industrial Revolution', in R. Swift and S. Gilley, *The Irish in Britain, 1815-1939* (London, 1989) pp. 156-7.

11 J. S. Taylor, 'Speenhamland', *British Studies* (1991), p. 191; PP 1821, Vol. IV, [543], *Report of Select Committee on Vagrants*, p. 4.

12 59 Geo. III, C12 and 59Geo. III C 50; Under an Act of 1744 Justices of the Peace were empowered to have vagrant Irish rogues and vagabonds shipped back to Ireland. (17 Geo. II, C5).

13 PP 1820, Vol. I, [259], Bill *to amend Removal Laws.*, p. 1 ; PP 1821, Vol. IV, [543], *Report of Select Committee on Vagrants*, p. 5 .

14 PP 1820 *Report of Select Committee on Vagrants*, Vol. IX, [212], *Correspondence . . . Paupers*, p. 3.

15 PP 1820, Vol. IX, [212], pp. 6, 7; PP 1821, Vol. IV, [543], *Report of Select Committee on Vagrants*, p. 111.

16 PP 1833, Vol. XVI, [78], *An account of the number of Irish poor shipped . . . from Liverpool*; see also PP 1828, Vol. IX, [513], *Report Select Committee*, p. 4.

£4.11s.3d. The scheme was also open to exploitation and witnesses at the select committee believed that Irish harvest workers operated a system whereby one of a group took charge of all the earnings and bought a passage home. The remaining members then sought relief and were sent home at public expense.[17] Similar allegations were made at the commission into the operating of the Poor Laws in 1833.[18]

Irish Poor shipped through Liverpool 1824-1831

	FROM LANCASHIRE	OTHER COUNTIES	TOTAL
1824	1606	875	2481
1825	1867	1161	3028
1826	4291	2137	6428
1827	3765	2290	6055
1828	2478	1871	4349
1829	2964	2122	5086
1830	3481	2198	5679
1831	3318	2545	5863
Total	23770	15199	38969

(*Source*: PP 1833, Vol. XXXII, [78], *Irish Poor . . .*, pp. 2-3)

By 1833 there was general opposition against granting poor relief to any Irish or Scottish vagrants in England. Witnesses at that year's select committee on vagrancy reiterated the earlier complaints about the costs incurred in removals. The expense of relocating the 35,614 Irish and Scottish vagrants who had passed through Middlesex between 1828 and 1832 was estimated at £4 each.[19] Paupers bound for the north of Ireland were shipped through Liverpool and those destined for the south went via Bristol. The passmaster responsible for processing Irish poor through London moved 3,071 paupers from Kent, Sussex, Surrey and Hampshire in 1832. To cut down on expenditure, it was advocated that the paupers be transported directly from London and not carried overland to the west coast for shipping.[20]

Parishes were almost paranoid about preventing people gaining

---

17 PP 1828, Vol. IX, [513], *Report from Select Committee*, p. 4, 7, 12. See also John Archer Jackson, *The Irish in Britain* (London, 1963), pp. 73-4; Keith Laybourne, *The evolution of the British Social Policy and the Welfare State* (Staffordshire, 1995), p. 30; See also PP 1830, Vol. VII, [665], 3rd, *Report on the state of the poor in Ireland*, pp. 603-4.

18 PP 1834, Vol. XXVII, [44], *Report of Commissioners on Poor Laws* Appendix A, p. 189.

19 PP 1833, Vol. XVI, [394], *Select Committee*, pp. 4, 24.

20 PP 1833, Vol. XVI, [394], *Select Committee*, pp. 5, 22.

settlement. In some areas cottages which became vacant were demolished and the construction of new ones was prevented. Accommodation was refused to non-locals so they had to reside outside the parish and commute to and from work. English labourers were reluctant to leave their own parish as they feared that they could lose their entitlement to relief. Also, non-residents who earned a settlement would not endanger their situation by leaving the parish.[21] This reluctance to travel was given as a reason for the influx of Irish workers into areas such as London, when labour was scarce, and the Poor Law Commissioners' report for 1836 noted that, in England and Wales, 'the Irish at present are very numerous in every great town'.[22] The fear of removal was a disincentive to labour mobility and it had a negative influence on local industry because 'more enterprising country dwellers moved in search of higher wages while the more apathetic and less capable remained behind'.[23] Without the annual influx of Irish labourers many English farmers would not have been able to save their harvest.[24] Very few of the Irish immigrants gained a settlement. They were not entitled to a birth or derivative settlement, apprenticeship was rare amongst them and they seldom succeeded in gaining a settlement as a result of hiring or service. The few settlements which were acquired were usually as a result of renting a tenement. The authorities in Manchester and Liverpool were more lenient than those in other areas and after a residency of ten years the Irish immigrant usually acquired an equitable claim to relief. It was, said one official report, 'an Irishman's ambition to gain a settlement, or live here long enough to have a claim for relief'.[25]

The Settlement laws and the Cork workhouse

According to Section 41 of the Irish Poor Law Act, regardless of their place of residence, destitute applicants could not be refused admission to Irish workhouses. The guardians had no power to charge another union

21 See: S.G. and E.O.A, Checkland (eds.), The *poor law report of 1834* (London, 1974), pp. 36-7, 247; George R. Boyer, *Economic history of English Poor Law* (N.Y, 1990), pp. 244-5, 254-5.
22 *First Poor Law Report – Britain*, PP 1834 [44], pp. 86-88; *Second Report of the Poor Law Commissioners for England and Wales* (London, 1836); p. 472; see also *Minutes of Select Committee on Poor Laws (Ireland)*, 6th Report, PP 1849, Vol. XV, [194], p. 8.
23 Ursula R.Q. Henriques, *Before the welfare state: Social administration in early industrial Britain* (London, 1978), p. 58.
24 *Second Report from the Select Committee on the Poor Law Amendment Act*, PP 1838, Vol. XVIII, [138], pp. 9-10.
25 PP 1836, Vol. XXXIV, [40], Report *on the state of the Irish poor . . .*, Appendix G, pp. XXIII, XXIV.

for the maintenance of inmates and, unlike their English counterparts, they could not remove non-residents to their homes or 'place of settlement'. Applicants could be refused admission when a workhouse was full.[26] The number of poor people transported from England increased rapidly following the declaration of the Cork Workhouse. The guardians discussed the situation, and in response to a query on the matter, the Poor Law Commissioners were emphatic that if these applicants were destitute they would have to be admitted to the house.[27]

The numbers of paupers being transferred from England increased steadily, and in one week in September 1840, over 150 poor Irish people from London were landed at the Cork quays. Of these, 120 were from Dublin and other parts of Ireland.[28] The arrivals continued and during 1840 Jeremiah Thomas, who took charge of Irish paupers deported by the Middlesex magistrates, brought 1,600 people to Cork.[29] Threats that the Cork guardians would not pay the maintenance costs of transported paupers were occasionally made. In December 1841 when 51 year old Catherine Carr was admitted to the Cork workhouse, the guardians contacted the Clerkenwell authorities to warn that the cost of maintaining the woman would be charged to their account. The threat was unsuccessful, expenses were not reimbursed and Catherine Carr remained in the Cork workhouse until she sought her discharge on 20 April 1842.[30]

Some of the transported paupers had horrific experiences. On 26 November 1841, 118 paupers arrived from London. They had spent most of the six-day passage on the ship's deck in cold, wet and windy weather. One young child who died was buried at sea by its parents.[31] The normally compliant *Cork Constitution* was roused to ask: 'Is it in a Christian country atrocities so iniquitous are perpetrated? Is there any humanity – are there Hearts in the bosoms of the brutes by whom the pains of poverty are thus wantonly augmented?'[32] The plight of some of the individuals seeking

---

26 *SR* 25 February, 27 February 1840, 17 June 1845; also *Poor Law Commissioners Annual Report*, 1850, p. 127; See also PP 1837, Vol. LI, [69], *Report of George Nicholls, Esq., to their Majesty's principal Secretary of State for the Home Department on Poor Laws – Ireland*, pp. 25-7; PP 1837-8, Vol. XXXVIII, [104], *Second Report of Geo. Nicholls, Esq., to their Majesty's principal Secretary of State for the Home Department on Poor Laws Ireland*, pp. 14-19.

27 *SR* 7 May, 18 June 1840.

28 *SR* 8 September, 29 September 1840; *CC* 3 September, 8 September, 17 September, 3 October, 24 November 1840.

29 *CE* 13 December 1841; *SR* 9 November, 30 November 1841.

30 *CUL* – (outward letters) 13 December 1841; *Cork Union Indoor Register* BG69/G2, 24 January 1842.

31 *SR* 27 November 1841, also 9 November, 30 November 1841.

32 *SR* 7 December 1841.

admission to the Cork workhouse during that winter was particularly harrowing. On 6 December one 'poor old woman, bent almost double by the united effects of old age, disease and poverty', sought admission for herself and three young children. A stranger who had been given charge of the children en-route from London had brought them to her door with the message that they were the offspring of her nephew. The children were under three years of age, and as the old woman was unable to support them, they were admitted to the workhouse.[33]

Another 'emaciated, wretched, half-clad female' who applied for admission had been born in Cork but had lived in London for 39 years. Her husband was a bricklayer and they had three daughters who worked as servants. When her husband was hospitalised after a fall, she was forced to apply for workhouse relief. The authorities promised her employment and one morning at 6am. she was taken from the work-house but, to her dismay, she was put on board a Cork bound steamer. "I thought I was going to get the work promised me the day before! I had not the least idea where I was going, for I was not asked a single question! I am most anxious to get back to my family for they don't know where I am or what has become of me!" she told the authorities when she was put ashore at Cork.[34] A couple of weeks later a boy named John Saul arrived on the *Jupiter* and sought admission to the Cork workhouse. He was a native of Clonmel and had been taken to London by his father, six years previously. The father went to Australia in search of work and left young John with an aunt. Subsequently, he sent £10 to cover the boy's fare to Australia but the aunt refused to send him unless she and her own family were also paid for. She sent the boy to Peckham work-house from whence he was promptly shipped to Cork.[35]

These and many similar tales provoked comments from the Cork guardians who equated the behaviour of English officials, or 'cold-blooded miscreants' as they were described by the *Cork Examiner*, with that of kidnappers and slave-dealers.[36] On occasions the ships from England moored at the Cork quays in the early hours of the morning when there were few people around to witness their arrival. Some of the passengers remained in Cork and for days there were 'living spectres, wandering through the city, reeling from weakness against house walls, and in half articulate sounds, calling on the passer by, "for God sake, to direct them to the Poor House."'[37] In disgust the *Southern Reporter* concluded that 'England as a nation, feels no real sympathies for the

33 *CC* 7 December, 11 December, 14 December 1841.
34 *SR* 7 December 1841.
35 *SR* 4 January 1842.
36 *CE* 6 December 1841.
37 *SR* 15 December 1841.

miseries of Ireland. Her policy is to exhaust the best years of Irish manhood, in increasing her wealth, and in return to transport to our shores cargoes of living skeletons, with scarcely as much life in them as keeps soul and body together'.[38]

At the end of 1841 the Cork guardians prepared a memorial criticising the constant removal of Irish poor from London to Cork. Because many were unable to reach their homes they entered the Cork workhouse where some of them remained for lengthy periods in already overcrowded wards. Some of the applicants were distressed people who had sought short-term relief in London and because the English magistrates frequently failed to send a warrant and a copy of the statement made by each pauper, the legality of many of the transportations was questionable.[39] Before the end of January 1842 the Cork guardians received a letter from the London authorities, signed by Henry Gill, the City of London passmaster, explaining the removal system. Gill maintained that the Irish poor were returned at their own free will and consent, that they were landed at the nearest port to their homes and that they were provided with adequate rations en-route. In an attempt to justify the actions of the English officials, Gill complained about the large number of Irish paupers continually arriving at English and Welsh ports, many of whom had had their fares subsidised.[40]

To prove that the paupers had been landed at a particular location, the official in charge was expected to bring a receipt back to the port of discharge. As a protest against the methods being used to remove the poor people, the Cork authorities refused to supply any documentation unless each passenger was inspected before landing. They also instructed the local police to prevent paupers from landing until the magistrates had been appraised, and then each case could be investigated.[41]

This inconvenience was easily surmounted and when the *Jupiter* steamer next arrived in Cork, the paupers were discharged without any attempt being made by crew members to have official documentation signed. Some of the passengers entered the Cork workhouse and when the guardians discovered that two women had links with Clonakilty, they gave them a day's supply of bread and had them transferred to the Bandon workhouse.[42] The Bandon guardians, who correctly said that the

38 *SR* 15 December 1841.
39 *CUM* 20 December 1841; *CUL* 13 December 1841; *CE* 22 December 1841; *SR* 6 January, 20 January 1842.
40 *SR* 27 January 1842.
41 *SR* 22 January 1842; *CE* 24 January 1842; *CC* 22 January 1842.
42 *SR* 5 February 1842; see also *Cork Workhouse Indoor Register* BG69, G2 in which it is recorded that they were sent from England against their will, 3 February, 7 February 1842.

Irish Poor Law did not sanction such transfers, promptly returned them to Cork. They also complained to the Poor Law Commissioners about the illegal behaviour of the Cork guardians who had provided outdoor relief in the form of bread and had also introduced a law of settlement, neither of which was recognised by the Irish Poor Relief Act.[43] The Commissioners wrote to the Cork guardians and advised them to refrain from their illegal expenditure of money.[44]

In the autumn of 1842 the Cork guardians decided to close the workhouse against further admissions and to transfer paupers from outside Cork Union to their native places. When news of this reached the Commissioners they immediately contacted the guardians and warned that relief could not be withheld from deserving applicants by refusing admission to the workhouse. Also, paupers could not be transferred from one union to another, 'which would be practically to enact a law of settlement and removal'.[45]

Removals subsided at the end of 1842 but during the following year 200 paupers who landed from the *Tiger* on 15 October were described as 'penniless, shivering with cold, and in a most pitiable state'.[46] Two of the people admitted to the workhouse that year were Jane Harvey and her daughter and both of them were still there in 1854.[47] In the autumn of 1844, large-scale removals re-commenced and people were landed at Cork's quays 'as if they were *debris* collected by a dredging boat'.[48] During late October and early November over 400 paupers from London were landed at Cork. Many were in a state of extreme destitution. One of them, a sixty-year-old man, was found starving at Great George's Street, and he died soon afterwards. The *Southern Reporter* lamented that while he had lived and worked in London 'they had used him there, and, as they could not send him to the Knacker's when his work was done, they shipped him here, and generously gave his bones to the land where he was born'.[49]

The laws of settlement were renewed regularly.[50] When the issue was under discussion in 1846 many people were opposed to a proposal which would grant a settlement to Irish persons with five years continuous

---

43 *CUM* 28 February 1842; *CC* 19 April 1842; *SR* 1 March 1842.
44 *CUL* 26 February 1842; similar criticisms were received from the guardians during the next couple of years – see *CUL* 1 June 1844, 2 August, 1845; NAI, Poor Law Commissioners, Letters to James Burke 1845, 27 June, 2 August 1845.
45 *CUM* 26 September 1842 and *CUL* 24 September 1842.
46 *CE* 16 October 1843.
47 PP 1854, Vol. XVII, [396], *Select Committee on Poor Removal*, p. 147.
48 *SR* 15 February 1845, see also 27 February 1845.
49 *SR* 26 October, 9 November 1844; *CC* 26 October 1844.
50 7&8 Vict. Cap. 42; 8&9 Vict., Cap. 117; see also *13th, Poor Law Commissioners Annual Report*, 1874, pp. 8-9.

residence in an English parish.[51] In spite of their apprehension, the Poor Relief Act, which was passed in August 1846, conferred the status of "irremovability" on people who had resided for five consecutive years in a parish and also permitted them to claim local relief.[52] Irremovability differed from a settlement in that the latter was a permanent status which could not be lost. The condition of irremovability was unique only to that parish. This status was forfeited it a poor person left the parish, even for a few days in search of work. Five further years of continuous residence would be required to regain the lost status or to acquire a new irremovability status. As a result of the Act some parishes noted an increase in the number of Irish people applying for relief. These destitute Irish would formerly have shunned the authorities during periods of hardship, as they feared deportation.[53] In other areas, officials interpreted the Act in a selective manner, which conferred irremovability after five years only to English paupers.[54] It was of course difficult for parish officials to ascertain the exact duration of the residency of some immigrants, and a number of officers wanted the irremovability clause deleted as it merely encouraged Irish immigrants to London and other centres.[55] Some parish officials contrived to remove Irish applicants before they completed the residence necessary to claim irremovability.[56] Though there was a decrease in the volume of forced removals to Cork, poor people did arrive during the famine years.[57]

Frank Neal in his study of Irish famine immigrants in England distinguishes the two methods used by English authorities to transfer Irish people back to their homeplaces. Destitute Irish who wished to return to Ireland applied to magistrates for voluntary repatriation. If their application was granted the English parish paid the fare and the Irish were *passed* home. *Removal* was an involuntary repatriation and frequently involved a forced deportation from England, Scotland or Wales.[58]

---

51 See *SR* 1 August 1846, 26 January, 6 March, 6 April 1847.

52 9&10 Vict. Cap. 66; see also C. Kinealy, This *Great Calamity – The Irish Famine 1845-52* (Dublin, 1994), p. 335; L H. Lees, The Solidarities of Strangers – The *English Poor Law and the people, 1700-1948* (London, 1998), p. 219; also, Keith Laybourne, *Evolution of British Social Policy . . .* (1995), pp. 29-30.

53 PP 1847. Vol. XI, [82], *Removal . . . 1st. Report*, p. 8.

54 See PP 1858, Vol. XIII, [374], *Report from the Select Committee on Irremovable Poor . . .* p. 3.

55 PP 1847, Vol. XI, [518], *Removal, 6th. Report*, pp. 184, 296; also PP 1847, Vol. XI, [518], *Second and Third Reports from Select Committee on Settlement and Poor Removal; together with the minutes of evidence, appendix and index.*

56 M.E. Rose, '*Settlement*, Removal and the new Poor Law', in D. Fraser (ed.), *The New Poor Law* (1976), p. 39.

57 See *SR* 6 March 1847.

58 F. Neal, *Black '47* (London 1998), p. 218; F. Neal, 'Lancashire, the Famine Irish and the Poor Laws: A study in crisis management', in *Irish Economic and Social History* (1995), Vol. XXII, p. 29.

Removal from England was not as straightforward as this implies. To avoid the connotations associated with the forcible removal of paupers the terms *passed* and *removed* were used interchangeably – indeed the more frequently used and passive expression, *passed* was merely a euphemism to disguise the true nature of the deportations.[59]

During the summer of 1847, 18 paupers from Middlesex were landed from the *Preussischer Adler*. Twenty more were landed on 1 July; 120 came from Liverpool a few days later and on the following week 52 paupers were brought to Cork on the *Bristol* steamer under an agent named John Frost. He left 18 of them in the city with allowances of between 1s. and 2s.6d. each for lodging money, and arranged for the others to be removed to Dublin or Limerick. Any connection that the immigrants had with Cork was tenuous.[60] Frost, who was employed by the Middlesex magistrates, continued to land deportees at Cork. He brought 80 paupers to the city in mid-August and another batch of 25 in the first week of September. Up to that date 600 poor people had been brought from Middlesex to Cork during 1847. On 29 September a further 34 deportees were landed from the *Juverna* steamer.[61]

In June 1847 the Mayor of Cork asked his London counterpart to ensure that any poor people sent to Ireland were returned to the port nearest their own localities. The Cork guardians made a similar request to the Poor Law Commissioners because 'the great distress existing here will render it totally impossible to render assistance to any but those who have a legitimate claim upon us'.[62] The arrivals continued during 1848 and 1849. These cases frequently ignored the directions of the 1846 Poor Removal Act and were, said the *Southern Reporter*, 'a dark stain on the boasted benevolence of England'.[63]

The catalogue of persecution and illegal deportations continued during the next few years.[64] In May 1851 fourteen Irish paupers, under the charge of a man named Nicholson, were landed at Cork. Only six of them were from Cork, the others were from places such as Tipperary and Limerick.[65] In these and many similar cases, the deportees had no choice

---

59 See for instance, PP 1854, Vol. XVII, [396], *Select Committee on Removal*, p. 445.
60 *CE* 23 June 1847; *CC* 3 July, 24 July 1847; *SR* 24 June, 10 July 1847.
61 *CE* 1 September 1847; *CC* 30 September, 7 October, 16 October 1847; see also *CUL* 2 July 1847.
62 *CUM* 9 June 1847; *CUL* 24 April, 15 May 1849; *CE* 27 June 1847.
63 *SR* 9 September, 11 September 1847, 1 February 1849; *CE* 2 February, 6 April, 13 April 1849, also, PP 1854, Vol. XXII, [396], *Minutes Select Committee on Poor Removal*, Appendix No.15, p. 622; *CUM* 4 April, 9 May 1849; *CE* 8 July 1847.
64 *CUL* 31 January 1850, 13 May, 2 June, 24 November 1851.
65 *CUM* 14 May, 21 May, 11 June 1851; *CE* 14 May, 16 May 1851.

but to apply for workhouse relief.[66] In October 1852 John Frost sought a receipt for 14 paupers from London who were landed at Cork. Frost was now one of the principal English removal contractors and he transported paupers from seven unions for 22s. per head. On this occasion he failed to make provisions to transfer the paupers to homes at Killarney, Clonakilty and elsewhere, so the guardians who were not co-operating with the removal system refused a signed receipt.[67] In the following June eight paupers were brought from London to Cork by Bernard Curley, an agent of Frost's. One was a six-year-old girl named Margaret Hegarty who, it seemed, had been abandoned by her father. Along with the others, Curley merely deposited this helpless child on the Cork quayside. Curley's documentation related only to the child and, as the other passengers were not included, the Cork authorities refused to authenticate the receipt. Young Hegarty was admitted to the Cork workhouse on 27 June. The child's accent and demeanour indicated that she was English and the Cork guardians suspected that the not uncommon practice of acquiring a 'witness' to swear that a particular individual was Irish, or Irish-born, had been used as evidence in removing the girl.[68] Their suspicions were correct as it later transpired that the child had become separated from her siblings while playing on the streets of Westminster. She had been taken to the workhouse and, without her father's knowledge, removed to Cork. Cornelius Hegarty traced his daughter to the London workhouse and after Frost admitted taking her to Cork, she was located and returned to her family in London in 1854.[69]

In the early 1850s it was estimated that an average of 26 paupers per week were being landed at Cork from the London steamers.[70] Official figure show that in the years 1849-53 a total of 1,107 paupers, or an average of 221 per annum, were brought from Liverpool to Cork.[71]

---

66 *CE* 28 November 1851; On a number of occasions during 1850 and 1851 the Cork guardians corresponded with the Poor Law Commissioners on the matter of forced removals from England. PP 1854, Vol. XVII, [396], *Select Committee on Poor Removal*, p. 83; also *CE* 17 February 1854. See Cork Union *Letter Book* (outward), BG69/B1 – 28 January 1850, 6 May, 1 November, 15 November 1851.

67 *CE* 27 October 1852.

68 *CC* 30 June 1853; *CE* 1 July 1853; *CUM* 29 June 1853. In the workhouse register entry number 1853 / 30103 it is recorded that Mary (sic) Hegarty had been deserted by her father and sent to Cork by the London authorities; she left the workhouse on 17 May 1854. Cork Union *Indoor Relief Register* BG69 – No.G8, 27 June 1853.

69 PP 1854, Vol. XVII, [396], *Minutes, Select Committee on Poor Removal*; pp. 78, 148 and Appendix No.15, p. 624. See also pp. 78-86, 146-8 for details of other cases; *CUL* 5 July, 25 July, 9 August, 6 September 1853.

70 *CC* 25 May 1854; *CUM* 8 February, 15 February, 22 February, 29 March 1854.

71 PP 1854, vol. LV, [374], *Poor Removal – Return*, pp. 1-3; PP 1854, Vol. LV, [488], *Poor Removal, Return*, p. 1.

Many of the paupers arriving at Cork were admitted to the workhouse. Included amongst them were families of up to seven individuals, some of whom had lived and worked in England for up to 30 years.[72] On a few occasions Cork magistrates and poor law guardians, using their personal finance, shipped families back to England.[73] They believed that 'the only way to stop this cruel system is to tire the English authorities out by immediately sending their victims back'.[74] On 6 July 1854, at the Select Committee on Poor Removal, the M.P., John Francis Maguire explained that when a family had been broken up, or if their employment was still available in England, the guardians endeavoured to send them back. He had often given money to have paupers returned.[75] As the removals continued, the guardians became more frustrated with the harshness of the one-sided legislation. In the autumn of 1855 a 35 year old woman, whose infant died while she disembarked from the steamer at Cork, applied to the guardians for assistance to get back to her seven year old son in London. Commenting on those who had deported the woman, a local newspaper concluded that 'flesh and blood are not the components of their harsh humanity. They have no more *nature* than if they never drew milk from gentle breasts. They shipped the mother and the infant died'.[76]

Select Committee on the Settlement laws

In April 1854, the House of Commons ordered that a Select Committee be appointed to inquire into the operation of the Poor Removal Acts.[77] Among the 58 witnesses were Robert John O Shaughnessy, clerk of the Cork Union, Richard Longfield Jameson, chairman of the Cork Union, Constable John Duross of the Cork Constabulary and George Carr, master of the Liverpool workhouse and former master of the Cork workhouse. Included on the Select Committee was John Francis Maguire, proprietor of the *Cork Examiner* and M.P. for Dungarvan.

The working of the Poor Removal Acts was subjected to a detailed

---

72 *CC* 23 February, 30 May, 12 December 1854; *CE* 11 December 1854, see also PP 1854, Vol. XVII, [396], *Select Committee on Poor Removal,* Appendix No. 15, p. 624-5.
73 *CC* 16 February, 1854; 13 October 1855; PP 1854, Vol. XVII, [396], *Select Committee on Removal,* p. 88.
74 *CC* 23 February 1854.
75 PP 1854, Vol. XVII, [396], *Select Committee on Removal,* p. 440.
76 *CC* 13 October 1855.
77 8&9 *Victoriae,* C117 and 8&9 *Victoriae,* C83; PP 1854, vol. XVII, [396] *Select Committee on Poor Removal;* PP 1854-5, Vol. XIII, [308], *Report from the Select Committee on Poor Removal; together with the proceedings of the committee, minutes of evidence, Appendix and Index; CUM* 17 May 1854.

examination and many anomalies were exposed. The evidence showed that the five-year irremovability clause was repeatedly ignored. English parish authorities deported large numbers of Irish people who were legally entitled to remain in areas where they had earned the status of irremovability by a residency, in many instances, of a far longer period.[78] English parishes gave at least three weeks notice of an intended removal within the country. This luxury was denied to Irish unions who received no such notice, thus depriving them of any chance to contest one of the many suspect removals. To retain irremovability it was necessary for a settler to remain in the specific parish in which the status had been gained. This was sometimes difficult, particularly during periods of work scarcity, and it seems that on occasions hapless settlers were tricked into leaving their parishes so that they could be removed. Witnesses at the Select Committee thought it unlikely that children born in England to an Irish father would be removed to Ireland, but they could legally be removed to the parish of their birth, i.e. their legal settlement parish. English born children were often admitted to the Cork workhouse after a forced removal to Ireland and, according to R.J. O Shaughnessy, the Cork guardians rarely corresponded with the Poor Law Commissioners on the matter, as they believed that this was a waste of time. Instead of taking proceedings against English authorities they supported the paupers in the workhouse. In general, Irish unions were reluctant to appeal against removals because of the expense.[79]

In his evidence, George Carr provided details on the working of the removal system at Liverpool. Paupers who were to be passed to Ireland did not enter the workhouse itself, instead they were kept in a vagrant shed which was situated near the main building. The shed had basic sleeping accommodation. Food allowances were minimal and discipline was rigid 'in the extreme'. Carr believed that some Irish workers sought Parish relief in the anticipation that they would be refused, and shipped home at no cost to themselves. So as to discourage this exploitation, the vagrant Irish were forced to work in the holding shed. The procedure was recognised as 'a sort of ordeal that they had to go through if they desired to be passed home'.[80]

Constable John Duross frequently interviewed paupers who had

---

78 PP 1854, Vol. XVII, [396], *Select Committee on Poor Removal*, pp. 2-3, 20, 24-6.
79 PP 1854, Vol. XVII, [396], *Select Committee on Poor Removal*, pp. 18, 30, 69, 75, 89.
80 Ibid., p. 407. George Carr paid a visit to the Cork board of guardians in September 1856. When it was suggested that Carr should address the board, John Francis Maguire, M.P., protested. He criticised Carr for his unhelpful and anti-Irish evidence before the Select Committee and he left the boardroom. The meeting broke up shortly afterwards. *CC* 4 September 1856.

disembarked from ships at the quays. En-route from England they were usually kept on the ship's deck, which they sometimes shared with cattle or horses. If the horse stalls were unoccupied the poor people were allowed use these during bad weather. At Cork the paupers were frequently abandoned and left to fend for themselves. On a number of occasions pregnant women were found on the quayside in a distressed state. Duross estimated that up to one third of these paupers applied for workhouse relief.[81] He found that more paupers were returned during the winter months and that most had come from London. The Irish poor in England avoided applying for relief and medical assistance until all other options were exhausted.[82] During winter months sickness and unemployment were common, so the increase in transportations reflected the rise in applications for assistance and the response of the English authorities.[83] In 1854 alone 1,668 Irish poor were removed from London, and of these 1,070 were brought to Cork.[84]

The evidence of James Rankley, one of the contractors for removing Irish poor from London, gives an insight into the treatment of these people. Paupers selected for removal were brought to his Thames-side depot in carts by a parish official. The paupers were well fed, said Rankley, in fact 'better than I really ought to feed them, because I should have an uproar with them if I did not'. The Cork-bound paupers received 2lbs. of bread, six ounces of cheese, one ounce of coffee and two ounces of sugar each day. Each Thursday morning paupers were shipped from London and at Plymouth they were handed over to another employee who took them to Cork. The majority were deposited on the quayside, but on occasions arrangements were made to transfer individual sick or old paupers to another destination. In some cases, paupers who feared that they might not be admitted were accompanied to the house, as also were blind and other handicapped people. Occasionally, unaccompanied young children were also delivered to the workhouse.[85] In Rankley's experience the Cork workhouse was always willing to receive the paupers. During the 1840s the contractors had received a fee of £2 for each pauper removed to Ireland, and on landing at Cork a few shillings were usually given to the paupers to help them on their overland journey. When the fee was reduced to 26s. in the early 1850s the paupers' allowances were discontinued and they were left to fend for themselves on the quayside. Rankley had rarely seen instances of people applying for

---

81 PP 1854, Vol. XVII, [396], Select *Committee on Poor Removal*, pp. 96-7.
82 PP 1854-5, Vol. XIII, [308], *Select Committee on Poor Removal*, pp. 12-13.
83 PP 1854-5, Vol. XIII, [308], *Select Committee on Poor Removal*, pp. 95, 100.
84 PP 1854-5, Vol. XIII, [308], *Select Committee on Poor Removal*, pp. 115-18; see also PP 1854, vol. XVII, [396], *Select Committee on Poor Removal*, p. 559.
85 PP 1854-5, Vol. XIII, [308], *Select Committee on Poor Removal*, pp. 546-47.

relief solely to get a passage back to Ireland, but he had taken the same people back to Cork on a couple of occasions. He had seen some unjust removals, one of which involved a woman who had been in England for 19 years and had gained a settlement at Bishopgate. Her husband went to America to get a better job and arranged to send the fare for her and their children when he earned it. Eventually the woman had to apply for parish relief but she declined entering the workhouse because, as was the practice in many English workhouses, the children of inmates were taken to a separate institution in the country. Unwittingly, she accepted advice and applied to St. Leonard's workhouse in nearby Shoreditch. This forfeited her settlement and she and the children were removed to Cork a few days later. During her stay in Rankley's depot she learned that her husband had lost an eye in an industrial accident in America. Consequently, there was no chance of his being able to send her any money.[86]

James Carder, clerk of the Birmingham poor law guardians, acknowledged that many of those who had been removed from Birmingham were illegally transported. Their irremovable status had been ignored. When asked for his opinion on the entire removal system, he replied that 'abstractedly considered, I think that removals to Ireland are wrong; but politically considered, I am afraid they are right'. He defined 'politically considered' as 'a matter of policy; in fact almost necessity, arising out of the state of things,' that is 'the number of Irish who would, I think, fly to this country, as soon as employment ceased, having made no provision, they would apply to the parish'. Although Mr. Carder was not anxious to have Irish people seeking relief in England he did acknowledge that they were excellent workers.[87] In a calculated assessment of the laws, G. Coode, a member of the English Bar, and a former Assistant Secretary of the Poor Law Commissioners, said 'it appears to me to be a characteristic of the law that it is thus unjust, that every parish in this country takes the best of Irish ability, the very best of Irish wealth, the very best of Irish talent and enterprise, and yet rejects the poor man the first moment that he becomes unprofitable to itself; that is parochial liberality and justice'.[88]

At the conclusion of the select committee's work it was agreed that the period necessary to earn irremovability should be reduced from five to three years. It was also advocated that the area of residence, on which irremovability was based, should be enlarged from a parish to a union.[89]

---

86 PP 1854-5, Vol. XIII, [308], *Select Committee* on Poor Removal, pp. 548-49, 551-53.

87 PP 1854-5, Vol. XIII, [308], *Select Committee on Poor Removal*, pp. 12, 13, 14, 22; 25, this was acknowledged by other witnesses, p. 40; PP 1854, vol. XVII, [396], *Select Committee on Poor Removal*, p. 371.

88 Ibid, p. 198.

89 PP 1854-5. Vol. XIII [308], *Select Committee on Poor Removal*, pp. III-V.

Select Committee on Irremovable Poor

The removal laws were subjected to another in-depth investigation in the summer of 1860 when a Select Committee again questioned a variety of witnesses on the operation of the system as it applied to the irremovable poor.[90] The clerk of the Birmingham union, from which 100 people had been removed in 1859, believed that the Irish poor were not treated in the same manner as their English counterparts. Unlike the English poor who were delivered directly to the workhouse in their own union, the Irish were disembarked from ships in places generally unknown to them, and often many miles from their intended destination. He was sympathetic to those who had been removed from the 'natural affection' of their equally poor relations and friends after 30 or 40 years in a parish.[91]

John Frost, the well-known pass-master for Middlesex, Surrey and Kent, was questioned on 10 July 1860. He gave the impression that he had great concern for the welfare and feelings of those who were transported under his charge. In addition to removing people to Cork he was responsible for transporting others to Dublin, Waterford and Limerick. During 1859 he removed 483 people to Ireland. Prior to sailing, the poor people were accommodated in his depot at 46 High Street, Wapping. The majority of those bound for Cork sailed directly from London port, but between November and February they were taken by train to Bristol so as to avoid a lengthy sea passage. Frost was paid £1.4s. for each adult, 12s. for each child under 10 years of age and 5s. for each infant under 12 months that he removed to Cork. This included maintenance for up to two days before embarkation. If extra accommodation was required it would be charged to the removing parish at the rate of 1s. per day. If clothing was required for any pauper, money expended by Frost was also re-imbursed by the parish. Frost's charges were generally shipped as deck passengers and sometimes a bed was provided for sick or aged passengers. He assured the committee that all were well treated on the steamer, that sleeping accommodation was available and that sheltered areas were allocated in adverse weather conditions.[92] The daily food allowance for each pauper was 2 lb. of bread, 6 oz. of cheese, coffee and sugar. Half of the food was issued at the commencement of the voyage, and the ship's cook distributed the remainder after two days. The voyage to Cork generally lasted for four days and three nights but in bad weather

---

90 PP 1860, Vol. XVII, [520], *Report from the Select Committee on Irremovable Poor*; p. 11; see also PP 1858, Vol. XIII, [374] *Report from Select Committee on Irremovable Poor*.

91 PP 1860, Vol. XVII, [520], *Irremovable Poor*, pp. 69, 72, 231-2; *CE* 10 February 1860.

92 PP 1860, Vol. XVII, [520], *Irremovable Poor*, pp. 278, 286, 287, 291.

this could be six days – it is not clear if the passengers were given additional rations during the extra days on board. Frost claimed that when the poor arrived in Cork they were met by his agent, taken to lodgings for a night and then dispatched by coach or train to their destination. He was in regular contact with his Cork agent, William Fitzgerald of 21 Leitrim Street, and they exchanged weekly reports.[93]

Scale of charges used by John Frost

PORT	ADULT	CHILD UNDER TEN	INFANT
Belfast	£2.	£1.	5s.
Cork	£1.5s.	12s.6d.	5s.
Derry	£2.	£1.	5s.
Dublin	£1.5s.	12s.6d.	5s.
Dundalk	£2.	£1.	5s.
Limerick	£1.10s.	15s.	5s.
Waterford	£2.	£1.	5s.

In addition to the above, John Frost charged the removing unions 2d. per mile for each pauper brought from a port to a receiving workhouse. A similar charge was made for the conductor's expenses on the journey to and from the workhouse. A separate charge of 3s. per day for the conductor's maintenance on the overland journeys was also levied.

(*Source: Poor Law Commissioners Report*, 1865, p. 49)

During Frost's presentation, he was confronted with evidence which clearly showed that paupers under his care had been mistreated. He denied that paupers were removed against their will and that their shipboard accommodation was primitive. An allegation was also made that he had dispatched paupers to Cork regardless of weather conditions. A subsequent assessment in a *Cork Examiner* editorial stated that Frost's evidence had been presented in an 'angelic' style, and that he gave the impression of being 'the sweetest gentleman that ever made a humble profit by pauper deportation'.[94]

A week later, Frost's evidence was subjected to a thorough scrutiny when four Cork witnesses were questioned. Barry Sheehan, a Cork businessman, related that he had seen groups of 'wretchedly and miserably clad and half starved looking creatures' on the Cork quayside. They had arrived from London and had received bread as 'hard as a paving stone' on the ship. No one met them from the vessel, they were distressed and

---

93 PP 1860, Vol. XVII, [520], *Irremovable Poor,* pp. 279-80, 284; see also *CUL* 15 March 1864, 23 May, 6 June, 14 July, 27 August, 31 August 1865.
94 PP 1860, Vol. XVII, [520], Irremovable Poor, p. 283; *CE* 31 July 1861.

had neither the money nor the local knowledge to continue their journey. This was reiterated by John MacManus, a Cork police sergeant, who stated that it was a regular occurrence for paupers to be left unattended on the quayside. The unfortunate people were taken to the bridewell, given shelter and brought to the police office on the following morning. MacManus was familiar with John Frost and had seen him a number of times in London. MacManus was also familiar with a man named John Phillips who was employed by Frost to bring paupers from London to Cork. Phillips was frequently drunk in Cork and he often left the ship and his charges en-route to the city. He 'actually ran away from them at Passage [West], and left them without taking any further care or charge of them'. Many complaints had been made against Phillips and once he had been charged with 'an assault upon female virtue'.[95] When he appeared before the Cork police office in July 1855 charged with spending the money entrusted to him for a group of paupers, a newspaper described him as 'a most repulsive looking object, being dirty and ragged, and looking much more like a pauper than the paupers whom he had been placed in charge of'.[96]

Paupers from England applied to the Cork workhouse almost every week and 71 were in the institution in the summer of 1860. Forty of those removed from England and Scotland during the 12 months to March 1859 became chargeable to the Cork Union. According to R.J. O Shaughnessy, just 17 of these had been born in the Cork Union. For a number of years as many as 400 returning paupers had applied for workhouse relief. The demand gradually decreased and during 1859 there were about 100 applicants. During his 13 years as clerk of the Cork Union, O Shaughnessy had heard many paupers complain about treatment they received during their custody in England and on the passage to Ireland. Because they were booked as deck-passengers, they were not entitled to any covering, so John Frost's claim that they had access to shelter in the ship's barrack-room was not true.[97] O Shaughnessy gave the committee many examples of individual hardship endured by paupers. He instanced the case of Catherine Keane, a 50-year-old widow who had spent the entire voyage from Liverpool on deck in pouring rain. No agent met her at Cork and she was admitted to the workhouse hospital. Similar treatment was given to Bridget Dillon and her five children, aged from two to eleven years. They got little to eat on the voyage and were offered no assistance to reach their destination in Clare. Margaret Shackwell, the widow of an Englishman, was taken from St. Pancras

---

95   PP 1860, Vol. XVII, [520], *Irremovable Poor*, pp. 320, 321, 325.
96   *CC* 19 July 1855.
97   PP 1860, Vol. XVII, [520], *Irremovable Poor*, pp. 331-2; 336; PP 1860, Vol. LVIII, [331], *Poor Relief*.

workhouse hospital and put on a steamer to Cork. Because of a leg injury she was unable to stand and was obliged to lie on deck for the entire four-day journey. Prior to leaving London she had not been allowed to contact her two children. One aged eleven was at work, and a friend was caring for the other, aged 8 years. O Shaughnessy cited numerous other cases in his evidence.[98]

When William Fitzgerald sent the paupers out of Cork it was often found that the fare which had been paid on their behalf was inadequate and they were left stranded many miles from their homes. Henry Humphrey, the chief clerk of the Cork justices, was very familiar with the plight of the removed paupers because of his work in the police office. He had found that in general the poor people had merely applied for temporary relief in England. They had no intention of remaining in an English workhouse and were frequently whisked back to Ireland without any opportunity of informing a husband, parent, other family members or friends. As there was usually no one at Cork to meet them they frequently arrived at the bridewell and were often admitted to the workhouse. Many of those he had seen in court were English-born and were 'perfectly Anglicised in their manners' and their dress. He recollected that Phillips, the employee of Frost, had a 'mean miserable appearance' and that on one occasion he had been detained for appropriating property or money belonging to a passenger under his charge.[99] In his opinion, responsibility for the welfare of transported passengers was not a suitable role for a person of Phillips' character.

It was clear from the evidence of the Cork witnesses that Frost and his network of co-workers had little interest in the comfort or welfare of the paupers under their charge. Equally, the authorities who entrusted their helpless poor to these people showed a lack of concern for their wellbeing. Their sole objective was to transfer the problem to another area.

In their published report the Select Committee noted that:

> during this inquiry evidence has been submitted to them of some peculiar evils which attend the removal of Irish Poor when chargeable in England. These chiefly relate to the mode and form of conducting removals.[100]

The 1860 committee's proposals, which echoed, or indeed reiterated those of previous committees, included recommendations that the period for acquiring a status of irremovability should be reduced from five to three years, and that the area of consideration should be extended

---

98   PP 1860, Vol. XVII, [520], *Irremovable Poor*, pp. 332-4.
99   PP 1860, Vol. XVII, [520], *Irremovable Poor*, pp. 246, 335, 345, 350.
100 PP 1860, Vol. XVII, [520], *Irremovable Poor*, p. III.

from a parish to the whole union. To prevent abuse of the removal Acts, it was recommended that warrants would be issued only by 'justices assembled at a petty session, or by a stipendiary magistrate', that these would not be issued unless the head of the family was present, and that the health of those to be removed was given consideration. The full costs of removal to Irish destinations were to be paid by the removing parish, and no woman or child under 14 years of age was to be transmitted as a deck passenger during winter months. Also, a copy of the removal warrant and depositions was to be available to the board of guardians of the union to which the parties were destined.[101]

Legislation

The recommendations of this Select Committee were enshrined in parliamentary legislation on 1 August 1861 (24&25 Victoriae, cap. 55) and on 6 August 1861 (24&25 Victoriae, cap. 76). Under the former Act, orphans under the age of 16 years were able to inherit the status of irremovability acquired by their parents, and deserted wives were enabled to acquire irremovability after three years residence in a union.[102]

The latter Act, which dealt specifically with removals to Ireland, introduced a new element into the Irish Poor Law system. Sections 4 and 5 authorised the removal of Irish people to the workhouse at the port nearest to their ultimate destination. The Irish Poor Law Commissioners were not enthusiastic about this development, seeing it as 'quite repugnant to the spirit of the Irish Poor Law' which heretofore fixed chargeability on the place in which destitution was relieved. The guardians of the port union had the option of giving the paupers workhouse relief or of transferring them to their own union. To facilitate the transfer, boards of guardians in the port unions were empowered to appoint a removing officer who would deliver the paupers to the workhouse named in the English removal warrant.[103] The receiving union had little option about refusing to accept paupers for a Poor Law Commissioners circular of 1 November 1861 advised that 'the officers of the Workhouse at which he is delivered must accept the pauper without hesitation or objection on any ground whatever – all questions affecting the legality of the removal having been finally adjudicated in granting the warrant'. All expenses involved in transferring the paupers were to be

---

101 PP 1860, Vol. XVII, [520], Irremovable Poor, pp. III-IV.
102 24&25 Victoriae, cap. 55; see also *Poor Law Commissioners Annual Report* (1862), p. 25; see also, Michael E. Rose, 'Settlement, Removal and the new Poor Law', in D. Fraser (ed.), *The New Poor Law in the Nineteenth century* (London, 1976), p. 30.
103 *Poor Law Commissioners Annual Report* (1862), pp. 26-7, 44.

repaid by the English union which initiated the removal.[104] For a period after the passing of the Acts in August 1861 removals to Ireland decreased, but by the end of the year they were again on the increase and the law as administered by the English authorities was described as 'unsatisfactory'.[105]

The section of the Act authorising Irish workhouse officials to transfer the removed paupers to their ultimate destination was repealed in July 1863. (26&27 Victoriae, cap. 89, Section 4.) English or Scottish removing agents were compelled to deliver the paupers directly to the relevant Irish union, thus guaranteeing 'continuous safe custody'.[106] From March 1866 the period of residence required to gain irremovability was reduced from three years to one year but removals and hardship persisted. (28 &29 Vict., Cap79, Sec. 8; see also, 30 & 31 Vic. Cap. 61) The still common practice of removing families to Ireland while husbands were away from home was a cause of distress to all parties involved. Removals continued and during 1886 the people brought from England included 86 year old Patrick Cummins and 67 year old Ellen Shea from Cardiff workhouse. In February 1887 William Scannell died of acute pneumonia in the workhouse fever ward after being returned from the Liverpool workhouse. In June 1888 William Robinson was brought to Cork from Croydon workhouse. The 58 year old man, who was too ill to work, had spent 55 years in England. Again, in November 1888, the workhouse master reported that one of the men removed from Cardiff to Cork had spent 48 years in England.[107] The removal of Irish people from Scotland also continued with many poor people being returned from Glasgow to Cork.[108] The concept of irremovability for Irish residents was enshrined in Scottish law

---

104 On 25 March 1863 there were 48 inmates of the Cork workhouse who had been born in England, Wales or Scotland. PP 1863, Vol. LII [192], *A return of the names and ages of all paupers in the workhouses in Ireland on the 25th day of March, who were born in England, Wales or Scotland*, pp. 4-5.

105 For details of removal cases, see: *CUM* 13 November, 20 November, 27 November, 4, December, 11 December, 18 December, 23 December 1861, 1 January, 8 January, 15 January, 22 January, 12 February, 19 February, 12 March, 26 March, 9 April, 30 April, 7 May, 14 May, 28 May, 4 June, 11 June, 25 June, 22 October 1862; *Poor Law Commissioners Annual Report* (1862), pp. 30-41; *Poor Law Commissioners Annual Report* (1863), pp. 10, 80-104.

106 *Poor Law Commissioners Annual Report* (1864), pp. 24-25, .30.

107 *CE* 20 August 1886, 25 February 1887, 8 June, 6 July, 9 November 1888, see also 22 March 1878, 11 February, 18 February 1881; 13 December 1889; See also *CUM* 3 May, 10 May, 17 May, 7 June, 30 August, 6 September 1888, 9 May, 5 June 1889, 24 April, 2 August 1890.

108 PP 1871, vol. LIX, [8], Return of poor persons removed from England and Wales . . . pp. 30, 52; see also PP 1876, Vol. LXIII, [206], *Return re relief . . .*, p. 3; PP 1879, Vol. LX, [58], *Return of persons born in England . . .* p. 3; PP 1880, Vol. LXII, [358], *Poor Removal*, p. 6.

in 1898.[109] Under section four of the Scottish Poor Law Act (61&62 Vict. C.2) an Irish poor person who had resided continuously in Scotland for not less than five years was deemed irremovable. Provided that the person had resided for 12 months in the same parish, relief would be available in that area.[110]

Conclusion

The purpose of the settlement and removal laws was to rid an area of poor and destitute people who were in receipt of, or seeking, poor relief or charitable assistance. Those subjected to the laws were predominantly the sick, the disabled, and generally the most vulnerable and unprotected members of society. The removal laws were administered locally by poor law guardians, magistrates and other officers who carried out their tasks in a methodical and bureaucratic fashion.[111] The system 'operated on the basis that it was relatively unimportant to poor people whether, and where they were removed'.[112]

People who applied for assistance during periods of financial hardship or illness were often admitted to the workhouse. Pregnant or sick applicants were admitted to the maternity or infirmary wards. As inmates, they were free to leave the institution after a short period of notification. As part of the admission procedure, all applicants were questioned on their background, place of birth, family connections and other details, which identified potential removal candidates. Those who had an Irish name or accent, or who revealed any links with Ireland left themselves open to summary removal. People who were not legally entitled to work-house relief or hospital treatment were frequently prevented from leaving the institution. Because of the threat of removal, sick people were slow to seek assistance.[113] Lack of medical attention caused unnecessary misery and suffering, and prolonged minor ailments. When infectious diseases were involved, the presence of the sick endangered those around them and spread illnesses. The removal system itself also helped spread infection and during the smallpox epidemics of the 1870s a number of cases of the disease were brought from England to Irish workhouses.[114]

---

109 See letter from William D'Esterre Parker to the Chief Secretary of 12 January 1889 in NAI, CSORP 1903 2963.
110 *Local Government Board Annual Report* (1899), p. 19.
111 See N. Longmate, *The Workhouse* (London, 1974), p. 22.
112 R. Cranston, *Legal foundation of the Welfare state* (London, 1985), p. 24.
113 M.E. Rose, 'Settlement, Removal and the new Poor Law', in Fraser (ed.), *The New Poor Law* (London, 1976), p. 37.
114 *Poor Law Commissioners Annual Report* (1871), p. 135. *Local Government Board Annual Report* (1877), p. 22, and (1878), p. 27.

The removal system was a cruel method of ridding an area of individuals who had fallen on bad times. Frequently those removed had been residents for many years, or in some cases, for their entire lives. Many of those returned from England had very weak linkd with Ireland; some had been born in the country but had spent the greater part of their lives in England. Others were old people who had gone to England as youths, married English spouses, reared families and worked their entire lives in England. Regardless, they were deported, and landed in a country with which they were totally unfamiliar. In 1875 the *Cork Examiner* summed up the removal system by saying that: 'the law is carried out by the English and Scotch boards with cynical cruelty; and cases are continually occurring in which hardships of a shocking character are disclosed. Families are broken up, men and women are taken by force from the midst of friends and old associations, from the spots in which all their interests and affections are centred, and transferred to places which they had quitted perhaps in childhood, and where they are totally unknown'.[115]

The unfeeling removal machinery ignored many factors and considerations. All that mattered to the authorities was that they cleared their own areas of poor relief candidates. Settlers were sometimes prevented from gaining irremovability by parish authorities who forced them to move to another area before the adequate residence requirement had been completed. The system as practised in England itself was also considered to be 'expensive and useless' because many of the removed parties returned almost immediately.[116] Mothers were sometimes deported without all, or any of their offspring, and children were often shipped without their parents.[117] Sometimes, those who had been removed ended up in an Irish workhouse far from the intended destination. This made the task of retracing a lost spouse, parent, relation, sibling or friend almost impossible. Husbands returning home from a period of work in another city or town in England were frequently confronted with this dilemma. Without doubt many of these broken families were never re-united, and relationships severed by removal remained so.

Christine Kinealy's claim that the 'power of removal was generally employed with restraint throughout the course of the nineteenth century'[118] is clearly at odds with the evidence presented in the foregoing

---

115 *CE* 23 July 1875; see also speeches of McCarthy Downing M.P. at House of Commons in *CE* 24 July 1875 and 5 July 1878.

116 F. Finnegan, *Poverty and Prejudice* (Cork, 1982), p. 115; *Second Report from the Select Committee on Poor Relief* (England), PP 1861, Vol. IX, [323], p. 164; See R. Cranston, *Welfare State*, pp. 24-5; *CE* 4 September 1857.

117 See F. Neal, *Black '47*, p. 228.

118 C. Kinealy, *Great Calamity* (Dublin, 1994), p. 338.

account. Her subsequent comment that some British boards of guardians 'displayed less concern for the niceties of the English Poor Law' is nearer to the reality.[119] The plight of the poor in Ireland during the 1840s received widespread publicity in the English press. Few of the population of England would have been unaware of the situation in the 'sister' island. Certainly poor law officials and magistrates would have known of the hardship, starvation, disease and famine in Ireland. They were fully aware that deportation meant privation and possible sickness and starvation. Michael E. Rose remarked that 'the practice of settlement and removal reflected the intensely local nature of the English poor relief system'.[120] It can perhaps be described as the epitome of parochialism.[121]

---

119 C. Kinealy, *Death dealing famine* (London, 1997). p. 124.

120 M. E. Rose, 'Settlement, Removal and the new Poor Law', in Fraser (ed.), *The New Poor Law* (London, 1976), p. 42.

121 The laws of removal and settlement were on the British statute books until 1948 and during the early years of the twentieth century thousands of people were being removed annually between poor law unions in England. M.E. Rose, 'Settlement, Removal and the new Poor Law', in D. Fraser (ed.), *The New Poor Law* (London, 1976), p. 31. The 1948 National Assistance Act finally abolished the removal laws. 11&12 Geo. 6, Chap. 29 – see in particular 7th schedule.

4 School

Although the workhouse may not have offered the ideal environment for education, its isolation from external distractions did present some unique opportunities. A varied but imaginative and integrated timetable incorporating elements of classroom education and work skills would have prepared the children for life outside the workhouse. On more than one occasion attempts were made to revise the workhouse education programme by incorporating subjects like music and drawing. The changes were generally rejected by the majority of guardians and, instead, the young charges were treated more like prisoners or unpaid slaves and subjected to monotonous classroom lessons and repetitive work tasks. The children were at a disadvantage by virtue of their isolation from outside life. This was obvious to many parties and some efforts – most notably by the Ladies Visiting Committee – were made to resolve this problem.

The 1838 Act for the more effectual relief of the destitute poor in Ireland pays little attention to the educational needs of workhouse children and the reference to education is contained in the section dealing with religious services in workhouses. Article 22 of the official workhouse rules specified that 'boys and girls who are inmates of the workhouse shall, for three of the working hours at least, every day, be instructed in reading, writing, arithmetic, and the principles of Christian religion; and such other instruction shall be imparted to them as shall fit them for service and train them to habits of usefulness, industry and virtue'.[1] The importance of a good education for workhouse children was recognised by George Nicholls who wrote that 'if rightly educated and well trained, they will, in fact be sought after'.[2]

The duties of the teaching staff were covered by the rules, and article 64 specified that the schoolmaster and mistress were:

---

1 PP 1844, Vol. XL, [577], *Copies of four orders of the Poor Law Commissioners to Unions in Ireland (Workhouse Rules)*, Article 22; PP 1843, Vol. XLVI, [616], *Correspondence between the Poor Law Commissioners and the Guardians of Poorhouses (Ireland), Education of paupers*, p. 271.
2 PP 1843, Vol. XLVI, p. 233.

1. To instruct the boys and girls according to the directions expressed in Article 22.
2. To regulate the discipline and organisation of the school, and the industrial and moral training of the children, subject to the directions of the Board of Guardians.
3. To accompany the children when they quit the workhouse for exercise, unless the guardians shall otherwise direct.
4. To keep the children clean in their persons, and orderly and decorous in their conduct.
5. To assist the master and matron respectively in maintaining due subordination in the workhouse.[3]

Inmates were occasionally appointed to the position of schoolmaster or schoolmistress. Such was the case in 1840 when the schoolmistress was an inmate with three children. She received no salary or benefits, but to avoid the estimated £30 per annum spent on maintaining her children some guardians were anxious to have the woman discharged and re-employed as a teacher at £20 per annum. She could then live outside with her children and provide the same service at a cheaper rate. The suggestion was not accepted but it generated a discussion and the guardians decided to set the salaries at £30 per annum for the schoolmaster and £25 for the mistress. They were not to receive workhouse food and were expected to teach for five hours each weekday. Thomas Hyde was appointed schoolmaster and Mrs Mary O Keeffe schoolmistress in April 1840.[4]

During 1842 the guardians decided that teachers would have to live on the premises and take responsibility for supervising the children and distributing their food which was usually consumed in the classroom. For these duties the teachers were granted workhouse meals. They had little choice but to accept the new conditions for, in the words of one guardian, Captain Rogers, if they did not, 'the Board could very easily get rid of them, and he believed no great loss would be sustained'.[5]

Corporal punishment was used to enforce discipline and in February 1842 the guardians ordered the schoolmaster 'to use a rattan [cane] instead of a cat o' ninetails for punishing the boys'. The children's

3 PP 1844, Vol. XL, [577], *Workhouse Rules*, Article 64.
4 *CUM* 30 March, 27 April, 15 June 1840; *SR* 12 March, 23 April 1840; *CC* 2 May 1840. Mrs O Keeffe died in August and a Mrs Cunningham replaced her. In January 1842 two inmates: Susan Murphy and Margaret Keane were appointed as assistant schoolteachers – for their services they were rewarded with rations similar to those of the workhouse nurses. *CUM* 24 August, 31 August 1840, 17 January 1842; *SR* 22 September 1840.
5 *SR* 3 May 1842; *CUM* 23 May, 29 August 1842, 19 June 1843; *CUL* 27 August 1842.

education was hindered by inadequate textbooks and to remedy this problem, the guardians applied to the Commissioners of National Education for a supply of up-to-date schoolbooks.[6] Following initial reluctance, the guardians agreed to place the workhouse schools under the inspection of the Board of National Education, which allowed schools to purchase books and materials at reduced costs.[7]

During 1843 when James Reilly, the Catholic teacher, provided physical exercise for the boys, he was criticised for encouraging them to play football in front of the workhouse. Rev. H. Clifford, the Protestant chaplain, questioned Reilly's religious impartiality and complained that the Sabbath was being desecrated by the boys' activities which gave the workhouse the appearance of a 'lounge for idlers'. The Catholic chaplain, Rev. George Sheehan, defended Reilly as a 'kind, careful person', who took great interest in the 200 boys under his charge. The Commissioners intervened and demanded that the guardians discourage the ball playing.[8]

By 1846 about three quarters of the 130 workhouse schools were connected to the Commissioners of National Education which acknowledged that the inmates required more extensive instruction than that given in the general national schools. They were in favour of introducing farm and industrial training to prepare the children for life outside the institution.[9] This was the practice in many Irish workhouses. For instance, in the Tipperary institutions boys and girls were taught a variety of skills such as farm work, weaving, baking, shoemaking, sewing and embroidery.[10] In the Cork workhouse some boys received training as tailors, carpenters and shoemakers, and a seamstress instructed girls.[11]

---

6 *CUL* I5 June 1840, 14 February 1842; *SR* 18 April 1840. For an account of the early years of the Commissioners of National Education, see: John Coolahan, *Irish Education: Its history and structure* (Dublin, 1983 edition) pp. 10-19.

7 *CC* 25 April, 2 May 1840; *SR* 18 June 1840; *CUM* 24 October 1842. See also correspondence on this topic in PP 1843, Vol. XLVI, [616], pp. 279-80; see also Gerard O Brien, 'Workhouse management in pre-Famine Ireland', *Proceedings of Royal Irish Academy*, Vol. 86c. (1986), p. 122.

8 *CUL* 19 January 1843; *SR* 10 January, 26 January 1843; see also PP 1843, Vol. XLVI, pp. 280-81; Gerard O Brien, Workhouse Management, op. cit. (1986), p. 126.

9 13th *National Education Report* (1846), p. 5; see also Appendix to 20th *National Education Report* (1853), p. 625; *14th National Education Report* (1847), pp. 140-41; Jane Barnes, *Irish Industrial Schools, 1868-1908, Origins and developments* (Dublin, 1989), pp. 29-31.

10 Anne M. Lanigan, *The Poor Law children of county Tipperary and their education 1840-1880* (M. Ed. thesis, UCC, 1988), pp. 98, 98, 100, 140-1, 145-8, 190-4, 212-7, 291.

11 PP 1843, VOL XLVI, [616], p. 280; PP I845, Vol. XXXVIII, [351], *Return of the number of children sent out to service . . .*, p. 5.

Unfortunately this training had little lasting benefit or relevance. Although many children made great progress in the house, most of those who worked with the tradesmen were not given an opportunity to continue these skills when they left.[12] During the period of constant disruption and unrest in the late 1840s progress did not continue, and when the education inspector visited the workhouse on 10 September 1847, he lamented that 'the schools can only be regarded as in nominal operation; they will take much time to recover the effects of the late disastrous year'.[13]

During 1847 national education inspectors undertook a survey of workhouse schools. Among the matters examined were teachers' qualifications, duties and classes conducted; the progress and activities of children; the conditions of the schools and equipment. The results were disappointing – of 206 teachers examined, the Commissioners had trained only 30 and in total just 63 were deemed to be suitably qualified. The teachers' remunerations were inadequate, with 61 receiving salaries of less than £15 per annum plus board and lodgings. Another 114 received between £15 and £20 and just 27 had salaries in excess of £20. Teachers in many workhouses – for instance those in Tipperary[14] – had to perform duties other than instructing and, no doubt with justification, they claimed that the extra work interfered with their education programme. Perhaps as a result of their poor qualifications, the status of workhouse teachers was low amongst the other staff. Over half of the schools had inadequate furnishings, books and equipment and many classrooms were overcrowded.[15]

As a result of the survey, the Commissioners made a number of suggestions, which would improve classrooms, facilities and the lot of the workhouse teachers. It was recommended that the minimum salary for male teachers should be £30 per annum plus an apartment and food and for female teachers a minimum payment of £25 with similar conditions. No teacher was to undertake the instruction of more than 100 children and if this were exceeded assistant teachers would be provided. This apparent concern was negated by a clause which stated that 'the whole time of the teachers shall be devoted to the literary, moral and industrial

12 NAI, Poor Law Commissioners, Letters to James Burke 1845, 12 November 1845; also PP 1846, Vol. XI, [694], *Poor Relief and Medical Charities*, part1, Evidence of T.R. Sarsfield, pp. 276-7.
13 *CUM* 21 December 1846; *CUL* 11 December 1846, 11 November 1847; NAI, Poor Law Commissioners, Letters to James Burke 1847, 27 February 1847.
14 Anne M. Lanigan, *The Poor Law children of county Tipperary* (thesis, 1988), pp. 102-4, 189, 296.
15 14th *National Education Report* (1847), pp. 60, 61; J. Robins, *The Lost Children A study of charity children in Ireland 1700-1900* (Dublin, 1981), p. 226.

education of the children, and to the superintendence of them, during the hours of recreation and manual labour'. Conditions were to be improved with a minimum space for each child of 'at least six square feet', and classrooms were to have 'suitable furniture and apparatus'. In reality many of these innovations were not implemented.[16]

Disorder and chaos reigned in the workhouses of the late 1840s and Inspector James Kavanagh noted that the 'already sadly inefficient' work-house schools 'now might be said to be *schools only in name*'.[17] The Cork boys' school was situated in a temporary timber shed without any toilet facilities. Classrooms were overcrowded, furniture, books and equipment were insufficient, teachers were saddled with duties far removed from education and real schooling was largely neglected.[18] Such was the case when the inspector visited on 24 January 1849 and about 400 boys were under the casual control of unqualified pauper inmates and another 100 were breaking stones outside the school windows.[19]

The Commissioners were dissatisfied with progress.[20] Following his appointment as headmaster in August 1848, Edward Walsh often complained about the many extraneous duties and the need for addi-tional teaching staff. A proposal by the Cork guardians to appoint assistant schoolmasters from the inmates was rejected by the Poor Law Commissioners on the grounds that competent candidates would not be found in a workhouse; also, they doubted that respect would be shown to teachers who had formerly been inmates of the house.[21] Captain Bran-dling, the Poor Law Inspector, had sympathy for headmaster Walsh's predicament in being responsible for the education of almost 900 school-boys. The Commissioners advised the guardians to appoint assistants from outside the house and within a couple of months Peter McSwiney was employed.[22]

The area allocated for girls' education was totally inadequate. The schoolroom had accommodation for about 200 girls, but on occasions attendance exceeded 500. As a result 'the younger children squat on the floor – the older ones are huddled together on the forms – all are jostling and struggling for space'. The schoolmistress was unacquainted with

---

16 14th *National Education Report* (1847), pp. 60-61.
17 20th *National Education Report* (1853), p. 627. Appendix L, pp. 623-758, of this report contains a particularly interesting account on the state of schools and education in Irish workhouses.
18 20th *National Education Report* (1853), pp. 627, 646; *CUM* 10 May 1847; *SR* 1 March 1849.
19 *CUL* 12 February 1849.
20 16th *National Education Report* (1849), P. 13; 17th *National Education Report* (1850), p. 12 and appendix p. 151.
21 *CUL* 24 April 1849.
22 *CUL* 4 June, 10 July 1849; *CUM* 9 May, 30 June, 11 July 1849.

geography and she had only a 'very slight knowledge' of the school's reading books. Under examination, none of her pupils gave the correct answer to a multiplication question, and spelling was generally bad. One ratepayer who visited the girls' school department at South Terrace, was highly impressed with the pupils. 'I examined their copy books and was truly surprised when, comparing their progress with the date of each girl's commencement, it showed attention and talent in the pupils, and told much for the ability and care of the school Mistress. Many were engaged at needle work, which was well done, and thanks to the Monitor system, none were idle or neglected in this densely crowded room'.[23] The infants were also impressive, and 'after three lessons were sung, they gave correct answers to several questions in the multiplication and pence tables'. In 1850 the infants' school had 210 pupils in a good room and although the teacher had no formal qualifications, an efficient programme, which included basic spelling, grammar, reading and singing, was being conducted.[24]

The boys' school room was 150 feet long, 19 feet wide and 10 feet high, it was well lit and ventilated and accommodated 475 pupils who also dined in the apartment. During 1850 the average daily attendance was 468 boys but on a few occasions there were up to 752 pupils 'packed and crushed together to the peril of health and decency'. When James Kavanagh visited during 1850, 170 boys, many suffering from 'cutaneous diseases', were in the sick wards, and 45 others were employed on various tasks in the workhouse. To keep order in the schoolroom one teacher 'is wholly engaged, with ruler in hand, in suppressing noise and riot'. Neither of the two teachers was trained. The head, Edward Walsh, was 'ignorant of geography' and 'deficient in arithmetic', and he was 'somewhat broken down in spirit from long toil in teaching'. His brother, the assistant, 'has neither taste nor qualification for his duties, he can read in a medium style, and can write legibly, but here his scholarship ends. He is unacquainted with the elements of grammar, geography and arithmetic'.[25] The inspector recommended that four teachers should be employed in this school. Not surprisingly, the standard of scholarship

---

23 *CE* 21 February 1849.
24 17th *National Education Report* (1850), Appendix, pp. 149, 181.
25 The head master, Edward Walsh, died just a few days after the inspector's visit. Walsh was, said the *Southern Reporter*, 'a man of much acquirement, undoubted talent, and sincere patriotism, and through the pages of the *Spirit of the Nation* his poems have made their way to the hearts of many'. *SR* 22 August 1850. The guardians were unable to assist his widow and family, but a public appeal raised sufficient funds to enable them emigrate. *CE* 23 August 1850; *SR* 22 August, 29 August, 31 August, 5 September, 12 September, 14 September, 16 September, 19 September 1850; *CUL* 10 September 1850; *CUM* 27 March, 10 April, 19 June, 7 August 1850.

was lamentable and of 511 pupils examined just 36, or 7%, could read a simple narrative in words of two syllables. The absence of books, stationery and visual aids created difficulties for the teachers and certainly failed to stimulate the children. Distractions were common and no attempt was made to suppress external noise. The infants' school was infested with rats and during the inspector's visit, many 'walked freely round the room to pick crumbs'.[26]

The inspector returned on 25 September 1850 and examined the female and infants schools. There were 323 pupils in the female class and the overworked teacher could instruct few of them. Just 154 were learning arithmetic and subjects such as reading, grammar and geography were taught to limited sections of the class. The teacher was assisted by six pauper girls who were 'utterly unfit for such an office, being ignorant of the very elements of grammar, geography and arithmetic'. Again the inspector pleaded with the guardians to employ a well-qualified teacher and assistant. He was happy with changes in the infants' department where marked improvements were evident in reading, arithmetic and grammar, and the young children were enjoying their singing classes in particular. He did voice his concern about the workload on the solitary teacher in this department.[27]

A deterioration in the quality of teaching was again noted in February 1852. The inspector was horrified by the behaviour of the unqualified assistant, particularly as 'his extremely injudicious management of the classes, including the punishment by striking on the head with a thick rough heath rod of many young children who failed to answer his questions *was sanctioned* by the principal teacher'.[28] An earlier suggestion that monitors should be appointed to help reduce the pupil teacher ratio had been implemented, but they too had been authorised to inflict corporal punishment for trivial offences.[29] Under the monitorial system of education, the teacher instructed selected pupils; they in turn were responsible for instructing junior pupils, while the teacher acted as 'supervisor, examiner and disciplinarian'.[30] In the girls' school the teacher was assisted by a couple of young monitors but the 319 pupils were generally neglected and 'a few of the third class can read fairly but their intelligence is very low, their minds being hardly ever exercised on the subject

---

26 *CUL* 31 August 1850; 17th *National Education Report* (1850), pp. 186-7.
27 *CUL* 8 November 1850. In July 1851 the workhouse had a schoolmaster and a schoolmistress plus an assistant for each department. PP 1851, [591] VOL. XLIX, Salaries of Officers . . ., p. 4.
28 *CUL* 3 April 1852.
29 18th *National Education Report* (1851), p. XXVII; *CUL* 25 August 1851.
30 David Wardle, *English popular education, 1780-1975* (London, 1976), p. 86; *CUL* 28 May, 1 June 1852.

matter of the lesson'.[31] During the inquiry into education for criminal and destitute children in April 1853, Walter Berwick, assistant barrister for the Cork East Riding, described the education system in the Cork workhouse as 'frightfully defective'.[32] The Poor Law Commissioners told the guardians to make improvements and in the autumn, the board purchased slates, paper, pens and ink for the school. At the end of the year the Commissioners sanctioned the appointment of a temporary instructor to teach the female inmates the skills of net making.[33]

Outside the workhouses the national education system had been growing steadily – the Education Commissioners' first report in 1833 showed that there were 789 schools with 107,042 pupils; the 1853 report gives a total of 5,032 schools with 556,478 children connected to the national education system. The Commissioners were at that time reviewing the management of workhouse schools and their head inspector, James Kavanagh, made a number of suggestions on improvements and modifications.[34] Kavanagh was particularly critical of workhouse schools with their low literacy standards and defective industrial training.[35] Efforts to assess the ability of the Cork workhouse school staff were resisted by the male teachers who objected to a proposed examination in 1853. The principal teacher used a system of 'self instruction' for the pupils. Consequently, after years of fruitless attendance, minimal attention and little stimulation, many hapless children were still pursuing the mysteries of the alphabet or the first lesson book. Thus, lamented the inspector, instead of progressing, the schoolboys actually 'forget what they had known'.[36] The programme in the female school was equally mundane. The head mistress had no teaching method, no control over the children and 'pursues no particular arrangement as to the occupation of time'. During the inspector's visit 'the utmost noise and uproar prevailed in the school. . . notwithstanding the continued efforts of the teacher and her assistants to obtain some degree of silence'.[37] In this school also, girls who had spent up to five years in attendance were still on the first book.

The infants had the only trained teacher in the house, but her class-

---

31 *CUL* 28 May, 1 June 1852.
32 PP 1852-3 Vol. XXIII, [674], *Report from select committee on criminal and destitute children; together with the minutes of evidence and appendix*, p. 344.
33 *CUL* 8 June, 4 August, 3 November 1852.
34 20th *National Education Report* (1853), p. X, XVI; vol. II Appendix, L, p. 630.
35 E. Ó Heideain, *National School inspection* (Dublin, 1967), footnote, p. 126, pp. 69-71; Kavanagh resigned from the National Education Board in February 1858, mainly as a result of the reaction against his report on Irish workhouse and prison schools which was published in the 1853 National Education Report.
36 *CE* 25 March l853; *CUL* 14 March 1853.
37 *CUL* 14 March 1853.

room lacked basic teaching equipment such as a blackboard, charts or visual aids to stimulate the children. Although the inspector was treated to many fine songs, few of the pupils wrote well and 'whole masses of children hardly received any instruction'. A radical intervention would be necessary to effect improvements, so Inspector Coyle suggested that school time should be extended from three to five hours a day to boost the children's education.[38] By comparison children in national schools outside the workhouse had six hours of classroom work each day.[39]

The guardians discussed the inspector's report and, with a characteristic lack of ownership, some of them denied that things were as bad as had been painted. Others agreed that the inspector had presented an honest assessment of the schools and their teachers. Following a lengthy deliberation, the guardians passed a resolution calling on the Poor Law Commissioners to initiate improvements. In turn, the Commissioners authorised the guardians to take action.[40] In an editorial, the *Cork Examiner* said that the Cork workhouse school was

> a model of scandalous incompetence and disgraceful failure. So far as the system has gone, it has been one by which the poor child has been sedulously kept in the most profound ignorance of everything which even a pauper child ought to know. In fact, the cotton planters of Carolina and Georgia could advance no objection to the system of training for which successive reports of Inspectors have rendered the Cork Union illustrious. They might safely transplant the whole system into the very centre of their slave community, without the slightest danger of the ignorance of their Sambos, Dinahs, Miss Luceys, and youthful Dan Tuckers.[41]

Because of the large class sizes and an inadequate number of teachers, the education inspector recommended that 'the teachers be permitted to devote their time *exclusively* to the legitimate duties of their office'.[42] In a letter to the chairman of the board of guardians, the headmaster complained that 'he was virtually a wardmaster, storekeeper, cook, purveyor, etc . . . that not only had he to look after the washing of the boys' dishes, tins, etc., but he had also to wash his own dishes, brush his own room, and dress his own bed'.[43]

Conditions for the children were also uncomfortable. The boys' school

---

38 20th *National Education Report* (1853), Appendix. L, p. 647.
39 J. Robins, *Lost Children*, p. 234.
40 *CUL* 26 March 1853; *CUM* 14 March, 23 March 1853. Some school furniture was replaced during the summer *CUM* 20 July 1853.
41 *CE* 25 March 1853.
42 *CUL* 28 April 1854; *CE* 31 March, 5 May 1854; see also 20th *National Education Report* (1853), Vol. II, Appendix. L, p. 646.
43 20th *National Education Report* (1853), Vol. II, Appendix, L, p. 652.

was constructed from ill-fitting timbers, it had no fireplace or heating, and during the winter of 1853-4 over 140 panes of glass were missing from its windows.[44] 'I have', said the inspector, 'never found in any work-house that I have visited more uncomfortable schoolrooms; and my conviction is, that during the cold weather, the business of teaching will be utterly profitless; unless more comfortable accommodation be provided for the teachers and pupils'.[45]

The Poor Law Commissioners were annoyed at the continuing bad reports and the lack of corrective action so they asked the guardians to replace the existing school staff and employ others at reasonable salaries. The guardians did their best to avoid making changes, and some wanted to withdraw the school from under the National Education Board. Eventually a motion to dismiss the male teachers and employ new ones was passed.[46] Some weeks later, John Donaghy was recruited as head schoolmaster, Michael Ring was appointed as an assistant and monitors were being trained.[47]

The children's education was frequently neglected and at the end of 1853 the school committee complained that the young boys were not receiving even their daily three hours. Instead, about 200 of the seven to ten year olds were forced to grind corn as a pretence for useful industrial training.[48] Writing on the matter some time later, the education inspector questioned the value of alternating the children's activities between school and industrial work. He had great sympathy for the school staff because 'each class comes before the teacher only in dribbles, and at different times of the day. . . . it is impossible to frame a timetable for a large school under such regulations'.[49] He was sceptical about the merits of the so-called industrial education at which 'fifty of the boys are employed at present from 9 to 1 o'clock, and from 2 to 4 o'c, each day, in planting cabbages. This is the only instruction they receive in *agriculture*'.[50] The house committee responded by transferring all blame to the teachers for failing to draw up a proper timetable.

---

44 *CUL* 24 December 1853; *House Committee Book, FM1* (Cork Archives), 3 December 1855; see also *CUM* 24 August, 14 September 1853.

45 *CUL* I3 December 1855; see also *CUL* 17 November, 5 December 1854; 16 February 1855.

46 *CUL* 26 March, 5 April, 27 June 1853; *CE* 25 March, 8 April, 11 April, 15 April 1853.

47 *CUL* 7 June, 23 August 1853; 28 February 1854; *CUM* 3 August 1853; *Poor Law Commissioners Annual Report* (1855), Appendix, A, p. 96.

48 *CUL* 24 December 1853; *CE* I6 December 1853.

49 *CUL* I3 December 1855.

50 Alternating classes between schoolwork and agricultural training was also practiced in Dungarvan workhouse. William Fraher, etc., *Desperate Haven: The Poor Law, Famine & Aftermath in Dungarvan Union* (Dungarvan, no date), p. 268.

The committee also took the inspector to task for his remarks about the farm work, and insisted that the boys were getting valuable experience at 'every description of manual labour required for tilling the workhouse land'.[51]

When the inspector visited the infant school in February 1855 he was full of praise for Eliza Murphy who was 'energetic and painstaking in the discharge of her duty'. Despite a large attendance and limited time, great improvements had taken place. The children's reading skills were satisfactory, writing was good and many knew their money, weight and measurement tables by heart. An assistant teacher would ensure that progress continued and the inspector also suggested that classroom aids should be purchased and a proper playground provided. 'Under existing arrangements, the poor little creatures (many of whom have lost the sight of one eye) are imprisoned during the greater part of the day in a large, gloomy shed, badly lighted and imperfectly ventilated and where, from the want of sufficient fuel and proper exercise they suffer from the extreme cold and severity of the season'.[52]

Because of the almost relentlessly critical reports, Poor Law Inspector Hall carried out an independent inspection of the schools in June 1855. In the boys' department he concluded that many pupils were 'backward'; answering in the girls' school was 'indifferent' and the junior classes were 'not generally satisfactory'. Having considered the matter, he concluded that the time wasted by teachers in fulfilling duties which should be carried out by minor officers was having a totally adverse effect on the children's education.[53]

During March 1856 the school inspector spend six hours examining the most advanced female pupils, he concluded that the junior classes were 'learning little or nothing', and that progress in the senior classes was 'of very little value' with most of the pupils being poor at reading, writing and arithmetic. Out of 203 girls aged between nine and fourteen years, each of whom was supposed to attend school for six hours per day

> only two are able to write small hand freely – not one well; only five were able to work an easy sum in short division of money – and not one such a sum in simple proportion as the following: If 41 lbs. of tea cost 24s. 8d., how much may be bought for £42.7s.8d? Of the 16

---

51 *House Committee Book, FMI* (Cork Archives), 31 December 1855.
52 *CUL* 31 March 1855; also *CUL* 16 February 1855, 28 November 1854. It is interesting to note that in the letter book of 31 March, 1855 the inspector's remarks have been qualified by a supplementary, but undated note, which tells us that the children are taken outdoors for exercise during fine weather. The note also says that the school is sufficiently lighted and ventilated, and it emphasises that no child has lost the sight of an eye during the previous three years.
53 *CUL* 9 July 1855.

most advanced pupils, only four were able to set down correctly the number 1,030,103; only three were able to write down with correct orthography a few words dictated to them from the third Lesson Book; and only one wrote down the names of the days of the week without an error in spelling.

The inspector was still concerned about the lack of discipline:

> The children seem not to have acquired the habit of observing silence, when seated at the desks, and moving in an orderly manner to and from their class-stations, and of yielding a ready and respectful obedience to their teachers. During the entire time that I was engaged in the classroom there was one continuous uproar which the unceasing exertions of the assistant were quite insufficient to restrain. The principal teacher plied her large bell rigorously and repeatedly, but without any lasting effect, and at length I was compelled to request that all the children except those under examination should be sent into the playground. This total absence of order and discipline appears to me to be the real cause of the remarkably unsatisfactory state of the school as regards the proficiency of the classes.[54]

Although critical reports were made during the next twelve months or so, and the inspector lamented that every class in the workhouse was 'fully short of the minimum standard laid down in the National School programme',[55] the education inspector acknowledged that the workhouse teachers were making a genuine effort to introduce improvements.[56] By the end of 1856 good progress was recorded in the boys' school with many pupils advancing to higher classes. The inspector gave the head master full credit for this transformation and described him as 'the most effectual workhouse teacher I have ever met with'. Again he criticised the poor condition of the boys' building which he blamed for retarding the progress of some pupils.[57]

Some improvements, which were perceptible in the girls' department,[58] continued and by the autumn of 1857 they were 'completely habituated to the strict observance of order and discipline'.[59] In April 1858 the inspector mentioned that some of the assistants were very talented and one girl, Kate Larkin, was particularly noticeable 'both for

54 *CUL* 22 April 1856.
55 *CUL* 22 April, 14 November 1856; 2 April 1857.
56 *CUL* 10 July 1856.
57 *CUL* I4 November 1856. Some repair work was undertaken to the wooden building during 1857. *CUL* 24 February, 11 March, 19 May, 23 May, 23 September 1857.
58 *CUL* 2 April 1857.
59 *CUL* I2 August 1857.

her quickness in answering, and her aptitude and love of teaching. If appointed assistant teacher in a school, and with sufficient time for study, there is no doubt that in a few years she would become one of our best and highest classed teachers'. Although the guardians were willing to appoint her as an assistant teacher, the Poor Law Commissioners were slow to give their support because the girl had been an inmate of the house for a long time, but as the guardians were so enthusiastic, they withdrew their objection. The inspector was also impressed with the answering and enthusiasm of four other girls so he nominated them for training as monitresses.[60]

The tuition in the infants' department was of a poor standard and the 16-year-old teacher taught in an 'unsystematic and abrupt' manner. The monitresses were of little use and five of them were 'suffering from some affliction of the eye'. The teacher in charge of the hospital school had no academic skill but her compassion and dedication were of benefit because 'she appears very successful in gaining the affection and promoting the happiness of her afflicted pupils'.[61]

When the education inspector visited the male school in July 1857 some of the brightest pupils had left the workhouse to pursue apprenticeships. Nonetheless, results indicated that great progress had been made during a two-year period:

Comparison between boys' school results July 1855 and July 1857

	JULY 1855		JULY 1857	
	NO.	%	NO.	%
Present at time of inspection	148	—	109	—
Able to read 2nd Book correctly	18	12.1	35	32.1
Able to read 3rd Book intelligently	18	12.1	17	15.6
Acquainted with parts of speech	4	2.7	26	23.8
Able to parse syntactically	0	—	2	1.8
Answered fairly in geography	6	4.0	16	14.7
Able to write from dictation fairly	0	—	14	12.8
Able to write from dictation well	0	—	5	4.6
Able to set down a number of seven places	7	4.7	21	19.2
Able to work correctly, sums in proportions etc.	3	2.0	24	22.0
Able to write small hand freely	6	4.0	36	33.0
Able to write small hand well	2	1.4	17	15.6

(*Source*: *CUL* 12 August 1857)

---

60 *CUL* 13 May, 18 May, 1 May 1858; *CE* 2 April, 21 May 1858.
61 *CUL* 9 January 1858.

The positive transformation pleased the inspector who remarked that 'I am not acquainted with any school in which more remarkable progress has been made within the same time'. The commitment of the teachers was rewarded and during 1854 John Donaghy received a £3 gratuity. In 1858 the headmaster, Francis McCormack, received gratuities totalling £5 for work with different classes, and assistant teachers Jeremiah Desmond and Michael King were awarded £2.[62] In the following year, Mc Cormack was awarded two further gratuities and Frances Shaughnessy, the second class teacher in the girls' school, received a gratuity of £1.10s.[63]

The children continued to receive practical training to supplement their education. Girls repaired clothing for two hours each day; between thirty and forty of them were instructed in crochet and others were taught washing and the care of their own clothes. Boys were involved in trades; twenty learned weaving, 16 tailoring, 14 shoemaking, four baking, 4 carpentry, 5 tinwork and a number of others worked in the vegetable and flower gardens.[64] Conditions in some departments were unpleasant and boys in the tailoring and shoemaking workshops had to sit on cold, crude floors while at work. Punishment was often severe in the classroom and boys were occasionally flogged on their bare backs.[65] One boy named William Coughlan died in the workhouse hospital after receiving a severe kicking from an impatient teacher named O Leary. In spite of the boy's injuries, an inquest recorded a verdict of death 'by the visitation of God'. Although an attempt was made to dismiss O Leary for his 'extraordinary want of self-control', he was retained because of his previous good behaviour.[66] When another boy named Dan McCarthy ended up in the hospital after a savage kicking by O Leary, the teacher tendered his resignation. Incredulously, the guardians gave him a testimonial in which they recorded 'much pleasure in expressing their entire approval of the integrity, which he evinced in the discharge of the duties appropriated to his office'.[67] On another occasion when a schoolteacher caught a boy copying a maths answer from another pupil's slate, he lost his temper and gave the lad a 'most unmerciful flogging', which left the boy with severe marks on his back.[68] Sometimes children engaged in tough or dangerous play antics such as a risk game which included an element of stone

---

62 21st *National Education Report* (1854), Appendix, p. 374; 25th *National Education Report* (1858), p. 235; 26th *National Education Report* (1859), Appendix, pp. 100, 244, 266.

63 26th *National Education Report* (1859), Appendix, VI, p. 244.

64 *CUL* 12 August 1857; *CUM* 26 August 1857; see also *CUM* 25 March 1857.

65 *CUM* 9 September 1857; *CE* 7 May 1858.

66 *CUM* 7 January, 21 January 1852.

67 *CUM* 28 April, 5 May 1852.

68 *CE* 6 March 1861; *CUM* 5 February 1861.

throwing. This sometimes resulted in damage to property or personal injury. When a young lad was hospitalised after receiving an injury to his head, the teacher punished the perpetrators 'by taking up their clothes and whipping them with a birch. The mother of one of them, Anne Crean, on hearing that her little boy was chastised, and seeing the marks left by the birch, attacked the infant-school mistress and beat her into hysterics'.[69] Subsequently teachers were ordered to be present during playtime to supervise the children and on one occasion some boys received six lashes each for throwing stones at a schoolteacher.

At the start of the 1860s the education inspector considered the boys' school to be 'the best conducted and best taught of some 30 or 40 work-house schools' he examined, and 'not inferior to the best ordinary national school in the country'.[70] The boys continued to spend half of their day in school and the remainder at agricultural or trade work and the girls spent a couple of hours sewing, knitting or making clothes.[71] Such mundane and routine tasks limited employment opportunities for workhouse girls and, says Annmarie Turnbull, merely 'anticipated their assumed adult domestic roles'.[72]

In May 1860 the children's examinations were carried out in the presence of the public. The ability of the boys was impressive and Admiral Talbot offered naval apprenticeships to several of the older lads. The girls were examined on the following day but 'they by no means acquitted themselves in a creditable manner, on the contrary, their answering contrasted most unfavourably' with that of the boys.[73] Constant distractions from building activities in and around the girls' school did not encourage good results and during the previous 12 months almost 60 of the best girls were employed outside the house. Just three teachers and one assistant were responsible, not alone for the education of the 228 girls and infants, but for their training, housekeeping and ward duties. It was no surprise, then, that the results from the girls' school were disappointing.

Early in 1862 the workhouse chaplains sought to bring attention to

---

69 *CUM* 16 May 1860; see also School Committee Minutes 15 May 1860 in *House Committee Book FM1*.

70 *CUL* 24 September 1858, 2 February, 22 October 1860; *CE* 3 September 1858, 8 February 1860.

71 *CUL* 21 July 1859, 2 February, 3 August, 26 October 1860.

72 A. Turnbull, 'Learning Her Womanly Work: The elementary school curriculum, 1870-1914', in F. Hunt (ed.), *Lessons for life The schooling of girls and women 1850-1950* (London, 1987), p. 84.

73 *CUM* 25 April, 2 May 1860; Visiting Committee Minutes 23 April 1860, in *House Committee Book FMI* (Cork Archives); School Committee minutes, 25 August, 11 November 1860, in *House Committee Book, FMI* (Cork Archives); *CE* 4 May, 31 August 1860.

the situation, and in a scathing evaluation of the workhouse school, they were particularly critical about the paucity of teachers. In the infants' school just one teacher supervised 71 boys and 59 girls. As a stopgap measure she was helped by nine children – some as young as seven years of age – who acted as assistants. As some of them were barely able to read, the system merely deprived them of their own education – this was truly a case of 'the blind leading the blind'. The situation in the girls' school was little better, with 143 pupils aged nine to nineteen years, plus 63 infirm girls, under the teacher Miss O Sullivan and an assistant. Again, four young monitors provided assistance, which limited their own education. The chaplains were not impressed with the boys' school, which had 115 pupils, of whom 24 were unable to read and another 28 were barely able to understand the junior books. In the infirm boys' class, the teacher endeavoured to educate 55 young lads, but the presence of two 'idiots' created constant disruption and distraction which merely wasted time and effort.[74]

In many cases the school system was little more that a child-minding or child-control intervention and education, when and if it occurred, was often the product of the pupils' own determination or ability. Some guardians were blinded by an anxiety to save money; others were motivated by a determination not to provide the children of paupers with a worthwhile education. In an environment where they could have capitalised on the children's natural curiosity and isolation from distractions, their penny-pinching attitude, meanness of spirit and lack of imagination merely deprived the young inmates of a basic, or indeed a minimum, education. Their short-term view of the situation had a negative result for the ratepayers. The provision of basic life-skills would certainly have assisted, and probably motivated the young adults into leaving the workhouse and, as had been demonstrated by the navy's interest in recruiting capable and educated boys, a reasonable education would have made the children attractive to employers outside the workhouse.

A workhouse committee investigated the chaplains' complaints and, having dismissed most of their criticisms, it conceded that teaching assistants were required in the infirm and hospital schools and that a ward mistress should be deployed to instruct girls in needlework and care of their clothing.[75] The chaplains' criticisms were somewhat premature because changes which had been initiated by a new head mistress some

---

74 *CE* 26 February, 28 February 1862. For details of religious instruction and teaching staff in the workhouse during 1862, see: PP 1864, Vol. XLVII, *Return of all schools in connection with the Board of National Education in Ireland in operation on 31 December 1863*, pp. 84-87.
75 *CE* 6 March 1862; School committee minutes, 4 March 1862, in *House Committee Book, FM1 (*Cork Archives).

months earlier were in the course of maturing and when the education inspector next visited he noted that the female school was 'fast approaching in point of efficiency the male [school]'.[76] The transformation continued and when the inspector visited during the summer of 1862, he recorded that the headmistress 'has raised it from being one of the worst, to one of the best female schools in my entire district'.[77]

Favourable reports continued during the next couple of years and, as well as praising the girls' ability at reading, spelling and general interest, the inspector made particular reference to their standard of singing.[78] The senior classes impressed him with their knowledge of mathematics, geography (including elementary astronomy) and writing. The boys' ability at penmanship was so impressive 'that I procured specimens of it from each class in order to show them to the teachers of the ordinary national schools with the view of getting them to pay increased attention to this important branch of instruction'.[79]

Some changes were introduced in the mid-1860s. Drawing classes for senior boys were inaugurated and, following the inspector's suggestion, one teacher studied navigational techniques, which he in turn introduced as a subject for boys in fourth class during 1865.[80] This, it was envisaged, would give the boys a good preparation for naval exams.[81] The schools continued to receive favourable reports from education and poor law inspectors.[82] Towards the end of the 1860s the education inspector said the 'the boys and girls of the Cork workhouse school are receiving a sound English education, such an education as will qualify many of them for situations outside the workhouse'.[83]

Senior girls were taught needlework from 2 to 4pm and those in junior school learned plain sewing and knitting from 10am to noon which enabled them to repair their own clothes. A number of boys were exposed to tailoring and shoemaking and, although few developed any

---

76 *CE* 9 July 1862; *CUL* 6 June 1862.
77 *CUL* 3 July 1862; *CE* 4 July 1861, 28 May, 12 June, 9 July 1862.
78 *CUL* 21 October 1862, 13 January, 8 June 1863; *CE* 15 January, 23 July, 28 November 1863, 8 September 1864.
79 *CUL* 13 January 1863, also 12 January 1864; *CE* 15 January 1863.
80 *CUL* 5 September 1864, 16 March, 3 July 1865, 23 October, 16 February 1866; *CC* 8 September 1864.
81 *CUL* 16 March, 3 July 1865.
82 *CUL* 21 October 1862, 8 June 1863, 2 February, 5 September 1864, 12 February, 23 October 1866, 15 November 1867, 18 June, 17 December 1868, 27 April, 31, August, 6 November 1869, 15 February, 2 April, 2 November, 22 December 1870; *CE* 23 July, 28 October 1863, 13 January, 8 September 1864, 22 February 1866, 28 November 1867, 28 July 1871; 7 July 1876.
83 *CUL* 16 February 1866.

real skills, many were 'picked up the moment they begin to be useful'.[84] At the end of 1867 there were 604 pupils in the workhouse schools and of this number, 20 boys worked at trades and 130 assisted on the farm, eighty girls were also receiving training in the house.[85] During 1870, 70 boys got outside employment as clerks, farm servants and trades assistants and 56 girls left the house for domestic service.[86]

Reports by visiting inspectors' continued to express dissatisfaction with conditions in some departments. The boys' school was still singled out for criticism. Its principal entrance on a first floor was reached by a 'wretched stepladder or gangway, the steps of which are worn away, and very dangerous for young children'.[87] The flooring itself was defective and the lower room was difficult to light and ventilate. The principal schoolroom was 'in the middle storey of a wretched wooden building, cold, full of draughts, and comfortless, and although a dormitory intervened between it and the roof, the rain comes down freely to the schoolroom floor'.[88] Parts of the building were rotting and the structure was in danger of collapsing because 'when the wind blows strong from one particular point, the house, I am told shakes to an alarming extent'.[89] In spite of requests from the Poor Law Commissioners, the structure was not improved. Its dangerous state was regularly mentioned by the education inspector who scathingly remarked that 'an ordinary school held in such a building would not be taken into connection by the Board'.[90] The Poor Law Inspector concurred, and lamented that the facilities 'must exercise a depressing influence on both the teachers and pupils'. Following a visit to the workhouse during 1872, however, the vice chairman of the Nenagh board of guardians said that the arrangements in the girls' school were 'as perfect as can be and far superior to those he has seen elsewhere'.[91]

The number of pupils in the institute continued to fluctuate. In June 1869, the school had 223 boys, 287 girls and 114 pupils in the nursery plus 223 in the various hospital wards. Just over twelve months later, the number had decreased with 184 boys, 103 girls and 127 infants on the roll. The girls transferred to a new school in the workhouse grounds during 1871. It had spacious dormitories, large schoolrooms, WCs, and baths. The disposition of the pupils improved and the inspector noted that

---

84 *CUL* 15 January 1867.
85 *CUL* 14 December 1867, also 20 April, 27 April 1869.
86 *CUL* 2 November 1870.
87 *CUL* 18 June 1868.
88 *CUL* 15 February, 2 April 1870.
89 *CUL* 22 December 1870; *CUM* 29 February 1870.
90 *CUL* 9 January, 24 July 1871, 21 January, 20 February 1872.
91 *CUM* 19 December 1872.

they became 'more cheerful' in spirit.[92] Their academic ability continued to improve and he was particularly impressed with their writing. Overall, the standard was 'as high as could be reasonably expected'.[93] Extending, levelling and gravelling their playground improved their surroundings and regular exercise helped keep them healthy.[94] The Commissioners were anxious to provide the children with exercise outside the workhouse grounds. As well as giving them a 'change of air and a change of scene', this would put the children on public display and possibly arouse interest in fostering or adoption by outside parties.

A number of new teachers were appointed in the mid 1870s and workhouse boys and girls continued to be successfully placed in outside employment.[95] During a discussion about placing the workhouse teachers under the National Education Act, some guardians protested at what they saw as a further attempt to improve the quality of education. In their opinion, workhouse children did not need a 'very high class education', which would be of little use when ploughing or shoemaking. Instead, they suggested that additional industrial training should be provided.[96] The former interest in training had waned and Dr McCabe, the Poor Law Inspector, was critical that some of the older girls had not been absorbed into the 'working population' outside. He, too, favoured a reduction in the number of teachers and the recruitment of a housekeeper to provide training in household duties. Under the circumstances this was a realistic approach to workhouse education. The formal classroom subjects would provide the children with useful personal skills and talents, but the stark reality was that few would secure a position in which a totally classroom oriented education would prove useful as a marketable skill. 'The defect of workhouse education', said one observer, 'appears to be the want of systematic, well-organised industrial training. Too much is sacrificed to merely literary advancement'.[97] Nonetheless, the blend of academic education and practical training did produce successful placements as the following table shows.

---

92 *CUL* 12 July 1871, 23 January, 18 March, 20 October 1872.
93 *CUL* 24 July 1871, 2 July 1873; *Local Government Board Report* (1876), Appendix A, Circular No. 1, pp. 37-8.
94 *CUL* 24 July 1871, 2 July 1873.
95 *CE* 7 June, 13 June, 20 June, 27 June 1873, 24 April, 29 May, 7 August, 26 August, 30 October 1874, 2 July, 24 September, 8 October 1875; *CUL* 18 June 1873.
96 *CE* 22 October 1875.
97 PP 1878-9, Vol. XXXI [c.2239], *Poor Law Union and Lunacy Inquiry Commission (Ireland), Report and Evidence with Appendix*, p. lviii, also p. lix.

Girls' School 25 March 1862 to 25 March 1877

Total number of girls	1,255
Did not return	1,148
Died	26
Emigrated	40
Returned to workhouse	33
'Turned out bad'	8

The girls who returned to the house were distributed as follows: To hospital 9, to infirm ward 8, working in laundry 9, hospital assistants 4, one girl in the nursery, one married and one unmarried girl in the Lock ward. Those who 'turned out bad' were accounted for as follows: In government Lock hospital one, six in Good Shepherd's Refuge and one in the Protestant Refuge. (*Report of Local Government Board*, 1879, Appendix A, III: Report of Dr F. McCabe, p. 63)

Some guardians were dissatisfied with the agricultural training which merely served as a free labouring service for the workhouse garden and it was suggested that a programme which would give the young lads some formal qualification should be introduced.[98] Inadequate and substandard tools were provided so few boys benefited from this training. On average about twenty boys worked in the gardens. During September 1878 they worked on 20 days, in October on nine days and during November they were employed on just twelve days.[99] The industrial classes were also of little value and the boys learned almost nothing from the tradesmen, many of whom were 'confirmed old drunkards'. The few good shoemakers were reluctant to betray their secrets. Craftsmanship and production were poor; the workshop was disorganised and untidy and old stock such as children's clogs and timber-soled shoes cluttered the storage areas.[100] During 1879 the board of guardians decided to discontinue manufacturing footwear, so just a few operators were retained to undertake repairs.

Boys Daily Programme – 1879

6.30-8.30 a.m.	Rise, wash and make up dormitories, etc.
8.30-9 a.m.	Breakfast

---

98 *CE* 15 November 1878, 11 April, 25 April 1879.

99 *CUM* 31 October, 5 December, 19 December 1878.

100 *CE* 21 February, 5 September 1879, 28 May, 11 June, 25 June 1880, 28 July, 8 September, 15 September 1882; *Poor Law Commissioners Annual Report* (1879), p. 67; *Eagle and Cork Advertiser*, 1 November, 1884.

9 a.m.-12.30 p.m.	Secular and religious instruction
12.30-2 p.m.	Recreation and walking exercise
2-2.30 p.m.	Dinner
2.30-3 p.m.	School
3-5.30 p.m.	Agricultural instruction in gardens
5.30-6 p.m.	Supper
6-7.30 p.m.	School, preparing lessons for following day
7.30-8 p.m.	Recreation; Bed at 8 p.m.

(*Source: Local Government Board Report* (1879), Appendix A, III, p. 62.)

By mid 1878 the 70 girls in the senior school were given basic industrial training for two hours each evening in knitting, cleaning and polishing. Another twenty girls got extra domestic training at washing, ironing, table laying and other skills to prepare them as house servants.[101]

Girls Daily Programme – 1879

6.30-7a.m.	Rise, wash and make beds
7-7.15 a.m.	Morning prayers
7.15-8.15 a.m.	Sweeping, dusting and scrubbing dormitories
8. 15-8.40 a.m.	Breakfast
8.40-10 a.m.	Out for exercise, walking in suburbs
10am-1.30 p.m.	Secular and religious instruction
1.30-2 p.m.	Dinner
2-4 p.m.	Industrial training, sewing, knitting etc. On Fridays ironing
4-6 p.m.	Mondays, Tuesdays and Wednesdays – industrial training at laundry; Younger children bathed – once a week each
6-6.30 p.m.	Supper

(*Source: Local Government Board Report* (1879), Appendix A, III, p. 63.)

For a long time, the workhouse teachers were included in the results-fees scheme whereby they received a bonus based on pupils' achievements in annual exams. This was withdrawn in 1879 and within months standards at the boys' school plummeted to a level which was described as 'a disgrace to humanity'. Although one teacher was sick and another was on leave the deterioration was unacceptable to the guardians. As compensation for the discontinuance of the results-fees

---

101 *CE* 25 October 1878; *Local Government Board Report* (1879), p. 67.

system, the board agreed to revise the salary scale, and a new head teacher was appointed.[102] Some months later the board agreed to Dr Brodie's suggestion about employing a skilled supervisor to take responsibility for the girls' industrial household training. Unlike their peers outside, the duties of workhouse teachers did not end at school finishing time. The workhouse teacher had to supervise children at all times, he 'probably oversees his conduct in the playground, watches him during meal-times, superintending him during evening hours, and may even be on duty in the dormitory at night'. Some guardians were in favour of paying results-fees to the workhouse staff whom they believed were just as entitled to the bonus as teachers outside.[103] As usual, other guardians, who must have been oblivious to the resentment their attitude caused among the workhouse teachers, opposed the paltry extra expenditure. In mid 1883 the guardians agreed to reintroduce the results-fees system and pay the outstanding entitlements from the current exam.[104]

A certain amount of industrial training was still provided for the children. About three dozen boys spent a few hours each day in the various workshops and six dozen were employed in the gardens. All attended school for three and a half hours each day. The timetable incorporated a number of breaks; the boys had an hour's outdoor exercise on fine days and in the evening they spent one and a half hour at study and revision. This regularity did not receive general approval, for, commented one observer, 'the child is roused by a bell, and wakens to find his day carefully arranged for him. Tasks, which rarely vary, are performed in rotation, each succeeding each with unfailing regularity, meals are served punctually, he knows today precisely what he must do to-morrow, and his will, his judgement and his powers of decision are slowly impaired, while his sense of dependence upon others is equally slowly but no less inevitably fostered by the rigid discipline under which he serves'.[105] The placement record of the school was excellent. In the ten years prior to 1884 nearly 1,000 boys had passed through its doors; only 16 had returned as inmates, of whom eight were incapacitated from illness or injury.

---

102 PP 1876, Vol. LXIII, [100], Return *for the year 1875 of the names of Poor Law Unions in Ireland, which have agreed to become 'contributory unions', under 'The National School Teachers (Ireland) Act, 1875' with the Annual Valuation of each, and the total of the whole'*, pp. 4, 16; *CE* 2 April, 16 April, 23 April, 1880; for information on the results-fees system, see Donal H. Akenson, *The Irish Education Experiment, The national system of education in the nineteenth century* (London, 1970), pp. 229-30.

103 *CE* 1 April 1881; Susanne R. Day, 'The workhouse child', *Irish Review*, Vol. II, No. 16, June 1912, p. 173; *CUM* 26 May 1881.

104 *CE* 22 June 1883, 30 May, 6 June 1884; see also *Local Government Board Report* (1888), Appendix A, Circular No. 5, pp. 64-5.

105 Susanna R. Day, 'The workhouse child', op. cit., p. 172.

The guardians could not agree about the benefit of exposing the boys to skills such as shoemaking and repairing, which some saw as an introduction to the world of trades. Because this training was casual and unstructured, the boys learned little and cultivation of the workhouse grounds was counter-productive and gave the young workers a totally misleading impression about agricultural production.[106] The Cork Ratepayers' Association complained to the Local Government Board that the girls had no proper training unit and that the boys' programme in gardening and shoemaking was purely a casual arrangement. The ratepayers' assessment was correct because many of the guardians had no interest in giving the children skills. Children working as garden helpers, trades assistants, kitchen hands, laundry workers or merely mending their own clothes, were doing jobs which assisted the workhouse machine. The exposure to industrial, domestic and agricultural skills was for the most part, basic exploitation.

In March 1886, the guardians agreed that the appointment of a music and drawing teacher would add an interesting and entertaining dimension to the schoolboys' curriculum. When the time to elect a suitably qualified teacher arrived, narrow preconceptions about the limits of paupers' education resurfaced and the matter was postponed when some guardians complained that 'ratepayers' children are not taught music and drawing'. William D'Esterre Parker wrote to the Local Government Board about the benefit of expanding the range of school subjects. Drawing would be of immense benefit he maintained, because, along with reading, writing and arithmetic, it 'forms the foundation of industrial and technical education'. The value of music had been shown in earlier years when the subject was taught to workhouse pupils. Boys who liked music frequently joined the army and were quickly promoted to the service bands. His conclusion that guardians opposed the change because they resented the idea that workhouse children would receive a better education than their peers outside was probably not without foundation. One guardian suggested that if the board wanted to start a 'first-class boarding school', they should publicise this because ratepayers would be interested in sending their children to such an institution. In the event, the guardians decided that drawing and music were not required and Cornelius Murphy, who had no qualifications in these subjects, was elected as a new workhouse teacher.[107] In disgust, Parker

---

106 *CE* 24 January, 29 January, 15 February, 18 July 1884.
107 *CE* 2 April, 9 April, 16 April 1886; *CC* 9 April 1886. Limiting the education of workhouse children to purely basic levels was not an uncommon practice by poor law guardians, see: Frank Crompton, *Workhouse Children* (Gloucestershire, 1997), p. 165.

wrote that 'it is not because ignorance prevails outside the workhouse, that it is to be continued inside'.[108] He continued with his attempt to have compulsory drawing included in the curriculum. The Office of National Education did not concur with his 'somewhat utopian views' and it advised the Local Government Board that drawing lessons would be a waste of time for many workhouse children.[109] Even when the Cork School of Art offered to teach free-hand drawing to the boys in a series of two-hour classes over 40-weeks, some guardians dismissed the idea as it would make 'jacks-of-all-trades' of the boys.[110]

The school inspector's reports for spring 1887, 1888 and 1889 were very positive. Exam results in the boys' department were 'highly gratifying', discipline was excellent and the teachers were 'earnest and interested in the advancement of their pupils'. The girls also achieved good results as did the infants, into whose school the Kindergarten system had been introduced in 1885.[111] The boys' school had been relocated, but an old timber shed, which served as their dining hall, was condemned in 1887.

A limited amount of industrial training was still undertaken with girls concentrating on domestic oriented chores and boys on vegetable cultivation. Plans to introduce structured training in agriculture and other skills failed, but the ladies' committee organised cookery lessons and classes in general household duties for senior girls. They established a small library in the house and the lapsed prize-giving ceremony was revived. By mid-1887 over 30 girls were successfully placed in outside employment. Between February and October 1888, 50 boys left the house to work with farmers. Three returned because of ill treatment – one was given no bed clothing, just a couple of old bags for blankets and sheets, also he did not get a coat but had to care for cattle in cold and wet weather. During 1888, 60 girls went into service and 12 others emigrated; some returned to the house – one from overwork and another from a 'disinclination' to work.[112]

---

108 *CE* 13 April 1886.
109 NAI, CSORP 1886 19469.
110 *CE* 25 February 1887.
111 *CE* 4, 11, 18 December 1885; 8 April, 26 August 1887; 14 February, 4 May, 30 October 1888, 26 April 1889, 25 April 1890; *CC* 26 April 1889; CUM 3 December, 10 December 1885; NAI, CSORP 1886 19469.
112 *CE* 30 October 1888; see also *CE* 21 February, 11 April, 5 September 1879, 23 April, 28 May, 11 June, 25 June, 2 July, 16 July, 6 August 1880; 3 February, 8 September, 22 September, 29 September, 24 November 1882; 10 January, 21 November 1884; 12 January, 14 January 1885, 18 January 1889; *CUM* 28 August, 4 September 1879; 22 April, 10 June 1880; 2 February, 8 March, 30 March 1882; 10 October, 12 November 1885.

Conclusion

Some guardians viewed education and training more as a necessary evil than a beneficial or rewarding experience. This is shown by the reluctance with which they greeted the numerous innovations suggested by other guardians and the feeble response to repeated poor reports from education inspectors. The quality of workhouse education and training was largely dependent on the goodwill and enlightenment of the guardians. Conflicting priorities of board members determined the quality of care provided for children. A reasonable programme would have gone some way towards preparing the young inmates for life outside the workhouse. Because this was largely denied, many of the children were not adequately prepared for the sudden and stark transition to a climate in which they were expected to make rational and independent decisions and contributions about the many day-to-day matters influencing their lives. Away from familiar surroundings and former companions, some of the liberated inmates were overwhelmed, and soon returned to their erstwhile home. Others, no doubt scarred by the negative experiences of former years, also had difficulty coping with the change. Some succumbed to illness and in a few cases girls who became pregnant were forced to return to the workhouse.[113] This problem was not unique to Cork and many ill-prepared workhouse children had difficulty in making the transition to life outside the institution. The majority of course did survive, they surmounted difficulties and, unscathed, settled into their new identities away from the workhouse.[114]

---

113 See PP 1879, Vol. XXXI, [c2239], *Inquiry*, Appendix B. p. 199.
114 See for instance: E.S. Turner, *What the butler saw, Two hundred and fifty years of the servant problem* (London, 2001 edition), p. 242.

5 Training

On occasions attempts were made to prepare young workhouse inmates for a career outside the institution. The range of activities pursued in the house was confined to making and repairing clothing and footwear, preparing and cooking food for inmates and hospital patients, cleaning, maintaining and painting buildings, grounds and fittings, and the control of workhouse stock. A formal system of training was not pursued but boys and girls participated in the general workhouse activities. This involvement gave them some basic practical skills and also kept them occupied for part of the day. During the late 1850s a committee was formed to organise apprenticeships for workhouse boys. A couple of years later, a group of ladies established a committee to provide formal training in household skills for young workhouse girls.

Land and sea training

In May 1850, young people in the workhouse numbered 278 under five years of age, 842 aged five to fourteen and 486 aged from fourteen to twenty years. Poor law guardian Francis Hennis expressed concern about the absence of constructive training and suggested that the guardians acquire some land near the workhouse on which the boys could be housed and taught agricultural skills. Another guardian, Mr Drew, spoke in favour of naval training and urged the board to apply to the government for a hulk, which could be used to inculcate 'moral and industrial habits' in the workhouse boys and enable them get jobs in the merchant or Royal navy.[1] As this would necessitate additional expenditure on shipboard staff the board was divided on the issue and some guardians were of the opinion that this type of training could be accomplished on a simulated vessel which could be constructed in the workhouse grounds. Mr Drew continued with his efforts to have boys enlisted in the navy and in September 1851, shortly after the passing of an Act which empowered boards of guardians to apprentice workhouse

---

1 *CC* 16 May 1850; *SR* 16 April, 16 May, 27 June, 4 July 1850; *CUM* 26 June, 3 July, 14 August, 10 October, 17 October 1850.

boys in the merchant or Royal navies, he furnished the admiral at Queenstown with a list of suitable candidates for flagship duties.[2] The idea of naval training was revived during 1853 when Captain William Martin suggested that a group of boys be instructed in splicing, knotting, sail and rigging work and other sailors' duties, either on a hulk at Queenstown or in a simulated vessel.[3] When the guardians discussed the proposal they voted in favour of constructing the deck, masts, rigging and sails of a brigantine in the workhouse grounds. They also agreed to acquire two rowing boats to teach the boys the basic techniques of rowing and manoeuvring. A naval instruction committee was appointed and it recommended the construction of an 84 feet long by 22 feet beam decking in the workhouse grounds, at a cost not in excess of £295.[4] Unfortunately the chance to give the boys some useful experience was lost when the project collapsed, after Captain Martin's name was withdrawn from the official list of ex-officio guardians in October 1853.[5]

Despite an initial reluctance to recruit boys from the workhouse, the Royal Navy did enrol some young inmates during the 1850s and 1860s. Some boys were recruited in the mid 1850s and in June 1861 ten Cork workhouse lads were among a delegation of over 30 who attended an inspection on the *Sanspareil* at Queenstown. The entire delegation of Cork boys was chosen but not one of the other candidates was deemed suitable for Her Majesty's Navy.[6] Some months later a group of Cork boys was rejected because they had a bad rash and others were not allowed enrol when their mothers objected. In January 1864, 24 boys from the Cork workhouse were taken as naval apprentices on the *Ferret* and five more were taken on the *Hawke* in October. The recruitment of nine more boys in January 1866 brought the total number of

---

2 *Poor Law Commissioners, Annual report* (1852), p.111; *SR* 4 September 1851; *SR* 4 July, 11 July 1850; CUM 13 August 1851. In December 1854, seven workhouse boys were appointed to the North Cork Rifles. *CUM* 13 December 1854.

3 *SR* 18 June 1853; *CC* 18 June 1853; see also *SR* 28 July 1846. Earlier in the year a list of boys suitable for naval training had been compiled. *CUM* 27 April, 21 September 1853.

4 *CUM* 29 June, 6 July, 13 July, 21 September, 28 September, 5 October, 19 October 1853, 30 December 1857; *SR* 30 June, 15 July, 22 September, 29 September, 6 October, 11 October 1853. When Sir George Nicholls visited the workhouse in 1853 he expressed his support for nautical training in the visitors' book. *CC* 8 September 1853.

5 *SR* 13 October, 20 October, 10 November 1853; see also *CUM* 3 May 1854.

6 *CUM* 4 May 1859, 29 May, 5 June, 12 June 1861, 23 July, 30 July 1862; *CE* 29 May, 5 June 1861; *CC* 30 May, 6 June 1861 see also *SR* 4 May 1854; *CE* 9 May 1855, 4 May, 9 May 1860; 18 July 1862; also PP 1861; Vol. X, [408], *Report from the Select Committee on Poor Relief*, p. 321.

workhouse lads enlisted in the navy to 56 in five years.[7] During 1867, a further 15 boys from the workhouse were taken on naval vessels at Queenstown.[8]

A discussion on the benefits of training outside the workhouse resulted in an agreement among the guardians that 25 acres of farmland should be hired for agricultural training. The practice of cultivating land adjacent to workhouses was not uncommon in England, and at Clogheen, in Tipperary, twelve acres of farmland were hired and an instructor trained boys as labourers.[9] At Cork the guardians were hopeful that a properly organised scheme would facilitate the instruction of about 150 of their better-behaved boys in farm work.[10] The production of vegetables for the workhouse table and the utilisation of the institution's manure as fertiliser would, it was estimated, save £300 per annum. It was planned to divide the boys into three groups. Classes would then be arranged so that the boys would spend about two thirds of their time at normal school activities and the remainder working on the farm. As well as providing 'time-consuming and physically exhausting toil'[11] the farm work would teach the boys useful skills and develop 'their muscles and sinews and not leave them stunted and unfit for the labours of life'. Residence on the farm would have another important benefit, as it would remove the boys from the negative influences of the 'old and confirmed paupers in the workhouse'.[12] Some guardians believed that 25 acres would be too small to accomplish any worthwhile agricultural training. John Rogers Wiseman was in favour of taking up to 150 acres in the vicinity of the city and erecting an auxiliary house to accommodate 1,000 boys. This would enable

7 *CE* 24 June 1863, 2 February, 24 February, 20 October, 3 November 1864, 2 January, 18 January 1866; *CUM* 18 May 1865.

8 *CUM* 20 February, 29 May, 5 June, 11 September 1867. This recruiting continued into the 1880s, see *CUM* 13 January and 20 January 1881.

9 See: PP 1852-3, Vol. LXXXIV, [513], *Return from each of the Poor Law Unions in England, Wales and Ireland, showing what kinds of employment are carried on in the workhouses, or on land attached; the number of adult able-bodied persons in the books as recipients of relief on 1 July 1852, and the proportion engaged in handcrafts and agricultural industry, etc*; PP 1854, Vol. LV, [77], Statement *relating to the industrial employment of the juvenile inmates of union workhouses, Ireland, in the month of September 1853.*

10 *SR* 29 November 1849, 30 May 1850; *CC* 30 May, 13 June 1850; PP 1851, Vol. XLIX, [646], *Report on Education and Training*, pp. 44-7; *CUM* 28 November 1849, 29 May 1850. Agricultural training was successfully conducted in many Irish workhouses at that time, see: John Forbes, *Memorandums made in Ireland in the autumn of 1852* (London, 1853), Vol. II, pp. 246-50.

11 Anne M. Lanigan, *The Poor Law children of county Tipperary and their education 1840-1880* (M.Ed thesis, UCC, 1988), p. 37.

12 *CUM* 12 June, 17 July 1850; *SR* 13 June, 20 June, 11 July 1850; *CUL* 11 June, 2 July 1850.

the board to discontinue renting the auxiliary store which it had occupied since 1846 and thus save £400 per annum.

Because of deaths, migration and emigration, skilled male and female farm workers were in short supply in the countryside, and suitable replacements were not to be found amongst the general workhouse inmates.[13] Some agricultural training at ploughing and the use of farm tools such as reaping hooks, scythes and spades, would enable boys and young men leave the workhouse and find employment with farmers on general or specialised farming tasks.[14] The demand for workers was particularly acute during harvest time and inmates were occasionally dismissed from the workhouse in the hope that they would locate employment. Farmers had little interest in unskilled workers and frequently unsuccessful applicants were refused re-admission on their return to the workhouse. This was illustrated by the case of Mary White, a mother of 12 children, three of whom were still in her care. She was directed to a farm where a wage of 6d. per day was being paid. As this was inadequate to feed herself and the children, one of whom was still an infant, she re-applied for a workhouse ticket. The relieving officer refused her application but when she went before the workhouse admission board, she was re-admitted despite the protests of some guardians. The Poor Law Commissioners were apprehensive about the initiative and instructed the guardians to discharge inmates only when immediate employment was available. Applicants who failed to locate work had to be re-admitted when they returned to the institution.[15]

The Poor Law Commissioners showed a keen interest in the proposal to take farmland and various sites were inspected.[16] The Commissioners disapproved of a property at Lapland, and when farmland at Grange in Douglas was leased at £50 per annum from John Gould, some of the ratepayers objected.[17] The cost of developing the land, constructing the various buildings, paying wages, and purchasing stock was prohibitive

---

13 *SR* 28 August 1851; 26 August 1852; 25 August 1853; *CUL* 27 August 1853.
14 *SR* 23 October, 28 October 1851; 24 August 1854; See also Poor Law Commissioners Annual Report (1854), pp. 35-6 re wages and demands for agricultural workers in the Cork area.
15 *CUM* 30 August 1854; SR 31 August, 7 September 1854; CE 26 August, 2 September 1853.
16 *CUM* 7 August, 27 August, 25 September, 16 October 1850, 30 July 1851; *SR* 23 July, 22 August, 5 September 1850; *CUL* 17 December 1850. The Poor Law Commissioners were particularly supportive of agricultural training for workhouse boys. *Poor Law Commissioners Annual Report* (1850), p. 10, *Poor Law Commissioners Annual Report* (1852), pp. 13-14; see also Circular on Industrial Training of Workhouse children, *Poor Law Commissioners Annual Report* (1854), pp. 17-21, also p. 7.
17 *CUM* 11 December 1850, 8 January, 29 January, 10 September 1851; *SR* 17 October, 10 December 1850, 9 January, 23 January, 24 July 1851; *CUL* 28 January, 14 February, 12 March, 9 April 1851, see *General Valuation of Rateable*

and the farm committee was prevented from working the land. The lease was retained and under pressure from a group of interested guardians, a committee was appointed to report on its viability. The Commissioners were also anxious to have the land used for training, and although the guardians failed to agree on the level of utilisation, grazing rights were sold. Twenty-one workhouse inmates were employed on the farm, and eight acres of oats were planted in spring 1853 and sold in the autumn. The agricultural work continued and during summer and autumn 1855 about 6 cwts. of cabbage was supplied each day to the workhouse kitchen.[18]

The Poor Law Commissioners remained enthusiastic about the farm and were anxious to have the land cultivated and, if possible, buildings erected on the grounds. The workhouse agricultural committee was also in favour of providing buildings, or indeed, an auxiliary workhouse on rented land.[19] As before, economic advantages, such as a ready supply of vegetables, career training and improved health, were cited as justification for the project, but, as the farm was two miles from the workhouse, the guardians were unwilling to spend money on developments and it was finally surrendered in 1855.[20] A site near the workhouse was inspected by the committee and on its recommendation the guardians voted in favour of taking the land. As the site was only about five acres in extent, the Commissioners deemed it inadequate for the training of the 202 boys under 15 years of age in the workhouse, and refused to sanction the project.[21] A seven-acre site was acquired from a man named Mehegan in the autumn of 1854.[22] Some cultivation work was carried out during 1855 on an acre at Fitton's field, adjacent to the workhouse. The institution's manure was used as fertiliser and 12,000 cabbages were produced. Two acres of corn were planted at Mehegan's field and another acre was prepared for turnip plants. Even if the boys were only

17 (cont.) properties in Ireland, County of Cork, Barony of Cork, Parish of Carrigaline, townland of Grange (Dublin, 1852), [Griffith's Valuation], p. 9.
18 SR 21 August, 28 August 1851, 16 September, 21 October 1852; 6 January, 7 April, 16 June, 18 June, 23 June, 7 July, 23 August, 3 November 1853; CC 25 October 1855; CUL 25 May 1852, 7 June 1853; see also CUM 6 April, 27 April, 7 September 1853; CUL 3 May, 14 May, 1 July, 27 October, 29 November 1853, 14 March 1854; PP 1852-3, Vol. LXXIV [904], Land under crops, p. 2; PP 1855, Vol. XLVII, [345], Workhouse farm and manufacturing accounts, p. 2.
19 CUM 3 May, 10 May, 9 August 1854; SR 11 May 1854; CUL 16 February, 14 March, 25 April 1854, 30 January 1855; NAI, CSORP 1859 5550, enclosure No. IV.
20 PP 1854, Vol. LV, [77], Industrial Employment, p. 2; SR 23 February, 4 May 1854; CUL 20 March, 14 August 1855; CUM 22 June 1853, 7 March 1855.
21 SR 25 May, 15 June, 17 August 1854; CE 19 May 1854; CUM 17 May, 14 June 1854, 3 January 1855; CUL 16 May, 23 May, 30 May, 20 June, 18 July, 8 August 1854, 23 January, 6 March, 20 March 1855.
22 SR 10 August, 24 August 1854; CUM 24 October 1854.

'fiddling' with the ground, it was agreed that this would be better for their health than long periods of idleness in the workhouse.[23]

In 1856 Francis Hennis spoke at length on the benefits of employing an agricultural instructor to train the workhouse boys and he put this as a proposal to the board. As usual, he sought to achieve change with the minimum of expenditure, and a condition of the appointment was that the salary of the workhouse headmaster would be reduced and a junior teacher discharged. He argued that the reduction in the number of boys in the house during the previous few years would enable classes to be rearranged, so that half their number could be at school while the others were being trained at farm work. John Francis Maguire agreed with the proposal to appoint an agricultural instructor, but he believed that it was not necessary to dispense with any teacher. Almost £150 had been realised by the cultivation of vegetables during the previous year, he argued, and this saving would more than compensate for the wages of the instructor. To compensate for the loss of a teacher, it would be necessary to increase class sizes which would have a negative effect on education, and which would also mean that younger boys, many of whom were 'afflicted with a loathsome disease', would be in contact with the older boys. Hennis's proposal, with its condition that one of the teachers be dismissed, was eventually passed and a Michael Smith was employed as the agricultural instructor.[24] The debate about the number of teachers was resumed a couple of weeks later when Mr Drew proposed that the teacher should be retained. Though it was opposed by T. R. Sarsfield, who believed that the boys 'should be instructed, but in a way that became their position', and that the emphasis should be on agricultural training and not classroom work, Mr Drew's motion was passed. Later in the year it was agreed to increase the meal allowance for boys engaged at farm work from four ounces to six ounces for their breakfast.[25]

Farmers sometimes employed children who had been trained at agricultural work. The transition to outside life was generally successful but on occasions dissatisfaction resulted. For instance, in May 1859 the guardian Thomas Wiseman complained that three boys he had placed in employment as cowherds left their employers after a short time. One of the boys named Callaghan, who was blind in one eye, commenced work at between 3 and 4 am each morning when he cleaned out stalls and

---

23 *CE* 8 August 1855; *CUM* 21 December, 28 February, 15 August, 22 August 1855, 19 August 1857.
24 *CUM* 12 December 1855, 2 January 1856; *CE* 4 January, 18 January 1856; *CUL* 1 March, 12 April, 22 April 1856. The behaviour of the boys towards the agricultural instructor was 'most disgraceful'. *CUM* 5 March 1856.
25 *CE* 13 February, 17 December 1856; *CUM* 17 December 1856, 28 January 1857; *CUL* 29 July 1856.

then herded cows, pigs, sheep and geese which were to be found in all parts of the farm. He absconded from the farm of Daniel Humphreys when the family was at Sunday service. When he returned to the refuge of the workhouse he explained to the guardians that he had found the farm work too demanding. The boy was castigated for his ingratitude in leaving the employer who had provided good food and a comfortable bed. Though there were unsubstantiated reports that the boy had pawned some of his clothing, some guardians wanted to give him a 'good flogging'. Only when the legality of inflicting this sentence was questioned by the local media, did the guardians withdraw the threat.[26]

In a similar incident some months later, two other boys who refused to remain working with farmers were forced to break stones when they returned to the workhouse. One of the boys had returned without his workhouse clothing and Mr Wiseman thought the punishment too lenient and wanted to have the boy flogged instead. Nicholas Mahony commented that, in general, the guardians did not take sufficient care when selecting candidates for outside work, which he ascribed as the principal reason for boys returning to the workhouse.[27] When one boy was reluctant to leave the house to work with a farmer for 10s. a quarter, the guardians threatened to expel him. The *Cork Constitution* was outraged that the boy was slow to leave and it recommended that all the 'skulking, scheming labour-shunners' in the workhouse should be forced to earn their livelihood.[28] The selection of employers was haphazard. One employer named Benjamin Cross regularly whipped a servant boy.[29] Another boy who was nursed out, and then adopted by a farmer named Patrick Walsh from Ballineaskin, was also treated badly and frequently hired out to neighbours. When the board learned of the abuse they allowed the Foley family at Whitechurch to adopt the boy.[30] In the mid 1870s a girl named Bridget McCarthy left the workhouse to act as a childminder with a farmer named Denis Higgins at Grenagh, for which she was to be paid 7s. per quarter. As time went on, the girl was given other duties such as milking cows, to perform. Instead of the agreed wages, she merely received pennies and an occasional item of clothing. Her health eventually declined and she returned to the workhouse in a broken down state from ill health and overwork. During her nine years with the farmer, the unfortunate girl was paid just 6d. The matter was investigated by the board of guardians and the farmer provided details of

---

26 *SR* 19 May, 21 May, 25 May, 26 May 1859; *CC* 21 May 1859; *CUM* 25 May 1859.
27 *CE* 11 April, 23 April, 27 April 1860; *CC* 12 April 1860.
28 *CC* 6 June 1861.
29 *CE* 19 July, 27 July 1866; *CC* 27, July 1866.
30 *CE* 10 October 1867; *CUM* 9 October 1867. See also *CUM* 4 March 1875.

the clothing he provided to the girl. When this was deducted from the sum owed to the girl he agreed to pay the outstanding money.[31] The work placements of the children were usually successful and these few incidents are not representative of the results generally achieved.

Apprentices

During 1853 an English firm contacted the Cork workhouse with an offer to take a number of boys as cotton spinning apprentices at their mill near Manchester. The firm undertook to provide food, clothes and lodgings for the boys who would be paid wages when they became skilled at the work. The apprenticeship, until the boys were 21 years of age, would consist of carding, spinning and reeling cotton yarn. The clerk of the company, a Mr. Mason, visited the workhouse in October and selected 14 orphans aged between 14 and 17 years for his business. He was very particular about the selection procedure and was accompanied by a specialist who interviewed the boys and made a 'phrenological examination of their heads, and see what bumps were most prominent'. The company paid the travelling expenses to the cotton mill at Bankwood near Manchester and the Cork Union gave an allowance of 11s. to each boy to cover the cost of new clothing.[32]

At the Bankwood cotton mill they were joined by 15 other Irish orphan boys including some from the South Dublin Union. The Cork boys were accommodated in one house and the other lads occupied an adjoining premises. An Irish woman managed the houses and the boys were fed regularly. Unfortunately, all was not well. The boys were not provided with extra clothing, their bed clothes were not changed regularly and, instead of the promised weekly pocket money, they were given ½d. to spend after one month's work. Some of the boys were sick and although a number developed 'itch', no precautions were taken to isolate the healthy lads. They worked from 6am to 6pm and they were often ill-treated at the mill.[33] 'Besides being often worked [at] overtime, they were severely belaboured for trivial offences; they were knocked down and beaten by the over lookers [supervisors] with a strap while they were only partly dressed, and often they considered that the faults of others were visited upon their shoulders'.[34] Within a few months nine of the boys ran away and sought admission to the Manchester workhouse. Their cases

---

31 *CE* 28, 29 November, 5, 12, 19 December 1884.
32 *SR* 10 September, 15 September, 13 October 1853; *CUM* 14 September, 28 September, 12 October 1853.
33 *SR* 3 December 1853.
34 *CC* 15 April 1854.

were investigated and, instead of granting them relief, the guardians decided to ship them back to Ireland.[35]

On a few occasions, employers recruited workhouse boys as apprentices.[36] Usually just a few left the house but the industrial department report for March 1852 notes that 27 orphan boys from the shoemakers' shop and 22 from the tailoring department were recruited by local employers. Those who went out as tailor apprentices were:

Robert Cassills age 16 years
Robert Connor age 14 years
Michael Corcory age 16 years
Denis Cotter age 16 years
John Dawson age 16 years
Daniel Dawson age 14 years
William Fennell age 15 years
John Hanlon age 15 years
Timothy Herlihy age 14 years
Timothy Lyons age 14 years
John M'Donnell age 16 years
John Mahony age 16 years
Mark Moloney age 14 years
John Murphy age 12 years
Thomas Murphy age 15 years
Thomas Regan age 16 years
Patrick Reily age 18 years
Owen Riordan age 15 years
Edward Scully age 16 years
Patrick Sliney age 15 years
Francis Sliney age14 years
John Shannessy age 16 years

The following went out as apprentice shoemakers:

John Barry age 15 years
John Barry age 17 years
John Busteed age 15 years
Daniel Byrnes age 16 years
Jerry Callaghan age 15 years
Patrick Calnan age 16 years

---

35 Twelve months later Edmund Burke Roche, M.P., took 50 females from the house to work at his flax mill in Kildinan. The girls were provided with food and accommodation and received 6d. per day in wages. *SR* 21 September, 24 September 1854; *CUM* 20 September 1854; *CC* 5 October, 10 October 1854.

36 See, PP 1854, Vol. LV, [77], *Industrial Employment*, p. 2. An orphan named Richard Kenneddy was bound out as a shoemaker apprentice in July 1853, and William Scott was bound to a tinsman in February 1856. *CUM* 20 July 1853, 20 February 1856.

Thomas Daly age 15 years
Augustin Driscoll age 17 years
David Hannon age 15 years
John Hannon age 17 years
Daniel Harrington age 16 years
Thomas Lane age 15 years
John Long age 15 years
Thomas Long age 17 years
John Neill age 16 years
John Regan age 19 years
Michael Shea age 17 years
Michael Shea age 16 years
Jerry Sheehan age 15 years
Owen Sheehan age 18 years
Kerns Walsh age 16 years
Robert Walsh aged 16 years

In addition to these orphans, five who trained as shoemakers and two who trained as carpenters were assisted to emigrate.[37]

To encourage more involvement by local employers, the guardians attempted to introduce a reward system for farmers in 1853. The farm apprentices were to be paid 2s.6d. per quarter and on production of a certificate of good treatment, signed by a clergyman or magistrate, employers were to receive £1 at the end of the boy's first year of employment.[38] Because existing legislation only permitted the apprenticing of workhouse boys into the merchant sea service, this proposed scheme was not authorised by the Poor Law Commissioners.[39] The Cork guardians believed that more opportunities should be available to provide apprenticeships or other useful occupations for inmates, and viewed the existing legislation as 'disgraceful'.[40] Some guardians were confident that the number of children taken from the house would increase if a proper selection and introduction system was formulated.[41]

A committee was appointed to investigate, and in January 1857 it reported that 131 boys in the house were suitable for training as

---

37 *SR* 25 March 1852; see also *CUL* 12 July, 19 July 1853; *CUM* 27 July, 3 August 1853. The five shoemakers were: William Creedon (16), John Keeffe (16), William Keeffe (15), Daniel Murphy (15) and Daniel McCarthy. The two carpenter apprentices sent money back to Cork which helped their families join them in America.
38 *CUM* 3 August, 31 August, 14 September 1853; *SR* 1 September, 15 September 1853.
39 *SR* 6 October 1853; *CUL* 30 September 1853, 27 April 1854; See circular of 11 January 1853 in *Poor Law Commissioners Annual Report* (1880), pp. 22-3.
40 *CUM* 12 April 1854.
41 *CE* 2 January 1857.

apprentices. Eighty-four of the boys had no living parent and another 47 had only one parent living. To save the children from the mandatory transfer to the able-bodied ward, with its negative influences, when they reached 15 years of age, the committee suggested that a Benevolent Apprentices Society be established to indenture boys to farmers and other employers.[42] The objectives of the society, which was under the patronage of the board of guardians, included the annual enrolment of workhouse children as apprentices with tradesmen and farmers. They were to be selected from orphans of good character who had been in the workhouse for at least two years.[43]

The good will towards the society was reflected by the rate at which contributions were made to its funds once news of its establishment became known. By the start of March 1857, over £75 had been contributed, which included £2 from the Lord Lieutenant. At an early meeting of the committee Dr D. C. O Connor, the former workhouse medical officer and the main instigator of the scheme, spoke on the plight of the workhouse children, who were, he believed, 'as much slaves from their position, as were those in America with the black skin and curly hair'. It was agreed that competitive exams would be the fairest method of selecting the most deserving and suitable candidates for apprenticeship.[44]

The first examination of 130 boys over 13 years of age took place in the workhouse schoolrooms on 16 April 1857. The boys were examined in reading, writing, arithmetic, geography and grammar, and their competence, particularly at writing from dictation, surprised many observers. All of the boys read very well and on verbal examination they 'actually astonished their examiners'. Many very competent candidates were eliminated before the 25 boys for the first apprenticeship scheme were selected. Almost immediately, applications from employers were received. The guardians undertook to provide 26s. with each boy taken from the house, and the Benevolent Apprenticeship Society gave £5, which was paid as an initial sum of £2 with two further donations of 30s.[45] Within weeks the society had six boys placed with employers and

---

42 *CUM* 29 March 1854, 20 February, 31 December 1856, 21 January, 18 February 1857; *CE* 2 January, 12 January, 19 January, 18 February 1857; *CC* 15 January, 24 January 1857.

43 *CE* 19 January 1857; also PP 1861 Vol. X, [408], Report *from Select Committee on Poor Relief*, pp. 108-9.

44 *CE* 12 January, 6 February, 14 March 1857; For biographical details of Dr D. C. O Connor, see C.J.F. MacCarthy, '"The Angelic Doctor", Denis Charles O Connor, M.D., L.L.D, 1807-1888', *Bandon Historical Journal*, No. 9, 1993, pp. 24-28.

45 *CUM* 22 April 1857; *CC* 18 April, 23 April 1857; *CE* 17 April, 24 April 1857; PP 1861, Vol. X, [408], *Report on Poor Relief*, pp. 89-90.

another employer had independently recruited a boy of his own choice.[46] The boys were provided with new clothes and at the formal signing of indentures they and the employers were advised on their responsibilities and obligations, and the society undertook to visit the boys regularly and monitor their progress.[47] By the end of June 1857, 21 workhouse boys had been bound out to masters.[48] The innovation had a positive effect on the other orphans in the workhouse and there was a noticeable improvement in their conduct and attention to educational matters.

The committee's first annual report noted that no complaints were received about any of the boys, although a few minor problems had been sorted out during the visits to employers. When business declined at two of the companies, the apprentices refused to return to the workhouse while matters were being sorted out; instead, they remained with their masters where they had to endure various privations.[49] In 1858 the scheme was extended and girls were given training as children's maids and domestic servants, and it was also hoped to place some of them as servants and shop assistants. The provision of such training for girls required little effort. This stereotyping of future career options is underlined by a contemporary opinion which stated that 'the industrial training of the girls in workhouses is comparatively an easy task, as the domestic and economical duties of the house itself furnish the means of employing them in almost all the kinds of occupations which will hereafter fall to their lot in private life'.[50] Examinations were held in April 1858 and suitable boys and girls were selected for apprenticeships and for service. Some vacancies were already available for girls and it was agreed to allocate 40s. to provide clothing for each girl.[51] The Benevolent Apprentice Society placed 32 boys with employers in 1857 and 1858 but, as it would have been necessary to approach the same donors for funds, it was decided not to undertake a third scheme.[52] Though the

---

46 *CE* 22 May 1857. These six boys were Patrick Sullivan aged 17, Matthew Prendergast (13), Rob O Callaghan (14), R. Lyons (14), J. Connor (13) and R. Cunningham (13); the other boy was Maurice Burke who was apprenticed to W. McCarthy of Donoughmore. *CUM* 26 May 1857.

47 Two of the employers were Daniel Daly, a baker of Devonshire Street and Edmond Power of Nile Street; *CE* 22 May 1857.

48 *CE* 1 July 1857; for further names of apprentices, see: *CE* 3 June, 1 July 1857; *CUM* 13 May, 3 June, 1 July 1857; *CC* 2 July 1857.

49 *CC* 3 April, 15 April 1858; *CE* 2 April 1858; PP 1861, Vol. X, [408], *Select Committee on Poor Relief*, pp. 108-9.

50 John Forbes, *Memorandums made in Ireland. . .* (London, 1853), Vol. II, p. 247.

51 *CE* 9 April, 16 April 1858. The first batch of girls included Mary Sullivan (16), Mary Anne Collins (16), Margaret Desmond (16), Mary Bexley, Eliza Desmond and Anne Harrison. *CUM* 7 April, 14 April, 21 April, 5 May 1858, 25 January 1860.

52 PP 1861, Vol. X, [408], *Select Committee on Poor Relief*, pp. 89-90.

work of the apprentice society had a very positive effect on the general conduct of the workhouse boys, the Poor Law Commissioners were not in favour of the initiative. They believed that it was unfair to poor parents outside the workhouse who could not afford to have their own children bound as apprentices. The Commissioners were also of the opinion that boards of guardians did not have the power to pay premiums or to legally bind children as apprentices to employers.[53] By the summer of 1861 the workhouse boys had been excluded from training at trades in the workshops and their physical work was confined to agricultural training, at which 74 were employed. The girls were receiving varied training, to which 'cooking of a plain and rough description' was added. At that time 106 girls were being instructed at sewing, knitting and housework, 40 worked in the laundry and ten were engaged at delicate sewing and embroidery.[54]

Ladies Visiting Committee

Surveys in London by the newly established Workhouse Visiting Society in 1859 and 1860 established that most of the young able-bodied female inmates were 'leading useless lives' although there was a huge demand for servants outside. Education and training was a misnomer as the general activity consisted of oakum picking with a handful of women participating in cleaning or laundry work. The more demanding and interesting skills like cooking and dressmaking were reserved for older female inmates. The Society concluded that any value in oakum picking was outweighed by its negative aspects for 'there is abundant time and opportunity for communication and conversation between each other, and the worst women rapidly bring all the rest down to their own level'. Salvation for the girls would only be achieved by removing them from contamination, so the Society initiated the establishment of an outside training house.[55]

In Cork, local observers acknowledged that a similar society would benefit inmates of the workhouse. Dr D. C. O Connor, the former

---

53 PP 1861, Vol. X, [408], *Select Committee on Poor Relief*, pp. 56-7.
54 PP 1861, Vol. X, [408], *Select Committee on Poor Relief*, Appendix No. 61, p. 562; *CUM* 23 May 1860. For subsequent details on training see: *CE* 21 February, 11 April, 5 September 1879; 23 April, 28 May, 11 June, 25 June, 2 July, 16 July, 6 August 1880; 3 February, 8 September, 15 September, 22 September, 29 September, 24 November 1882; 10 January, 21 November 1884; 12 January, 14 January 1885; 30 October 1888. *CUM* 28 August, 4 September 1879; 22 April, 10 June 1880; 2 February, 8 March, 30 March 1882; 10 October, 12 November 1885.
55 See article from *Daily News* in *CE* of 23 April 1860; also evidence of Louisa Twining in PP 1861, Vol. IX [474-1], *4th Report from Select Committee on Poor Relief (England)*, pp. 1-15.

workhouse medical officer, agreed that such a society could organise domestic training for household servants. The training, particularly if undertaken outside the workhouse, would remove the young women from contact with adult inmates 'whose companionship is not of the most edifying character'. Isolating well-behaved girls from the bad influence of street wise peers was a recurring concern. When the girls reached 15 years of age, they were removed to the adult wards, and 'exposed to an immoral taint' which rendered any corrective intervention as good as useless. A guardians' committee did suggest that a separate ward for well-conducted girls of 15 years and older should be set up away from the influence of the coarser females. The committee also advocated that new arrivals be admitted to an intermediate ward until 'some proof of their conduct can be obtained'. In the able bodied female wards, refined women mixed freely with the 'evil conducted' and the nursery division accommodated married and unmarried mothers. The morality of this was questioned by some guardians who said that the absence of segregation was destroying 'order and regularity' in the house. In the adult wards young newcomers would almost certainly have been regaled with sordid tales and inculcated with an uncensored and unbalanced view of city life. Abandoning girls and boys to mix freely with a miscellaneous range of characters was tantamount to the destruction of innocence and ambition.

Young female inmates were unable to carry out everyday tasks such as sewing, washing or cooking and during 1859 poor law guardian Nicholas Mahony suggested that a domestic tutor be employed to teach these skills. Some guardians were in favour of establishing a ladies' visiting group to train the girls and 'educate them to be useful servants to the upper, and useful wives to the working class'.[56] The suggestion that workhouse girls be instructed in needlework and shirt making was raised on a number of occasions during 1860. Nicholas Mahony, a member of the Blarney woollen manufacturing family, was particularly anxious that the girls be taught basic skills. His firm had taken workhouse inmates as factory hands from time to time and they had generally proved satisfactory. He once persuaded a city firm to provide shirts for washing in the workhouse, but when they were returned to the company the laundry work was unacceptable. Needlework had also been a failure, and involving girls in workhouse cooking merely showed them how to 'turn a big stick in the boiler'.[57] Mahony and other guardians were willing to provide sample products, to help the girls develop some confidence and prepare

---

56 *SR* 22 December 1859; see also PP 1861, Vol. X, [408], Report *from Select Committee on Poor* relief, pp. 50-51.
57 *CE* 4 May, 16 May, 18 May, 4 July, 28 September 1860. Such work was also dangerous and on one occasion a kitchen hand was scalded to death when she tumbled into the stirabout vat. *CE* 1 August 1851.

them for outside employment, but the board would not authorise the project. Another guardian suggested that the board purchase a cow, 'to learn the girls to milk', which would encourage farmers to employ them as milkmaids.[58]

From his observations of workhouse girls and young women, Sir John Arnott concluded that 'when they leave the house, they either become a prey to vice, or are driven back to its shelter again. They have been taught nothing, know nothing, and are fit for nothing useful'.[59] At the very least, the girls should be taught how to prepare simple meals, for, without training, they were like 'birds in a cage – when they are set at liberty they are totally helpless'.[60] A positive move was made when William J. Shaw presented notice of his proposal to establish a ladies committee which would visit the workhouse and teach basic domestic skills to a selected group of a dozen girls.[61] Shaw suggested that seven ladies be admitted to the workhouse to prepare girls and young women for service outside. Isaac Julian seconded the resolution, but a section of the board lodged an amendment, which opened a discussion. Speaking in favour of the plan, Nicholas Mahony said that during the previous year the guardians had sent 186 females out to service but within a few months over 60 had returned to the workhouse. The harsh reality was 'that girls, from want of proper instruction, were utterly unfit for service, and many of them were incapable of fulfilling the meanest domestic office'. The failure rate was particularly high among children who had been in the institution since birth, and most of these returned to the workhouse. The sudden transition from institutional life must have caused many traumas. The children were confronted with a variety of problems. They had no experience of outside life, were unskilled, had no friends and were unknown to anyone

---

58 *CE* 20 June 1860; *CC* 21 June 1860. This was rejected at the time, but ten years later the guardians did agree to acquire two cows for the purpose. *CE* 5 August 1870. Nicholas Mahony's interest in a womens' visiting group was encouraged by the work of his sister Ellen Woodlock. In the years after the famine, she was instrumental in setting up two industrial schools in Cork. Along with her friend Mrs Sarah Atkinson, she later founded and managed the St. Joseph's Industrial School in Dublin, and she was also involved in the establishment of Temple Street Hospital for Children. Workhouse girls were among the children trained at industrial and domestic skills in her school. She encouraged women in Cork and elsewhere to visit workhouses and take an active interest in the training and well-being of young inmates. PP 1861, Vol. X, [408], evidence of Mrs Woodlock, pp. 216-227; see also M. Luddy, *Women and Philanthropy* (London), 1995, p. 38 and M. Luddy, *Women and Philanthropy in nineteenth century Ireland*, Phd., thesis (UCC, 1989), pp. 45, 67-8. For obituary of Ellen Woodlock, see *CE* 16 July 1884 and *Freeman's Journal* 15 July 1884.

59 *CE* 27 July 1860.

60 *CE* 30 October 1861.

61 *CE* 11 July 1860; *CC* 9 August, 11 August, 14 August 1860; *CUM* 11 July 1860.

in the outside world. After some discussion, the board voted in favour of implementing the training scheme which would provide the children with interpersonal and manual skills.[62] Following initial reluctance to open the workhouse to 'irresponsible parties', and a stubborn denial that the existing system was little better than useless, the Poor Law Commissioners gave their authorisation, and a committee of guardians consisting of George Smith, Isaac Julian, Nicholas Mahony, Thomas Lyons and William J. Shaw was selected to implement the scheme.[63]

By the first week of December 1860 the ladies' committee was ready to visit the workhouse and select a dozen girls for their attention.[64] The objectives of the group, as presented to the guardians, included a commitment to train 12 to 15 year old girls as needle-women and domestic servants, and to locate outside employment before the girls were transferred to the able-bodied ward at 15 years of age. The progress of the twelve selected girls was to be discussed with their teachers each week and detailed records were to be kept on their ability at household tasks such as cooking, washing and cleaning. These reports would be reviewed at the committee's monthly meeting and, whenever necessary, extra help or instruction would be organised. Before the end of November 1860 the ladies placed 13 year old Margaret Kearney in employment. That Christmas, the Committee organised a ceremony at which gifts were presented to 326 children in the institution. Perhaps for the first time since its inception, the Cork workhouse witnessed scenes of 'delirium and delightful hubbub' in its infants' and children's wards.[65]

At the ladies' first annual general meeting on 8 November 1861 their

---

62 *CUM* 29 August, 12 September, 19 September, 26 September 1860; *CE* 12 September, 19 September, 21 September, 26 September, 28 September, 3 October 1860; *CC* 13 September, 20 September, 27 September 1860; also PP 1861, Vol. X, [408], *Report from Select Committee on Poor Relief*, p. 91; see also M.E. Rose, 'The crisis of Poor Relief in England, 1860-1890', in M.J. Mommsen (Ed.), *The emergence of the Welfare State in Britain and Germany* (London, 1981), p. 58.

63 *CE* 12 October 1860; PP 1861, Vol. X, [408], *Report on Poor Relief.*, pp. 50-51, 101, 322, 329, 334; *CUL* 18 September 1860; *CUM* 10 October 1860; for the rules of the Women's Workhouse Visiting Committee in London, see: PP 1861, Vol. IX, [323], *2nd Report from the Select Committee on Poor Relief (England)*, p. 189.

64 The members of this first committee were Mrs W. J. Shaw, Mrs N. Mahony, Mrs T. Mahony, Mrs William Townsend, Mrs Tracy and Mrs P. McSwiney. *CE* 7 November 1860, 9 November 1861; *CC* 5 December 1860. For a contemporary opinion on the benefit of women visiting workhouse inmates, see: Mark S. O Shaughnessy, 'Some remarks ... on befriending pauper girls', *Journal of Social and Statistical Inquiry Society of Ireland*, 1862, Part XX, pp. 143-57; see also Margaret H. Preston, 'Lay women and Philanthropy in Dublin, 1860-1880', *Éire-Ireland*, XXVIII: 4, Winter, 1993, pp. 74-85.

65 *CE* 3 December, 28 December 1860; *CC* 29 November, 29 December 1860.

report showed that of the 12 girls selected for training, all but one were orphans. A timetable had been arranged and a competent pauper inmate was recruited to instruct the girls at sewing and other skills. A rota system allowed two girls to work in the hospital kitchen, two to assist in cleaning the boardroom and matron's quarters and two to keep a selected ward in good order. At the end of each month the girls were assigned to different duties. In addition to the twelve selected youngsters, some grown girls who requested training were included in the scheme, but they were not allowed to fraternise with the others. They too were under a pauper tutor who taught them laundry, kitchen skills and plain needlework.

An external committee worked in conjunction with the visitors and within a few months girls were placed with families. Fourteen girls were put into service during the year and two left their employers 'entirely from a love of change'. A few others returned to the workhouse because they were unable to cope with their situations, which sometimes amounted to 'hard labour'. Alternative jobs were usually located, but in some cases the girls were not permitted to remain in the workhouse when they returned. One girl who had been born in the institution, and had never left its precincts until she got her job, became 'quite a treasure to her employer, most correct in her conduct, faithful and trustworthy in every respect'.[66] The Ladies Visiting Committee was satisfied with its initial progress but its members were hopeful that a separate apartment could be provided for the girls to prepare and cook their meals and wash their clothes and those of house officers. They were concerned that the girls should be protected from the 'corrupt and wicked' influences of some inmates. Commenting on the first year's report, the *Cork Examiner* observed that without the help of the ladies' committee, 'there is little hope for the poor girl trained in the workhouse'.[67]

During the summer of 1862 another group of skilled girls was available for service outside, but training seems to have faltered during 1863.[68] John Francis Maguire spoke at length on the necessity to revitalise the commitment to training and he proposed that a separate apartment be set aside for this purpose.[69] The Ladies Visiting Committee was also anxious to have its own premises because it had found that some household servants would not associate with girls from the workhouse. To remove the workhouse stigma, they asked the guardians to acquire an outside house in which to train the girls under a qualified

66 *CE* 12 February 1862, See also *CE* 18 September, 10 October 1861.
67 *CE* 9 November 1861.
68 *CE* 17 May, 1862.
69 *CE* 2 April, 15 April 1863; *CC* 13 March 1862; PP 1861, Vol. X, [408], *Select Committee on Poor Relief*, pp. 91-2.

supervisor.[70] The guardians concurred with the view that 'a girl of 14 or 15 years of age, reared in a workhouse, is as unlearned in the experience of life as a child of five years old in the general population'.[71] At the start of May 1863 the board voted to take a house and employ a matron at £30 per annum to train the girls. This would remove them from the influence of 'persons who would represent vice in the most alluring forms, and ridicule virtue'.[72] Perhaps, more importantly, it would provide the girls with some scope for developing social skills and self-confidence.

Getting suitable premises proved difficult, and various locations were considered before the ladies located a house at No. 31 Mary Street which was suitable for conversion as a training establishment.[73] In reply to a query from the Poor Law Commissioners, the committee explained that in the new facility the girls would be trained in

> a variety of needle work such as would be useful in families; cleaning a home in a proper manner, preparing their food in different ways, so as to give them some knowledge of cookery, keeping the kitchen, laundry, etc, and all necessary utensils there in proper order, learning how to handle ware and glass, making, mending and keeping their own and the house clothes in a proper manner and acquiring a knowledge of the various details connected with domestic service that cannot be acquired in any workhouse . . . No efforts hitherto have been undertaken for this youthful class, except the questionable and expensive one of sending them untrained and useless out of the country, whereas the training of them for a short time may save the ratepayers the cost of emigration or many years of their support in the workhouse. With this object in view the ladies will be thankful for any advice or suggestions the experience of the Commissioners may afford.[74]

The Commissioners were not opposed to the idea, but they asked the guardians to ensure that the regular industrial experience offered to other girls was not neglected in the workhouse. In reality, this had little formal value and was merely unpaid labour; for instance, in May 1863, 91 girls were employed at knitting, 61 served meals or scrubbed floors, 40 were employed at washing and 20 helped with the cooking.[75] In the

70 Such an institution for training workhouse girls in domestic skills had been established at 22, New Ormond Street, Dublin during the previous year, and one was also opened at Belfast. *CE* 22 March 1862, 28 January 1864.
71 *CE* 16 April 1863.
72 *CE* 6 May 1863; *CUM* 6 May 1863.
73 *CE* 9 December 1863, 7 April 1864; *CUM* 9 December 1863; 10 February, 9 March, 27, April, 4 May, 11 May, 8 June, 1 October 1864; *CUL* 18 February, 15 March 1864.
74 *CC* 28 January 1864; *CE* 28 January 1864.
75 *CE* 11 February 1864; *CC* 11 February 1864; *CUL* 21 April, 15 December 1863, 19 January, 2 February, 9 February 1864.

period August 1861 to April 1864, the committee placed 85 girls in employment and just 13 returned to the workhouse. Funds were allocated for furniture and bedding, renovations were made and accommodation was provided for a matron and 15 girls in the new building.[76] On 1 September 1864 Nicholas Dunscombe, a guardian who had taken an active interest in the project, performed the official opening of the Mary Street home. The house was provided with an extensive range of domestic equipment and it was intended that 'neatness, tidiness, smartness, activity, attention, willing obedience, industry and honesty' would be inculcated in the girls.[77] The normal workhouse diet was modified and the Mary Street girls were allowed more meat, and instead of milk they had tea for their breakfast. At the end of 1864, the purchase of a new cooking range brought the amount expended on the Mary Street premises to almost £200.[78]

Within a couple of weeks of the opening, seven girls, four of whom were orphans, and a woman from the workhouse were residing at the home. Few of the girls had ever been in a private house; most had never used cutlery, cups and saucers, or handled glassware. The art of cooking was a mystery. None of the girls had ever seen fowl, and they had no idea of how to prepare potatoes or meat. Producing quality servants was not going to be a simple task because 'their deplorable want of knowledge connected with domestic service – their slow way of moving – their look of utter helplessness when asked to do the simplest things, made it at first a laborious work to teach them; but as they began to learn something and found that they had a better fortune to look forward to than spending their lives in the workhouse, their dormant facilities were roused'.

Members of the committee took it in turns to visit the home and two ladies spent four hours each day instructing the girls. Despite fears about the small stature and youth of the girls, four were employed as servants and another was on trial at a household by the spring of 1865. The pauper helper had also learned how to cook and do housework, so she too got a job outside the house. Because of a demand for children's maids, the ladies organised needlework classes at the workhouse, and as an incentive to the girls, prizes were offered for the best quality workmanship. As another incentive, the visiting committee undertook to provide a financial reward to any servant who remained with her

76 *CC* 7 April 1864; *CE* 7 April, 20 July 1864; *CUM* 13 July, 20 July 1864.
77 *CUL* 6 September 1864; *CE* 2 September, 8 September 1864; see also William D'Esterre Parker, *The Irish Poor Law is a national grievance, with suggestions for its amendment* (Cork, 1868), pp. 27-8.
78 *CE* 15 September, 21 September, 12 October 1864; *CC* 6 October, 13 October 1864; *CUM* 5 October 1864; *CUL* 11 October 1864.

employer for a period of 12 months.[79] The training scheme was treated very seriously, discipline was severe and it was not uncommon for girls to be subjected to corporal punishment for misdemeanours.[80] Unfortunately, the pool of suitable workhouse girls was soon exhausted, and when it became difficult to get enthusiastic candidates, the Poor Law Commissioners opposed a suggestion that new arrivals at the workhouse should be sent directly to the home.[81]

By the end of 1865, 40 workhouse girls aged from nine to eighteen years had received training at the home. Seventeen had been successfully placed with households, six had returned to the workhouse because of illness, eight were still being trained and nine failed to secure permanent work. Of the latter, three were discharged because of their lazy attitude, three were impertinent, two ran away from employers, and one returned directly to the workhouse. Eventually, all but 17 came back to the workhouse. Little sympathy was shown for those who failed to integrate into outside society and as a punishment they were subjected to laborious and irksome work. This unsympathetic attitude must have shattered any remaining enthusiasm the girls had for a career outside the workhouse. The home had then cost almost £320 and as the placement of the 17 girls was saving the union £136 per annum, the venture was deemed successful by most of the guardians.[82]

During 1866 another 36 girls were received into the home and 20 were placed in service. When the home's annual report was presented to the guardians in January 1867, the lease had just three weeks to run. The premises was in need of repair and the ladies' committee was anxious to acquire a larger house to accommodate up to thirty girls. No progress was made, and when the lease expired, the nine remaining residents were returned to the workhouse. In total 77 girls had been trained in Mary Street and over 40 remained in permanent employment.[83] There was still a large amount of good-will towards external training. Suitable girls were identified, a new 12 month training programme was drawn up and the ladies and their supporters were determined to find another house.[84] Some guardians opposed the idea and its inherent expense. They

79 *CE* 10 November 1864, 9 March, 14 March 1865.
80 *CUM* 19 October, 2 November 1865.
81 *CE* 2 November, 9 November 1865; *CUL* 4 October, 18 October, 7 November 1865; *CUM* 9 November 1865.
82 *CE* 25 January, 26 January 1866; *CC* 26 January 1866; see also undated report in *CUL*, bound between 26 July and 1 August 1865; *CUM* 9 November, 7 December 1865, 25 January 1866.
83 *CE* 10 January, 24 January, 12 February, 21 February 1867; *CUM* 9 January, 23 January, 13 February, 27 February 1867.
84 *CE* 26 February, 27 February, 28 February, 18 April, 2 May 1867; *CUM* 17 April, 1 May, 8 May, 22 May 1867.

favoured workhouse-based training, which could be conducted at little cost and would provide services such as laundry and cooking.[85] The matron of the Mary Street home resigned and the chairman of the board of guardians suggested that girls who had been trained there could instruct the eligible inmates. Instead, an industrial superintendent was appointed at a salary of £20 and 20 girls were put under her charge. Their tasks consisted principally of housekeeping, laundry and sewing skills and they also cooked the hospital food.[86] Although this venture was merely exploitation under the guise of training, it did have some merit as it prepared candidates for internal posts. Some of the girls were later appointed to permanent positions such as hospital assistants and domestic servants in the institution.[87] The great success of the Mary Street home was that by removing inmates from their workhouse routine it opened a door to the outside world and made the transition a natural progression. The closure of the home and the failure to resume outside training deprived the girls of this opportunity to break the link with the workhouse and its many negative influences and perceptions.

Although another outside training unit was not acquired, the instruction of female domestic servants continued in a new domestic training unit. Ever ready to exploit the inmates, some guardians were anxious to profit from the training and they were in favour of commencing large scale manufacturing operations in the workhouse. They argued that the removal of the regime of 'forced idleness' would give the inmates training and experience, and could help the workhouse budget by producing clothing and other items.[88] In his annual report to the board of guardians in April 1869, the chairman spoke highly of the girls' training unit, which had produced about 700 articles of clothing during the previous year. These girls prepared food for male hospital patients and made and repaired clothing. They were also instructed in domestic skills such as washing floors, making fires and polishing household equipment. Since the commencement of the unit at the start of 1868, some 54 girls had passed through its doors. Twenty-four had been placed in situations outside and 17 had successfully integrated into their employment; the others had returned either to the workhouse or its hospital.[89]

A limited amount of industrial training was undertaken during

85 *CE* 9 May 1867; see letter from D. L. Sandiford PLG of 4 May 1867 to Poor Law Commissioners in *CUL* 7 May 1867.
86 *CE* 18 July, 25 July, 8 August, 19 August, 29 August 1867; *CUL* 3 September, 14 December 1867; *CUM* 29 January 1868; *CUM* 17 July, 24 July, 7 August 1867.
87 *CE* 9 April 1868; *CUM* 19 February 1868.
88 *CE* 25 February, 11 March, 12 March 1869.
89 *CE* 8 April, 22 April 1869; *CUL* 20 April, 27 April 1869; *Irish Times* 24 April 1869.

subsequent years with girls concentrating on domestic oriented chores and boys on vegetable cultivation. At the very least, said the *Cork Constitution*, children leaving the house to work as servants should know 'how to light a fire, cook plain food, sweep out a yard, or dig a square of garden'.[90] At the start of 1885, the ladies' committee organised cookery lessons for senior girls. They extended the training to include general household and servants' duties and this department continued to operate on a reduced scale for some time. There was a great demand for properly trained girls and in the four year period up to the end of 1889, 97 were successfully placed in employment outside the workhouse.[91] Plans to introduce structured training in agriculture and other skills were not achieved, but a limited number of boys did work on cultivation and a few were employed at trades. Although about 50 boys left the establishment to work with farmers during 1888, in the house, they still lacked proper facilities, and they often laboured with rough adults, 'neer-do-wells' and 'broken-down old drunkards'.[92] The work of the Ladies Visiting Committee and the Benevolent Apprentice Society certainly provided valuable training and industrial placements for the young workhouse inmates. This enlightened attitude did not represent the general approach. Frequently, training was linked to the institution's day-to-day activities and the young participants merely augmented the labour force in the garden, wards or workshops. The training usually consisted of unstructured repetitive tasks with little value other than that it provided an element of physical exercise for the hapless participants.

---

90 CC 25 February 1882.
91 *CE* 19 November, 29 November, 13 December, 19 December, 20 December 1889; *CC* 28 March 1887, 29 November 1889.
92 *CE* 8 April, 26 August 1887, 14 February, 4 May, 30 October 1888, 27 June, 18 July, 15 August 1890; *CUM* 10 June 1880, 13 January, 26 May 1881, 3 December, 10 December 1885; *CC* 12 February 1886; NAI, CSORP 1886 19469.

6 Work

For a comparatively short period during its history, the Cork workhouse functioned as a large-scale industrial workshop. During that time a majority of its inmates were engaged in some form of industrial activity. Frequently the work amounted to little more than punishment. Such was the case with the capstan mill and stone breaking ordeals, which made the workhouse more like a penal institution. In place of such degrading and punitive activities, a properly organised system of 'industrial training' would have benefited the inmates and rewarded them with useful skills and a positive attitude towards work. This was particularly true in the case of children. In spite of opportunities for inculcating a healthy work ethic, time was wasted on the repetitive and soul-destroying ordeal of rotating a capstan mill. The other chosen options of basic farm work, mundane household chores and assisting second-rate craftsmen were also of little value.

Inmates, particularly women, were appointed as 'pauper assistants' in locations such as the workhouse hospital and nursery. In return for demanding and exploitative labour, they were begrudgingly issued with extra food rations or even a little alcohol which were withdrawn at the whim of the board of guardians. The women were rarely given a permanent position because the Poor Law Commissioners and Local Government Board frowned upon appointments from the pauper cohort. Nonetheless, these roles did have a positive side as they imparted self-respect and an identity to the workers.

Industrial activities

During the late 1840s and early 1850s attempts were made to establish industrial departments in Cork and other Irish workhouses. For instance, in the Clonmel auxiliary house, about 40% of adults were engaged in industrial activities. Women worked at spinning, weaving and laundry tasks, men were employed at white washing and girls were taught knitting, sewing and hat making. Similar activities were conducted at Kilkenny, Naas and Larne workhouses; at Mallow, the industries included wool and linen processing, agricultural activities

145

and baking which, as well as giving the inmates skills, saved an estimated £775 during 1849.[1] Female inmates at Macroom made and
repaired their own clothes and the men were employed at breaking
stones to the size of 'marbles'.[2] Many workhouses, including those at
Cork, Ballina, Killarney, Midleton, Nenagh, New Ross, Skibbereen and
Wexford had efficient industrial departments, which in some cases
included capstan mills.[3] The range of industrial activities was extensive
and included skills such as net-making, embroidery, locksmith's work
and water pumping.[4] Goods produced by inmates were usually
consumed in their own workhouse.

For a number of years during the 1840s and early 1850s the Cork
workhouse did have an efficient industrial department which produced a
variety of goods. The venture commenced with the purchase of some
looms at the start of 1848. A few men were put weaving and some
women commenced knitting and spinning but as the operations did not
result in financial savings, they were discontinued.[5] When George Carr,
the former store man, became master in January 1849, inmates were
deployed at levelling the grounds, workshops were erected and a variety
of industrial operations recommenced. During the half year 1 January to
23 June 1849 the weaving and woollen department produced 2,006
yards of frieze, 907 shawls knitted by female paupers, 51 blankets and
37 yards of linsey woolsey (a cloth made from a combination of linen
and wool). If purchased from an outside supplier, these items would have
cost £249, but as they had been produced for £187 in the workhouse,
the ratepayers had been saved £62 by their manufacture. Similarly, the
shoemaking department, which produced 1,498 pairs of clogs and 27
pairs of leather shoes, realised a saving of £103. The saving at the

---

1 *SR* 18 January 1849; *CC* 20 September 1849; *CE* 22 August 1849.
2 *CC* 21 November 1848; *SR* 21 November 1848.
3 *CC* 25 November, 28 November 1848; *CE* 21 December 1849.
4 See: PP 1852-3, Vol. LXXXIV, [513], *Return from each of the Poor Law Unions in England, Wales and Ireland, showing what kinds of employment are carried on in the workhouses, or on land attached; the number of adult able-bodied persons in the books as recipients of relief on 1 July 1852, and the proportion engaged in handcrafts and agri-cultural industry, etc . . .*; PP 1854, Vol. LV, [77], *Statement relating to the industrial employment of the juvenile inmates of union workhouses, Ireland, in the month of September 1853.*
5 *SR* 16 November 1848; *CE* 17 November 1848; A.G. Stark tells us that during 1847, John Sadlier Foster was engaged to establish an industrial system in the Cork workhouse. Because the results were unsatisfactory, operations ceased until they recommenced under George Carr. A.G. Stark, *The South of Ireland in 1850; being the journal of a tour in Leinster and Munster* (Dublin, 1850), p.112; see also *Cork workhouse visiting committee book* (Cork Archives), BGFM, FM1, 8 December, 15 December 1847, 22 May 1848; *SR* 11 November, 9 December 1847, 3 October 1850, 14 August 1852.

workhouse bakery, which made 274,120 four-pound loaves of bread, was recorded as £750.[6]

In the period from July to September 1849, 559 shawls, 1,173 yards of frieze, 133,389 loaves of bread, 124 pairs of shoes and 696 pairs of wooden clogs – 194 being of a 'superior' quality for emigrants – were manufactured. In addition, many items of clothing were made in the tailors' shop and female workrooms. An estimated saving of £461.3s.6d. had been realised by the industry during that quarter. The industrial area was extended and additional looms for linen and flannel were installed. In total about 800 inmates were employed 'reproductively' in the institution. In its report, the industrial committee boasted that on completion of two more workshops, employment could be extended to include oakum picking for aged and infirm males. Plans for employing all the females were to be accomplished in a wool-processing department where woollen drawers and flannels for aged, infirm and sick inmates would be knitted. This department was in operation before the year's end and 150 women were employed there at carding, spinning, picking wool and operating a dozen looms.[7] In the nearby linen department, 60 women, 5 men and 5 boys worked on spinning wheels, looms and other equipment, and another team of 100 women repaired clothing. Men's clothes were repaired in the tailoring department, where some new items, including clothes for emigrating girls, were also manufactured. The *Cork Constitution* was pleased with progress and declared that 'the result of the experiment is highly creditable to everyone concerned in it, and will be highly gratifying to the ratepayers. More, we have no doubt, might be successfully attempted if the guardians . . . were but free to follow the suggestions of their own judgement and experience'.[8]

Some officials and guardians did not see exploitation of workhouse inmates as unfair. A half dozen skilled weavers, who were inmates at the time, oversaw the institution's weaving operations. Following intervention by poor law guardian John S. Foster, some of these weavers were assisted to leave the house in search of employment. Consequently some looms ceased to operate and production in the department decreased when up to 400 women became idle. For its success the department depended on a ready pool of workers who could be supervised and directed by inmates with specific skills. The board discussed the situation

---

6 *SR* 5 July 1849; *CUM* 16 May, 30 May 1849; see also *CE* 21 February 1849.

7 *CUM* 9 January 1850; *SR* 11 October 1849. Susan Aubrey, the superintendent of this department later emigrated to Australia. *CUL* 20 February, 23 March 1850, 20 August 1852.

8 *SR* 10 January 1850; *CC* 10 January 1850. Industrial operations showed a profit of £943 for the three months 29 October to 29 December 1849. *CUM* 9 January 1850.

and some guardians criticised Foster for his action, which deprived the workhouse of key personnel and threatened the viability of industrial operations. Foster argued that funds had been saved because the guardians were no longer required to maintain the weavers at the ratepayers' expense. At an investigation into the matter it was established that Foster had actively encouraged weavers to leave the workhouse and had sought employment for them in England. Some guardians accused him of deliberately sabotaging the workhouse industrial department by this action. Eventually a majority of the board exonerated him from any wrong doing and agreed that his actions were well intentioned and designed solely to improve the conditions of the men.[9]

During February and March 1850 the number of inmates in the institution remained at around 6,000. The workhouse itself had 3,050 residents, 1,200 were in temporary buildings on the site, the former house of industry had 800 inmates and 1,800 others were located in two storehouses in the city. The continuing success of industrial operations was indicated by the figures in the first report for that year. The number of loaves of bread produced exceeded 131,686 and 244 pairs of shoes and 628 pairs of clogs were manufactured. Though production at the capstan mill (see below, pages 156-160) showed a decrease to 670 sacks of wholemeal and 504 sacks of Indian meal, the various other departmental returns indicated that industrial operations were thriving.[10] The industrial committee credited the physical activities with a noticeable improvement in the behaviour of the inmates. Instead of 'depressing and demoralising inertness' inmates were now engaged in 'active, cheerful, heartful employment'.[11] Visitors to the workhouse in April 1850 recorded that

> the great temporary building, erected within the walls during the famine year, enlarged by the excavation of a basement storey, and the cells formerly appropriated for the purposes of punishment, are now one continuous scene of busy and cheerful industry. Upwards of 600 women are employed carding, hacking, spinning and sewing, in large and admirably ventilated apartments, all looking healthful and contented, and performing their work without the slightest symptom of sullenness or apathy. The spinning rooms, indeed, present a scene of busy, active, cheerful occupation that is about the last thing one associates with the idea of an Irish pauper asylum.

9 *SR* 7 March, 14 March 1850; *CUM* 13 March 1850; see also editorial in *CE* 20 March 1850.

10 See A.G. Stark, *South of Ireland*. pp. 108-9; *CUM* 8 March, 10 April 1850; *SR* 11 April 1850; *CC* 11 April 1850. Inmates were also involved in a project to install floors in the recently excavated timber buildings.

11 *SR* 16 April 1850; NAI, Poor Law Commissioners, Letters to James Burke 1850 – circular of 4 December 1850 with cutting from *Daily News* (London), of 28 September 1850.

In the male department, weavers, tailors, shoemakers, blacksmiths, tinmen, etc., were equally busily engaged. Blankets, coverlets, etc., were in process of manufacture in the looms, and some excellent specimens of strong grey calico, made from cotton wool, which had been carried through all the intermediate stages of preparation, in the Workhouse, by unassisted pauper labour. Besides the matters already enumerated, we saw the capstan mill, for grinding the corn used by the inmates in the establishment, and the bakery where it is finally converted into bread; the whole being contrived and brought into the present condition, within, we believe, a single year, under the super-intendence of the present active and most intelligent master.[12]

Though workhouses were not permitted to manufacture in excess of their own requirements, the industrial committee was anxious to extend its activities and produce goods for charitable institutions in the city.[13] The aspiration to extend activities beyond the confines of the workhouse was seen as a threat to the standard of living of workers in the city. In a departure from its enthusiastic support of industrial operations in the workhouse, the *Southern Reporter* questioned the accuracy of the profit claimed in the institution's reports.[14] It acknowledged that the inmates were engaging in activities designed to improve 'their health, their self-respect and their morality', and that ratepayers' money was being saved, but the *Reporter* was convinced that the amount was exaggerated. As an example, it singled out the bakery, saying that the work of paid labour outside the house was now being done by unpaid workers in the institution. This diminished the livelihoods of the outside workers and ultimately resulted in some of them and their families entering the workhouse. When a baker and his family were driven to the workhouse, other trades such as shoemakers, tailors, weavers, hatters etc., also suffered from the consequent decrease in the demands for their services. If goods which were formerly imported, or purchased in other parts of the country, were being replaced by articles manufactured in the workhouse, only then could it be claimed that the local economy was not being damaged.[15] Because the expenditure on workhouse industry took no one out of the institution and actually damaged local businesses producing similar goods, the system was in effect encouraging pauperism. The Poor Law Commissioners were in favour of industrial employment, particularly for able-bodied inmates, because, as they warned, 'if labour of an unattractive kind is not provided for this class and they are not steadily kept at work by competent subordinate officers, the workhouse ceases to

12 *SR* 16 April 1850.
13 *SR* 1 August 1850; *CE* 31 July 1850.
14 See *SR* 11 April 1850.
15 *SR* 8 January, 8 August 1850.

be an effectual test of the destitution of this class, and discipline and order cannot be duly maintained'.[16] Nonetheless, the Commissioners were apprehensive that competition between workhouse inmates and outside labour would be detrimental to the latter.[17] This was well illustrated by the plight of Cork's nailers who were fighting a losing battle against competition from cast and machine made fasteners. As their trade disappeared, the craftsmen worked longer hours for less money, but their plight was ignored by the guardians who authorised the production of nails for the workhouse by the institution's inmates.[18] Some commentators disagreed with the *Reporter*'s views and saw the industrial work as an appropriate 'test' to discourage casual poor from applying to the workhouse.[19]

In an editorial on 20 August 1850 the *Southern Reporter* suggested that an industry such as the manufacture of linen, which would process flax through the various operations of scutching, hacking and weaving, would not damage the local economy. Likewise, the manufacture of cotton, the weaving of sailcloth, sewed muslin work or knitting would be preferable to shoemaking, tailoring and baking which did threaten the jobs of local workers.[20] A contemporary assessment of workhouse industry by Professor W. N. Hancock argued that first class workers were required if a profit was to be realised. In general there were few skilled able-bodied workers in workhouses and without an adequate number it would be virtually impossible to compete with outside industries.[21] Professor Hancock argued that inducements beyond the general workhouse entitlements would be necessary to ensure that the skilled workers maintained a high level of productivity. Thus, the retention of the workers in the house would require some form of reward, which was contrary to the principle of workhouse relief. He warned that the labour for skilled workhouse inmates would have to be interesting because 'nothing could be more dispiriting, nothing would be more calculated to make them sullen and discontented, than to employ them at useless work as a test of destitution'.[22]

By the end of 1850 a reduced number of inmates resulted in a decrease in the volume of goods produced in the workhouse. The employment of younger inmates was extended and 80 girls aged between

16 *CUL* 18 May 1852.
17 *Poor Law Commissioners Annual Report* (1850), p. 10; *Poor Law Commissioners Annual Report* (1852), pp. 12-13.
18 *SR* 29 April, 26 June 1851.
19 *SR* 6 August, 8 August, 13 August, 17 August 1850.
20 *SR* 20 August 1850.
21 W. N. Hancock, '*Should Boards of Guardians endeavour to make Pauper Labour self-supporting. . .'*. (Dublin, 1851), p. 6.
22 Ibid, p. 10.

11 and 14 years of age were brought to the spinning room for two hours each day after school. They were instructed in the art of spinning flax and some even managed to produce sewing thread of a very fine quality. A number of the girls were shown how to knit shawls for their own use, and the industrial committee was anxious to extend their training by employing an instructor to provide classes in lace embroidery work. This was discussed during the reading of the industrial report for autumn 1850, and some guardians opposed the idea as they believed that the girls would abuse their skills, and possibly make items to sell outside; others feared that parents would send children into the workhouse to learn how to produce embroidery work.[23] The venture was seen in a positive light by other observers who believed that the acquisition of skills would encourage inmates to leave the workhouse so the guardians sought an embroidery teacher at 10s. per week.[24] Before the year's end some new skills were being used in the workhouse – inmates made all the institution's buttons, hooks and eyes, and mops and the embroidery school had commenced operating. By January 1851 thirty-four girls had mastered the art of embroidery and their work was said to be of an excellent quality.[25] The training at embroidery work did have some success and a number of girls were able to leave the workhouse for full time employment. The names of these girls were: Hannah Allen, Margaret Barrett, Hannah Bourke, Mary Coleman, Bridget Connell, Margaret Daly, Abby Lyons, Alice Maguire, Mary Anne Maguire, Ellen Mulqueeny, Jane Scanlon and Jane Sullivan.[26] Their skills were in demand and because most of their work was sold outside Cork, their introduction into the local labour market had a positive effect on the local economy. The possibility that boys trained in crafts such as shoemaking could displace established workers was a genuine concern. Some observers advocated that all the boys should be sent abroad when trained or, alternatively, the range of skills taught in the workhouse should pose no threat to local workers.[27]

The industrial committee's report for the quarter ending December 1850 listed an extensive range of items which had been manufactured or processed in the various workhouse departments. These ranged from flour and bread, frieze, gingham and sheeting, thread and twine, shawls, suits, caps and jackets, shoes, boots and clogs to nails, tinwear and wooden tubs. Repairs and modification work were undertaken on

23 *CUM* 30 October 1850; *CC* 31 October 1850; SR 3 October 1850.
24 *SR* 31 October 1850; *CE* 4 November 1850.
25 *CUM* 1 January 1851; *SR* 12 December 1850, 11 January, 20 January, 30 January 1851.
26 *SR* 25 March 1851.
27 *SR* 1 April 1852.

clothing and footwear, and inmates also carried out maintenance on the grounds and buildings.[28] Subsequent reports indicated that during 1851 and 1852 large savings continued to be realised from the industrial work.[29] In the tailoring department suits were made up for a small expenditure; the shoemakers made men's footwear for 2s.9d. a pair, women's shoes for 2s.2d., and canvas clogs for between 1s. and 1s.2d. a pair.[30] The large range of items produced by the smiths and tin workers included dishes, mugs, lanterns, candlesticks and spittoons, and, as well as making household items and furnishings, the carpenters produced the coffins used for house burials. Workers from these areas helped with the construction of a new building to accommodate 1,200 paupers and the painting and glazing was undertaken by inmates. Unskilled inmates sunk a new well in the yard and also carried out excavation work. Old and infirm inmates were not excused and they were required to break a certain quantity of stones each day. Of the 4,995 inmates in the workhouse during the summer of 1852, a total of 914, which included 67 boys and girls, were engaged in industrial activities.[31]

The weavers in the industrial department were expected to produce five yards of cloth per day, for which they received the normal workhouse food allowance. On occasions when a large volume of material, such as gingham, was urgently required the weavers worked until 9pm and were given a supper as a reward for their labours, but, of course, some guardians objected to the provision of this extra food. The Poor Law Commissioners also were opposed to the policy of providing any reward for labour carried out in workhouses. This, they believed, could encourage workers to enter the institution. 'Success in the management of a Workhouse was', they said, 'evinced rather by the absence of persons able to work profitably for the Ratepayers, than by a display of profitable results obtained from the labour of a large number of persons reconciled to a continuous residence in the Workhouse'. Fluctuations in the quality and quantity of goods produced in the workhouse often resulted in a shortage of some items. The absence of raw material, such as flax, also caused idleness in the industrial department.[32] Such was the situation in early 1852 when up to 10,000 yards of ticking and bed linen were urgently required. Few wards had the luxury of a change of linen and in the boys' department most of the inmates were actually lying on bare

28 *SR* 30 January 1851; *CE* 31 January 1851.

29 *SR* 22 May, 6 November 1851; 25 March 1852; *CUM* 5 November 1851.

30 *SR* 6 November 1851; 25 March 1852; *CC* 6 November 1851.

31 PP 1852-3 vol. LXXXIV, [513], *Abstract of Returns/Employment*, p. 26; see also, PP 1853, Vol., LXXXIV, [904], *Return from each Union in Ireland showing . . . the number of persons employed . . . for the year ending 29th September 1852*, etc.

32 *Poor Law Commissioners Annual Report* (1852), p 13; *SR* 1 April 1852.

straw and their beds were in a 'most shameful and disgraceful state and the ticks were fallen in pieces from rottenness'.[33]

Part of the problem arose from a reluctance by guardians to become involved in committees and proper stock checks were hardly ever undertaken in the house.[34] Many of the elected guardians rarely came to the workhouse, so meetings were badly attended. Internal committees, such as the house committee and finance committee, were riven by cliques and factions, often the result of religious or political affiliations, or sometimes simply personality differences, with some guardians refusing to work alongside others. As a result, the duties of large groups fell to a few willing members.[35] The efficiency of the house committee was undermined by the unwillingness of members to carry out their duties. The problem was highlighted in April 1852 when Richard Star, the new workhouse master, was unable to get adequate assistance from the guardians to carry out a proper stock check.[36] The indifference displayed by guardians was causing problems in other areas and the quality of work in the industrial department deteriorated during 1852. Frequently, members of the industrial committee were so disillusioned by the experience that they either resigned, or refused to allow their names go forward for a second term.[37] In disgust at the evident disorder and apathy, the *Southern Reporter* blamed the board. The 'condition of the paupers as to bedding, bed clothes, and habiliments, is asserted and admitted to be disgraceful; and everything indicates disorder and inattention. Surely this is discreditable to all parties concerned. What business have men seeking to be nominated guardians if they thus fail to discharge the duties they assume? We can find no excuse for their doing so, and we cannot avoid expressing our surprise at finding such an institution as the Workhouse, so shamefully managed in a locality like ours'.[38]

Little was done about the lack of bedding material and just a few beds were improved. The majority remained in a disgraceful condition with bed clothes rotting and filthy, the straw mattress filling had been

---

33 *CUM* 28 April 1852; *SR* 29 April 1852. This was not a new occurrence and on previous occasions extra inmates had to be put into each bed when fresh straw was unavailable for new mattresses. *CUM* 5 February 1851.

34 *SR* 15 April 1852; *CUM* 1 June, 17 August 1853, 5 April, 17 May 1854; *CUL* 7 June 1853.

35 *SR* 5 August, 7 August 1852.

36 *SR* 22 April, 29 April, 1 May, 20 May 1852; *CUL* 23 March 1852; *CE* 23 April 1852; Richard Star replaced George Carr as workhouse master. Star drowned in an accident at the Western Road Baths on 7 September 1852. William Fitzmaurice replaced him as workhouse master.

37 *SR* 29 July 1853; 20 January 1853.

38 *SR* 1 May 1852.

reduced to dust and the health of all the inmates was under threat.[39] Because of the lack of linen, most of the inmates could not wash their clothes and they were forced to wear the same underwear for weeks on end. Conditions in the boys' ward were appalling and one guardian complained that:

> On going through the house one day this week I found about forty or fifty of them huddled together in one corner of the room; to seeing them all miserable and dejected, I asked them why they sat there, and they said they sat together for the purpose of trying to keep them-selves warm; and in fact the rags upon their bodies were quite inadequate for the purpose; they were a mass of filth and rags, and the fetor arising from them was most disgusting. I went to another portion of the room and saw about forty or fifty more seated down, and on my asking them why they sat there instead of running about and trying to keep themselves warm, they said they were not able to do so, as their feet were too sore from the cold. Upon looking at their feet I saw that a good many had them bound up.[40]

In addition to footwear, the boys also needed clothing and Richard Dowden observed that so many of them required breeches that they were like 'highlanders'. The inadequacy of the industrial department as the sole source of materials for clothing was highlighted by this disgraceful situation, and before the end of 1852 the union had to spend £1,500 to purchase workhouse clothing.[41]

Some guardians believed that the industrial department was of little benefit to the ratepayers, and its only real value was that it helped keep inmates busy and boosted their morale. For others the department was a source of trouble, and was 'pregnant more with mischief than with good, and if continued should be purged and reformed'. This faction was convinced that many of the inmates in the industrial department did no work and although people were sitting at spinning wheels and other machinery, their contribution to the department's output was question-able. Guardians were of the opinion that many of the women who sat around in the department would be better employed at the capstan mill and a new rota was drawn up to include them at this work.[42]

The principal workhouse hospital department was situated in an old part of the complex, and the possibility of transferring its patients to the newer industrial building was discussed in 1853. Contributions to the

---

39 *SR* 1 July 1852, see also *CUL* 10 May 1853.
40 *SR* 18 November 1852.
41 *SR* 27 November 1852, 20 January 1853. The appalling condition of the male wards was recorded in an internal report *CUM* 17 November 1852.
42 *CUM* 7 April, 28 July 1852; *SR* 29 July, 5 August 1852.

discussion indicated that the former enthusiasm for workhouse industrial operations was on the wane. The justification for expending a large
amount of money in transferring the hospital and moving the industrial
machinery was questioned by some guardians. During the previous year,
up to 100 skilled women had received employment outside the workhouse and they in turn helped 50 friends leave the institution. As this had
saved the ratepayers up to £600 in one year, the city's Mayor, John
Francis Maguire, suggested that inmates be trained at plain work and
shirt making because skilled women were urgently required in these
industries. If the guardians scaled down the industrial department this
would result in 'an injury that all their cheese paring, their nibbling,
grinding, diminishing of salaries and harassing of officers, would never
compensate for'. The pleas of the Mayor were heeded and a committee
was appointed to investigate and report on the status of the industrial
activities.[43]

The next industrial department report, for the quarter ending March
1853, showed that goods were still being produced in the various workshops. The spinning room had 60 woollen wheels, 60 carders and three
winders at work, and flax was being processed by a variety of operators.
Goods such as men's and boys' shirts, women's and girls' wrappers,
petticoats, shifts and ticks had been finished and brought to the workhouse store. Production was down in the weaving room because
machines were out of order, skilled hands were scarce and boys were
operating the looms. Nonetheless, during March 1853, almost 2,000
yards of gingham, flannel and coarse linen had been manufactured. A
range of goods was made in the tailoring workshop but because 500 suits
were urgently required, it was decided to employ a skilled tailor to make
them on contract. The shoemaking and metalwork shops produced some
goods and although the carpentry workshop manufactured 209 coffins, a
skilled tradesman had been employed to supervise a small staff of
unskilled workers.[44] As the year progressed, demands for extra hands
occasionally disrupted the work of the industrial department.

Unlike the majority of Irish workhouses, the number of inmates in the
Cork institution increased during the 12 months to mid 1854. Factors
such as the large workhouse hospital were believed to have contributed,

---

43 *SR* 20 January 1853. During October 1853 applications were made to the work-
    house for able bodied workers. The few labourers in the house left for wages of 1s.
    6d. per day. This was the first ever application to the Cork workhouse for labour-
    ers. *CE* 2 October 1853.

44 *CUM* 6 April, 10 August 1853; *SR* 7 April 1853; *CUL* 22 February, 19 March, 27
    October 1853. During September 1853 fifty-six boys were receiving training as
    weavers, tailors, shoemakers and tinsmiths in the workhouse. Fifty-two girls were
    being trained at needlework. PP 1854, Vol. LV, [77], *Industrial Employment*, p 2.
    See also PP 1855, Vol. XLVII, [345], *Workhouse farm accounts*, pp. 2, 12-13.

but some observers blamed the decline in industrial operations for attracting lazy applicants. The lack of experience or training for inmates deprived them of the opportunity to develop a work ethic and made it almost impossible for them to leave the institution.[45] By September 1854 little industrial work was being carried out and most of the inmates were idle. Because of improvements in conditions outside, the skilled workers who formerly spearheaded the industrial operations had left the house and unskilled inmates or children carried out the work. Most of the industrial activities consisted of repairs and modifications, rather than the variety of manufacturing processes previously undertaken.[46] Although some fabric was produced, the majority of the materials for workhouse clothing had to be purchased from outside contractors. The absence of skilled hands made it necessary to put boys working in the bakery. The bread quality declined and the possibility of closing the bakery was discussed. To lose this department would have been a retrograde step, so the responsibility for improving conditions and providing better bread was transferred to the master baker.[47] The bakery workers were obliged to toil in hot and dusty conditions and when they applied for an increase in their daily allowance of milk from ½ pint to one pint, their request was sanctioned.[48] Because of a continuing deterioration in the quality of bread, the baker was dismissed in June 1855. A new master baker was employed at an increased salary of £1 per week, and thereafter few complaints were heard about the workhouse bread.[49]

The Capstan Mill

During the late 1840s the Hive Iron Works installed a capstan mill in the Cork county gaol, and soon after, a similar machine was ordered for the workhouse.[50] The workhouse industrial committee inspected the completed instrument and found that the machine

---

45 *CUM* 3 May 1854; *SR* 4 May, 17 June 1854.

46 *SR* 7 September 1854. Because of the lack of experience, unskilled hands frequently damaged raw materials. *CUM* 15 June 1853, 17 January, 7 February 1855.

47 *SR* 14 September 1854; *CUM* 12 July, 6 September 1854.

48 *SR* 31 March 1854; 9 February, 23 February, 3 March, 7 September, 19 October 1854; *CUM* 22 February, 1 March 1854; *CUL* 28 February, 2 March, 7 March, 13 September, 26 September, 3 October, 14 October, 24 October, 31 October 1854.

49 *CE* 6 June, 22 June 1855.

50 *SR* 16 November 1848, 6 January 1849; *CE* 17 November, 24 November 1848; see NAI, Poor Law Commissioners, Letters to James Burke 1849, 4 January 1849; PP 1849, Vol. XXVI, *27th Report of Inspector General of Prisons in Ireland*, Appendix, p. 75.

more than realises their most sanguine expectations as a labour test for the able-bodied male paupers; it is found to be most effective while it can be worked by all classes, boys, girls, men and women with advantage, and in the most satisfactory manner supplying the Establishment, at the cheapest rate, with an abundance of Indian meal and wholemeal of best quality, and thus materially improving the quality of the food, and thereby adding to the health and comforts of the inmates.[51]

The mill was manufactured and installed at a cost of £250 and from its commencement on 1 August 1849 to mid-September 321 bags of wholemeal and 184 sacks of Indian meal were produced. The mill was about the size of a threshing machine; it had two pairs of stones and was propelled by a wheel with 24 iron handles, each of which could be pushed by up to four people. Depending on the strength of the operators and the amount of work to be done it was possible to engage either one or both pairs of stones. When operated by able bodied men the two pairs of stones were engaged, but when manned by women or boys just one pair was used. A team of boys could grind about 1½ bags of wholemeal in an hour. Similar machines were installed in many Irish workhouses and most of the Tipperary institutions had capstan mills, which were regularly operated by children.[52]

While turning the mill, the women usually sang bawdy songs such as the *Jolly Butcher*, which had particularly offensive lyrics. On several occasions the workhouse chaplains came to the mill yard and spoke to the women about their behaviour and bad example to other inmates. The Poor Law Commissioners were also concerned about 'the corrupting influence which these songs are calculated to exercise on the minds of the female inmates especially the younger members of this class'.[53] As the mill was located near the women's quarters, a new WC had to be provided to prevent men 'straying from their work' and a ten feet high wall was built to enclose the mill yard. The miller in charge of the machine was paid £1 per week and a wardmaster was employed at 6s. per week to supervise the mill workers.[54]

The mill operated for eleven hours each day and work alternated between different categories of inmate. People who refused to participate

---

51 *CUM* 19 September 1849; *SR* 20 September 1849.
52 Anne M. Lanigan, *The Poor Law children of County Tipperary and their education 1840-1880* (M.Ed. thesis, UCC, 1988), p. 293.
53 *CUL* 17 June 1854; *SR* 20 September 1849, 10 December 1850, 25 March 1852, 27 May, 30 May 1854; see also *CUM* 16 September 1849, 20 February 1856.
54 *CUM* 2 May, 20 June, 29 August, 5 September, 16 September 1849; *SR* 21 April 1849. John Griffin, a former employee of Listowel workhouse replaced this miller John McCarthy, in January 1850. *CUL* 26 January 1850, 17 June 1851.

were either prosecuted or expelled from the house. Sometimes their diet was reduced to the 'idlers' allowance', as was the case when a group of women refused to work because they wanted to see 'how much annoyance they can give to subordinate officers placed over them'. Men were employed in teams of 100 for five hours, 150 boys operated the mill for three hours, 150 girls spent one hour at the task and 100 women turned the machinery for two hours each day.[55] The exercise of pushing the mill and breaking stones probably benefited the children but it also deprived them of exposure to school subjects which could have been useful in their future lives. Poor Law Commissioner John Ball was not impressed with industrial training in the Cork workhouse which was, he said, in June 1852, not 'by any means what it should be'.[56]

Commenting on the mill, a group of visitors recorded that they never saw

> a merrier set of fellows, than the boys, working the capstan-mill, singing in uproarious chorus, and varying the harmony with an occasional cheer; while grinding half a ton of flour an hour, for their own consumption. There was not a squalid or dejected face amongst them, and we are convinced that their natures are far less demoralised than those of the same class as we have seen them, in former years, loitering around the doors of filthy hovels.[57]

The enthusiasm witnessed on that day was not characteristic of the boys' normal behaviour. On many occasions the miller or the boys' teacher treated the lads like animals and used a stick or whip to force them to drive the mill faster. One day when the miller was particularly agitated, he threw a large stone at the group, causing serious head and facial injuries to one hapless lad.[58]

Because of the design and weight of the mill structure, it was virtually impossible to damage its mechanism under normal use. Close observation by the pauper operators eventually revealed some design defects and the women succeeded in breaking the mechanism by violently rocking the hand-wheel while turning the machine. Some of the ringleaders were put into solitary confinement and others were sentenced to a fortnight's

---

55 *CUM* 3 October 1849, 9 January, 13 May 1850, 20 May, 4 August, 18 August 1852, 1 September 1853, 5 December 1855; *SR* 10 January, 17 January, 3 October 1850.

56 PP 1852, Vol. VII, [515], *Report from the select committee on criminal and destitute juveniles; with the proceedings of the committee, minutes of evidence, appendix and index*, p. 347. See also *PP 1852-3, Vol. XXIII, [674], Report from the select committee on criminal and destitute children; together with the minutes of evidence and appendix*, p. IV.

57 *SR* 16 April 1850.

58 See also 3 October 1850; *CUM* 16 April 1851; *CUL* 28 April 1851.

hard labour in the county gaol. The other women on the mill at the time of the breakage had their milk allowance stopped, and were assigned to extra work duties. This dissatisfied guardians who believed that offenders should be severely reprimanded, and they sought to introduce a 'corrective element' into the industrial work.[59] The mill was so seriously damaged by male workers on 23 August 1852 that the machinery had to be completely dismantled and was out of action for a few weeks. Again, the ringleaders were punished and the guardians warned the inmates that if the mill was broken again, the entire workhouse, with the exception of children and infirm inmates, would have their food allowances 'reduced to the lowest possible scale, consistent with health'.[60]

Because of a reduction in the number of mature inmates, it became necessary to use young inmates to turn the mill, which disrupted their education. When hands were scarce they were taken to work at 10am and contrary to regulations, children under 10 years of age were often included in the team of 200 boys. After their time on the mill and a lunch break, the children went to their classrooms for just 1½ hours, instead of the regulatory 3 hours. Dr O Connor complained to the guardians that including the children on mill work 'merely made idiots of them, by sending them round and round'. The three sacks of meal ground by the boys saved the workhouse just 1s.10d. each day. In the opinion of many guardians, this paltry sum was worth more than the education of the children.[61] Dr O Connor later wrote on the plight of the children working the capstan mill: 'nearly one hundred of them being required to turn the mill, they clung to the handles as close as clustering bees; some pushed it, others only held on, and were dragged round; whilst the miller, being required to grind a certain quantity per hour, if the wheel did not move fast enough, came out and lashed the young slaves to his heart's content, without the possibility of his knowing who was the delinquent . . .'.[62]

Other than the bakery, the capstan mill provided the only regular industrial pursuit in the workhouse. During a review of industrial activities in October 1854, some guardians said that the milling operations were degrading, particularly for women who had come from respectable backgrounds. Frequently it proved difficult to get suitable inmates to turn the mill. The industrial committee recommended that the operation

---

59 *CUM* 4 August, 11 August, 18 August 1852; *SR* 12 August 1852.
60 *SR* 30 September 1852; *CUM* 25 August, 1 September, 29 September 1852. The Poor Law Commissioners advised that food could be stopped only from persons involved in damaging the machine. *CUM* 6 October 1852; *CUL* 5 October 1852.
61 *CUM* 25 May, 31 August 1853, 25 January 1854; *SR* 15 December 1853; *CC* 15 December 1853.
62 D. O Connor, *Seventeen years* of workhouse life (Dublin, 1861), pp. 49-50.

be discontinued and, instead, pumping water, 'the hardest labour in the house', be substituted as a workhouse test.[63] The board decided to discontinue using the mill and ground meal was purchased from outside contractors.[64] There were some subsequent discussions about modifying the mill to pump water but when the plan was not implemented, the guardians accepted an offer of £35 for the equipment[65] and its stones and machinery were dismantled before the end of 1859.[66]

Staff issues

Although unnecessary and irregular contact between workhouse staff and inmates was not encouraged or tolerated, many examples indicate that such interactions did occur. At the end of 1849, a wardmaster named John McDonnell was dismissed for repeated drunkenness and assault, and for using improper expressions to female inmates. On a number of occasions, he had invited women to his sleeping quarters and he regularly used indecent language towards them.[67] At around the same time a nurse named Kearney and a wardmaster named Thomas Collins resigned when the nurse gave birth in the house.[68]

Two years later a wardmaster named O Sullivan resigned when the workhouse master discovered 'that he had been guilty of acts of gross immorality' in the auxiliary house at South Terrace.[69] Again, on Monday 16 August 1852, the workhouse cook resigned from her post without notice. On the previous Saturday morning, shortly after midnight, the workhouse master had found her in the storekeeper's apartment 'under circumstances apparently calculated to excite suspicion'. Rather than face a probing interview, she left the institution without a regular

---

63 *CUM* 31 August 1853, 8 November 1854. When people applied for poor relief and were offered admission to the workhouse, it was anticipated that only those who were desperate for assistance would enter the institution. Thus, the concept of a 'workhouse test' was based on the premise that only the truly desperate would enter the workhouse.
64 *SR* 26 October 1854; *CC* 14 December 1854; *CUM* 27 December 1854, 31 December 1856.
65 *CUM* 14 January, 18 February, 25 February 1857.
66 *CC* 11 March 1859. That same year the position of workhouse weaver was abolished and the unused materials in storage were sold off. *CUM* 13 September 1854, 15 June, 24 August, 5 October, 12 October 1859; *SR* 9 May, 27 May, 10 August, 17 August, 30 November 1854.
67 *CUM* 12 September, 26 September 1849; *CC* 27 September 1849; SR 27 September, 11 October 1849; *CE* 27 September, 3 October, 11 October 1849. *CUL* 9 October 1849.
68 *CUM* 9 May, 16 May 1849.
69 *CUM* 29 January 1851.

discharge and the storekeeper also resigned.[70] Similarly, when the work-house master detected the baker and some patients in company with female deputy nurses, he asked the guardians to replace the deputies with males 'for the better preservation of morality and classification'.[71] An allegation that a wardmaster named John Clark had caught hold of an inmate and had taken 'liberties of a highly improper nature with her', was investigated in April 1855. When the inquiry failed to establish that the man was not guilty of the charge, a sealed order for his dismissal was issued.[72] Again, in August 1858 two staff members were dismissed when Rev. Clifford found that a wardmaster named Hudson had gone to the quarters of wardmistress Berry without authorisation.[73] During November 1860, the master carried out a search of the workhouse premises for two prostitutes who were missing from their wards. He noticed that a privy door near the female hospital was open and 'on entering cautiously with his dark lantern, he found the girl Cunningham, and Con Mulcahy, a pauper assistant in the stores, lying together; a little further on he found the other girl Hanora Horgan' with Richard Barrett, a porter's messen-ger. A number of bottles of alcohol were later found on the premises. The two men were prosecuted for their action and received sentences of one month's imprisonment with hard labour.[74]

Sometimes serious consequences resulted from unauthorised liaisons in the workhouse. When a nursing assistant named Margaret Mahony threw herself from a window in the workhouse a subsequent investiga-tion established that she was having an affair with John O Connor, a ward master. O Connor's mother, Mrs Knowles, who worked as a hospi-tal nurse, had intervened to break up the relationship and attempted to have Mahony dismissed from her job in the hospital area. In desperation, Mahony, who had previously aborted a pregnancy, attempted suicide by jumping from the window. Following the investigation, O Connor and his mother were dismissed from their employment at the workhouse,[75] and it seems that Mahony survived the attempt on her own life.

In their weekly report of 10 October 1878, the workhouse visiting committee criticised night watchman Thomas Moore for having, some time previously, taken a girl named Mary Egan out of the house, to work as a servant. Although they had interviewed the girl's mother and some

---

70 *CUM* 18 August 1852; *CUL* 31 August 1852.
71 *CUM* 28 April 1852.
72 *CC* 19 April 1855; *CUL* 17 April 1855
73 *CUM* 13, 20, 27 October, 3 November 1858.
74 *CUM* 14, 21 November 1860; *Visiting Committee Minute Book, BGFM– FM1*, 13 November 1860.
75 *CE* 15, 30 June, 6 July 1865; *CC* 7 July 1865; *CUL* 14, 27 June, 5 July 1865; *CUM* 8, 15, 22 June 1865.

workhouse staff, they found no evidence against Moore who was living with his wife and family. Nonetheless, they were uneasy about the incident and concluded that the girl had been removed under very suspicious circumstances.[76] Further inquiries brought mixed results but no evidence of any actual wrongdoing. Some witnesses thought that Moore had used the influence of his position and 'coaxed' the girl out of the house against the wishes of her mother and the Sisters of Mercy. Even though it was said that the girl had subsequently gone 'on the town', the Local Government Board were reluctant to initiate a full-scale inquiry.[77] Moore may have escaped, but within days, an inmate named Mary Lynch alleged that he had been guilty of immoral conduct with her in the workhouse. The Board lost no further time and an inquiry under Poor Law Inspector, Dr Mc Cabe commenced on 10 December 1878.[78]

In a preliminary statement, the inspector outlined the charge against Moore. Evidence was then heard. Mary Lynch recalled that on 31 December 1876 she was sentenced to two days in the workhouse punishment cell for singing an improper song. During the night Moore came to the cell and asked if she was asleep; she answered and he returned a little later at around midnight. This time he came into the cell 'and committed an indecent offence on her against her will'. In her submission she claimed that 'in consequence of her fall with Moore she became unfortunate' (i.e. a prostitute).[79] In her evidence at the hearing Lynch repeated these details. She claimed that, although she did not scream, she resisted Moore as much as she could. She left the workhouse two days later but did not tell anyone about what had taken place. On the following April she was refused admission to the workhouse. During the next year and a half she spent periods of time in a variety of locations. Following her refusal at the workhouse she met an agent of the Protestant Refuge on Patrick Street and accepted an offer of accommodation. She remained in the refuge for about six months but after a row with another inmate, she was transferred to a Protestant Home in Dublin. After another eleven months or so, she left the home and went to the Catholic High Park Convent, from where she was placed in employment in a private house. Her unsettled existence continued and she returned to Cork, and spent time in the Protestant Refuge, the city gaol and the Good Shepherd's Convent. Through the agency of a letter from Rev Michael O Flynn CC, St Peter and Paul's, she was readmitted to the workhouse on 23 November 1878. During her two months stay at the Good Shepherd's Convent she became

76 *CUM* 10 October 1878; *CE* 11 October 1878.
77 *CUM* 17 October, 7, 14 November 1878; *CE* 8, 15 November 1878.
78 *CUM* 28 November 1878; *CE* 29 November, 6 December 1878.
79 *CUM* 28 November 1878; *CE* 11 December 1878.

friendly with Mary Egan and they exchanged stories about Thomas Moore.

The inquiry lasted for three days and much of the evidence sheds light in a side of workhouse life which was generally obscured beneath the mundanity of the everyday routine. Moore's former servant Mary Egan, was brought from the Good Shepherd's Convent to testify at the hearing. The 20-year-old young woman, who had had a baby when she was fourteen years of age, claimed that Moore had seduced her; it is not clear if this took place in the workhouse or during her four months service at his house. Julia Byrne related that she worked as a night assistant in the hospital kitchen and that she and Moore had frequently been intimate both there and in other parts of the workhouse. She claimed that Moore had first 'committed himself' with her in the kitchen during 1877. Under questioning she admitted that she had previously accused another man of taking advantage of her, but she qualified this by saying that on that occasion, she thought that she was pregnant. She claimed that she knew of the relationship between Thomas Moore and Mary Lynch for some time, and her main reason for giving evidence was because she believed that Moore had wronged her. Mary Lynch's professed innocence was somewhat undermined by George Irwin who worked as a special hospital assistant. In his evidence he related that he and Lynch had engaged in 'repeated acts of immorality' in the workhouse prior to December 1876, and that she had even visited his wife in their home.

Evidence was also taken from staff members and Richard Steele, the workhouse master, said that Mary Lynch had first come to his attention in September 1876 for refusing to go to Mass and for singing immoral songs. She had been confined in the punishment cells on a number of occasions but no complaints about Moore's behaviour had been made by her, or by any other inmate subjected to solitary confinement. In view of the evidence, he admitted that the policy of having females inspected by male staff would have to be reviewed, as also would the practice of allowing female staff work during the night.

In his own evidence, and predictably, Moore denied that there was any truth in the accusations by Mary Lynch and Julia Byrne. He was emphatic that he had never entered the punishment cells when he checked the occupants at night. Although he had never received written instructions, he had performed his duties as conscientiously as possible during the six years he had been employed in the workhouse. Fr Timothy Murphy who also gave evidence, admitted that he had advised workhouse staff that certain keys in Moore's possession should be given instead to a female night nurse. Fr Murphy had been alerted to this danger in a conversation with Sr. Paul, the principal Sister of Mercy in the workhouse. He had also received indications about Moore's behaviour from other sources – no doubt the workhouse gossip had found its way to his ears.

The Local Government Board was satisfied that the weight of evidence against Moore, although conflicting in some details, proved his guilt. It ruled that 'he is unfit to be longer employed as a paid servant of the union'. On receipt of this judgement, Moore was dismissed from his position in the Cork workhouse.[80]

The almost unrestrained movement of inmates throughout the workhouse received some attention in the wake of the revelations at the Thomas Moore inquiry. This had long been a problem in the institution with women almost routinely going to different departments to talk and gossip. Many of the women moving around the complex were hospital employees bringing food and refreshments from the kitchen to different wards. Laundry workers and messengers also roamed through different areas.[81] Following an evaluation of the situation the guardians agreed that a number of changes should be introduced. These included:

- The introduction of separate visiting days for male, female and dangerously ill inmates.
- Repositioning the workhouse entrance gate.
- Controlling and regulating visits to the workhouse chapel by prior arrangements between chaplains and the master.
- Locking all departmental dividing doors
- Introducing different lock patterns for male and female divisions.[82]

In spite of these precautions, irregularities continued. In March 1882 Dr Brodie conducted an investigation into the circumstances surrounding the birth of a child to an unmarried inmate named Margaret Gates. The 22-year-old woman who had entered the workhouse with her mother and brother a few years previously, and had left the institution only on one occasion for five and a half hours in April 1881, gave birth to her infant in February 1882. An anonymous letter to the workhouse master credited Gerard Fitzgerald, the son of the institution's storekeeper and his hospital nurse wife, with fathering the baby. The Fitzgerald family's quarters were on the workhouse premises and 22-year-old Gerard, who lived outside, enjoyed unhindered access to his parents' residence. He usually took his meals in the workhouse and often remained on the premises until a late hour in the evening. For a few months between May and August 1881 he worked as a temporary workhouse clerk but he resigned this position on 18 August because of alleged ill-health.

---

80 *CUM* 26 December 1878; *CE* 29 November, 6, 11, 12, 14, 27 December 1878.
81 *CE* 11 July 1861, 8, 15 October 1875, 9 February 1877
82 *CUM* 2, 9 January 1879; *CE* 3, 10, 17 January 1879.

During questioning at the inquiry Margaret Gates told of how she had met Fitzgerald when she worked in the house laundry and kitchen. Prior to their meeting, she never had sexual experience and she became pregnant in the period before Fitzgerald worked as an officer in the house. When it became known, at four months, that she was pregnant she was spirited away to the hospital. For the remaining five months of her pregnancy no doctor examined the hapless girl. The workhouse authorities must have had a good idea of who fathered the child but the woman's rejection was accentuated because 'no officer of the house nor anybody ever asked me how the thing occurred or inquired of me who was the father of the child'. Perhaps it was not without coincidence that three months before the baby was born, the workhouse authorities prohibited male relations of staff from visiting their families in the institution.

Although evidence was taken from Margaret Gates and her mother and from various staff members, inmates and the Catholic chaplain, almost inexplicably, it was decided that there was no necessity to examine Gerard Fitzgerald. Before the hearing ended its emphasis changed and it was concluded that 'the only question was the credulity of the girl, Margaret Gates, and the unsatisfactory character of her evidence was shown by the discrepancy between her statement and that of her mother'. The young woman was certainly treated shamefully by her banishment to the infirm ward for the concluding months of her pregnancy. The failure by the authorities to pursue the matter and publicly identify the child's father was a dereliction of responsibility and it must be concluded that they were not interested in pinpointing the perpetrator.[83] For their part, the Local Government Board concluded that Dr Brodie's investigation had revealed 'a lack of discipline and absence of supervision, very much to be deplored'. They criticised the matron for her failure to have the pregnant woman medically examined. The master and porter were also criticised for allowing people to visit the workhouse without recording the relevant details.[84] A couple of years later a ward master named Mulligan was dismissed for an alleged indecent assault on a girl in the workhouse.

Indiscretions were not confined to workhouse employees and sometimes external agents were penalised for poor behaviour. The Cork Union relieving officers were expected to establish if applicants were in need and entitled to workhouse relief. Occasionally, undeserving applicants, such as women who claimed to have been deserted by their husbands, succeeded in getting workhouse tickets. Subsequent investigation established that their husbands were at work outside the

83 *CC* 8 March 1882; *CE* 8, 10 March 1882; *CUM* 9, 16 February, 23 March 1882.
84 *CE* 24 March 1882; *CE* 18 June 1886.

institution.[85] In general, it was difficult for strangers to get a workhouse ticket from the relieving officers, and as a result many poor people ended up as vagrants, or in gaol. Relieving officers were occasionally criticised by the guardians for refusing tickets to people who were genuinely destitute. Desperate applicants sometimes retaliated and attacked the officers, for which they were later jailed.[86] On one occasion when a former inmate named Ellen Mahony wanted to return to the workhouse, a man at the dispensary told her to bark at the official when she met him and he would give her the ticket. A short time later, the simple woman located the official in the city market. She commenced barking and when he ambled away, she ran after him and bit him on the leg. Although she was charged with assault, the magistrates dropped the case and she was admitted to the workhouse.[87]

The relieving officers were not above reproach and abuse of their positions was sometimes detected.[88] An allegation by Rev. Alexander Peyton, parish priest of Blarney, of immoral behaviour against Robert Wiseman, the local relieving officer led to an inquiry in May 1853. Wiseman was accused of being a person of immoral and intemperate habits, and of having impregnated a woman named Margaret Donoghue and seducing a Mary Lenihan. In evidence at the inquiry, Rev. Peyton stated that a daughter had been born to Wiseman and 26-year-old Donoghue in the Cork workhouse. Wiseman admitted that he had a poor reputation in his parish, but dismissed the allegations as hearsay. The workhouse records were produced to show that the child had been born on 28 March and baptised in the house on 8 April. The midwife confirmed that the baby had been registered as Margaret Wiseman, and Rev. Peyton said that it was well known that the couple had had another child. Constable William Hannan of Whitechurch confirmed that Wiseman had a reputation of associating with loose women, and he was aware of Donoghue's claim that Wiseman was the father of her child. Under subsequent questioning, Wiseman eventually admitted that he had connections with both Donoghue and Lenihan.[89] Having considered the evidence, the Poor Law Commissioners were not convinced that Wiseman's behaviour was immoral, but they directed the board of guardians to take careful notice of his future behaviour.[90] Wiseman was arrested for being drunk and disorderly in

---

85 *SR* 30 May 1850.
86 *CUM* 6 November 1850, 12 February 1851; *SR* 7 November 1850, 11 January 1851.
87 *CC* 23 and 24 July 1867.
88 *CUM* 23, 30 July. 13 August 1851.
89 *CC* 21 May 1853; SR 5, 12, 21 May 1853, *CUL* 26 April 1853.
90 *SR* 2, 6 June 1853; *CUL* 31 May 1853.

the city during August 1853. His behaviour was reported to the Commissioners and he was dismissed from his position.[91]

Able-bodied inmates

In return for board and lodgings, able-bodied applicants were required to carry out labour tasks in the workhouse. This could consist of routine duties such as unloading carts, breaking stones, sweeping and tidying, burying deceased paupers, or more specialist tasks like repairing and maintaining buildings and grounds, catering, or nursing duties. Few guardians appreciated that this contributed to the efficient running of the workhouse machine, but the value of this labour became painfully clear when the guardians spoke of discharging able-bodied residents. In July 1874, when it was decided to discharge 58 men, an evaluation of their status showed that over 50 were engaged at different activities around the house. Despite the incredulity of some guardians, money was actually saved by the presence of the able-bodied inmates.[92] On another occasion when there were about 80 male and 160 female able-bodied inmates in the house, it was established that 17 men worked as hospital assistants, six worked as scavengers, 10 assisted in the bakery and others were employed in the store, the dining hall, the shoemakers' workshop and elsewhere. The women also worked at various tasks, with the majority being employed in the hospital.[93] Although some inmates were classed as able-bodied, in reality many were unfit, and when a recruiting sergeant came to the workhouse during 1876 he identified only five men who were fit enough to join the army.[94]

Many guardians were opposed to admitting able-bodied men and, as a deterrent or labour-test for frivolous applicants, short-term residents or tramps were expected to break a quantity of stones before their breakfast and leaving the house. Other methods were also used to discourage casual applicants. Occasionally the regulation that new arrivals should be given a bath, in water heated to a temperature of 80°, was ignored. Instead, casuals and tramps were subjected to a cold bath – frequently in water which had been used by other applicants – and reminded that they would have to break a certain quantity of stones before breakfast. The normal practice of fumigating or disinfecting clothing was rarely implemented for these short-term residents. The consequences were not

---

91 *SR* 11, 18 August, 8, 22 September 1853; Wiseman resigned officially in August 1853 and Christopher Crofts was elected as replacement relieving officer for Whitechurch in September. *CUM* 24, 31 August 1853; *CUL* 5, 16 August 1853.
92 *CE* 3 July, 10 July 1874, 9 April, 10 September 1875; see also *CC* 28 March 1861.
93 *CE* 28 January, 7 April 1876.
94 *CE* 2 February 1877.

always pleasant or healthy, and occasionally casuals with clothing 'full of vermin, and in the most loathsome state', mixed with other inmates in the probationary ward. The tramps got little sympathy from the guardians, one of whom contemptuously observed that 'it was monstrous to be making the place pleasant for tramps and casuals'.[95] The contempt with which the casuals were held is illustrated by the guardians' decision to feed them on waste bread which formerly had been assigned to the workhouse pigs. Singling out tramps and able-bodied applicants for a cold bath was a breach of regulations. The policy was reviewed and, the guardians decided that if the master wished to single out applicants for a cold bath, this would first have to be approved by the medical officers.[96]

Many guardians resented the presence of tramps and other able-bodied casuals and at harvest time in 1881 the board decided to expel most of the 80 able-bodied men from the house. About two dozen were brought to the board room and, on being informed of the decision, many protested, saying that they didn't have suitable clothing. Some guardians were sympathetic but the master warned that most of the men would pawn the clothes, drink the money and return to the house in a destitute condition. His views were accepted and when the men left the house they were given the worst possible clothing from the store. This ensured that the clothes would be of little value to pawnbrokers, but it also diminished the men's chances of getting employment. A more civilised method of clearing the house was adopted in 1883 when notices on the availability of harvest workers were posted in churches and other public places.[97]

The deterrent of stone breaking continued and many of the able-bodied inmates spent about seven hours each day in a large shed smashing an average of 1¼ cwts. of material. To make the task more soul-destroying, some guardians wanted to increase the quantity of stone broken and others sought to separate the men by confining each of them to a small compartment. From a safety point of view, this may have been sensible because flying chips of stone certainly posed a danger to fellow workers. This was recognised by the medical officers who asked the guardians to issue wire mesh eye protectors to the stone breakers. Road contractors and builders used the finely pounded stone but frequently, hundreds of tons were accumulated in the workhouse grounds because customers were unwilling to pay the 2s. 6d. per ton demanded by the guardians.[98] Many of the casuals admitted to the workhouse were 'tramping' workers en-route to employment or searching for jobs. They

95 *CE* 10 October, 19 December 1879; *CUM* 9, 23 October 1879.
96 *CE* 12 September, 24 October 1879; *CUM* 9, 23 October 1879.
97 *CE* 5, 12 August 1881, 31 August 1883.
98 *CE* 4 November 1881, 2 June 1882; *CUM* 6 January, 27 October, 10, 17 November 1881.

could not afford to pay for accommodation and had no choice but to seek workhouse relief. This practice was resented by some guardians who wanted the men to be jailed for vagrancy; others took a more humane approach and accepted that the sojourn in the house was in fact a temporary inconvenience for the men. Because the men had to break stones before leaving the house, it was usually around mid-day before they got on the road. Then, they were faced with the prospect of tramping for days or even weeks, before they located employment. Although there was a market for the broken stone, little profit was realised because the raw material cost 2s.5½d. per ton, and the finished product was sold for 2s.6d. or even less. By the end of the 1880s the demand for broken stones had slackened and few were being broken in the workhouse.[99]

The Local Government Board was fully aware that casual labourers frequently used the workhouse ward as an overnight stopover while searching for employment. During 1887 a circular issued by the Board advised boards of guardians that, because the current trade depression was forcing workers to migrate in search of employment, they should be lenient when approached for provisional relief. Nonetheless, the Local Government Board stipulated that everyone admitted to a workhouse would have to be subjected to the regulations regarding searches, clothing, cleanliness, etc.[100]

Workhouse inmates were employed as pauper assistants in various locations throughout the house. As a reward for their labour they were given extra rations, which sometimes included expensive food or beverages when the work was particularly onerous. Between 1870 and 1884 the number of such assistants increased from 113 to 244. Although they were a convenient labour force, some of them were costing between 3s. 0¼d. to 4s.10d. per week, which was considered excessive when compared with the 1s. 4½d. needed to maintain an able-bodied inmate with the cheapest diet in the institution. During 1884 a workhouse review committee made some sweeping suggestions about reducing the number of paupers receiving extra allowances. This, it was calculated would save about £140 per annum. Included was a suggestion that the food allowances for cleaners, laundry workers, servants and assistant teachers should be reduced.[101]

Pauper assistants in the hospital and other parts of the workhouse were usually supplied with uncooked rations of meat and tea which allowed them make their own arrangements for preparing their meals.

---

99 *CE* 22 September 1882, 26 October 1883, 10 January, 11 April 1884, 11 January 1887; *CUM* 12 January, 16 February 1882; see also NAI, CSORP 1883 1192.
100 *CE* 10 June 1887; *Poor Law Commissioners Annual Report* (1888), pp. 61-2.
101 *CE* 18 July, 3 October, 19 October 1884, see also *CUM* 18 September, 25 September 1879.

When the guardians decided to discontinue this privilege in 1886 the assistants withdrew their labour. Chaos resulted in some parts of the workhouse and in the hospital the medical officers found great difficulty in carrying out treatments. Although some guardians relished the confrontation, the majority decided to resume the food allowances before a stalemate was reached.[102] Following a recommendation by the Poor Law Inspector, Colonel Spaight, the extra food allowances were again withdrawn in 1888. An assistant, who was detailed to the task of regularly cleaning a faulty sewer pipe, discontinued his work as a reprisal against the new directive. Within a short time, the area around the male hospital became flooded with liquid and raw sewage. The master was directed to order each of the 97 able-bodied inmates in the workhouse to undertake the cleaning operation. This was not successful and within a couple of weeks the medical officer reported that as the faulty sewer pipe had not been cleared, the basement division of the hospital, which contained 70 patients, was again flooded with sewage and foul water. Soon, other pauper assistants discontinued working when their extra rations were stopped. Wagon-men refused to clean the yards. Hospital work was neglected and when the assistants refused to remove the body of a deceased woman, a number of lunatics were deployed to do the job.

When bakery helpers left their work three extra bakers had to be employed immediately at 5s.4d. each per day. The guardians were working to the letter of Colonel Spaight's directive that no able-bodied men should receive extra rations, but when they discussed the situation they decided that because of its heavy and onerous labour, the bakery could be considered as an exception. Such concern for hardship inflicted on the inmates was uncharacteristic of the Cork board of guardians. In reality, the rations were re-introduced because it had become necessary to replace able-bodied assistants with paid workers from outside. The practice of deploying workhouse inmates to assist with labour tasks in the institution was set to continue for many years.

By the start of 1884 the little industrial work carried out in the Cork workhouse consisted mainly of stone breaking by able-bodied men. A certain amount of industrial activity was provided for children. About three-dozen boys worked for some hours each day in the various work-shops and another six dozen were employed in the gardens. All the boys attended school for three and a half-hours each day. They had three half hour breaks during the day, were taken for an hour's outdoor exercise and in the evening they spent one and a half hours on home exercise and revision. The somewhat casual approach to cultivating the workhouse grounds was counter-productive and gave the young workers a totally

---

102 *CE* 13 August, 1 October, 22 October 1886.

misleading impression about agricultural production.[103] The Cork Ratepayers' Association was annoyed about the lack of a structured approach and in a letter to the Local Government Board it complained that the girls had no proper training unit and that the boys' programme in gardening and shoemaking was casual.[104] The ratepayers' assessment was correct and many guardians had no interest in inculcating skills. Children working as garden helpers, trades assistants, kitchen hands, laundry workers or merely mending their own clothes were doing jobs which assisted the running of the workhouse machine. The exposure to industrial, domestic and agricultural skills was for the most part incidental and amounted to basic exploitation.

Conclusion

As well as benefiting the workhouse budgets, industrial pursuits kept occupants busy, but, in general, a reluctance to develop a worthwhile industrial programme deprived inmates of useful new skills. The attitude of the Cork guardians towards the workhouse inmates is clearly illustrated by their cruel and insensitive approach to industrial activities. The children's experience was limited principally to sewing or house work for girls or a little gardening, shoemaking or tailoring for boys. This gesture was of little value and merely clashed with classroom work. Because of the absence of quality training in the South Dublin Union, it was said that many of the girls who were discharged from that workhouse 'had no means of earning their bread honestly, and that there was scarcely a resource left to them when turned from the workhouse door, but prostitution'.[105] It has been remarked that training for boys in workhouses was 'not intended as a future livelihood but a general experience of work discipline in a skilled but demonstrable craft, in which output was clearly related to effort'.[106] The primary objective was to make the workhouse as unattractive as possible. Inmates were exploited by being forced to engage in 'irksome' employment and others were rewarded with a token helping of extra food in return for long hours of labour. Applications for a short residency in the house were discouraged by a regime of degrading treatment and penal stone breaking. The poor did not benefit from this image of the workhouse. The only winners were the ratepayers who saved money because unpaid inmates were carrying out many duties,

---

103 *CE* 24 January, 29 January, 15 February, 18 July 1884.
104 *CE* 4 April 1884; NAI, CSORP 1884 23794; *Amended Report of committee into internal management of Cork workhouse* (Cork, 1884), pp. 6-7.
105 *CE* 22 June 1861.
106 Francis Duke, 'Pauper Education', in, D. Fraser (ed.), *The New Poor Law in the nineteenth century* (London, 1976), p. 84.

applicants were discouraged and the expenditure on rates was reduced. In the adult sphere, industry was used as a form of discipline and the penal tasks of stone breaking and oakum picking have an enduring and negative connection with the popular image of workhouse life.

7 Health I

In common with other aspects of workhouse life and administration, the provision of health care was inextricably linked to concerns about expenditure. The quality of care for inmates was dependent on decisions made by the guardians at their weekly meetings. Some guardians were determined to keep workhouse expenditure at the lowest possible level. Consequently, ill-considered, hasty or mischievous decisions often resulted in misery in the hospital and workhouse wards. Misery and discomfort also resulted from the practice of overcrowding beds and wards; again, the cause was frequently related to an unwillingness to raise the required finance by increasing rates. An ambivalent attitude towards improving sanitation and hygiene also contributed to poor health in the workhouse. The spread of sickness and disease was assisted by the poor diet, overcrowding and bad sanitation.

In the post-famine years, the workhouse gradually assumed the role of Cork's largest hospital for the poor. To cater for the change, additional buildings were provided for fever and other patients. Additional staff were employed and nursing nuns entered the hospital in the early 1870s.

Care of Children

During 1849 and 1850 numerous complaints were heard about the poor conditions and treatment accorded to the workhouse children.[1]

The quality and quantity of their food was questioned and one guardian warned that they 'were literally pining away from downright want of proper nourishment'.[2] Periodic investigations and reviews of

---

1 *CUM* 13 June, 11 July 1849; 16 January, 11 July, 1 July, 22 August, 11 September, 18 September, 9 October 1850; *CUL* 7 July, 1849; 28 February, 6 April 1850; *SR* 14 June, 12 July, 1849; 12 September, 19 September 1850. For the Poor Law Commissioners' guidelines on workhouse dietary scales, see *Poor Law Commissioners Annual Report* (1849), Appendix, A, Guidelines on workhouse dietary scales, Article, 13, pp. 63-5.
2 *CUM* 25 September 1850, *SR* 19 September, 26 September 1850; *CE* 20 September 1850; *CC* 19 September, 26 September 1850.

the food allowances were undertaken by internal committees. On one occasion, when it emerged that the 1s.6d. per day required to maintain an inmate in Cork exceeded other workhouses by up to 4½d., some guardians attributed this to excessive food allowances. Further investigation showed that the allowances in some of the unions were below the Poor Law Commissioners minimum recommendations. The investigating committee recommended that the coarse bread issued to Cork's two to five year old children be replaced by household quality bread. The matter was debated at subsequent meetings and opposing guardians vied with each other to secure an increase or a decrease in the dietary scales. Guardian Foster presented evidence to show that most of the dietary classes were in receipt of excessive allowances. Other guardians were concerned that the health of young children was being damaged by the substitution of skimmed milk in place of the fresh produce. Captain Martin accused the board of targeting 'those who were unable to state their case themselves – who were unprotected either by strength or friends – who were unable to tell that board their sufferings – their distress – and the actual starvation they were labouring under'. Eventually, following an address by Dr D. C. O Connor on the necessity of providing proper food to young children, the board agreed to implement a new dietary scale, which did produce improvements in the children's health.[3]

During September 1850 the workhouse medical officers carried out an investigation, which showed that infants under two years of age were accommodated in a new, well-ventilated building. Most were in good health and cared for by their mothers or by nurses. Women who breastfed the orphan children were given a small gratuity as a reward for this service. The Poor Law Commissioners frowned on this and advised the guardians to discontinue the practice. Should an 'unwillingness of nursing females to render this service to motherless infants' result', the Commissioners advised the guardians that 'the course often adopted in private families of bringing up children by hand, should be resorted to'. The Commissioners had already criticised the guardians for rewarding inmates who acted as hospital nurses or assistants. Such remuneration was not permitted under the 21st article of workhouse regulations, but the Commissioners conceded that they would 'not object to such allowances of rations to nurses who sit up at night, as the medical officers may deem to be actually necessary'. The allowances were withdrawn in November 1850 and soon the workhouse officials were urgently seeking wet nurses for some neglected children.[4]

---

3 *CE* 27 June 1851.
4 *CUM* 23 January 1850, 19 June, 23 October, 6 November, 27 November 1850, 25 June 1851; *CUL* 13 February, 13 March 1849; 27 June, 16 July 1850.

Classification of Inmates for workhouse dietary scale

Class 1	Able-bodied working males
Class 2	Able-bodied working females
Class 3	Aged and Infirm persons, of either sex and adults above fifteen years of age, not working
Class 4	Boys and Girls above nine and under 15 years of age
Class 5	Children above five and under 9 years of age
Class 6	Children above two and under five years of age
Class 7	Infants under two years of age.

(From *PLC Annual report* 1849, Appendix A – workhouse regulations, p. 63)

The medical officers were particularly concerned about the 389 two-to-four year-old children, of whom 227 were deserted or orphans. Just 52 remained under the care of their mothers. The others 'are either without parents or separated from them by the rules of the house at an age when they have not intelligence to state their wants'. Because of an absence of suitable accommodation, 86 of these children were detained in hospital or infirm wards and interspersed with other children; consequently they received little attention and mortality was high. Overcrowding was common in the hospital and in some wards four patients occupied each bed; in the children's area, six to eight boys or girls slept together in one bed.[5] Their clothing and footwear were inadequate and although the medical officer's report was compiled in the late autumn of 1850, the young girls were still clad in light summer dresses. The doctors recommended that these children should be provided with first-class or, 'household' quality bread, given better accommodation, a spacious day-room and a grassed area for outdoor exercise.

When the guardians discussed the medical officers' report it emerged that just two nurses were in charge of five wards that housed 250 children. Some of the children were unwell and because of the nature of their illness they 'broke out in eruptions'. The guardians eventually resolved to give the infants fresh milk, and voted in favour of providing household quality bread to the two-to-five year-old children.[6] On receipt of the guardians' minutes, the Poor Law Commissioners responded by pointing out that according to the workhouse rules, children under five years of age should be provided with three meals a day. As the children were unable to consume their entire meal at dinnertime,

---

5 See *CUM* 23 January 1850. Overcrowding of hospital and workhouse beds was not uncommon, see for instance Helen Burke, *People and Poor Laws* (West Sussex, 1987), pp. 93-4; Eamon Lonergan, *A workhouse story: A history of St. Patrick's hospital, Cashel, 1842-1992* (Clonmel, 1992), p. 36.

6 *CUM* 2 October, 9 October 1850; *SR* 3 October 1850.

many retained their bread and nibbled on it for the rest of the day. This was unsatisfactory, as there was no guarantee that each unsupervised child was allowed to consume a proper allocation of food. The Commissioners demanded that children aged between two and fifteen years should be provided with a supervised supper to ensure that each of them had a sufficient quantity of food.[7]

Poor food and conditions did have serious consequences for the workhouse children, and during 1851 the Commissioners alerted boards of guardians to the danger of ophthalmia in workhouses and asked for co-operation in controlling the disease. They recommended the separation of ophthalmia cases from other hospital patients and the regular fumigating and disinfecting of wards. Other measures suggested were the provision of exercise facilities, a good supply of fresh water and utensils, and towels for washing.[8] The Commissioners' advice was based on investigations undertaken by Dr Arthur Jacob in December 1849 and by Sir William Wilde in August 1850. Dr Jacob's examination of children stricken with ophthalmia during an outbreak in Athlone workhouse established that about 16 per cent of the girls and 5 per cent of the boys were affected. Blaming a poor diet, lack of exercise and overcrowding for the prevalence of the disease, he made a number of suggestions for improving the children's dietary scale.[9] Following Sir William Wilde's investigation into an outbreak of the disease in the Tipperary workhouse, he also made some recommendations. These included the provision of 'good wholesome bread and milk or stirabout and milk, as well as some broth containing fresh vegetables' for the young inmates. For sicker children, he suggested that cod-liver oil should be issued once or twice during the day. He was critical of the workhouse washing facilities

---

7 *SR* 19 October 1850; *CUL* 5 October, 15 October 1850. The divergence between the diet of Irish and English workhouse inmates is starkly evident in published dietary scales. See for instance the menus of Islington and Whitechapel unions in 1860. In the latter workhouse, children received meat and potato dinners, fruit jam and rice puddings on a number of days in the week. PP 1861, Vol. IX, [323], Second *Report from Select Committee on Poor Relief (England)*, pp. 185-88. In 1852 Dr John Forbes also highlighted the contrast between the Irish and English workhouse diets. John Forbes, *Memorandums made in Ireland in the autumn of 1852* (London, 1853), Vol. II, pp. 229-34.

8 *CUM* 2 July, 16 July 1851; *SR* 3 July, 17 July 1851; *20th Annual Report of Strand Road Dispensary, for year ending 30 June 1851*, in NAI, CSORP 1852 H6025; *Poor Law Commissioners Annual Report* (1852), pp. 14-15, 114; see also *Poor Law Commissioners Annual Report*, (1851), pp. 127-9.

9 *Poor Law Commissioners Annual Report* (1851), pp. 130-33.

and the scarcity of water buckets and towels, which meant that up to 60 children had to share face cloths, thus facilitating the spread of contagious disease.[10]

Although over 3,000 cases of ophthalmia were treated in the Cork workhouse between 1849 and 1851, the local medical officers were satisfied that few suffered any long-term injury to their sight.[11] The Cork guardians implemented some of the Poor Law Commissioners' recommendations relating to sanitation and organised a number of physical activities for the children. Proper diagnosis of ophthalmia was complicated because children who wanted to be admitted to hospital or escape school put irritants such as lime, urine or the juice of the 'birds' milk' plant (euphorbium) into their eyes. As a response to this 'vicious practice', the medical officers altered the diet for children suffering from certain eye complaints, and staff were warned to be vigilant in detecting self-mutilation. Captain George Huband, the Poor Law Inspector, investigated the matter and discovered that the practice of self-mutilation among school children was common in the Cork workhouse. In order to make their eyes sore workhouse schoolgirls put threads containing blue indigo dye under their eyelids, which caused severe watering and swelling.[12] At the end of July 1851, there were 48 boys and 69 girls in hospital with ophthalmia and 98 others had milder eye complaints. The disease continued to occur in the house in subsequent years and serious outbreaks were recorded.[13] The majority of workhouse children whose eye complaints were identified as the contagious infection ophthalmia were in fact suffering from the nutritional deficiency disease xerophthalmia, an eye disease caused by a lack of vitamin A in their diet. Prolonged deprivation of vitamin A – potatoes and most cereals do not contain the nutrient – leads to xerophthalmia, which if untreated leads to blindness. Foods such as fish oils, including cod-liver oil, liver, butter, cream, cheese, milk and egg-yolks are rich in vitamin A.[14] Substituting skimmed milk in place of whole milk contributed to the problem as it

---

10 *Poor Law Commissioners Annual Report* (1851), pp. 143-45; See also Anne M. Lanigan, *The Poor Law children of county Tipperary and their education 1840-1880* (M. Ed. thesis, UCC, 1988), pp. 48, 90-4, 119-20, 304.

11 *CE* 25 July 1853; *CUM* 20 July 1853.

12 *SR* 17 July 1851; *Poor Law Commissioners Annual Report* (1852), pp. 14-15, 113-15; *CUM* 2 July, 16 July 1851.

13 *SR* 31 July 1851, 2 March 1854; *CE* 1 August 1851; 30 November 1855; *CUM* 30 July 1851, 30 March, 25 May, 6 July, 20 July 1853, 1 March, 16 August, 24 October, 28 November 1854, 28 November, 19 December 1855, 9 January, 16 January 1856; *CC* 22 November 1855; Ophthalmia was a serious problem in other Irish workhouses – see Patricia Kelly, *From workhouse to hospital* (M.A. thesis, Gaillimh, 1972), pp. 42-3.

14 E. M. Crawford and F. L. Clarkson, *Feast and Famine* (Oxford, 2001), p. 150.

reduced the amount of vitamin A available to the children.[15]

Other health problems also affected the children and 38 died in one week at the start of June 1851. Dr O Connor reported that although numbers of the children were weak, of those who died most had just pined away. This he attributed principally to inadequate exercise, the lack of fresh air and a transient population bringing new diseases and illnesses into the workhouse. The guardians agreed that the children should be permitted to take walks in the larger yards, or even into the countryside, in groups of about 50.[16] An outbreak of measles, which had raged in the house since a woman had been admitted with the disease at the beginning of May also contributed to the high death rate. Between 7 May and 21 June, almost 200 cases had occurred and those affected were principally orphans and young people already weakened by earlier sicknesses.[17]

In early 1854 the medical officers were again concerned about diet and conditions in the workhouse and they suggested that the allowances for the aged and infirm inmates should be increased to 6 ounces of meal and one pint of milk for breakfast and 14 ounces of white bread and a pint of milk for dinner. They were also critical of the quality of the milk being distributed to the children and infants. In many cases this class was being supplied with skimmed milk instead of the regulatory fresh product. To compensate for the inferior quality, the doctors suggested that the allowance be increased by ½ pint per day, which was sanctioned by the Poor Law Commissioners.[18] The Commissioners were outraged to discover that, instead of the mandatory sixteen ounces of bread for dinner, the master was issuing only twelve ounces to able-bodied

---

15 E. M. Crawford, 'Dearth, Disease in Ireland, 1850', *Medical History*, 1984, Vol. 28, p. 157. Following visits to a number of Irish workhouses during 1852, Dr John Forbes was in no doubt that inferior menus contributed to poor health. He condemned the diet 'not merely for its extreme unchangeableness, but for its great inferiority in regard to actual nutriment', as a definite link to the high incidences of ophthalmia. See John Forbes, *Memorandums made in Ireland . . .*, (London, 1853), Vol. I, p. 85, Vol. II, pp. 46, 230-9; Crawford and Clarkson, *Feast and famine* (Oxford, 2001), pp. 149-51; Kennedy, Ell, etc, *Mapping the Great Irish Famine* (Dublin, 1999), pp. 111-2; See also *Census of Ireland for the year 1861*, Part III, Vital Statistics, Vol. 1, Reports and tables relating to the status of diseases (Dublin, 1863), PP 1863, Vol. LVIII, pp. 94-6; Mary C. Karasch, 'Ophthalmia (Conjunctivitis and Trachoma)', in K. F. Kipple (ed.), *The Cambridge World History of Human Disease* (Cambridge, 1993), pp. 897-905.
16 *CUM* 4 June 1851, 28 November 1855; *SR* 12, 19, 26 June 1851.
17 *CUM* 4 June, 25 June, 2 July 1851; *CE* 27 June 1851. Another measles outbreak occurred at the end of 1854. *CUM* 13 December 1854; see also *CUM* 19 December 1855.
18 *CUM* 8 February, 29 March, 5 April 1854; *CUL* 21 March, 4 April 1854. See also *CE* 22 May 1854 for Dr D.C. O Connor's opinion on illness in the workhouse.

inmates. They warned the board that 'a subject of so much importance as depriving workhouse inmates of so large a portion of the food allowed to them by the guardians, requires serious consideration'. During the next couple of weeks, the able-bodied allowances were revised and changes were made to the infirm inmates' diet. Before the end of 1854 the Commissioners asked the guardians to discontinue their practice of providing an inferior diet as a method of discouraging applications from able-bodied poor. Instead, they suggested that casual applications could be discouraged by 'a strict system of discipline and classification and continued employment for able-bodied inmates'.[19] The general food serving regulations were also revised and the visiting committee recommended that 'the food be laid upon the tables of the dining hall at the several meals by the hall assistants before the classes are called to meals, that the inmates be marched in two by two, and take their places at the tables, beginning at those nearest the door, that the attention of the officers be called to the previous orders directing that none but the hall assistants be permitted to be in the hall, except at meal times'.[20]

The city's Mayor, John N. Murphy, visited the workhouse in January 1854 and he was surprised to see so many paupers without shoes or stockings. The workhouse clogs were made of canvas which turned down at the heel and gave little protection from the cold and caused feet to become sore. Paupers who found it more comfortable to walk on their bare feet discarded them. The clogs were also noisy and disturbed patients in the hospital wards.[21] The Mayor estimated that it would cost about 1s.1½d. per year to supply paupers with three pairs of stocking and another 1s. to provide durable leather clogs. If each inmate wore out three pairs of inferior canvas clogs which cost 8d. each, the transition to stockings and leather footwear would cost about 1s. extra per annum for each inmate At that time the Mayor was endeavouring to clear the city streets of beggars and prostitutes. As an option, they were offered workhouse relief, but, influenced by stories of hardship inside its walls, many refused this alternative.[22] The estimated additional expenditure of about £500 per annum on leather footwear would, he believed, have been beneficial, but as usual, one section of the board was preoccupied with cutting costs. They feared that inmates would steal the leather footwear and they introduced the usual argument against

19 *CUL* 7 March, 28 March, 25 April, 31 October, 7 November, 14 November 1854; *CC* 19 October, 2 November, 9 November 1854, during subsequent years, changes were occasionally made to the diet of inmates. *CUL* 16 March 1858.
20 *CUM* 20 June 1855.
21 *CUM* 29 June 1853.
22 In January 1854, the guardians voted against improving the floor in the penitentiary ward's day room. *CUM* 18 January 1854.

making conditions attractive.[23] Mayor Murphy presented his proposals on 8 February and he produced figures to prove that a pair of leather clogs could be made at a cheaper rate than a number of pairs of inferior canvas shoes. Stockings could be made by inmates and the total cost of the footwear would amount to just over 2s., which was better value than the canvas clogs. He claimed that minor ailments from inferior clothing and footwear were leading to serious illnesses, which necessitated hospital treatment. People accustomed to wearing shoes and stockings before entering the workhouse, had difficulty in adjusting to the change. Some of the inmates tore strips off petticoats or other clothing to bind their feet and protect them from cold workhouse floors. The board would not vote on a proposal to provide leather clogs, but did agree to give woollen stockings to the inmates. Of the board members – Francis Hennis in particular – who refused to allow a vote on the footwear motion, the *Southern Reporter* asked 'is it not deplorable, is it not disgraceful, that unhappy human creatures should be left to the control of such men? Can there be a more solemn and disgusting mockery in this world than calling such men guardians of the poor? The thing is really too monstrous, and is a disgrace to all concerned'.[24]

Footwear was discussed again during the winter of 1857 when the clerk reported that the schoolgirls' canvas shoes were in a sorry condition. Others who had no footwear got wet when going between the school and dining hall. Despite the usual protests from some guardians, it was agreed to provide full leather shoes to all school children aged nine years and under.[25] During the following winter shoes were also ordered for inmates, including infirm women, who had to move about the house in their bare feet.[26]

Sanitation

In addition to contagion from fellow patients, other factors impinged on the health of inmates. The workhouse sewage was fed into four cess-pools which were agitated daily and emptied weekly by inmates. On these occasions the stench was terrible and the 'abominably insufficient' system

---

23 *CC* 5 January 1854; *CUM* 7 December 1853, 11 January, 25 January 1854; *SR* 5 January, 12 January 1854.
24 *CUM* 15 February 1854; *SR* 9 February, 16 February 1854; *CC* 16 February 1854; During 1854 the average weekly cost of maintaining a pauper in the Cork workhouse was 2s.3d. – this compared with 3s.0½d. in Belfast, 2s.8d. in Dublin South and 2s.4d. in Dublin North workhouses. PP Vol. XLVI, 1855 [424], *Return – Poor Relief . . . no. of paupers*, p. 10.
25 *CC* 5 November, 26 November 1857; *CUM* 28 October, 4 November, 11 November, 25 November 1857; *CE* 6 November, 27 November 1857.
26 *CUM* 6 October 1858.

frequently overflowed on to yards and passages. Foul discharges oozed from the pool in the women's department, and old bedding straw was heaped onto it to contain the smell.[27] Manure taken from the pools was stored nearby in heaps. One particularly foul receptacle was situated outside the male ward in an area surrounded by walls and buildings; because of its location, the stench found its way into the adjacent corridors and dormitories. The medical officers were alarmed with the disruption involved in cleaning the pools and suggested that, instead of removing a huge quantity, the waste should be emptied on a daily basis. They also recommended that the men moving the barrows get an extra ½ lb. of bread and a pint of porter each day.[28] The possibility of moving the cess-pools outside the workhouse boundary was investigated, but instead, the manure was stored and removed periodically from the establishment in covered wagons.[29] The workhouse wells were often contaminated or they ran dry, so fresh water had to be brought in during summer.[30] On occasions, water was so scarce that pumps had to be manned by inmates until past midnight, to ensure that a supply would be available for breakfast.[31] The supply was so unreliable during summer of 1852 that six water carts were borrowed from the city's water company to bring a quantity to the house. Frequently there was no water for washing, and when inmates finished their tasks they often had no water to drink.[32]

Women were often deployed to work the pumps and because the unit in their own yard had no protection from the weather, a shed in the men's yard was re-located to provide some shelter.[33] When the laundry water supply failed in 1854, fourteen women were forced to pump water. They were uncooperative and marched around singing songs 'some of them not of the most proper kind'. At lunch time the women were given bread but their soup was withheld. Some of those who protested were put in the punishment cells and their places were taken

27 *SR* 26 May 1853; see also *CUM* 21 March 1849; 30 June, 14 July, 7 August 1852, 29 June 1853.
28 *CUM* 20 June, 27 June 1855.
29 *SR* 26 May, 20 October 1853; 19 January, 26 January 1854, 13 May 1859; CUM 28 September 1853, 8 February, 19 July, 9 August 1854, 6 February 1856, 25 February, 4 March, 8 July, 12 August 1857; *CUL* 15 April, 22 April, 21 November 1854, 26 June 1855, 8 November 1856, 16 March 1857; see also NAI, CSORP 1859 5550, enclosure Nos. 14, 16 and 21. The workhouse sewage was sold to contractors for use as farm manure. *CUM* 19 September 1855, 26 August 1857.
30 *SR* 21 May, 26 May 1853; 9 May, 11 May, 25 May, 29 June, 27 July, 17 August 1854; *CUM* 24 May 1854, 27 July 1857; *CUL* 11 June 1853, 27 June, 14 November 1854.
31 *SR* 20 November 1851.
32 *SR* 17 June, 17 July 1852; *CUM* 2 June 1852, 24 November 1858.
33 *CUM* 29 September, 2 November, 9 November 1853.

by other women. Punishment continued on the following day and the women's milk allowance was withheld at breakfast and a different crew was put on the pump. After a few days, the unfortunate women realised that they were 'attempting to play a losing game' and they conformed.[34] Although the protest ended, the authorities were dissatisfied with the amount of water being provided. A suggestion to replace the pumps with newer models was not, however, implemented.[35] At the end of 1855 the pump workers were given an 'idler's allowance' of bread because of their lack of enthusiasm. They were kept in the yard until late in the evening and during 'the interval from dinner 'till then, they employed singing, shouting and jumping about the yard in the most boisterous manner and would not work the pumps'.[36] Again, the authorities resorted to withholding food as a punishment.

Just four buckets, each holding three gallons of water, were provided to wash and clean the 400 boys in one area during the summer season. In winter the same number were obliged to wash in the open air at 'two regular pig troughs' about six feet long by two feet wide.[37] The children were not as healthy as their counterparts outside. Skin problems and other illnesses were readily transferred from child to child so the guardians decided to install a new washhouse with separate facilities for sick and healthy children.[38] As Cork Corporation's new water works was nearing completion it was decided to see if a supply could be got from the new network.[39] By the end of 1858 the piped water had reached the workhouse and the master recommended that fountains be erected at four strategic points in the complex. Though some guardians were reluctant to dispense with manual water pumping and its 'labour test' element, the institution was connected to the piped water network by February 1859 and fountains were installed.[40]

---

34 *CUM* 29 November 1854.
35 *CUM* 10 January, 7 November 1855.
36 *CUM* 5 December 1855.
37 *CUM* 16 July, 19 November 1851, 3 August, 7 December 1853; *SR* 8 December 1853; see *CUM* 2 February, 22 June 1853.
38 *SR* 30 March, 11 April 1854; *CUM* 31 August, 21 September 1853. In a report on an alternative water source, the county surveyor suggested that a regular supply could be acquired from the Pouladuff stream, or from the Tramore or Douglas rivers. At a cost of £400, a three-inch pipe could be laid to the Pouladuff stream and this, he estimated, would provide the house with up to 15,000 gallons of fresh water per day. *CUM* 17 June 1857; *CE* 19 June 1857; *CC* 18 June 1857.
39 *CUM* 25 February, 24 June 1857; *CE* 26 June 1857; *CUL* 15 January, 1 March 1859.
40 *CUM* 27 April, 1 June 1859; *SR* 6 January, 10 February 1859; *CUL* 19 April, 5 May, 17 November 1859. There were some problems with bursting pipes for a while but the Cork Corporation was paid £228. 8s. for the installation work in November 1859. *CUM* 18 May, 2 November 1859.

Some guardians refused to acknowledge that sanitation, or the quality of food, contributed in any way to a high level of deaths. Instead, they blamed admissions of old and sick people by relations who sought to avoid the cost of burial.[41] Some relieving officers were known to connive in this practice and people who had gone directly to hospital, without encountering the regular admission procedure, were included in the list of fatalities. One guardian cynically observed that exhaustion frequently contributed to workhouse deaths. He wondered if the ordeal involved in acquiring an admission ticket was a contributory factor. To allay the public's fears that the guardians were killing off the inmates, Francis Hennis said that deaths did occur soon after admission but that, in general, the able-bodied inmates were 'as healthy as any of her majesty's subjects'.[42] Another board member believed that 'neglect and the want of proper nourishment and proper treatment during the winter months', contributed to the deaths of 280 workhouse children under 15 years of age who had died between 8 January and 4 June 1853. He had anticipated a high death rate and

> was quite prepared for that result, when he saw those boys with empty stomachs, supplied very indifferently with food, and taken away to work at the very time when they should have received it. They got a wretched breakfast of porridge about nine o'clock, and at two o' clock were taken to the mill to work, without receiving any food. . . . He often saw them himself with their blue, pinched countenances, going to work when they should have been taken into hospital or received the food they required.[43]

When Assistant Commissioner Crawford inspected the workhouse in the summer of 1853 he found that many hospital wards were overcrowded. Beds in some departments were occupied by up to three adults. In one male ward 85 beds were occupied by 183 patients; in the venereal department 79 patients shared 40 beds and in the lying-in ward 14 mothers and their infants had to share 10 beds. The purchase of bedsteads and clothing during the next couple of months helped to alleviate the overcrowding.[44] During Inspector John Hall's tour in January 1854 he found up to three people in beds and he saw numerous instances of two patients to a bed in the hospital.[45] Although this was also rectified, overcrowding was again noted in the able bodied, infirm and

41 *SR* 26 May 1853; *CUL* 9 August 1864; *CUM* 25 May 1853.
42 *SR* 9 June 1853; *CUL* 3 June 1853, 12 February 1854; see also NAI, CSORP 1854 13113.
43 *SR* 9 June 1853.
44 *SR* 2 June, 9 June 1853; *CUL* 31 May, 14 June 1853.
45 *CC* 19 January, 26 January 1854; *SR* 2 June, 7 July 1853; *CUM* 1 February 1854; *CUL* 17 January, 31 January 1854.

nursery wards in 1855 and many beds were shared by up to three occupants.[46] In the female infirm wards pauper assistants had a poor reputation and they were suspected of selling food and drinking the porter prescribed to patients. The Poor Law Commissioners frowned on their poor discipline and dishonesty, but they blamed the workhouse officials for poor supervision.[47] Dining facilities in the hospital were primitive and because of a scarcity of cutlery, patients on special diets were obliged to tear their meat apart with their fingers. The guardians were reluctant to order new knives and forks, and, instead, the nurses were ordered to cut up the meat for the patients.[48] Some guardians were not in favour of admitting male venereal disease patients to the hospital. They believed that the men should not be treated at the ratepayers' expense for their 'blackguardism'. In 1857 when the board instructed relieving officers to refuse workhouse passes to syphilis patients, the Commissioners promptly informed them that, if the men were in need, they would have to be admitted to the hospital.[49]

The Arnott Investigation

At a board meeting on 6 April 1859 a lengthy circular on workhouse diets was read to the assembled guardians. The Poor Law Commissioners had found that many workhouse medical officers were ambivalent about the amount of stirabout issued to inmates and they frequently placed aged and infirm inmates on the medical diet so as to avoid the dining hall diet of stirabout, which upset many patients. Because meat was usually included in the medical diet the expenditure on workhouse food increased. The Commissioners recommended that infirm patients and delicate children should be excluded from the stirabout regime and provided with bread and tea as an alternative to the expensive hospital diet. To vary the workhouse diet, the Commissioners suggested that bread and milk, bread and rice or potatoes and milk should be issued on occasions. They believed that the inclusion of fresh milk would not 'infringe on the principle that the inmates of the workhouse ought not be better fed, at the expense of the poor rates, than persons maintaining themselves by independent labour'. They said that the general workhouse diet could be improved by adding cheap meat, in the form of ox-heads, shin beef or other coarse meat to the soup. This would compensate for the cost of putting aged and infirm inmates or delicate children on the hospital diet. Such dietary improvements had already

---

46 *CUL* 27 February, 26 June 1855, also: *CUM* 23 January 1850, 16 February 1853.
47 *CUL* 26 September 1854.
48 *CUM* 6 October 1858.
49 *CUL* 25 August 1857; *CUM* 19 August 1857; *CE* 21 August 1857.

been adopted in the Dublin workhouses. The Cork guardians discussed the contents of the circular but, instead of making an immediate decision, they retained the existing diet (see table below), and voted by a majority of two to refer the matter to a committee which would seek the advice of the medical officers.[50]

Cork Workhouse – Dietary for Healthy Classes

CLASS	BREAKFAST	DINNER	SUPPER
1	8 oz. Indian Meal ¾ pint Milk	1 lb. Brown bread, 1½ pints of porridge	
2	8 oz. Indian Meal, ¾ pint Milk	1 lb. Brown bread 1½ pints of porridge	
3	¾ lb. White bread, 1 pint of Milk	¾ lb. White bread, 1 pint of Milk	
4	6 oz. Indian Meal, ½ pint of Milk	¾ lb. Brown bread, 1 pints of porridge	¼ lb. Brown bread ½ pint of Milk
5	1½ lbs. White bread	and one quart of Milk	Daily
6	1½ lbs. White bread	and one quart of Milk	Daily
7	4 oz. White bread, ½ pint of new Milk	4 oz. White bread, ¼ pint of new Milk	4 oz. White bread, ¼ pint of new Milk

Note: 8 oz. oatmeal and 3 oz. rice to each gallon of porridge, with vegetables, pepper, salt, etc.

(*Source*: T. Brodie, *Inquiry* . . . (Cork, 1859), p. 27)

While the guardians met and discussed the suggestions of the Poor Law Commissioners, the Mayor of Cork, John Arnott, was in the process of carrying out a minute inspection of the workhouse and its occupants. Although it was not uncommon for interested parties to undertake tours of workhouses, and the Commissioners believed that comments in the visitors' book would encourage guardians to take an interest in the institutions,[51] on this occasion, it is probable that Arnott's visit was part of a premeditated plan to expose the harsh conditions in the institution. On his tour of the establishment he was impressed with the cleanliness of various departments, furnishings, yards and exercise areas and with the commitment of staff and pauper helpers. He examined beds, bedding and clothing which he found to be clean and comfortable in the hospital. He was also pleased with the quality of food he sampled. He stated that,

50 *CUM* 6 April 1859; *SR* 7 April 1859; *CUL* 31 March 1859 – Circular No. 81; B. Banks, *Compendium of the Irish Poor Law: Containing the Acts for the relief of the destitute poor in Ireland, and various statutes connected therewith* (Dublin, 1872), pp. 790-92; also *Poor Law Commissioners Annual Report* (1859), pp. 25-6; PP 1860, Vol. XXXVII, pp. 86-88.

51 *Poor Law Commissioners Annual Report* (1868), p. 24.

although food in workhouses had to be of a quality to deter the 'lazy and vicious' from exploiting the ratepayers, it had to be good enough to provide sustenance to the sick, the aged and infirm and to children who had no option but to remain in the house. The sick were well cared for in the hospital, and the infirm had sufficient food, although the quality could be improved at a slight additional expenditure. But, he was 'appalled' by the diseased state of the children, many of whom were suffering from scrofula ('a tuberculous inflammation of lymph nodes of the necks of children')[52] in its various stages. In an upper schoolroom he found that 48 were 'so stunted in growth and intellect, and awfully affected, that no human man could look upon them without the deepest compassion'. In the girls' department a further 64 children were in a similar condition. The Mayor recorded his observations in the workhouse visitors' book and concluded his comments by calling for humane guardians on the board to 'provide against the continuance of this most disastrous and terrible condition in which I have found these destitute and unfriended children'.[53] The public greeted the subsequent publication of the Mayor's comments with outrage and disbelief.

Accompanied by Dr Albert Callanan, John Arnott made another inspection of the workhouse on 14 April. They examined the children and found that of the nine to fifteen year old males, 102 were attending school, 29 were infirm and 50 were sick in hospital. Of the females in that age group, 87 were in school, 23 were infirm and 29 were in hospital. Of the 163 male and female children aged from two to nine years, 82 were in school, 26 were in the nursery and 55 were sick and infirm. The remaining 110 children under two years of age had not been weaned so were not on the workhouse diet.[54] Elaborating on his earlier comments in the visitors' book, the Mayor lamented that

---

52 *Melloni's Illustrates Medical Dictionary*, 3rd Edition (New York, 1994), p. 430; see also *Cambridge History of Human Disease*, pp. 998-1000. Scrofula is a glandular form of tuberculosis and is charecterised by swelling and open, discharging sores on the faces and necks of sufferers. Although the disease was recognised as a killer of infants and toddlers, it frequently crippled its victims. Conditions in the workhouse were ideal for the spread of the disease as it was maintained by an improper diet and exposure to cold and humidity. Katherine Ott, *Fevered Lives Tuberculosis in American culture since 1870* (London, 1996), p. 177; F.B. Smith, *The retreat of tuberculosis 1850-1950* (London, 1988), pp. 8, 12.

53 *SR* 7 April 1859. The text of John Arnott's comments is transcribed in J. Arnott, *Investigation into Cork Workhouse* (Cork, 1859), pp. 5-8; *CUM* 13 April 1859; T. Brodie, *Report on Cork workhouse* (Cork, 1859), pp. 93-5; PP 1861, Vol. LV, [184], *Copy of a report . . . into the state of the Cork Union Workhouse . . .* pp. 3-4; NAI, CSORP 1859 5550, enclosure No. 1; PP 1861, Vol. X, *Select Committee on Poor Relief*, pp. 17-18.

54 *SR* 19 April 1859.

the growing children have been fed day after day, week after week, month after month, year after year, with the same monotonous scouring food, and I am really quite astonished that it never occurred to any of the guardians that a little variety would be necessary. . . . You can thus by a process of slow starvation protract their wearisome and unprofitable existence. They are not even allowed to attain the mercy of death.[55]

The matter was discussed briefly by the guardians but to avoid confrontation it was agreed to ask the Poor Law Commissioners for an independent investigation.[56]

The investigation under Dr Terence Brodie commenced on 10 May and lasted until the 17th of the month. Many witnesses, including the Mayor, workhouse doctors, chaplains and staff, the bishop of Cork and local dispensary doctors were examined during the six-day hearing. In his evidence, the Mayor reiterated what he had written in the visitors' book and he attributed the 'sameness of the diet and the want of vegetables' as a contributing factor to the poor health of the inmates.[57] Dr Callanan recounted that on his inspection of the workhouse on 14 April he had tasted the soup. It was little more than water and although it was called vegetable soup, it contained few if any vegetables. Most of the children did not finish the soup. The bread was also poor and had a 'heavy and gluey' texture. He saw many signs of scrofula in the workhouse children, and in the children's hospital ward 38 of the 53 inmates had the disease – 'they were half eaten away with scrofula, the eyes, the glands, the lips were eaten away with scrofula'.[58] He said that the diet and the lack of fresh air were contributing to the high levels of sickness. The diet was also criticised by the Protestant bishop of Cork, William Fitzgerald, who said that it should have more variety, and that potatoes should be served. He was also critical of the children's clogs and did not favour having two patients in one bed, as was the case in the hospital.[59]

Dr Edward Townsend, who had carried out an inspection of the premises over an eight-day period in the previous weeks, presented an interesting report on the current state of the workhouse. He had observed many cases of scrofula 'in all its various forms, attacking the different parts of the human frame, causing in many instances deformity of appearance and in others rendering the extremities of the body

---

55 *SR* 14 April 1859.
56 *CUM* 13 April, 20 April 1859; *CUL* 19 April, 23 April 1859; NAI, CSORP 1859 5550.
57 T. Brodie, *Report.* (Cork, 1859), pp. 45-7.
58 *SR* 11 May 1859; T. Brodie, *Report . . .*, pp. 47-9.
59 *SR* 12 May 1859; T, Brodie, *Report . . .*, pp. 51-3.

useless'.[60] Of 38 male patients in the main hospital, 22 had scrofula and the disease also affected 21 of the 46 females. He too felt that the diet was contributing to the poor health of the young inmates and he suggested that potatoes and fresh milk be supplied and that meat be given to the children on a couple of occasions during the week. The *Cork Constitution* ascribed a different cause for the bad health of the young workhouse inmates. Most of the children are, it said, 'the offspring of polluted parentage. They are the contributions of parts and places noted for their profligacy. They have a hereditary trait of which no practicable system of regimen will divest the blood'.[61] Dr D.C. O Connor, the former workhouse medical officer, also made observations about diet, exercise, bad footwear and the separation of children from their mothers at a very young age. He was critical that some of the guardians had periodically refused to sanction additional expenditure on better food for the children.[62] Suggestions about improving the diet were made by other medical witnesses such as Dr John Popham and Dr William C. Townsend. The latter admitted that he was puzzled by the large amount of scrofula in the workhouse and he feared that the healthy boys were waiting 'to glide into disease'. He had worked in the house for a couple of years, during which he 'never saw a decent bit of meat brought into the hospital; I reported over and over and over again, and at one time I made a personal canvass to induce guardians to get a better description'.[63]

Although figures presented by John Arnott on the workhouse death rate were subjected to intense scrutiny, and his method of calculation was questioned, the Mayor was successful in his effort to force attention on the plight of the most vulnerable inmates. The evidence collected at the investigation was transmitted to the Poor Law Commissioners.[64] Included in the report was a record of Dr Brodie's inspection of the workhouse. He did not criticise the food or its preparation but he did have reservations about the treatment of boys in hospital. In its wards he had seen 22 boys with scrofula, which was 'more severe in its form than I have ever before witnessed'. Dr Brodie did make a number of suggestions about the dietary scale. He said that a better quality bread should be given to the infants, new milk should be provided to the two to nine

---

60 *SR* 13 May 1859. The Cork board of guardians employed Dr Edward Townsend to carry out this inspection and because of the extent of the task, he was accompanied by Dr Harvey. *CUM* 20 April, 27 April 1859.

61 T. Brodie, *Report*, pp. 58-71; *CC* 14 May 1859.

62 T. Brodie, *Report*, pp. 71-6.

63 *SR* 16 May 1859; T. Brodie, *Report.*, pp. 87-91. For a discussion on Arnott's comments and the subsequent inquiry, see: Rev. C. B. Gibson, *History of the county and city of Cork* (Cork, 1861, 1974 edition), pp. 330-333.

64 NAI, CSORP 1859 5550 contains a large amount of original documentation relating to this inquiry.

year olds, and on three days a week, they should receive meat-soup. Potatoes and meat-soup should, he suggested, be provided to the nine to
fifteen year olds and to the infant school children.[65] He also suggested
that the children get more exercise and that ordinary shoes should be
issued in place of their clogs.

As a result of the evaluation of the evidence and Dr Brodie's report,
the Poor Law Commissioners recommended an improved and varied
diet, extra recreation and the disuse of clogs by young inmates.[66] This
was reiterated by the workhouse committee and in June it recommended
that leather shoes should replace the children's clogs and that an
improved dietary scale be introduced. As part of the new allowances, the
poor quality bread supplied to infants under two years of age was to be
replaced by a better product. The two to five year olds were to get new
milk instead of skim milk. The five to nine year old children were to
receive meat soup, fresh milk, plus meat and vegetables during the week;
the nine to fifteen year age group were to get white bread, meat and meat
soup, and a superior mixture of stirabout. Instead of skim milk, infirm
children were to get new milk and on at least two occasions during the
week they were to get meat soup. The aged and infirm inmates were to
receive tea instead of their breakfast milk.[67] The healthy school children's
timetable was rearranged; they were given a two-hour recreation period
each evening and on two or three occasions during the week they were
taken on supervised walks in the countryside. The infirm boys were
provided with literary instruction for three hours each day and girls
received two hours instruction.[68] Although John Arnott expressed
support for the dietary improvements, the visiting committee had reservations about providing meat to the workhouse children, as they feared
that a good menu would discourage them from leaving the institution to
take up employment. They also anticipated problems when the meat-fed
children eventually graduated to the adult ward and discovered that meat
was not included on its menu. These reservations were shared by the
Poor Law Commissioners who still believed that 'meat is not an ordinary
article of food in the diet of the Irish labourer at present, nor even in the
diet of the Irish farmer'.[69] Regardless of these reservations, the new
dietary scale was introduced on 17 July 1859.[70]

As the year progressed other changes were made to the dietary scale

---

65 T. Brodie, *Report.*, pp. 13, 18-19.
66 *SR* 2 June 1859; T. Brodie, *Report.*, pp. 101-115; *CUL* 24 May, 31 May 1859.
67 *CUM* 8 June, 13 June, 20 July 1859; *SR* 9 June 1859.
68 *CUM* 18 May, 25 May, 15 June 1859; *CC* 26 May, 28 May, 2 June 1859.
69 *CUM* 6 July 1859; *SR* 30 June, 7 July 1859; *CUL* 28 June 1859; NAI, CSORP
     1859 5550, letter of 7 June 1859 and enclosure No. 15.
70 *CUM* 20 July 1859.

and new play swings were constructed for the workhouse boys.[71] When the Mayor re-visited the institution in December 1859, he was pleased with the improvements in the health of the children and infirm inmates. These he attributed to the increased allowances and better quality food being served to the inmates.[72] In 1861 Alfred Power, the Chief Commissioner of the Irish Poor Law, spoke about John Arnott's intervention on behalf of the workhouse children. Power admitted that the Mayor's observations on the workhouse and the subsequent inquiry under Dr Brodie had ensured that 'all these beneficial changes were readily adopted by the guardians of Cork'.[73] Within a couple of years further changes and improvements were made to the dietary scales. A third daily meal was provided to all children and infants and some variety had been introduced by the inclusion of meat in their porridge on a couple of days each week.[74]

Children and infants still remained vulnerable in the workhouse. Diseases such as puerperal, or childbed fever (puerperal sepsis) were not uncommon in the maternity wards and when the disease occurred fatalities usually resulted. In cases where a mother died, her child was 'given to a pauper woman to spoon-feed, and she has no interest in it; she has another child to keep, or perhaps two, and her only care is to keep it quiet'. Almost invariably, the unfortunate orphan died.[75] Nursery children in particular had a high mortality rate, with almost 150 dying in the 12 months to March 1864. Some guardians attributed this to the admission of many very ill children.[76] The repetitive and nutritionally limited hospital diet of 4 ounces of bread and 1 pint of milk for breakfast, 4 ounces of bread and ½ pint of milk for dinner and 4 ounces of

---

71 *CUM* 2 November, 26 October, 28 December 1859; *CUL* 8 November 1859; *SR* 3 November, 17 November 1859.

72 *SR* 22 December 1859.

73 PP 1861, Vol. X, [408], *Report from Select Committee on Poor Relief*, p. 23.

74 See PP 1861, Vol. LV, [533], p.1; PP 1867-8, Vol. LXI, [322], *Unions in Ireland in which a third meal is not allowed . . .*, p. 4.; PP 1864, Vol. LII, [260], *Dietaries in use in certain workhouses in Ireland*, pp. 7-8; also PP 1888, Vol. LXXXVII, [83], *Scale of dietaries in workhouses in Ireland*, pp. 71-2.

75 *CUM* 11 January, 18 January 1860, 27 December 1877; PP 1861, Vol. X, [408], *Report on Poor Relief . . .*, p. 96. Puerperal fever remained the greatest killer of women in childbirth until the 1930s. Lara Marks, 'Medical care for pauper mothers and their infants: poor law provision and local demand in east London, 1870 – 1929', in *Economic History Review*, XLVI, 3 (1993), p. 526; see also: Irvine Loudon, 'Some international features of maternal mortality, 1800-1950', in Valerie Fildes, Lara Marks and Hilary Marland, *Women and children first* (London, 1992), pp. 5-28; K. Codell Carter, 'Puerperal Fever', in K. Kipple, *Cambridge World History of Human Disease*, pp. 955-957.

76 *CE* 28 April, 29 April 1864.

bread and ½ pint of milk for supper, for two to five year old children, could not have encouraged good health. The daily allowance for infants under two years of age consisted of 12 ounces of bread and one pint of milk.[77] The unhygienic location of the overcrowded workhouse nursery was not conducive to good health, for it was situated:

> within the inner circle of the workhouse, in the bottom of a basin, surrounded by high buildings, and in connection with the children's hospital, where many children at present lie sick: in the yard attached, and the only means of obtaining air, are the privies of the house, with apertures in the walls opening into the yard. Close to the hospital, is the children's day room and dormitory; and be it known that outside this place the infants are never taken, and have no possible means of obtaining a breath of fresh air, crowded together in unventilated apartments, with their mothers and nurses – 241 in number.[78]

Child Mortality Sept. 1857 to March 1864

HALF YEAR ENDING:	DEATHS OF CHILDREN UNDER 2 YEARS	DEATHS OF CHILDREN AGED 2-5 YEARS
Sept 1857	12	30
March 1858	17	76
Sept 1858	9	33
March 1859	3	19
Sept 1859	4	37
March 1860	3	36
Sept 1860	3	30
March 1861	21	68
Sept 1861	6	48
March 1862	42	87
Sept 1862	14	30
March 1863	26	59
Sept 1863	7	48
March 1864	42	98

(*Source: CUL* 10 May 1864; *CE* 11 May 1864; *CC* 12 May 1864)

Diseases such as scarlatina and smallpox made periodic visits to the workhouse. When smallpox was introduced into the house in December 1855, a rapid vaccination programme was inaugurated. Nonetheless, many children contracted the disease and over two dozen cases were recorded by early 1856. Women rambling through the wards were credited with spreading the disease and by mid-March almost 100

---

77 PP 1864, Vol. LII, [260], *Workhouse dietaries*, p. 8.
78 *CE* 29 April 1864; see also William D'Esterre Parker, *The Irish Poor Law is a national grievance, with suggestions for its amendment* (Cork, 1868), pp. 14-15.

cases had occurred. Most of the stricken were infants and very young children, and over one third of them died from the disease.[79] A serious outbreak of whooping cough and measles 'attended with sudden and great prostration of strength', contributed to a higher than average number of deaths in the spring of 1858.[80] (See table above) During the epidemic, the infant school children were not permitted to visit the dining hall and their daily diet was increased to 1 lb. of white bread and 1½ pints of new milk each day. Later in the year, the medical officers complained that because of a deterioration in the quality of bread, a large number of infants were in hospital with diarrhoea of a 'very intractable character'.[81] Before the end of 1860, new outbreaks of measles and diarrhoea occurred in the children's hospital; the atmosphere in the wards was 'absolutely pestilential' and by mid-November, 100 cases of 'malignant' measles were under treatment.[82] A diarrhoea outbreak in the lock ward was exacerbated by a supply of poor quality milk. The medical officers vainly attempted to quell the debilitating illness by prescribing flour as an antidote.[83] At the start of 1862 the workhouse hospital was overcrowded with up to three patients in many beds. Another measles outbreak caused further problems and by mid-February 100 children were receiving treatment.[84] The disease was of 'a very severe and fatal form', with 40 patients dying in one week. The Poor Law Inspector admitted that the outbreak 'caused more mortality in the Cork workhouse than he had ever known before'. During one five week period in February and March the average death rate in the workhouse was over 29 patients per week.[85] Again, in November 1863 a case of malignant measles was brought into the workhouse. The disease spread rapidly and soon over 60 cases were under treatment. Many children were stricken by measles and at the start of 1864 outbreaks of scarlatina attacked other children. Fever was also rampant with 72 inmates under treatment in the workhouse and another 84 cases referred to the city fever hospital.[86]

---

79 *CUM* 19 December 1855; 9 January, 6 February, 12 March, 2 April 1856.
80 *CE* 5 March, 12 March 1858; *CC* 11 March 1858.
81 *CUM* 10 March, 29 December 1858.
82 *CUM* 10 October, 7 November, 21 November, 28 November, 5 December, 12 December 1860.
83 *CUM* 13 March 1861.
84 *CC* 22 January, 20 February 1862; *CUM* 5 February, 12 February, 19 February; *Poor Law Commissioners Annual Report* (1862), p. 11.
85 *CC* 27 February 1862; *CE* 19 November 1863.
86 *CC* 14 January 1864; *CE* 6 January, 24 March 1864. Measles outbreaks did occur during subsequent years; see *CUM* 25 January, 8, 15, 22 February, 1, 8 March, 7, 14, 28 November, 5, 12, December 1866, 2, 16, 23 January, 20 February, 6 March 1867, 19 December 1872, 2 January, 9 January, 6 February, 13 February 1873; *CE* 19 October, 26 October 1877.

Following some correspondence between poor law guardian William D'Esterre Parker and the Poor Law Commissioners, the Cork guardians discussed the matter in May 1864. The Poor Law Inspector attributed unsuitable and overcrowded hospital accommodation as a contributory factor in some of the 195 young children's deaths in the year ending March 1864. Although he agreed that a separate hospital could be beneficial, he was not convinced that it would reduce the death rate. Parker restated his conviction that the location of the nursery wards, allied to the fact that the unfortunate children were 'cooped up from one end of the year of the other, and were never taken out into the fresh air', were the prime causes of their premature deaths. As an alternative to subjecting the children to a protracted and tortuous death, he suggested that, if the guardians did not want to make improvements, they should adopt the custom of primitive societies in disposing of unwanted children, and 'place them at a low tide and allow the water to cover them'.[87] The problem was not addressed and some years later the infant mortality rate again soared. The children still lacked a proper exercise yard and frequently wet nurses were unavailable to suckle infants. An unwillingness by the board to increase the rate from £6 to £7 per annum for wet nurses made it almost impossible to build up a file of people willing to take the infants out of the house.[88]

By the end of the 1870s workhouse infants and their nurses were permitted to leave the confines of the nursery for exercise and fresh air on a couple of occasions each week. These short outdoor breaks from the unhealthy wards were important for the infants. In the nursery, cot blankets were not changed very often and the infants frequently slept on filthy bedclothes. Matters of personal hygiene were also overlooked and during one inspection of the nursery, a healthy suckling infant was found to be sharing mother's milk with the woman's own 'very sickly sore-eyed' baby. Contagious diseases were easily transmitted by such carelessness and a claim by the medical officers that nursed out infants were healthier and lived longer than their workhouse counterparts is difficult to contradict. Figures were produced to substantiate this claim but the results were no doubt influenced by the fact that, in general, nurses took healthier infants while their delicate peers stayed in the house. The medical officers were in favour of removing as many infants as possible from the workhouse and they also suggested that a new nursery should be

87 *CE* 11 May 1864; *CC* 12 May 1864.
88 *CE* 31 March 1870; see also *CUL* 31 March, 14 April 1868, 29 March 1870; C. O Mahony, *In the shadows Life in Cork 1750-1930* (Cork, 1997), p. 273; *CUM* 12 December 1866.

constructed on idle ground near the institution.[89] The visiting committee was in favour of nursing out infants of sick and deceased mothers
because 'the present practice of giving strange suckling infants to
mothers who have already infants of their own to suckle is highly
objectionable'.[90] Nonetheless, the mothers continued to care for the
children of other women.[91]

No change occurred during the next couple of years and in February
1882 William D'Esterre Parker complained to the Local Government
Board that, because the infants lacked fresh air and sunlight, almost every
one of them had 'the picture of a living death in their faces'. He called on
the board to have as many infants as possible nursed out in the country
for the benefit of their health. This intervention annoyed the medical officers who observed that, although there were shortcomings in the 'aspect
and ventilation' of the nursery, the infants themselves were generally
healthy.[92] One shed used by the nursery women and infants was in fact
'tottering', and an observer described it as 'nothing more nor less than a
living grave for the unfortunate infants'.[93] At around that time also, the
visiting committee suggested that the old buildings could be replaced for
about £300. The guardians were not in favour of the investment, so Dr
Brodie berated them for allowing 'the lives of those unfortunate creatures
to be hazarded because you will not expend a couple of hundred pounds'.
Although some board members supported the inspector, most were indifferent to the suffering of the infants.[94] The nursing women also had little
comfort and their monotonous daily allowance consisted of '½ lb. of
bread and one pint of tea for breakfast, ½ lb. of bread and ½ pint new
milk for dinner and ½ lb. bread and one pint of tea for supper'.[95]

Hospital improvements

From about the mid-1850s the Irish poor began to accept that worthwhile medical treatment was available in workhouse hospitals and from
that period the noticeable increase in the number of poor people applying for admission to these institutions was acknowledged in the annual

---

89 *CE* 31 January, 7 February, 25 July, 12 September 1879, 25 March 1881; *CC* 25
    June 1880; *CUM* 31 July, 7 August, 28 August 1879, 17 March, 7 April, 1 Decem-
    ber 1881.
90 *CUM* 10 June 1880, 15 July 1879.
91 *CUM* 28 April, 5 May, 30 June 1881.
92 *CE* 17 February, 3 March, 10 March 1882; During 1881, 130 children under 12
    years of age died in the workhouse, PP 1882, Vol. LIX, [277], *Mortality of chil-
    dren*, p. 3.
93 *CE* 26 November 1883; *CUM* 11 October, 22 November 1883.
94 *CUM* 3 January 1884.
95 *CUM* 10 and 17 January 1884.

reports of the Poor Law Commissioners.[96] Between 1852 and 1857 the percentage of hospital patients increased from 15% to 33% of all workhouse inmates. The Commissioners acknowledged that because of this change 'the workhouses of Ireland are assuming, especially in large towns, the character of hospitals for the reception of destitute sick persons'. Assistant Commissioner Crawford inspected the Cork workhouse during 1853 and he found that many of the hospital wards were overcrowded, with some beds occupied by up to three adults. In one male ward 85 beds were occupied by 183 patients, in the venereal department 79 patients shared 40 beds and in the lying-in ward 14 mothers and their infants had to share 10 beds.

Workhouse Deaths 1852-4

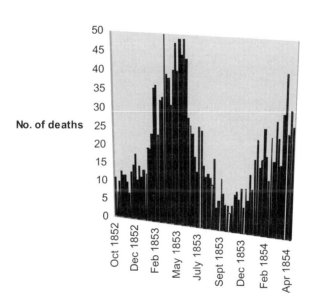

Chart showing large increase in the number of deaths in Cork workhouse between February and June 1853.

(Source: Cork Union Board of Guardians Records)

---

96 *Poor Law Commissioners Annual Report* (1853), p. 5; *Poor Law Commissioners Annual Report* (1854), p. 6; *Poor Law Commissioners Annual Report* (1855), p. 20; *Poor Law Commissioners Annual Report* (1856), pp. 12-13; *Poor Law Commissioners Annual Report* (1857), p. 5; *Census of Ireland for 1861*, p. 99; see also *CUM* 22 November 1883; *CE* 17 December 1856.

The workhouse death rate was also adversely affected by the admission of many seriously ill or 'hopeless' cases who died soon after entering its wards. The workhouse hospital admitted almost 1,300 fever cases to its wards in the nine months to June 1851. Mortality for this disease was about 8% or one in twelve cases. The number of workhouse deaths increased suddenly in the spring of 1853 and the medical officers attributed many of the deaths to the severe weather and the resulting bronchial and respiratory illnesses. Ophthalmia, or more likely, xerophthalmia, increased again at that period, but of the 130 cases in the workhouse, many had been weakened by previous attacks.[97] From early February to mid June the death rate in the workhouse increased from a maximum of about 20 per week, to 50, or an average of 40 each week during a 17-week period. This number of deaths, said an editorial in the *Southern Reporter*, converted the workhouse into 'one vast infection place and charnel house, for the poor. The destitute seem to be received into it, only that they may sicken and die – if, indeed, death kindly comes to relieve them, from some of the most distressing maladies which can afflict humanity'.[98] The 4,870 inmates in the institution at the start of May 1853 included 703 male and 1,103 females in the hospital wards. Among the hospital patients were numbered 90 male and 81 female ophthalmia cases, and another 200 patients, mainly children, suffered from ailments such as scrofula and ringworm. Between 100 and 200 females were suffering from 'night-blindness' (xerophthalmia), and the convalescent wards had 196 boys and 230 girls.

The duties carried out by the workhouse hospital staff were not appreciated by many guardians, some of whom did not trust the nurses and were reluctant to give them any authority. Their belief was that 'the position of a nurse is not such as to hold out much inducement to her to exert herself to protect property for which she is not responsible'. In matters of personal morals also, some guardians were suspicious of nurses. Because an 'improper intimacy' was suspected between a female nurse and a patient in the male ward, it was decided that only male attendant nurses would be allowed work in the male hospital. In defence of the hardworking female staff, the medical officer observed that 'the natural instincts of women, as well as their habits, point them out as the persons suitable for the painful and disagreeable office of attendance on the sick'. His chauvinistic opinion proved correct; the

97 *CUM* 30 March 1853; *CC* 5 January 1854; *SR* 5 January 1854; 31 March, 7 April, 26 May 1853; In 1854 there were eleven male and 28 female blind inmates in the workhouse. PP 1854-5, Vol. XLVII, [91], *Return of names and ages of blind Inmates in workhouses*, p. 2.
98 *SR* 21 May, 1853; *CUM* 25 May, 8 June 1853.

change was unsuccessful and female nurses were back in the male wards within weeks.[99] In most workhouse hospitals a few salaried nurses were employed and their numbers were augmented by 'the most eligible of the female inmates; by which latter class the menial services of the several sick wards, and sometimes services of greater trust and responsibility are performed . . . they receive a higher class of rations, to induce them to retain, by good conduct, this position of trust, and so as to remove, at the same time, the temptation to interfere, for their own advantage, with the diet of the inmates'.[100]

The guardians were insensitive about the feelings of women working in the hospital and during 1850 the nursetenders were offended when their uniform was modified without consultation. In place of their former cap, they were ordered to don an 'unseemly head-dress' shaped like an inverted water-jug. Around the front of the head covering was painted the legend "Cork Union Workhouse" in large red letters. The women protested about having to wear the "dowds", which was 'as villainous an appendage to the human face divine as it is possible to devise'. One journal interpreted the new head-dress as another 'irrational, vexatious, irritating' test of pauperism. It warned that, in preference to looking ridiculous, some of the more sensitive girls would leave the institution and possibly end up on the streets.[101] The Poor Law Commissioners intervened and advised the guardians not to force the women to wear the 'peculiar dress'.[102]

As a response to a demand for increased accommodation in the hospital, the Poor Law Commissioners suggested that the existing facility should be enlarged. A committee selected by the guardians drew up a report, which was presented to the board in August 1859.[103] The possibility of building a completely new unit was not addressed; instead the committee suggested that the occupants of various wards should be re-located so as to facilitate the conversion of the female school to a new male hospital.[104] Although the Commissioners favoured a new hospital, they did not object to the guardians' plans. Gerald Mahony, the Cork building contractor, was appointed to carry

---

99 *SR* 23 August 1849.
100 *Poor Law Commissioners Annual Report* (1861), p. 9.
101 *SR* 18 April 1850.
102 *CUL* 9 April 1850; *CUM* 20 March 1850; D.C. O Connor, *Seventeen years of workhouse life* (Dublin, 1861), p. 23.
103 *Poor Law Commissioners Annual Report* (1853), p. 5; *Poor Law Commissioners Annual Report* (1857), p. 5; SR 2 June, 7 May, 11 August 1859; *CUL* 16 August 1859.
104 *SR* 25 August 1859.

out repairs and modifications at a cost of £586.[105] The new hospital
facility was occupied in January 1861.[106]

Overcrowding of the hospital wards continued during the early 1860s
and it was still not uncommon for single beds to be occupied by two
patients.[107] At one stage each beds in the nursery was shared by up to five
patients and in the infirm area, patients were lying two to a bed. In an
attempt to reduce overcrowding in the nursery area, 33 infirm women
were transferred to an old ward above the dining hall. Dr Purcell did not
approve of 'thrusting' the women 'into a most detestable passage called
the tunnel, full of rags and bugs and so stifling for want of air, that to sleep
there is most prejudicial to health'. He was apprehensive that the move
would result in *'most lamentable consequences'*.[108] For a few months during
the spring of 1862 the guardians were obliged to rent 100 beds at the
North Infirmary to accommodate workhouse patients.[109] The Cork Union
authorities were often unable to cope with the demand for accommodation, and patients were regularly referred from the workhouse, by the
dispensary doctors and relieving officers, to the Cork City fever hospital.[110] During the autumn and winter of 1862-3 smallpox and scarlatina
cases were regularly brought into the workhouse hospital. In January up
to 10 cases of smallpox and a similar number of scarlatina cases were
admitted each week. To prevent an outbreak in the institution itself, these
patients were isolated in a ward some distance from other buildings.
Though the number declined in February, cases continued to arrive, and
victims of fever were also admitted.[111] As the facilities were obviously
inadequate, the suggestion that the workhouse should have its own fever
unit was discussed on numerous occasions.[112] Although this idea was

105 *SR* 8 September, 3 November 1859; *CUL* 6 September, 11 October, 15 Novem-
    ber 1859, 17 January, 12 April, 31 May, 5 June, 7 August, 31 August 1860; see
    also NAI, CSORP 1859 5550, letter of 7 June 1859.
106 *CE* 20 July, 17 August, 5 September, 12 September, 26 October 1860, 15 March
    1861; *CUM* 23 January, 30 January, 6 February 1861.
107 *CE* 19 June, 27 June 1861; *CC* 20 June, 17 October, 24 October 1861; *CUM* 16
    October, 23 October, 30 October, 13 November, 20 November, 4 December,
    11 December, 18 December 1861.
108 *CUM* 25 April, 1 May, 8 May, 29 May, 5 June, 17 July 1861, 8 January 1862; *CE*
    22 May, 5 June, 27 June 1861; *CC* 18 July 1861.
109 *CUL* 4 March 1862; *CC* 7 March 1862; *CUM* 15 January, 22 January, 29
    January, 5 February, 12 February, 19 February, 26 February, 2 April, 9 April
    1862; *CE* 29 January, 19 February, 2 April, 16 April 1862, 2 April 1863, also *CC*
    28 February, 7 March, 3 April, 17 April 1861.
110 *CE* 19 November, 26 November 1863; *CUM* 28 October, 4 November, 11
    November, 18 November 1863.
111 *CE* 24 September, 1 October, 8 October, 16 October, 22 October, 14 Novem-
    ber, 19 November, 10 December, 24 December 1862; 7 January, 15 January, 28
    January, 5 February, 18 February 1863; *CUM* 1 October 1862.
112 *CE* 3 December, 17 December 1863, *CUM* 2 February 1863.

supported by many guardians and even by the Poor Law Commissioners, a majority of the board would not sanction a proposal to build a new fever hospital.[113]

In March 1864 John Francis Maguire, a member of the board of guardian and Mayor of Cork, presented detailed plans and costings for a new fever hospital. He suggested that a four-acre site adjacent to the workhouse should be purchased for the hospital and following a discussion a committee was appointed to investigate and report on the viability of the proposal.[114] The committee rejected the idea and proposed that the workhouse garden should be utilised instead. Though it was more or less accepted that a fever hospital was necessary for the workhouse, this recommendation precipitated a protracted and bad-tempered debate on the issue.[115] This debate continued for some months and eventually it was agreed to purchase the additional ground and a design for the new hospital was drawn up.[116]

As the year came to a close, the city's fever hospital was finding it increasingly difficult to cope with the demands of the workhouse. Increasing numbers of patients were being admitted from the city and in November, of the 141 cases in that hospital, 73 were from the workhouse. The guardians acquired temporary accommodation at the South Infirmary for up to 70 fever patients. The first cases were received on 7 December 1864 and a part-time apothecary and medical staff were deployed there.[117] A hospital assistant from the workhouse was appointed as a nurse tender with responsibility for issuing medicines and stimulants. When some of her fellow nursing staff were dismissed for drunkenness, it was found that the volume of wine and spirits consumed in the auxiliary hospital did not correspond with the amount prescribed. This was soon explained when it was discovered that the nurse tender's inability to read or write had been detected by her subordinates, who withdrew extra rations for themselves.[118] This auxiliary hospital remained

---

113 *CE* 11 February 1864; *CUM* 16 December 1864; *CC* 1 October 1863, see also *CC* 16 November 1860; *CUL* 5 April, 10 May, 31 May 1864.

114 *CE* 23 March 1864; *CC* 24 March 1864; 23 March 1864.

115 *CE* 30 March, 31 March, 2 April, 13 April 1864.

116 *CE* 4 May, 18 May, 25 May, 1 June, 16 June, 23 June, 13 July, 18 July, 1 September, 8 September, 15 September, 12 October, 10 November, 1 December, 8 December, 10 December, 14 December, 28 December 1864; *CC* 26 May, 2 June, 7 July, 8 July, 23 July 1864; *CUM* 13 April, 4 May, 18 May, 1 June, 8 June, 15 June, 22 June, 6 July, 13 July, 27 July, 5 October, 12 October 1864; *CUL* 20 September, 24 November, 9 November 1864, 3 January, 12 January, 28 March, 25 April 1865.

117 *CE* 17 November, 24 November, 1 December, 2 December, 8 December 1864, 11 January, 19 January, 25 January, 21 April, 27 April 1865; *CUL* 29 November 1864.

118 *CE* 21 April, 27 April 1865.

in operation until mid-1865. At that time the workhouse had infirmary accommodation for 1,068 patients and a further 76 cases could be treated in a separate ward. External accommodation for 100 patients gave the institution a total capacity for 1,244 hospital patients and 2,133 pauper inmates.[119]

When the design and extent of the new workhouse fever hospital was finally agreed upon, Thomas Connor of Cook Street was employed in May 1865 to construct the facility for £1,500.[120] By April 1866 the hospital was being roofed, walls were being plastered and internal partitions were under construction. The building was completed that autumn but problems with plumbing, windows and chimneys postponed its occupation.[121] A description of the building tells us that a block of sick wards extended from each side of a central unit. The two blocks were identical

> they are each about sixty six feet in length by about twenty-four in width. These apartments are lofty and lightsome, and ventilated on a new and ingenious principle, and have water closets, lavatories, etc., attached. Overhead, and exactly of the same dimensions, are the dormitories, commodious, airy, and, withal, comfortable rooms. On the lower floor, a corridor communicates between one ward and the other, off which are the nurses' apartments, two convalescent wards, and clothes store. In like manner, in the upper portion of the house, a lobby runs from dormitory to dormitory, two other convalescent wards, nurses' quarters, surgery, and consultation chamber opening off it. The building, which is capable of containing a hundred patients, is said by men whose opinion in such matters is entitled to weight, to be one of the best designed and constructed hospitals in the kingdom.[122]

The hospital opened on Tuesday 18 December 1866. Within days numerous diseases, including typhus fever, were under treatment.[123]

119 *CE* 4 May 1865; *CUM* 15 June 1865; PP 1866, Vol. LXII, [309], *Infirmary Accommodation*, pp. 4-5.
120 *CE* 11 January, 19 January, 1 February, 9 February, 9 March, 17 March, 24 March, 31 March, 13 April, 27 April, 11 May, 27 July 1865; *CUM* 8 February, 15 February, 22 February, 18 May, 23 May, 8 June, 13 July, 31 August, 2 November, 30 November, 7, 21 and 28 December 1865; 11, 18, 25 January, 22 February, 1, 15, 22, 29 March 1866; *CUL* 23 May, 7 June, 12 June, 14 June, 19 July, 16 August, 17 October, 15 November, 5 December, 13 December 1865, 5 March, 27 March, 18 April, 29 May, 12 June, 27 June, 27 August 1866.
121 *CE* 8 September, 29 September, 22 December, 29 December 1865; 22 March, 31 March, 12 April, 10 May, 18 May, 9 August, 6 September, 15 November, 22 November, 29 November 1866; *CC* 29 November 1866; 26 April, 3 May 1866; *CUM* 14 November 1866.
122 *CC* 9 August 1866.
123 *CE* 20 December, 27 December 1866; 24 January 1867; *CUM* 19 December 1866, 23, 30 January, 20 February 1867, 27 May 1868; *CUL* 6 February 1867.

Accommodation in new Fever Hospital

WARD NO.	DIMENSIONS	DESIG-NATION	CAPACITY
1	65 feet 10 inches by 24 feet-1 inch, by 12 feet 8 inches high	Male fever	16
2	65 feet 10 inches by 24 feet I inch, by 12 feet 8 inches	Male fever	16
3	20 feet 2 inches by 17 feet 9 inches by 12 feet 8 inches high	Male convalescent	4
4	20 feet 2 inches by 17 feet 9 inches by 12 feet 8 inches high	Male convalescent	4
5	65 feet 10 inches by 24 feet 1 inch by 16 feet 9 inches	Female fever	21
6	65 feet 10 inches by 24 feet 1 inch by 16 feet 9 inches	Female fever	21
7	20 feet 2 inches by 17 feet 9 inches by 16 feet 9 inches	Female convalescent	6
8	20 feet 2 inches by 17 feet 9 inches by 16 feet 9 inches	Female convalescent	6
	TOTAL ACCOMMODATION		94

(*Source: CUL* 23 January 1867)

Shortly before the new hospital opened, the board of guardians discussed its management and staffing. Some board members saw the development as an opportunity to extend the working hours of Doctors Popham and Townsend. Both men had their own practices in the city and their attendance at the workhouse consisted of a visit to the house for a couple of hours each day. The guardians compiled a new timetable, which required extra attendance in the workhouse and a second daily or nightly visit by the medical officers. The doctors objected, and Dr Townsend only withdrew his resignation after considerable pressure from the alarmed guardians.[124] The Poor Law Commissioners intervened and their suggestion that a third medical officer be employed was eventually agreed to.[125]

---

124 *CE* 23 May, 28 May, 30 May, 13 June 1866; *CC* 31 May 1866; *CUM* 30 May 1866, 24 April 1867. Dr Townsend resigned to concentrate on his private practice in January 1867, and Dr Richard Callaghan was elected as a new Medical Officer in February. *CE* 17 January, 14 February, 25 February 1867.
125 *CE* 20 June, 11 July 1866.

The city fever hospital authorities were relieved when the workhouse opened its own fever unit. In their annual report they rejoiced that the new hospital ended the 'indiscriminate contact of destitution and squalor with the more orderly and comfortable classes resorting to our hospital'.[126] When the annual report of the new workhouse hospital was published in 1868 it showed that a total of 735 cases were admitted during its first year of operation. Although cases of 'pure' fever, such as typhus and typhoid, accounted for 401 admissions, the greatest proportion of the 71 deaths in the hospital occurred among patients suffering from measles and scarlatina.[127]

During the spring of 1866 some timber sheds used by female hospital patients were falling into decay and during rain showers, occupants 'had to take up their beds and bed clothes and crowd together for shelter and warmth'.[128] A large part of the female hospital consisted of a lock ward and, because of the inflexible classification system, it was unavailable to general patients. In order to increase accommodation, the board decided to utilise the hospital lofts,[129] but when the 'wretched tumble down' sheds were demolished their removal deprived the hospital of 50 bed spaces. Despite reorganisation, the women and children's wards were overcrowded and the lock ward had only 116 beds for 166 women and children.[130] The lock area was divided into three wards, 'one for cases under medical treatment; another for persons of immoral character, but not under medical treatment; and one for those who gave signs of reformation'.[131]

Before the end of 1867, new sheds were constructed for the lock patients and by converting an area above the nursery day rooms, a further 40 general hospital beds were provided.[132] Nonetheless, two, and sometimes three, general patients shared beds in some areas. In one ward where 68 patients shared 45 beds, the accommodation problem was eased by pushing two beds together to allow a third person sleep in the middle area.

126 *CE* 21 February 1867.
127 *CE* 25 August 1868; *CUM* 27 May 1868.
128 *CE* 14 April 1866; *CC* 22 December 1864; 6 September 1866; *CUL* 29 November 1864, 18 October, 31 October 1865.
129 *CE* 20 April, 3 May, 18 May, 23 August, 6 September 1866; *CC* 23 August 1866; *CUM* 17 May, 23 May 1866.
130 *CE* 4 October, 11 October 1866; *CC* 11 October 1866; *CUM* 19 September, 10 October 1866.
131 *CE* 18 October, 22 October, 25 October, 15 November 1866; *CUM* 12 September, 3, 10, 17, 24 October 1866. Workhouse accommodation was also used to care for victims of a cholera outbreak, which lasted from 8 October to 27 December 1866. A total of 132 cases occurred in the city. *CE* 11 April 1867; *CC* 18 October 1866. See also *CUM* 15 February 1866 for details of a suspected cholera case in the workhouse.
132 *CE* 19 December 1867; *CUM* 1 January 1868.

Some patients refused to share a bed and, instead, they slept on the floor.[133] This situation continued and some infirm wards were so crowded that during the night, beds were pushed together to make more room for the occupants.[134]

For a period during the early 1860s Sisters of Mercy visited Catholic hospital patients and Protestant ladies visited patients of their persuasion.[135] Though it was sanctioned in 1863 that the Sisters should be allowed into the house to attend the sick, nothing happened until the end of 1870 when the house committee was persuaded to investigate the matter.[136] The Catholic bishop, William Delaney, approved of the plan to allow Sisters of Mercy take charge of the workhouse hospital. At that stage he would not permit their involvement as nurses in the lock hospital, fever hospital or nursery wards, but they could visit these areas to give spiritual assistance and instruction. The nursing nuns would require accommodation in which to live as a community and would also expect to be paid a salary. As this would entail additional expense, the house committee and some guardians were disappointed that the bishop wanted to curtail the sphere of the nurses' activities.[137]

While these matters were being resolved, the Protestant interest stole a march on their rivals and the recruitment of two of their nursing nuns was sanctioned. The two ladies, Sisters Clara Augusta Jump and Mary Anne Goodwin, both veterans of the Franco-Prussian war, who had no problem about working in any part of the workhouse, took up duty during the summer of 1871.[138] The Sisters of Mercy finally entered the

133 *CE* 7 November, 14 November, 15 November 1867; 30 January, 6 February 1868; *CUM* 29 March 1866.
134 *CE* 27 August, 11 December 1868; *CUL* 18 August 1868.
135 *CE* 28 April 1864; 14 March, 18 July, 20 July 1865; *CUM* 6 July 1865.
136 *CE* 2 February, 10, 12, 18, 26 March 1863; 18, 20 July, 24 August 1865; 31 October 4, 12, 14 November 1867, 7 October, 14 October 1870.
137 *CE* 16 December, 23 December 1870, 6 January, 13 January, 20 January, 27 January, 3 February, 1 May, 2 June, 16 June 1871; *CUM* 15 December, 27 December 1870; 5 January, 2 February 1871; *CUL* 4 January 1871; The subject of admitting nuns to workhouse hospitals is covered in some detail by Patricia Kelly; see Patricia Kelly, *From workhouse to hospital*, Thesis (1972), Chapters 8 to 13; see also Maria Luddy, 'Angels of Mercy': nuns as workhouse nurses, 1861-1898', in Elizabeth Malcolm and Greta Jones, *Medicine, disease and the state in Ireland, 1650-1940* (Cork, 1999), pp. 102-117.
138 *CE* 10 February, 7 April, 28 April, 23 June, 30 June, 25 August 1871; *CUM* 18 May, 25 May, 22 June, 23 November 1871, 20 October, 27 November 1873, 23 April 1874; *CUL* 27 June 1871. Because of a domestic problem, Sr. Clara resigned from the house in October 1871 and was replaced by Ellen Fuller. Another Protestant nurse, Sr. Mary Gibbons resigned in June 1873, *CUM* 19 June 1873. *CUL* 31 October, 29 November, 5 December 1871; *CE* 27 October 1871; *CUM* 18 September, 18 December 1879, 25 August 1881. It was later remarked that the Protestant sisters introduced 'order and system' to their area of duty in the workhouse. *CUM* 24 April 1873.

workhouse on 3 November 1871 when eight of their community commenced duty as nurses. They resided in their own quarters and were paid £30 each per annum.[139] Although the role of the nursing nuns gradually expanded, the workhouse continued to rely on unpaid staff for many hospital duties. The following table shows the state of the hospital in 1881:

Hospital nursing staff and patients

FACILITY	AVERAGE NO. OF PATIENTS	PAID STAFF	UNPAID STAFF
Infirmary	961	9 nuns, 6 lay nurses	178 pauper nurses
Fever Hospital	53	3 nurses	9 pauper staff
Lunatic wards	28 male, 119 female	1 nurse 2 female attendants	2 male attendants 9 female attendants

(*Source*: PP 1881, Vol. LXXXIX, [433], *Return of hospital staff* p. 7)

---

139 *CE* 17 November 1871; 26 January, 16 February, 23 February 1872; *CC* 22 February, 26 February, 28 February 1872; *CUM* 18 May, 9 November 1871; PP 1873, Vol. LV, [246], *Return of nurses in workhouses*. One of the original nuns died during the 1872 smallpox epidemic and was replaced by Sr. Mary Paula Keyes. *CUL* 3 July, 15 November 1871, 29 May, 11 June, 26 June 1872; 14 May 1873; *CUM* 4 September, 9 October 1879. Sr. Agnes Wall took charge of the nursery in October 1879.

8 Health 1872–90

Although improvements had been made to administration and staffing, during the previous decades, deficiencies still existed in the hospital system at the start of the 1870s. Poor standards were frequently tolerated, and patients in the general wards and lunatic department were forced to suffer discomfort and embarrassment because basic sanitary and washing facilities were often absent. Outbreaks of disease still occurred and the workhouse was to the fore during the battle against smallpox in the early 1870s. Attempts by medical staff to provide appropriate medical care were often frustrated by the attitude of guardians – this was particularly true when the doctors sought to prescribe alcoholic stimulants and nourishing food for certain patients.

Smallpox

When a number of ship-based smallpox cases occurred in Cork harbour in 1871, it was apprehended that a major outbreak could result. Although the prospect of 'smallpox at our doors' alarmed the Cork Union medical officers, just a handful of cases and very few deaths were recorded.[1] When the workhouse fever hospital report was published in June 1871 the medical officers noted that they had treated just one case of the disease. With obvious relief they recorded that 'we are happy to add our testimony to the opinion expressed by the Poor Law Commissioners, that this disfiguring and dangerous ailment has been of late years almost completely stamped out in this country by careful attention to vaccination'.[2] By the first week of January 1872 it was painfully

---

1 *CE* 10 February, 14 February, 17 February, 20 February, 21 February, 27 February, 3 March, 7 March, 10 March, 17 March, 24 March, 14 April, 14 July 1871; *CUM* 9 February, 16 February, 8 June 1871; *CUL* 8 February, 23 February, 27 February, 8 March, 15 March, 20 March, 13 July 1871; *Poor Law Commissioners Annual Report* (1871), pp. 37, 257, 259, 262; NAI, CSORP 1874 10758; NAI, CSORP 1872 696.

2 *CE* 23 June 1871; The view that smallpox was on the decline was supported by official correspondence, see PP 1867-8, Vol. LXI, [196], *Circulars and Correspondence re smallpox*, pp. 6-11; see also *CUL* 20 September 1869; *CC* 13 February 1868.

evident that smallpox had not been stamped out. During the previous month 32 victims had been admitted to the workhouse. Soon, the workhouse fever hospital was given over to smallpox patients and a number of pauper inmates were appointed as nurses at 1s.6d. each per week.[3] A few cases occurred in the workhouse itself, but the number of admissions increased so rapidly that the workhouse hospital was barely able to cope with the demand. Service personnel were also under pressure and although a minimum of three women were required to wash the linen and clothing just one was available for the task. Hospital assistants were offered improved rations and 1s.6d. each per week to take up duty with the smallpox patients. None was willing to transfer and a stipulation prohibiting communication between the smallpox hospital staff and other workhouse inmates and personnel was a major deterrent to potential recruits. As a solution to the dilemma, the workhouse master was given carte blanche to select a number of women to act as nurses in the hospital.[4]

As the workhouse fever hospital was unable to cater for the influx of smallpox patients in addition to its regular quota of fever victims, arrangements were made to divert city fever patients to the city hospital for the duration of the outbreak.[5] Although it was anticipated that the outbreak would be short lived, by mid-January the workhouse fever wards were packed to overflowing with eight fever, three scarlatina and 86 smallpox patients. Even in this period of extreme personal danger, snobbery and pride came to the fore. Some smallpox victims, particularly those who did not wish to be associated with the workhouse and who preferred to pay for their treatment, insisted on applying for care at the fever hospital. To cope with the demand for accommodation, a joint committee of workhouse and fever hospital representatives decided that extra space would be made available. As an emergency measure it was agreed to construct a number of timber sheds for smallpox victims in the workhouse grounds. At the city fever hospital, some isolated buildings were reserved for people 'who would not take gratis relief'.[6]

By the first week of February 1872, of 232 smallpox cases admitted to the workhouse, 35 had died and almost 100 were receiving treatment. An analysis of the victims produced a convincing argument against the

---

3 *CE* 15 December, 29 December 1871; *CUL* 3 January 1872; *CUM* 7 December. 14 December, 28 December 1871, 4 January 1872; NAI, CSORP 1872 696. General fever cases were confined in the probationary wards which were commandeered for this purpose; *Poor Law Commissioners Annual Report* (1872), p. 192.

4 *CUM* 25 January, 29 February, 7 March, 21 March, 30 May 1872; *CE* 5 January, 12 January, 3 May 1872.

5 *CE* 5 January, 1 March 1872.

6 *CE* 17 January, 26 January, 9 February 1872; *CC* 26 January, 9 March, 22 March, 26 April, 3 May 1872; *CUM* 18 January, 8 February 1872.

anti-vaccination theories being propounded by a section of the population. Of the 232 victims, 100 had not been vaccinated, 93 of these had a most virulent form of the disease and 32 of them had died. Conversely, of the 132 vaccinated cases, only a small number had a serious form of the disease and just 3 had died.[7] The number of smallpox cases continued to escalate. By March, almost 500 victims had been admitted and 160 still remained in the workhouse. Lives were being endangered by limited accommodation, and it became necessary to mix seriously ill patients with convalescents. Even on this occasion, guardians who did not wish to incur the expense of further construction work, fought to have the probationary wards converted for convalescent patients. The medical officers intervened with a warning that a major outbreak would occur in the body of the house if such a plan were implemented. Common sense prevailed and the board of guardians agreed to construct another 100 feet long wooden shed in the workhouse yard.[8]

Child smallpox cases admitted to Cork Workhouse
3 Dec. 1871 – 4 June 1872

	ADMISSIONS	DEATHS
3 to 5 year olds	72	23
Vaccinated	21	2
Not vaccinated	51	21
Infants	82	43
Vaccinated	18	2
Not vaccinated	64	41

(*Source*: *CUL* 12 June 1872)

It became increasingly difficult to cater for the large number of inquiries, so a notice with details of each patient's progress was posted up at the workhouse gate each day. Visitors were not permitted to enter and to cater for the inquiries of illiterate relations and friends, the gate porter read out the details to the assembled inquirers at least three times each day.[9]

For a variety of reasons, but particularly from fear, many smallpox victims were unwilling to enter the workhouse, and some parents would not send offspring to the institution. Many victims were treated in their own homes in the city's lanes and alleys where they lived 'in small houses

---

7 *CE* 2 February 1872; *CC* 2 February, 9 February, 16 February, 1 March 1872; *Poor Law Commissioners Annual Report* (1872), pp. 33, 51-4, 188-194.
8 *CE* 1 March, 8 March 1872; *CC* 8 March 1872; *CUL* 22 March, 9 April 1872; *CUM* 29 February 1872; *Poor Law Commissioners Annual Report* (1872), p. 194.
9 *CE* 15 March, 11 April, 10 April 1872; *CC* 15 March 1872; 14 March 1872.

crammed together without sufficient light, air or space'. Patients who agreed to enter the workhouse were conveyed in the ambulance or 'sick van'. Rumours about poor care and treatment, and overcrowding in the workhouse wards, circulated in the city. The stories, although untrue, merely fuelled the popular imagination and gave justification to the people's distrust of the workhouse and its officials.[10]

Many of the city's working people believed that the hospital nurses were badly supervised and had no interest in their patients. They had, in the words of one observer, 'no social influence – they were mere scrubbers'.[11] In an attempt to change this image and encourage more people to enter the hospital, the Sisters of Mercy took up duty amongst the smallpox patients at the start of May. An immediate increase was noted in the rate of applications and soon patients from poorer parts of the city began to flock into the hospital. The Protestant sisters followed the example of the Sisters of Mercy and by mid-May the smallpox hospital was transformed 'into a perfect place of solace for the sick'. In its wards 'everything is order and purity; an atmosphere of tenderness seems to fold itself round the patients'.[12]

The hospital's medical officers received strict instructions not to release patients until they were clear of all signs of smallpox.[13] This put pressure on the available accommodation, so a joint committee of guardians and members of Cork Corporation agreed that a separate convalescent hospital should be established for recovering patients. A number of workhouse inmates were employed as nurses in this outside convalescent unit. They were given limited privileges and, as most had children, they were warned that they could not leave the institution unless they took their dependants with them.[14]

The outbreak gradually subsided. By the autumn of 1872 the convalescent hospital was closed and some of its furniture, including bedsteads, was removed to the workhouse. By the end of September, little trace of the disease remained and in the workhouse hospital, just a few smallpox patients were receiving treatment.[15] During the epidemic 3,365 known cases of smallpox occurred in Cork City, of whom 1,250 were treated in the workhouse. The city fever hospital treated 668 victims

10 *CUL* 20 February, 22 February, 17 April, 30 April 1872; *CUM* 11 April 1872.
11 *CE* 26 April 1872; *CC* 19 April, 26 April 1872.
12 *CE* 29 April, 1 May, 3 May, 14 May, 22 May 1872; *CC* 3 May, 24 May 1872.
13 *CE* 12 January 1872.
14 *CE* 22 March, 29 March, 17 April, 19 April, 26 April, 10 May 1872; *CC* 22 March, 26 April, 3 May, 10 May 1872; *CUM* 4 July, 11 July 1872.
15 *CE* 30 August, 20 September, 27 September, 4 October, 11 October 1872; *CC* 26 July 1872; *CUL* 30 October 1872; *CUM* 25 July, 17, 24, 31 October, 19 December 1872, 16, 23, 30 January, 6 February 1873. During the epidemic, just 13 children were attacked with the disease in the workhouse. *CUM* 22 October 1874.

and 150 died. The average stay of each patient in hospital was 30 days. The 1872 smallpox outbreak was 'unprecedented in its duration, its wide diffusion and its malignancy'.[16]

Smallpox admissions to Cork workhouse
April to September 1872

WEEK ENDING	ADMISSIONS		CURED	DIED		REMAIN-ING
	Vaccinated	Non-vaccinated		Vaccinated	Non-vaccinated	
11 Apr	28	17	34	7		134
18 Apr	18	21	35	2	9	130
25 Apr	36	22	21	0	15	154
2 May	47	24	53	3	6	167
9 May	32	14	44	1	10	158
16 May	33	31	38	3	9	170
23 May	18	19	45	1	14	150
30 May	28	20	34	2	15	148
6 June	41	16	34	0	8	155
13 June	20	13	29	2	11	140
20 June	17	7	40	0	4	126
27 June	12	12	29	1	4	115
4 July	14	1	33	1	7	93
11 July	18	5	33	0	1	78
18 July	7		29	0	1	58
25 July	3	5	27	0	1	35
1 Aug	3	4	14	0	1	27
8 Aug	1	2	10	0	1	19
15 Aug	2	1	4	0	1	17
22 Aug	4	6	8	0	0	19
29 Aug	1	1	2	0	1	18
5 Sept	2	0	4	0	0	16
12 Sept	1	2	3	0	0	16
19 Sept	0	0	4	0	0	12
26 Sept	0	0	5	0	0	9

(Source: Cork board of guardians' minute books)

Further outbreaks of small pox occurred in Ireland during 1874 and 1875 and again in the period 1878-79. The number of fatalities during the latter epidemic was high, with 254 deaths occurring in workhouses.

---

16 *CE* 31 January, 19 February, 28 February 1873.

These outbreaks were confined principally to Dublin and northern counties so the disease had little impact in Cork.[17]

Hospital Conditions

New arrivals to the workhouse were usually washed and isolated in the probationary wards prior to entering the body of the house. In addition to monitoring the behaviour of the new arrivals, isolation also helped to control the spread of disease. With the exception of any who were dangerously ill, all females were bathed in the probationary ward before they passed into the house itself. The water was rarely hot, and in any case, no method was available to check its temperature. Facilities for males were also rudimentary. On entry to the probationary wards, inmates were forced to stand in a bath of cold water, which barely reached their knees, and give themselves a thorough cleansing. The doctors complained that this system of washing new arrivals in cold water was almost useless. An investigating committee, which reiterated the view that hot water was essential, recommended that baths and hot water cisterns be acquired for new arrivals and hospital patients.[18]

Despite repeated requests, nothing was done to improve the situation, and few guardians had any interest in making changes.[19] Dr Wherland was satisfied with the existing arrangements, which he believed were adequate for the number of inmates in the house. Resorting to the oft-used stratagem of comparing the situation of the poor outside with that of their counterparts in the workhouse, he observed that the latter 'were in no worse position than the citizens of Cork, not all of whom had baths in their houses'.[20] This was his rationale for not making improvements, although he did concede that portable side-baths should be available for hospital patients who were unable to leave their beds. The matter was discussed at a number of meetings attended by Dr Charles Croker King, the Local Government inspector who spoke in favour of improving the bathing facilities.[21]

When Dr Croker King carried out his periodic inspection of the work-house during the summer of 1873 he reported that some bathing facilities had been installed, as also had a new ventilation system. He

---

17 *Local Government Board annual report* (1875), pp. 30-1; (1876), pp. 27-30; (1877), pp. 24-5; (1878), p. 26; (1878-9), pp. 26-9;(1880), pp. 26-7; (1884-5), p. 25; (1889), p. 20. Some cases were admitted to the Cork workhouse, see for instance: *CE* 15, 17 January 1879.
18 *CE* 24 January, 31 January, 21 March, 4 April 1873.
19 *CE* 12 June, 26 June, 16 October 1874.
20 *CE* 16 October 1874.
21 *CE* 23 October, 30 October, 6 November 1874.

found that although the general hospital wards were clean and in good order, there were some exceptions. The old wooden building, dating from 1847, in which male paupers were housed, was 'dark and gloomy'. 'The foundations of the entire building are rotting away and were it not for the massive timber crutches placed all round it, there is no question but that it would have given way at one side or the other. The danger now is that it will tumble in causing extreme loss of life, to the paupers, including the old people, the blind and the boys'.[22] One ward of the men's hospital, which was located on an incline, was partially below ground and its flagged floor was frequently covered with a few inches of rain water and liquid sewage, which made virtual prisoners of its aged and blind occupants. Although he condemned this ward as 'low and objectionable', others referred to it as a 'mouldy dungeon'. To ease the problem from water seepage and flooding, timber pallets were placed on the ground so that the occupants could move around without getting wet.[23] Nonetheless, the problem was not really solved and conditions in the 'catacomb', as the sister in charge called the ward, continued to cause discomfort for its occupants.[24] Further improvements, including the addition of a porch and the provision of extra windows for ventilation and light, did give some slight comfort to the occupants during fine weather. Dr Croker King noted a number of other inadequacies, including a lack of male hospital accommodation, the absence of toilets in the male and female hospital, and the necessity for a laundry at the children's hospital. As an interim solution to the lack of toilets, it was decided to install earth closets and W.Cs, in some departments.[25] Before the end of 1875 the guardians conceded that improvements were indeed necessary and proper baths and washing facilities were provided for the female lunatics and hospital patients, and also for the hospital surgical department.[26] Some weeks later old walls in the female hospital, which were infested with all sorts of bugs and insects, had to be plastered to save the women from constant annoyance.[27]

Facilities for insane inmates were poor and it was not uncommon to have two patients sleeping in one bed. Overcrowding was common in the dull and gloomy lunatic wards, and at one stage 19 men shared twelve beds.[28] The department's 104 female inmates had nothing to do all day

22 *CUM* 4 February 1875, also 4 March and 18 March 1875; *CC* 18 May 1875.
23 *CE* 23 February, 28 February, 7 March, 2 March 1873; 23 January 1874; *CUM* 27 February, 6 March 1873.
24 *CE* 23 January, 13 February 1874; 5 November 1875; *CC* 5 November 1875.
25 *CE* 4 July, 18 July, 25 July 1873; *CUM* 24 December 1874.
26 *CE* 2 July 1875.
27 *CUM* 3, 10 February 1876.
28 *CE* 3 March 1876.

and the solitary nurse was unable to give them adequate attention.[29] The female blind apartment was used for most of the patients' activities including eating, sleeping and passing their time. Its yard was small and lacked any form of covering to shelter the inmates from rain or sunshine.[30] Blind inmates were frequently sent to the Cork Blind Asylum and an allowance was paid for their maintenance. Ever suspicious of the motives of the public, a group of guardians feared that if outdoor relief – which amounted to about half the cost of maintenance in the workhouse – was granted, blind people would be encouraged to enter the workhouse to obtain the concession.[31]

Dayrooms and toilets were required for the nursery and its hospital and a covered outdoor exercise area was needed for convalescent fever patients.[32] The children's day room was 'unhealthy' and rudimentary, and, according to one observer, it resembled 'a kind of manufactory of disease', where the children developed like 'badly cared geranium plants dying out in a green house'.[33] Money for undertaking some improvements was borrowed, and by mid 1877 a new male ward was nearing completion and blind and insane inmates also had a new department.[34]

During the winter of 1877 an increase in sickness among the occupants in the new male infirm division was blamed on dampness from the construction work, so Dr Wall ordered extra coal for the wards.[35] Improvements resulted but, because some men had to sleep on the floor when their filthy beds were removed, chest and lung complaints increased. Poor quality blankets and day room seats placed against damp walls accelerated sickness and an uncharacteristic increase in deaths precipitated a discussion at a guardians' meeting in January 1878. Rev. Bowen, the Catholic chaplain, complained that since the beds were removed 83 aged men were sleeping on 'wretched beds laid upon [against] the cold, newly-built walls'. He also criticised the failure to return, or replace underwear, following the men's admission to the house. He instanced the case of a 'pretty hale old man' named John O Connell who came to the workhouse on 13 December 1877. On arrival, 65 year-old O Connell swapped his clothes for the workhouse uniform, but his flannel underwear was not replaced. He was taken to the infirm ward where

> the cold pierced him intensely, yet he continued to do his work as
> required by the rules of the establishment, until Monday night, the

29 *CE* 28 May 1876; 10 August, 31 August 1877.
30 *CE* 23 January, 13 February 1874.
31 *CE* 8 August, 26 September 1873; 26 June 1874.
32 *CE* 28 January, 28 May 1876.
33 *CE* 15 January 1875; *CUM* 14 January and 11 February 1875.
34 *CE* 22 June, 29 June, 20 July 1877; also 15 May 1874.
35 *CE* 23 November 1877.

31st December. That night he complained and on Tuesday morning he was brought before the doctor for 'medical treatment'. The doctor prescribed for him, and sent him back again to the infirm ward. He was seen again by the doctor on Wednesday, and again sent back to the 'infirm'. He was not seen at all on Thursday, although on the day he was not able to eat any food. On Friday inflammation of the lungs had clearly set in, and eventually he was ordered into hospital. I prescribed for him on Saturday, when he made this statement, and on Friday he was dead.

Dr Wall gave a similar account and he concluded that O Connell had died from inflammation of the lungs 'superadded to chronic bronchitis'. An increase in the death rate among the older inmates was usual during winter and in the corresponding period in 1876 eight fatalities resulted from a total of 40 chest complaints and in the following year seven of 48 cases succumbed. The incident did have a positive result and it was decided that any man with flannels would automatically get new ones on arrival at the workhouse; others would be supplied at the discretion of the medical officers.[36] Also new blankets were purchased for the old men's department.

During the early months of 1884 the male hospital was again over-crowded; forty-four patients were sleeping on straw beds on the floor and another six shared three beds. The medical officers made the usual appeal for more beds and suggested that an old wooden shed should be used as extra accommodation.[37] Dr Cronin, the medical officer in charge of the male hospital was responsible for a total of 963 patients in the workhouse. He had 438 patients in the general hospital, 278 in the infirmary, 139 in the boys' school and 108 in the male able-bodied area. When he complained, the guardians merely suggested that if the work was too heavy he should resign and concentrate on his private practice.[38] The infirm men were still obliged to share beds but one guardian said that this was 'quite comfortable enough for paupers'. The Poor Law Inspector was not impressed and when he voiced his objection to such a practice being permitted in a public institution, forty new beds were purchased.[39] Plans to extend the existing accommodation were drawn up and, as a stop-gap measure, it was suggested that some paupers should be sent to neigh-bouring unions with spare accommodation. The possibility of rearranging the school children's accommodation was also investigated.[40]

---

36 *CE* 4 January, 11 January, 18 January, 25 January, 8 February 1878; *CUM* 3 January, 10 January, 17 January, 24 January 1878.
37 *CE* 8 February, 22 February, 7 March, 21 March 1884; See also *CUM* 13 February, 20 February 1879, for reports of overcrowding in male wards.
38 *CE* 21 March, 28 March, 4 April 1884.
39 *CE* 11 April 1884, 16 January, 23 January, 6 February 1885.
40 *CE* 16 January, 20 January, 23 January, 24 January, 18 June 1885.

Some guardians could not accept that the overcrowding in the hospital resulted solely from sickness and hardship. Instead, they attributed it to conditions in the workhouse, which enticed applicants to where they would be better fed and clothed 'than the honest and decent people, that remained struggling and striving outside'. They also said that many hospital patients were well able to pay for their own treatment and they claimed that undeserving applicants gained access to the workhouse because of inadequate checking procedures.[41] The workhouse separation ward – a secure unit which ensured that its occupants did not fraternise with the general body of inmates – had about 80 prostitutes, some of whom were receiving the hospital diet because of ill-health, and others because they worked as nurses in the department. Col. Spaight believed that these women remained in the workhouse because of its good food and a policy which enabled them to stay 'idling and doing nothing at all – a life which must lead to mischief and discontent'.[42] He produced figures to show that the Cork Lock Hospital and Magdalen Asylum had greater success at reclaiming prostitutes 'from a life of sin and shame to one of comparative respectability'. This claim was contradicted by a newspaper correspondent who said that many of the workhouse prostitutes were 'leading truly penitent, Christian lives' and that most of them were determined not to return to their former careers.[43]

To make the hospital less attractive, its water supply was cut off each night between 8pm and 7am and a drinking supply was available from buckets. Conditions in the male hospital were unpleasant. The W.Cs were 'defective and offensive, the excreta now remaining some hours in the basin, till it reaches a certain point', and causes foul odours in the wards and passages. Colonel Spaight urged the guardians to install an automatic flusher and to erect wash basins. Toilet facilities for the women were also poor and they 'were somewhat like caged birds, with no accommodation but open buckets from which the stench was most abominable'. The inspector was shocked with conditions in some of the wards. When he arrived at the female hospital one evening he found the corpses of three women who had died in the early morning, still lying on their beds – 'the living and suffering patients having had to take their meals with those melancholy objects before them for so many hours'.[44]

The hospital also required a proper operating theatre for surgical procedures, so a glass porch in the nearby nuns' department, was modified and equipped for the purpose. The facility was frequently in use and

---

41 *CE* 16 January, 23 January 1885.
42 *CE* 6, 13 November 1885.
43 *CE* 13 and 14 November 1885.
44 *CE* 22 August 1884; 26 February, 9 April 1886, see also *CC* 9 April, 26 May 1886.

sometimes up to six operations were carried out in the course of one morning in an area in which the medical officer had 'barely room to turn'.[45] Patients were occasionally dissatisfied with their treatment. One such person was a man named Barry who had been admitted with a damaged arm. On the advise of Dr Cummins, the arm was amputated and replaced with an artificial limb. Barry claimed that he had undertaken the surgery only after Cummins had assured him that the new arm would be fully functional and would allow him pursue his livelihood as a boot and shoemaker. Things did not work out as planned and instead of a functioning arm, Barry was fitted with a stump, which had a hook at one end. He was unable to pursue his occupation and his complaints that the surgery had left him 'in a position of total helplessness and destitution', got little sympathy from the guardians.[46]

Treatment and attention in hospital wards was not always perfect. When a family named Morgan was admitted to the fever wards, the husband and one child died within a few days. During an inspection of the ward, at 6.10 a.m. two days later, Mrs. Murphy, the staff nurse, was missing from her post and her assistant was sound asleep. The inspector was shocked to fine Kate Morgan unattended and 'tied by a sheet to the iron bed'. The woman died shortly afterwards and Mrs. Murphy was dismissed from her position in the workhouse hospital.[47] On another occasion, Dr Cummins ordered two young medical officers to apply leeches to a poor man suffering from a painful swelling. Because of a misunderstanding and unfamiliarity with staff structures, the doctors waited for the staff nurse to order the leeches. She in turn believed that the doctors would get them, so nothing was done. When the leeches were eventually delivered no one was notified so they remained unused for another five hours and deteriorated in quality. The medical officers were severely criticised for their neglect, but, as the patient made a full recovery, no action was taken.[48] Friction sometimes resulted from the behaviour of skilled staff. During one of Rev. Webster's visits to patients in the female Protestant ward, a nurse entered and created a terrible noise by banging on a large tin dish. Although some of the women were terrified, the clergyman got little satisfaction when he complained. The matter was raised at the next meeting of the guardians and Dr Wall explained that, prior to his visits, a woman entered each ward and

---

45 *CE* 14 May, 9 June 1886; see also *CUM* 22 January 1874, 8 November 1877; *CC* 9 April 1886.
46 *CE* 26 March, 23 April 1886.
47 *CE* 30 October, 2 November, 23 November 1888.
48 *CE* 30 March, 6 April 1888. One source alleged that the leeches were useless when they did arrive because 'they had been used before, and were dripping blood'.

banged on the dish to silence the patients. The doctor had found that this was a reliable method of creating silence which allowed him use his stethoscope to its best advantage! Following Rev. Webster's complaint, the nurse was ordered not to disturb the clergyman and she was instructed to go to other wards when he visited the workhouse.[49]

Bodies

Considering that many guardians treated workhouse inmates with indifference and callousness, it is not surprising that little respect was shown for the remains of deceased paupers. When inmates died in the workhouse their bodies were removed by relatives or friends, or else buried at Carr's Hill graveyard. A burial service was usually held at the workhouse before corpses were removed to the graveyard at Carr's Hill. Because clergy did not officiate at the actual interment, some guardians said that the paupers were 'buried like dogs', and an attempt was made to have a chaplain attend the burial. This was not successful because the majority of guardians were happy with the existing arrangements whereby the rites were performed before the bodies left the workhouse. Although a mortuary chapel was constructed to facilitate the performance of burial services, the clergy made little use of the facility.[50] When it was suggested that the chaplains should be directed to use the chapel, one guardian observed that, as most of the poor people were interred without a ceremony 'it was introducing a luxury into the house, to provide a burial service for the paupers, it was wholly unnecessary and would only entail additional expense'.[51] Because the mortuary chapel was intended for the use of all religious denominations, it was found that most of the clergy were reluctant to use the facility. Rev. McCarthy, the Roman Catholic chaplain, explained that deceased paupers were prayed for at Mass every Sunday and also in the wards where they had died. Because the Catholic clergy would only be willing to make regular use of the mortuary chapel if it was fully equipped and dedicated to one creed, the guardians conceded; money was allocated and arrangements were made to hand the facility over to Rev. Mc Carthy.[52]

Inmates of the workhouse may have been disturbed by these discussions but other occurrences were perhaps more worrying and unnerving for the extra sensitive or superstitious amongst their ranks. In December

---

49 *CE* 30 January 1880.
50 *CE* 14 April, 4 May 1864; 4 November 1870; *CC* 14 April 1864; *CUM* 4, 11 May 1864.
51 *CE* 11 November 1870; *CUM* 10 November 1870; *CUL* 23 November 1870.
52 *CE* 16, 30 December 1870, 6 January 1871; *CUM* 15, 29 December 1870, 5 January 1871.

1863 the workhouse master reported to the board that two medical students had entered the workhouse morgue and carried out post mortems on the bodies of two children. It seemed that the intrusion was unauthorised, but Dr Townsend explained that it was a common practice for young medical doctors to visit the workhouse. Occasionally he requested the young doctors to carry out post mortems on the bodies of patients who had given prior consent. This was necessary for medical certification and it gave the medical officers more time with the living patients. There was some opposition to the practice, and Dr Wall advised his fellow guardians that it was necessary, and if they 'wished to object to *progress*, improvement and advancement in the healing art, they would get an unenviable notoriety for themselves'. His advice that physicians should be given 'every opportunity of exploring disease' was heeded. The guardians agreed that in future the young medical doctors would have to be accompanied by one of the house medical officers when they carried out post mortems.[53]

The unclaimed bodies of inmates were taken to the workhouse morgue where they remained for at least 24 hours, and sometimes for a couple of days. Most of the bodies were then buried at the workhouse graveyard but prior to removal, a message that a corpse was available for dissection purposes was sent to the professor of anatomy at Queen's College. The college required the bodies between September and May and usually about 40 were taken from the workhouse in this period. During the half-year ending 25 March 1866 there were 262 deaths in the workhouse, 125 corpses were removed for family funerals and of the remaining 137, 41 were sent to the college. The practice of sending the unclaimed bodies for dissection dated from the era of the house of industry, the predecessor of the workhouse, and the wishes of people who had expressed a desire not to have their bodies dissected were respected.

The issue was investigated in the late 1860s and it was pointed out that the 'bodies were taken out under certain conditions which did not at all make their removal the terrible and repulsive thing the public thought'. The city's high sheriff took a dispassionate view of the practice 'for my own part, I would have very strong objections to the removal of bodies, but at the same time no person should allow himself to be carried away by any mawkish sentimentalities; the Act was passed for the advancement of science, the study of disease, and the detection and prevention of crime'. The findings of the investigation were that the bodies were removed in 'the most careful and respectful manner, and subsequently buried in consecrated ground'. Although the authorities were exonerated of any irregularities or wrongdoing, the superstitions

53 *CE* 3 December 1863; *CC* 3 December 1863; *CUM* 2 December 1863.

and sensitivities of many workhouse inmates were undoubtedly activated by the revelations at this inquiry.[54]

Hospital care

On occasions the medical officers organised student visits to the workhouse hospital. It was not uncommon for the students to converge on the hospital wards and carry out medical examinations on hapless patients. Many patients resented these unsupervised interventions so the board intervened and restricted visits to students who had special permission. During 1885 it was again proposed to admit medical students who could carry out routine tasks such as changing dressings. As the patients could benefit from supervised medical examinations and because the guardians had a moral duty to help educate the students, it was decided to give them greater access to the hospital. The students, who had to be accompanied at all times, were not allowed to stay longer that three hours. They had to leave before 2 p.m., and, if the fever hospital was on their itinerary, no other wards could be visited afterwards. A maximum of 50 students would be permitted to visit the house in any one day. As the debate about students' visits concluded, Professor William K. Sullivan, president of Queen's College inspected the hospital and expressed satisfaction with the entire premises.[55]

A case of catalepsy, which attracted attention in the mid 1880s, was that of Jeremiah O Sullivan from Castletownbere. The patient aged about 50 years, was admitted to the workhouse in April 1885 by the Cork police who found him asleep in a city street. O Sullivan who had been employed as a wood chopper had returned from Boston just a few days earlier. Shortly after his admission, he fell into a deep sleep. When visited by Dr P.J. Cremen on the following morning

> he presented the appearance of a person in a sound sleep, or under the influence of an anaesthetic; and all ordinary measures were unavailing to awaken him from his trance-like condition. The limbs, when elevated, remained so on being released; the pulse and

---

54 *CE* 15, 20 September 1866; *CC* 20, 24, 27 September 1866; *CUM* 19, 26 September 1866. Complaints by some guardians that burials at Carr's Hill were hurried and unsupervised did not ease this disquiet, *CE* 7 April 1871; Bodies continued to be sent as 'anatomical subjects' to Queen's College, see *CUM* 18 May 1871, 21 May 1874, 18 May 1876, John A. Murphy, *A history of Queen's/University College Cork*, 1845-1995 (Cork, 1995), p. 68; See *CE* 18 July 1855 for correspondence on Queen's College Cork and the acquisition of bodies for medical dissection.

55 *CE* 18 September, 2, 9, 15, 16, 23 October 1885, 22 January 1886; *CUM* 1, 8, 10, 15 October , 10, 31 December 1885.

respiration were tranquil; the eyelids were firmly closed, and, on being raised, the eyes were found up turned, and the pupils contracted; the jaw was tightly clenched; the temperature stood at 96°. . . . There appears to be complete analgesia over the entire surface of the body, pins piercing the skin in any part causing no movement of withdrawal, nor any indication of pain. . . .

His senses were tested and it was found that, if liquid ammonia was held to his nostrils, the only reaction was that he coughed and his eyes watered. Likewise, no reaction was detected when sugar, quinine or other substances were placed directly onto his tongue.[56]

From an account, which was published in the press some 12 months later, we learn that

He remains sleeping fast day and night, and when roughly shaken, he will awake, and do whatever he is told, but it is only on some occasions that he will betray the faculty of speech, which he expresses with intelligence. When food is placed before him he will take it, but the attendant has to keep shaking him at intervals in order to prevent him from going to sleep before the conclusion of the meal. When he has finished eating, he falls asleep in whatever posture he happens to be in at the time, whether sitting or standing. If out in a standing posture, with his hands above his head and his fingers fixed in a certain way, he remains in that attitude until disturbed, without moving a muscle or showing any signs of life except regular breathing. If placed on two chairs, his head resting on one and his feet on the other, he remains so – the body being quite stiff and having the appearance of subjection to mesmeric influence. He is taken out into the yard for exercise every day and will walk about with very little assistance from those who have charge of him . . . such is the way Jerry spends his time – eating when wakened to do so; walking when put on his feet; looking about, and then returning to his uninterrupted slumbers with as much zest as ever. His case is exciting great interest in medical circles. . . .[57]

By the end of 1886 overcrowding was again evident in the male able-bodied and infirm dormitories. When Colonel Spaight discovered that many beds had two occupants he complained of this 'most objectionable practice'. The situation took a serious turn when one man was accused of 'an unnatural crime' and proceedings were initiated against him.[58] To help solve the problem, it was suggested that the then unoccupied St. Patrick's hospital wing in the workhouse, could be used to accommodate some of the extra inmates. One of the wards of this hospital was situated below

---

56 *British Medical Journal* 12 December 1885.
57 *CC* 13 May, 11 June 1886; see also *CC* 14 and 21 June 1886.
58 *CE* 24 December 1886.

ground; it was generally damp and cold and staff and inmates referred to it as 'Spike', which in the language of tramps, was a term used to describe workhouse casual wards.[59] When Colonel Spaight made his report in March 1887 he noted that 20 patients were sleeping double in the male hospital, in the infirmary nine male 'couples' were sleeping together, in the able-bodied area fourteen men shared seven beds and ten lunatics were also sleeping double – in total, he found 125 'couples' sleeping together in the house.[60] Staff were not excluded from this practice and, because of a bed shortage and inadequate accommodation, a new medical officer was forced to share a colleague's bed in February 1888.[61]

Some suggestions were made and, having considered the matter, the visiting committee proposed that the able-bodied day room should be converted to a dormitory for 52 inmates. The committee also recommended that the mattress size should be reduced to 2 feet nine inches and, to prevent intimacy, each should be separated from the adjoining mattress by a nine-inch timber plank standing on edge. To prevent lunatics sharing beds, the committee proposed that their dining area should be used as an additional night dormitory. If all the suggestions were implemented, up to 60 workhouse inmates would still have to share beds. Little seems to have been done to remedy the problem because when Colonel Spaight submitted his report at the end of summer, he again complained about overcrowding in various areas, which was, he noted in a restrained tone, 'very objectionable on various grounds'.[62] Again, the February 1888 report mentions overcrowding in the male wards. In St Joseph's hospital 22 single beds were occupied by 44 inmates which caused much suffering and inconvenience to the patients.[63] 'Just imagine', said one guardian, 'two men put to sleep together, probably total strangers, and probably one just out of gaol, in a bed too small for them, and this done by order of the Board of Guardians'.[64] Problems continued in the underground ward and because of periodic flooding, sometimes with raw sewage, it became necessary to transfer patients to other areas.[65] Personal hygiene also caused discomfort, and Colonel Spaight complained about the 'inexcusable carelessness and bad conduct of the able bodied men' in the upper ward of St. Patrick's hospital. Dampness in the lower floor resulted from the laziness of men who did not bother to enter the urinals at night time but

---

59 *CE* 28 November, 12 December 1884; see M.A. Crowther, 'The Tramp', in R. Porter (ed.), *Myths of the English* (London, 1992), pp. 91-113.
60 *CE* 11 January, 4 March, 11 March 1887.
61 *CE* 14 February 1888.
62 *CE* 26 August, 11 November 1887.
63 *CE* 12 February 1888.
64 *CE* 21 June 1889.
65 *CE* 25 January 1889.

insisted on 'making water against the walls of the urinal outside the door'.[66]

Although ophthalmia had contributed the largest number of patients to Irish workhouse hospitals at the start of the 1860s, the situation gradually changed. By the 1880s cases were usually isolated and it was rare for large-scale contagion to develop. One such outbreak did occur during the summer of 1887. Following initial reports from Dr Callaghan, a detailed inspection of the workhouse children was undertaken by Dr Arthur Sandford, a Cork eye specialist. This inspection established that 74% of boys, 80% of girls and 63% of the infants had problems with their eyes. Twenty-five boys were receiving treatment and eight of the 21 girls in hospital were suffering from eye complaints. Most of these sufferers had 'granulus ophthalmia' which varied from a latent form to 'an unsightly condition in which the eyes are a mass of disease and vision [is] hopelessly impaired or destroyed'. As the disease was highly contagious the overcrowding, poor ventilation and common washing facilities, with just one or two towels between many children, ensured that all were exposed to infection. Once contracted, the disease progressed rapidly. Eyes were irritated by strong sunlight streaming through blindless windows and from dust in the limestone gravelled play areas and pathways.[67] Hospital treatment gave some relief but the disease usually returned to damage already weakened eyes. Following his study of the institution, Dr Sandford advised the guardians to ensure that children with sore eyes did not use the common towels and wash basins. To restrict damage from glaring sun, he suggested that window curtains or blinds should be fitted in classrooms and that an open shed should be constructed at the playground. To eliminate dust irritation, he suggested that the playground should be covered with concrete. He also made a number of dietary suggestions, which included increases to the children's allowances of milk, vegetables and soup.[68]

Dr G. P. O Farrell, the Local Government Board's medical inspector for Munster disputed some of Dr Sandford's findings. Although he agreed that there was an 'abnormal presence' of ophthalmia in the workhouse, he concluded that many of the children were not in fact suffering from true ophthalmia but 'chronic unhealthy eyelids, granulus ophthalmia as it is called, which rendered them liable to contract acute inflammatory attacks from other children suffering from acute

---

66 *CC* 30 November 1888.
67 *CE* 26 June 1887.
68 *Census of Ireland for the year 1861, Part III, Vital statistics, Vol. 1, Reports and tables relating to the status of Diseases* (Dublin, 1863), PP 1863, Vol. LVIII, pp. 94-6; *CE* 15 July, 22 July, 29 July 1887; *CC* 15 July, 22 July, 29 July 1887; *CUM* 20 April 1864, 22 April 1880.

inflammation or from slight irritation apart from contagion of the eyes'.[69] In a report to the Local Government Board, Dr O Farrell made a number of recommendations. These included:

- Improving ventilation in the boys' dormitories
- Paying more attention to the cleanliness of younger children
- Isolating children with eye discharges or other active symptoms
- Providing each child with a numbered towel which would be replaced daily
- Increased medical inspections
- Increased physical exercise
- Separate beds, particularly for younger children

Some of these suggestions were implemented almost immediately – for instance physical exercise was introduced and footballs were provided for the boys – and gradually conditions for children improved. By the following year there were just a few cases of ophthalmia in the house. Unfortunately, children with sore eyes were still using the same facilities as their healthy companions.[70] Sharing facilities was not confined to children, and complaints were heard from healthy adults who had to share towels as well as beds with inmates who suffered from skin diseases.[71]

Stimulants

For many centuries and in many cultures, wine, beer and spirits had been prescribed to hospital patients for medicinal purposes. The associating of alcohol with health giving properties continued into the nineteenth century when it was commonly used as a medicinal stimulant for treating patients in hospitals and other institutions.[72] During a periodic review of costs, a full breakdown on the expenditure and consumption of wine and spirits was demanded by some of the Cork workhouse guardians. Dr Popham explained that the beverages were issued to the matron who measured each patient's allowance; this was consumed in the presence of the ward nurse to ensure that irregularities and wastage were avoided. During the second week of December 1860 the 437 patients in his wards consumed 361 glasses of wine, 481 glasses of whiskey and 240 pints of

69 *CE* 12 August 1887; *CUM* 12 August 1887.
70 *CUM* 16 August 1888; *CE* 2 September, 19 August 1887, 17 August 1888; *CC* 2 September 1887, 17 August 1888.
71 *CE* 25 January 1889.
72 See: Rod Phillips, *A short history of wine* (London, 2001), pp. 47, 58-9, 113-4, 149-50, 274, 277-9; R.P. Trail, Hist of Hospital finance and admin, in, F.N.L. Poynter, *Evolution of Hospitals* (London, 1964), p. 241. For an assessment of the medicinal properties of wine, see: Dr E.A. Maury, *Wine is the best medicine* (London, 1974), also Mark Grant, *Galen on food and diet* (London, 2000)).

porter at a cost of £10.0s.10d. The 620 patients in Dr Townsend's department were prescribed 306 glasses of wine, 102 glasses of whiskey and 923 pints of porter at a cost of £18.1s.0d.[73] Some guardians questioned this seemingly large consumption of alcohol and comparable details were acquired from other unions. Tables giving the number of patients and the number of deaths in six workhouses showed that the Belfast workhouse, with the highest number of deaths also had the lowest consumption of alcohol. In contrast, the Cork workhouse, with its generous use of alcohol, had a lower death rate than the other institutions.

The admission of patients suffering from the effects of insufficient food was a frequent occurrence and, for these, the medical officers usually prescribed a diet, which included some meat and porter. They were satisfied that the patients were treated as economically as possible, and that each received the best care, which sometimes necessitated wine and spirits. Thomas R. Sarsfield, the board's chairman, greeted this revelation with disbelief, and asked 'surely you don't say you are to treat paupers in the same way as you would treat a rich man?' Dr Townsend replied that, regardless of their status in life, all the workhouse patients would be given the best possible treatment.[74] Some of the guardians were suspicious that workhouse inmates, particularly women with children, feigned sickness in order to be transferred to the hospital with its alcoholic stimulants and better food. When the matter was investigated by the Poor Law medical inspector he found no evidence to support this allegation and his report showed that each of the 1,148 patients was receiving essential treatment.[75] Despite occasional dietary reviews and reductions, the Cork workhouse medical officers continued to prescribe generous quantities of alcoholic stimulants for their patients.[76]

The liberal use of alcoholic stimulants became a contentious issue in 1867 when Isaac Julian alleged that this was introducing patients to bad habits and was also undermining the morals of nursing staff who were frequently under the influence of alcohol, and incapable of performing their duties efficiently. Figures produced to support his claim showed that, even though the number of patients had hardly changed, the

---

73 *CE* 12, 21 December 1860.
74 *CE* 18 January 1861; *CC* 17, 21 January 1861.
75 *CE* 19, 27 February, 6 March 1862.
76 The seemingly excessive use of another medical interventions was also questioned by guardians. Leeches were frequently used to treat patients, and on average about two dozen were acquired each week. The creatures themselves were used for a maximum of three times, after which they were replaced. When fourteen dozen were used during a three week period in the summer of 1863, it was suspected that they were not receiving proper care. An investigation established that an unusually high demand for local bleeding contributed to the large replacement rate. *CE* 20, 28 May 1863; *CUM* 27 May 1863.

expenditure on alcohol had increased from £663.15s.7d. in 1861 to £923.2s.1d. in 1866. A number of guardians suggested that a more liberal distribution of broth and milk would have greater benefit and be preferable to alcohol. Other members of the board were not opposed to the use of alcohol and they suggested that the spirits should be diluted to make them less attractive to nursing staff.[77]

During a review of the dietary scales on 15 January 1868 a reduction of 4 ounces of bread was made to the daily allowances of the children and male infirm inmates. These changes were initiated because of alleged wastage. One guardian exaggerated the wastage and said that in the dining area, bread 'was thrown about and lying on the floor like paving stones', and that wheelbarrows were necessary to convey it to the house piggery. The topic was discussed at a number of subsequent meetings and it was decided to increase the infirm men's allowances to the previous level of 8 ounces of bread and a pint of milk for breakfast, 8 ounces of bread and a pint of soup at midday and 8 ounces of bread and a pint of milk in the evening.[78] This repetitive menu underlines the monotony of workhouse life. Within weeks the consumption of other commodities was under discussion. The expenditure on foods such as meat and eggs, which had only been allowed in the house since 1862, was objected to by some guardians who said that these items were 'luxuries'. During 1867 64,000 eggs and 130,000 lbs. of meat were consumed in the workhouse and in response to a motion by Daniel L. Sandiford, the guardians agreed to investigate the use of alcohol, meat and eggs.[79]

A report compiled by Isaac Julian and Dr James Richard Wherland was presented to the new board at their first meeting in April 1868. The report found that, although there had been little change in the number of hospital inmates, 'a progressive and most extravagant increase' had taken place in the use of alcohol and some foods. Embodied in the report were recommendations that some patients should be given Indian meal in place of bread, that milk should be used instead of meat and soup whenever possible and that, for the sake of economy, fresh bones should be crushed and boiled as an additive to the soup. It was also recommended that medical officers, and not nurses, should check the daily diet sheet for each patient. On the subject of alcohol and luxurious foods, the compilers objected to the large-scale consumption of eggs which, they

---

77 *CE* 7 February, 21 March 1867.
78 *CC* 13, 14, 20, 24, 26 February 1868; *CUM* 1, 15 January, 12, 26 February, 4, 25 March 1868.
79 *CE* 5 March 1867, 2 January 1868; *CC* 2 January 1868. For the Poor Law Commissioners' opinions on the use of meat in workhouses see *Poor Law Commissioners Annual Report* (1859), pp. 25-27; *Poor Law Commissioners Annual Report* (1860), pp. 28-30.

maintained, should be used only occasionally 'under pressing circumstances'. To discourage the use of wine and whiskey, they suggested, as
had an earlier Poor Law Commissioners' circular, that drugs such as
camphor or ammonia should be diluted with them. This, they believed,
would render the stimulants unattractive to anyone, other than patients
requiring the alcohol for medicinal purposes.[80] Included in the report
were figures detailing the current and projected consumption of alcohol
and eggs which showed that this expenditure was increasing more rapidly
than the rate of hospital admissions. During the subsequent discussion,
Isaac Julian implied that the medical officers were frequently intimidated
into prescribing unnecessary luxuries for some patients. The report was
subjected to detailed scrutiny and when some of its findings about the
use of alcohol were questioned, Isaac Julian lost his patience and alleged
that 'they had learned of numerous cases where the patients were so
drunk they were not fit to receive the rites of the Church when dying,
and in hundreds of cases, he believed, the patients were sent into the
other world drunk'. Although many guardians greeted this pronounce-
ment with shock and incredulity, the board adopted the report shortly
afterwards.[81]

   During the next few days, the report was analysed in the local press.
The *Cork Examiner* said that, because stimulants were frequently
prescribed for delicate children and aged patients, it would be 'cruel' to
have them diluted with unpalatable additives. The report was examined
at length and it was concluded that the data used by its compilers
produced a document in which 'facts are of the loosest and their figures
perfectly absurd'. The workhouse medical officers in particular were
offended by the allegations contained in the report. Rational debate on
its findings was overshadowed by demands that the allegations about
patients and the sacraments should be investigated.[82] The report's findings were not discussed by the *Cork Constitution*, which noted that Isaac
Julian had nothing personally to gain from the controversy. All he sought,
said an editorial, was to have 'Roman Catholic paupers protected against
being sent out of the world in a state that unfitted them for the rites of
that Church. Every respectable Romanist should feel obliged to him,
and, were there foundation for the fact, should forgive a mistake as to
the number'.[83] At the next board meeting Julian and Wherland

---

80 *CE* 2 April 1868; see also NAI, Poor Law Commissioners, Letters to James Burke,
    1849, Circular No. 8,806 of 21 February 1849.
81 *CE* 2 April 1868; *CC* 2 April 1868; *CUM* 1 April 1868.
82 *CE* 2, 9 April 1868; *CC* 9 April 1868.
83 *CC* 20 April 1868.

attempted to substantiate their findings on the use of alcohol, but many guardians were interested only in hearing an explanation about the reference to dying patients. Mr Julian apologised for using the expression, but as he refused to withdraw it, Poor Law Inspector Dr Croker King conducted an investigation into the allegation.

At the inquiry Julian and Wherland were questioned at length and they claimed that they had merely repeated what was already well known. Julian was unable to give any examples in support of the allegations which, under cross-examination, he admitted were merely hearsay, or speculation of his own imagination. The chaplains, medical officers and workhouse master were united in their evidence that patients had never died drunk in the hospital or that they had been refused sacraments because of drunkenness.[84] The Poor Law Commissioners were satisfied that there was no evidence to support the Julian and Wherland claims of alcohol abuse. An analysis of the use of alcohol, eggs and meat showed that there was an increase in the food items, but that in fact, the use of alcohol had actually decreased in the period prior to the inquiry. There were some references to the matter during the next few weeks but by the end of May, little was heard of the issue.[85]

Another attack on the use of stimulants was precipitated in the summer of 1871 when a delegation of the Cork Ratepayers Association attended the guardians meeting to protest about the amount of alcohol given to workhouse patients. They produced examples from other unions in support of their argument that the Cork paupers were being pampered with alcoholic beverages.[86] This seemed to be substantiated a month later when a comparison with an English workhouse, indicated that the expenditure on alcohol for each inmate, was less than half that of the Cork workhouse.[87] In response, the Cork medical officers produced figures, which showed that the cost of stimulants in their workhouse was 2s. per head while the expenditure in the North Dublin Union was 3s.3d. for each inmate. The expenditure in the Cork workhouse fever hospital was 2s.10¼d compared with 3s.10d. for alcoholic stimulants provided to each patient in the city fever hospital. Nicholas Dunscombe, chairman of the board of guardians disputed the figures, and he pointed out that ill effects did not result from the non-prescribing of alcohol in some small workhouses.

Because of their oversight in not realising that each hospital bed had been occupied by up to six patients during the year, the statistics of the

---

84 *CE* 24, 28, 29 April 1868; *CC* 23, 24, 25, 26, 28 April 1868.
85 *CE* 30 April, 7, 14, 21 May 1868; *CC* 30 April, 7, 1, 14, 15, 21 May, 17 September 1868.
86 *CE* 21 July 1871.
87 *CE* 15 September 1871.

anti-stimulant faction were easily discounted. Thereafter, the argument was based on emotion and rhetoric. Dr Thomas Wall, one of the guardians, and father of Dr John Wall, the workhouse physician, rounded on the chairman for the attempt to present an inflated and dishonest report on the expenditure on stimulants. Speaking of his inspection of the workhouse hospital on the previous day, he explained that he had found that it 'almost beggars description, the prostrate and almost down-trodden condition of your sick paupers'. Ignoring repeated interruptions, including a remark that the patients were prostrate from over indulgence in alcohol, he observed, that on average, patients were given a glass of Marsala wine and a little beef tea each day. The debate, with the oft-heard arguments from either camp, continued for some time. From one side, Nicholas Mahony pointed out that the repeated questioning of hospital practices was an insult to the medical officers while Isaac Julian, of the anti-stimulant faction, observed that in the workhouse hospital, many young people were supplied with alcohol for the first time, 'and, the taste sticking to them, became drunkards afterwards'.[88] The board came to no decision on the matter on this occasion. Because of an anomaly in the published figures relating to the cost of stimulants, repre-sentatives from the ratepayers attended the next board meeting and asked that the discrepancy be explained. Before leaving the board room, they complemented the chairman for looking after their interests; he was, they said, a 'staunch friend' of the ratepayers and 'the right man in the right place'.[89] The figures were rechecked by the workhouse master, who explained that, although the apparent discrepancy was the result of comparing two unequal time periods, it did not alter the medical offi-cers' conclusions on the cost of stimulants.[90]

Certain guardians continued to monitor the amount of alcohol and expensive foods consumed in the workhouse and the medical officers defended the regime by assuring the board that alcohol was issued only to patients whose condition could be improved 'by the judicious use of stimulants'.[91] Visitors sometimes commented on the quantity of food being supplied in the workhouse. One ratepayer complained about the expensive grades of tea, sugar, rice and coffee, which he said, were the 'same as supplied by grocers to the aristocracy'. As a cost-saving measure, he suggested that the coffee should be mixed with chicory and

---

88 *CE* 22 September 1871; *CUM* 21 September 1871.

89 *CE* 13 October 1871

90 *CE* 20 October 1871; In the year ending 29th September 1871, inmates of Irish workhouses consumed £12,456.12s.1d, worth of alcoholic stimulants which compared with the £319. 6s worth prescribed for out door paupers. PP 1872, Vol. LI, [388], *Pauper consumption of liquor*, pp. 2–3.

91 *CE* 6, 13 September 1872; 31 October, 7 November 1873; 9 January 1874.

that where possible, the inmates should be given cocoa instead of tea.[92] The guardians and medical officers had no objection to the substitution of cocoa in place of tea for able-bodied inmates, but the laundry women and hospital and school assistants were excused from the change because of the nature of their work.[93] When cocoa was issued for the first time in the summer of 1874, some of the inmates protested but little notice was taken of their objections. To economise further, a cheaper grade of tea was purchased and the guardians ordered that the amount being used should be reduced from 2 ounces to 1⅛ ounces per gallon of water, which, in actual fact, was in excess of the officially recommended proportion of 1 ounce per gallon.[94] Some of the hospital patients and house officers rejected the new tea, others became ill after drinking it and some staff members even bought their own in preference to drinking the house brand. They got little sympathy and Isaac Julian said they could well afford this expenditure, for whenever he met with them in the city, he was 'astonished at the silk and satins they wore'. Another guardian said that if they were dissatisfied, they should resign their positions.[95] In all, the changes relating to tea and cocoa, which was supplied to 569 inmates, including 427 aged and infirm people, realised a saving of about £10 per week. The original intention to confine the issue of cocoa only to able-bodied inmates was frequently ignored. On occasions others, such as blind inmates and nurses with infants, complained about the cocoa or the poor quality tea.[96]

On his re-election as chairman of the board of guardians in April 1875, Nicholas Dunscombe noted that during the previous 12 months the stimulants consumed in the workhouse included 726 gallons of wine, 219 gallons of whiskey, 212 bottles of brandy and 4,766 gallons of porter. He pointed out that this had cost £685.15s.7d., and asked the medical officers to initiate some reductions. His views found ready support among fellow guardians and ratepayers. The doctors responded with their usual justifications, saying that stimulants were issued only when required. Dr Cremen said that some of his patients were women with acute diseases and 'neither trouble nor expense' was spared in the effort to have them cured and discharged from hospital. Patients in the Lock hospital and its nursery 'whose constitutions were shattered by disease' were given every assistance, as also were fever patients. The doctors credited their own controlled distribution of alcohol with the

---

92 *CE* 16 March, 3 April 1874; *CUM* 23 April, 14 May 1874.
93 *CE* 20, 27 March 1874.
94 *Poor Law Commissioners Annual Report* (1859), p. 27; *CUM* 14 May 1874.
95 *CE* 3, 17 April, 15 May, 10, 24 July, 14, 21, 22, 28 August, 4, 11, 25 September 1874; *CUM* 19, 26 March, 2, 23 April, 7, 14 May 1874.
96 *CE* 11 September, 9, 16, 23 October, 4, 11 December 1874.

situation in the fever hospital where no death had been recorded during the previous year, despite some serious cases of typhus and typhoid. Reacting to the pressure for savings, the medical officers did make some reductions in the amount of alcohol issued to patients.[97] The situation had caught the attention of outside observers, and the *Londonderry Standard,* no doubt with tongue in cheek, lamented that if the use of alcoholic stimulants continued to decline, the Cork workhouse 'must soon become as dull and sober a place as one of its sister establishments in the North'. It was, said the newspaper, in danger of losing its appellation of 'the jolliest of Irish workhouses'.[98]

Some guardians kept an eye on the situation and when the consumption of wine and porter increased in June 1876, one board member caustically observed that, because of the amount of alcohol being prescribed to patients, the institution had earned the title of 'the Jolly Cork Workhouse'.[99] Although the medical officers explained that the increased consumption was caused by an outbreak of serious illness, including typhus and typhoid, the anti-stimulant faction made an unsuccessful attempt to have a committee of its own members appointed to investigate the matter.[100] No doubt weary of the recurring disagreements, Nicholas Mahony, the board's chairman, advised the guardians that they were faced with a simple choice – either 'get rid of your doctors or be guided by them'.[101] The activities of the anti-alcohol faction did, however, make an impression and when the figures for alcohol consumption were compiled at the end of 1876 a marked decrease was evident:

- In the year ending Sept. 1874 975 patients consumed £684.11s.4d. worth of stimulants;
- In the year ending Sept. 1875 979 patients consumed £556.15s.11d. worth of stimulants;
- In the year ending Sept. 1876 1,031 patients consumed £478.15s.9d. worth of stimulants.

---

97 *CE* 9, 30 April 1875, 11 June 1874; 7 April 1876; *CC* 16 March, 9, 16, 27, 30 April, 18 May, 10 June 1875.
98 Quoted in *CC* 18 April 1876.
99 *CE* 7, 14 July 1876; *CC* 7 July 1876. The Cork workhouse was not unique because other workhouses, such as the South Dublin Union, were also having heated discussions about alcoholic stimulants; see *CC* 14 October 1876. In England the value of alcohol for workhouse patients was also being discredited. PP 1876, Vol., LXIII, [202], *Correspondence re stimulants.*
100 *CE* 14, 21 July, 27 October, 10 November 1876; *CC* 14 July 1876; *CUM* 13, 20 July, 16 November 1876.
101 *CE* 14 July 1876; *CC* 27 October, 24 November 1876; *CUM* 23 November 1876.

As a reward for various duties, a small allowance of porter was granted to some inmates. Women rearing and nursing orphans and deserted children received a daily allowance of one pint of porter, as also did the house porters and other special assistants. In total, the nurses received 52 pints per week and the other recipients consumed 124 pints. Because of this system, one guardian referred to the workhouse as a 'great public house'.[102] As a cost saving measure, and because of their belief that the allowance would engender a love of alcohol, a group of guardians attempted to have the practice discontinued and suggested that a token cash payment be granted instead. Although other guardians were happy with the situation, which ensured that the children were nursed for the mere cost of a pint of porter to each nurse, the concession was withdrawn.[103] The outcome of such an action should have been obvious. When the porter supply ceased, the nurses withdrew their labour and 'positively refused' to nurse the helpless children. All interventions and offers of any kind of food they required, were declined by the women, who would not return to work unless the porter allowance was resumed. A stalemate resulted and the unfortunate children were the real losers. Concurrent with this decision, the board also decided to reduce the allowance of meat being supplied to the male hospital nurses and to able-bodied inmates who worked in the bakery.[104] When the male nurses also threatened to cease their duties, the medical officers pleaded with the board to devise some acceptable method of compensation before patients' lives were threatened. Following intervention by the Local Government Board, which said that it was permissible to employ inmates at workhouses duties, a local committee suggested that 20 pauper assistants should be dispensed with, and others employed in their place at 1s. 6d. each per week plus rations. The orphans' nurses rejected an offer of a weekly cash allowance, which could be accumulated and withdrawn on leaving the workhouse. An offer to grant soup at a cost of 3s. per week, as opposed to porter which cost 9d. for each nurse, was also rejected by the women. Eventually, common sense prevailed. The guardians concluded that the daily pint of porter, which would not make the women 'beastly drunk', was 'the cheapest and most harmless' option and they agreed by 14 to six votes to reintroduce this arrangement.[105] At the same meeting they decided that another cost-saving initiative should be rescinded. On their directions, the workhouse water supply had been turned off each day between 6pm and 8am. They were forced to reverse their directive

102 *CC* 23 April 1875.
103 *CE* 8, 15 June, 20 July, 16, 30 November 1877; *CC* 8 June, 16, 30 November 1877; *CUM* 7, 21 June, 19, 26 July, 23 August, 15, 29 November 1877
104 *CE* 7, 14 December 1877; *CC* 7, 14 December 1877; *CUM* 13 December 1877
105 *CE* 21 December 1877; *CC* 21 December 1877; *CUM* 22 December 1877.

when the clergy and nuns refused to visit any ward which did not have a ready water supply.[106] The use of alcohol for medicinal purposes continued and during 1880 the 2,249 patients were prescribed a range of drinks to a total value of £660. The prescriptions included 16,122 pints of porter and 64,585 glasses of wine as well as gin and brandy.[107]

Lunatics

The Cork workhouse lunatic department was frequently inadequate for the number of mentally ill patients it housed. In common with other workhouses 'no account is taken, or for practical purposes can be taken, of the mental condition of the pauper. He is simply consigned to the lunatic or idiot ward, as is the able-bodied pauper to his special department. In that ward or cell the lunatic is virtually a prisoner, without warrant for detention more than of committal'.[108] The department was often overcrowded and during March 1881 it had 148 'utterly demented, aged imbeciles' huddled together in a confined area, into which ten extra beds were crammed to provide additional sleeping accommodation. The day room was also inadequate and it generally became stuffy and unhealthy, particularly in damp or wet weather when the inmates were unable to venture into their 'bleak and cheerless' airing, or exercise yard.[109] In a report into the condition of the lunatics, Dr P. J. Cremen called for additional accommodation, including a larger day room and dining hall to accommodate at least another 70 patients. He also sought a larger exercise yard for 'it is almost impossible for melancholic patients to improve in the gloomy surroundings they have at present'.[110] An attempt was made to provide more activities to occupy the inmates and a number of women were employed at sewing, knitting, crochet and washing and some men were employed at simple gardening tasks such as weeding. Books and musical instruments were also supplied and some of the inmates were entertained with music and dancing.[111]

The nursery department had similar problems with inadequate sleeping and day room accommodation and an airing shed and exercise yard which were in poor repair. As a solution to both problems, the medical officers suggested that some vacant land, adjacent to the workhouse on Evergreen Road should be acquired as a site for a new nursery and infant

---

106 *CE* 21 December 1877.
107 PP 1881, Vol. LXXIX, [352], *Use of stimulants during 1880*, p. 4.
108 PP 1878-9, Vol. XXXI, *Poor Law Unions and Lunacy Inquiry Commission (Ireland), Report and Evidence with Appendix*, p. lxxi.
109 *CE* 26 March, 27, 28 May, 18 June, 6, 13 August 1880.
110 *CE* 1 March, 18 March, 25 March 1881; *CUM* 24 March 1881.
111 *CUM* 17 June, 24 June, 5 August 1880.

department. The vacated nursery could then be added to the lunatic department.[112] The suggestion was ignored and within weeks, twenty-two lunatics were sleeping on the floor of their ward and another twelve were sharing six beds. As an interim solution to the problem, 25 female patients were admitted to the city's lunatic asylum on 3 August 1881 and the guardians agreed to pay £8 per annum maintenance for each of the women.[113] The immediate problem was thus solved but within some months the number of lunatics in the house increased and, again, beds had to be laid on the floors for sleeping purposes. The possibility of renting accommodation was investigated. When nothing materialised Dr Brodie spoke in favour of a new building and the house committee recommended that an additional storey, at an estimated cost of £800 should be constructed to relieve the overcrowding.[114]

When Dr Nugent, the Inspector of Lunatic Asylums, visited the workhouse during the Spring of 1883, he found 122 persons in the department. He was pleased with their personal condition but, although their quarters were clean and well ventilated, he considered the bed space inadequate. He suggested that a new day room should be provided to give the residents some additional comfort and that at least one more nurse should be deployed to the female division.[115] The guardians discussed the report and, with their usual determination to save money, the inspector's proposition was twisted around and the possibility of building a new and much needed nursery quarters and installing the lunatics in the vacated area was discussed instead. The utility of renovating the old shed in an adjoining yard was also dragged into the discussion. The ideas were refined further until all proposals about erecting new buildings were excluded! Instead, a committee was appointed to establish which departments could be moved, divided or amalgamated so as to provide additional accommodation. In the meantime most of the lunatics were 'locked up like wild animals'.[116]

In a report which was presented to the board in June 1883, it was suggested that the girls school should be divided into two departments. The building which was capable of accommodating 536 pupils, was occupied by 170 girls, so if partitions were installed, the boys could move into its southern half and live as if 'they were miles apart' from the girls. The report also suggested that the infants and mothers could move into

112 *CE* 25 March, 1 April, 8 April 1881.
113 *CE* 1 July, 8 July, 29 July 1881; 10 March 1882; 8 March 1888; *CUM* 7 July, 14 July 1881; *CC* 8 March 1888.
114 *CE* 10 February, 6 October, 27 October 1881; 12 January, 19 January, 26 January 1883.
115 *CE* 6 April, 20 April 1883.
116 *CE* 16 February, 25 May, 1 June, 8 June, 29 June 1883.

the boys' school; the incurable females could be moved to the infants department and then the female lunatics could occupy the incurable hospital which adjoined their quarters. The problem of expanding the accommodation for the lunatics could thus be solved. Unfortunately the schoolgirls would have to sacrifice some of their comfort. As their condensed quarters would only accommodate 111 beds, it was proposed to give 67 older girls a bed each. Eighty-eight younger children would have to share the remaining 44 beds, so it was suggested that a section of the day room could be partitioned off and used as a dormitory. Critics of the report pointed out that although it seemed to solve overcrowding in the lunatic department, in reality it merely transferred the problem elsewhere. This assessment was confirmed by the medical officers who concluded that the health of the girls would be endangered, and that the day room accommodation for infants and nurses would be inadequate.[117] Dr Brodie, the Poor Law Inspector, agreed that the proposed changes would not solve the problem of overcrowding in the lunatic department; neither would they improve conditions for the girls or for the nursery women and infants.[118] The devious scheme was not implemented and overcrowding continued with the lunatics remaining 'like animals in a menagerie'. As an economic measure, their allowance of snuff was stopped, but when many of them became difficult to manage, the supply was resumed on the advice of the medical officers. As a reward for carrying out tasks in the house, many male patients were permitted to smoke. Little was really done to treat the lunatics in the workhouse and only those who became violent were sent to the city asylum.[119]

When the female lunatic wards became excessively crowded again in the summer of 1885, twenty-four of the women were removed to the city asylum in July on terms similar to those previously agreed.[120] By the following January the area was again overcrowded with 133 lunatics and assistants occupying a space suitable for a maximum of 100 people.[121] The city asylum couldn't take any of the inmates because it too had no spare accommodation. Col. Spaight, the Local Government Inspector, was anxious to have the problem resolved by the construction of a new building at the workhouse, so during April a tender of £220 was accepted for a new wing at the female lunatic ward.[122] When Dr Nugent

---

117 *CE* 29 June, 27 July, 24 August 1883.
118 *CE* 26 October 1883.
119 *CE* 10 January, 7 March, 4 April, 8 April 1884.
120 *CE* 8 May, 22 May, 26 June, 3 July, 10 July, and 17 July 1885.
121 *CE* 1 January, 12 March, 26 March 1886; see also *CC* 9 and 16 July 1886. In July 1888, the workhouse master requested that a padded cell be provided for the female lunatic department. *CUM* 26 July 1888.
122 *CE* 8 January, 15 January, 22 January, 12 February, 9 April, 30 April, 21 May 1886.

inspected the department during March 1887 he was pleased with the new additions. The dormitory accommodation was adequate but, as the number of patients had increased, day room facilities were already too small. One group of patients dined in their dormitory and then remained there for the rest of the day, and at night many male lunatics had to share narrow beds with a companion.[123]

During a review of finances the guardians decided to discontinue paying the maintenance allowances for 25 patients referred from the workhouse to the Cork lunatic asylum. The asylum governors demanded that the board of guardians honour the agreement. Many of the guardians protested about the decision and objected to breaking an agreement which had been 'honestly contracted'.[124] During the standoff, the workhouse lunatics suffered, and seriously ill patients who could have benefited from expertise at the asylum were effectively barred from transferring to its wards. When the workhouse medical officers contacted colleagues in the asylum about particular cases the governors intervened and insisted that there was no room for the patients. The workhouse guardians were outraged at this slight and they claimed that the asylum was obliged to take pauper lunatics because the institution had been constructed for this class.[125]

Despite negotiations and meetings, the impasse was not resolved; conditions for workhouse lunatics did not improve. The female day room was small so when the weather was bad they had to remain indoors 'huddled together without room to move or sufficient air'.[126] The male department was also 'far too small for its purpose' and the inspector found the practice of allowing two lunatics to share beds 'most objectionable'. The asylum governors demanded the money they were owed and the guardians refused to pay as they claimed that the asylum was obliged to take the lunatics. The asylum authorities were probably pleased with the turn that events had taken because one of them concluded that the workhouse lunatics and its 'drivelling idiots were an *incubus* on the asylum'.[127] Overcrowding continued in the male department with many inmates still sharing beds. At the end of 1889 a visitor found the patients 'shivering in the cold'. Many repeatedly tore their clothing into shreds, but the master arranged to have new uniforms and underwear provided. The female department was also overcrowded and

123 *CC* 26 August 1887.
124 *CE* 20 May, 10 June 1887; *CC* 10 June 1887.
125 *CE* 1 July, 29 July, 2 September, 7 October, 11 November, 18 November, 25 November, 23 December 1887.
126 *CE* 6 January, 13 January, 14 February 1888; *CC* 29 November 1889.
127 *CE* 8 March 1888; *38th Annual Report of Irish Lunatic Asylums*, PP 1889, Vol. XXXVII, p. 17; also *CE* 9 March, 8 June 1888.

the inadequate day room leaked badly during poor weather.[128] The Local Government Board inspector was not too concerned about overcrowding in the male ward because the patients 'were so closely jammed that it was impossible for them to injure each other'.[129] Describing this remark as 'a melancholy satire on the humanity of the guardians', William D'Esterre Parkker asked the public to 'imagine 58 lunatics, epileptics and idiots locked up together at night without any responsible person in charge of them'. He lamented that these male lunatics were 'immured within the dreary confined walls of their apartment dragging out a vegetable existence. Boys and men, no work, no recreation, no books to read, no effort made to mitigate their suffering'.[130]

Conclusion

Poor food, primitive standards of hygiene, overcrowded wards and the absence of basic exercise facilities for children were a common feature in Cork's workhouse hospital during the early 1850s. An inability to isolate infectious diseases made life hazardous, particularly for young inmates. In 1859 the Mayor of Cork brought public attention to the appalling conditions in the institution's children's wards. Following an investigation and widespread public attention, improvements were made to the children's diet, clothing and general treatment. Hospital conditions also improved and the provision of a new fever unit ensured that diseases such as typhus fever and smallpox were isolated from the general workhouse population. Innovations such as the deployment of nursing nuns helped erode the stigma associated with the workhouse. Gradually, increasing numbers of Cork's poor came to rely on the medical treatment available in its hospital wards.

---

128 *CE* 19 April, 26 July, 25 October, 29 November 1889, 27 June 1890; *CUM* 26 July 1888, 9 May, 20 June 1889, 8 May 1890.
129 *CC* 3 January 1890.
130 *CC* 7 January 1890.

9 Exiting

Workhouse inmates were assisted to leave the institution under a number of schemes. The workhouse was occasionally visited by prospective employers who took boys or girls to their farm, place of industry or residence to work as servants or at other labour. Infants and young children were sometimes given to applicants who wished to adopt a child. A formal system of nursing out young inmates was inaugurated in the early 1860s when new legislation was introduced. An informal system of providing financial help to enable workhouse inmates emigrate to America, Australia or Britain was constantly utilised to reduce the number of inmates.[1] Such help was frequently provided to wives who wished to join their husbands or to children whose parents had found employment overseas. Occasionally, large-scale emigration schemes were adopted to transport groups of inmates to a new life abroad. The motivation was usually based on financial considerations as opposed to high-minded ideals or altruistic considerations about the future wellbeing of the people involved. This was exemplified by the fact that many of the participants were knowingly dispatched to Australia or Canada without any skills to enable them to earn a livelihood.[2] The provision of outdoor assistance, or outdoor relief, was successfully deployed to keep families or individuals out of the workhouse. As well as proving cheaper than indoor relief, the outdoor relief allowances helped keep families together.

In response to the demand for female settlers, assisted emigration schemes were usually dominated by girls and young women. The majority of the earlier emigrants to the colonies had been males and by the

---

1 See for instance: *CUM* 24 April, 12 June 1850, 11 April, 14 November 1860, 5 March, 4 June, 9 July, 20 August 1862, 10 October 1878, 29 September 1881; *CUL* 27 April 1852; *CE* 9 January 1868, 2 June 9 June 1871, 30 April, 24 December 1875, 10 October 1878, 17 November 1882, 16 March 1883.

2 See Eric Richards, 'The importance of being Irish in colonial South Australia', in John O Brien and Pauric Travers (eds.), *The Irish Emigrant experience in Australia* (Dublin, 1991), pp, 78, 79. See also Gerard Moran, "Shovelling out the poor": assisted emigration from Ireland from the great Famine to the fall of Parnell', in Patrick J. Duffy (ed.), *To and from Ireland: Planned Migration Schemes c. 1600-2000* (Dublin, 2004), p. 151.

1840s women were urgently required to redress the imbalance and 'become servants, wives and mothers'.[3] The shortage of women constituted 'a continuing social problem' and in the province of Victoria, Australia, for instance, the population consisted of 155,887 males and 80,911 females in the early 1850's.[4] The unmarried Irish workhouse girls were introduced, says Eric Richards, 'to solve the labour, sexual and reproductive requirements of the colonial population'.[5]

Early in 1849 the possibility of assisting paupers to emigrate from the Cork workhouse to Australia was discussed by the guardians. As the estimated cost of £7 per head was deemed too expensive, the workhouse master suggested a method by which finance could be raised, or in fact diverted, for the scheme. He proposed that female inmates could be divided into groups of 20 and employed at knitting clothes for fellow inmates. Financial savings realised by the venture would be put into a fund and used to finance emigration. Eligibility for the emigration scheme was confined to women who had been in the workhouse for at least three years. Some of the suitable candidates had been in the house from birth and had already cost up to £90 each in maintenance.[6] The master's proposal to give the girls some practical training was enthusiastically supported by an editorial in the *Southern Reporter* which observed that many of the girls had grown up 'like young savages' and because of their institutional upbringing they were 'totally ignorant . . . of any of the means by which human beings contrive to obtain a livelihood'.[7] Although the Poor Law Commissioners were not enthusiastic about rewarding inmates for their labour, the master's plan was favourably received as it presented an opportunity to teach the girls discipline and some basic skills and the financial savings would benefit the emigration fund.[8] In the

---

3 David Fitzpatrick, 'The Settlers: Immigration from Ireland in the nineteenth century', in Colm Kiernan (ed.), *Ireland and Australia* (Cork, 1984), p. 25, see also Cecil J. Houston and William J. Smyth, *Irish Emigration and Canada settlement: Patterns, links and letters* (Toronto, 1990), p. 65; A. James Hammerton, *Emigrant Gentlewomen – Genteel poverty and female emigration 1830-1940* (London, 1979), p. 129; Stanley C. Johnson, *A history of Emigration from the United Kingdom to North America 1763-1912* (London, 1913, 1966 edition), pp. 256-7; Dympna Mc Loughlin, 'Superfluous and unwanted deadweight', in P. O Sullivan (ed.), *Irish Women and Irish Migration* (London, 1995), p. 80; Joseph Robins, 'The emigration of Irish workhouse children to Australia in the 19th century', in John O Brien and Pauric Travers, *The Irish emigrant experience*, pp. 29, 35.
4 A. James Hammerton, *Emigrant Gentlewomen*, p. 112.
5 Eric Richards, 'The importance of being Irish', in John O Brien and Pauric Travers, *The Irish Emigrant experience*, p. 75.
6 *SR*, 8 March 1849; *CE* 14 March, 21 March 1849.
7 *SR* 20 March 1849.
8 See *Poor Law Commissioners Annual Report* (1851), Appendix, A. *Emigration . . . training*, pp. 114-5; *CUL* 19 March, 27 March 1849.

autumn of 1849 an emigration committee of six guardians was appointed to oversee the scheme. Its suggestion that a separate rate of 1d. in the pound be introduced to finance the emigration of up to 150 females to the colonies was agreed to and the committee was authorised to purchase outfits for up to 100 girls.[9] Within a few weeks some orphan girls were ready for inspection by an official of the Poor Law Commissioners and 61 were provisionally selected to go to Australia.[10] The guardians were advised to send only girls of 'unblemished moral character and of sound health' and 36 girls aged from 14 to 18 years were presented to the board for inspection on 27 November. At the conclusion of the meeting the girls addressed the board and thanked the workhouse officials and guardians for arranging their departure to Australia.[11] Under the supervision of Mrs Connell, former matron of the auxiliary workhouse, the girls left for Plymouth on the first stage of their journey on 4 December 1849. Another 24 girls were sent to Australia before the year's end.[12]

During April 1850 the Cork Union signed a contract with emigrant agent, Gregory O Neill, to transmit 183 paupers to Quebec at a cost of £700.[13] These emigrants were mainly families but a number of young men and women were also shipped on the *Sophia*. All were supplied with clothes and other items. Three of the emigrants died on the sea passage, and on landing in Canada each surviving member was given 15s.[14] Some of the male paupers found work on the railway in St. Andrew's at the equivalent of 4s. per day and females located work at 7s. per week.[15] One emigrant's claim that she had secured a position as a servant in Montreal at $28 per month seems extravagant when compared with these rates of

---

9 *CUM* 29 August 1849; *SR* 23 August, 30 August 1849.

10 *CUL* 18 September 1849; *SR* 20 September 1849; *Poor Law Commissioners Annual Report* (1850), Appendix. B, table XV11, Emigration to Australia, p. 133; *SR* 22 October 1849.

11 *CUL* 14 November, 20 November 1849; *CUM* 7 November, 21 November, 28 November 1849; *CC* 29 November 1849; *SR* 29 November 1849.

12 *SR* 6 December 1849; *CUL* 6 December, 7 December, 11 December, 15 December, 18 December, 19 December 1849, 16 January, 19 January 1850, also *CUL* 24 December 1851, 7 January 1851; *CUM* 21 November, 26 December 1849. In his book: *Barefoot and Pregnant? Irish famine orphans in Australia* (Melbourne, 1991), Trevor McCloughlin provides useful lists of Irish female orphans who were assisted to emigrate to Australia in the immediate post-famine years.

13 *SR* 25 April 1850; Helen I. Cowan, *British emigration to North America The first hundred years* (Toronto, 1961, edition), p. 223; see also Stanley C. Johnson, *A history of emigration from the United Kingdom to North America 1763-1912* (1913, London, 1966 edition), p. 256; *CE* 29 April 1850.

14 *CUM* 6 March, 13 March, 20 March, 24 April, 15 May, 10 July, 17 July, 24 July, 23 October, 30 October 1850; *CUL* 5 February, 26 March 1850; *SR* 7 March, 21 March, 25 April 1850; *CC* 18 May, 25 July, 24 October 1850; CE 25 October 1850.

15 *SR* 14 November 1850.

pay.[16] A party of 67 workhouse emigrants left Cork for Quebec on the *Try Again* on 27 July 1850 and on 7 August another 78 sailed for St Andrew's on the *Susan*.[17] In total, 253 emigrants, consisting of 55 males and 157 females over 15 years of age, with 41 dependants were sent to Quebec that year. A further 80 – 45 men and 31 females with four children – were sent to St. Andrew's, New Brunswick.[18]

During the summer of 1852 the guardians again discussed emigration. In support of his motion that the union should send a large group to America or Australia, Mr Wiseman said that this could clear the house of over 1,000 inmates and make further emigration unnecessary for a number of years. The pattern of workhouse admissions had indicated that when inmates remained in the house for three years or longer, they generally became permanent residents. Wiseman emphasised that in order to qualify for emigration, candidates would require a minimum period of residence in the house. This would discourage admission applications from people who merely wished to be considered for inclusion on the emigration list.[19] As the workhouse had over 1,500 healthy paupers under 21 years of age – there were 1,064 in the 9 to 15 year old group, 158 aged 5 to 9 years and 285 aged 2 to 5 years – some guardians advocated that the majority of emigrants should be selected from this class. Otherwise, it was feared that when young people left the house and married, they would eventually return with families when life outside became difficult. To increase the employment prospects of the emigrants Mr Fisher suggested that they sign blank indentures, which could be used to tie them to future employers. This, he observed, would 'give the colonists servants that could not leave them'. Of course such an insensitive and one-sided arrangement could also bind the emigrants to a cruel or unsuitable master.[20] The Poor Law Commissioners were unwilling to arrange another large-scale emigration scheme, but between April 1852 and March 1853, 11 males and one female, plus one dependant were sent to the U.S., and another woman was sent to Australia by the Cork guardians.[21]

The subject of emigration came before the board again in January 1853 when Richard Dowden spoke on his proposal to send girls to

---

16 *SR* I August 1850.
17 *CUM* 31 July, 14 August, 9 October, 23 October 1850; *CUL* 2 July, 3 July, 16 July 1850; *CC* 8 August 1850. All these emigrants arrived safely in Canada.
18 *Poor Law Commissioners Annual Report* (1851), Appendix. B, Return of No of Emigrants, p 192.
19 *CUM* 19 May, 26 May, 30 June 1852; *SR* 27 May 1852.
20 *SR* 3 June, 19 June 1852.
21 *Poor Law Commissioners Annual Report* (1853), Return of Emigrants, Appendix. B, p. 147; *CUL* 5 June, 7 June, 28 June, 13 July, 15 July 1852, 8 February 1853; see also NAI, CSORP 1852 O3060, letter 29 May 1852.

Australia or Canada. As well as providing careers and independence, this would help to reduce the rates. He did not wish the workhouse to become 'a stepping-stone to emigration' but suggested that up to 300 girls be sent abroad. Mr Drew, who spoke highly of the earlier schemes to America and Australia, seconded the proposal. Correspondence indicated that virtually all of the American emigrants had found employment and the most recent communications claimed that many of the Australian emigrants had married. Not everyone was in favour of the emigration and Thomas R. Sarsfield lamented that he and fellow farmers were unable to employ workers to carry out everyday tasks. He opposed the plan on the grounds that there was plenty of work in the Cork area. This was countered by Mr Wiseman who said that few of the inmates were good workers. Regardless of this drawback, he felt that they would progress in a foreign land because 'it was said that Irish people got on better when they breathed another air from the one they were born in'. A committee was chosen to investigate Mr Dowden's proposal and it identified 200 girls who were deemed suitable for emigration.[22] It was subsequently decided to limit the number of girls being sent off at any one time.

Gregory O Neill was again contracted to transport the girls to Canada at £4.10s each. Before leaving the workhouse, a deputation of five 'strong, healthy looking and neatly and elegantly dressed female paupers' went to the boardroom and addressed the guardians. The girls spoke of their time as inmates of the house – 'we have passed many and sad years within these walls, wasting, in comparative uselessness, the best portion of our lives. To a fate so dreary as this – to a life so degraded, as the life of a pauper must be, we seemed consigned without hope'. They thanked the guardians for freeing them from the workhouse and promised to endeavour to prosper in their new careers.[23]

Ninety-nine workhouse girls left for Quebec on the *Urania* on 11 April 1853 and arrived safely in Canada on 26 May. A covering letter, which was sent with the girls, assured the emigration officer at Quebec that all were well conducted and in good health. Despite the Cork guardians' confidence that the girls were 'a valuable acquisition to the Colony', a couple of them were found to be almost blind, and were sent back to Cork.[24] Another party of girls departed on the *Sultan* in early May and

---

22 *CUM* 26 January, 2 February, 9 February, 23 March 1853; *SR* 27 January, 10 February, 17 February, 3 March 1853; *CUL* 26 March, 9 April 1853.

23 *CUM* 6 April, 13 April 1853; *CUL* 25 April 1853; *CC* 12 April 1853; *SR* 7 April 1853.

24 *CUL* 21 April 1853 – R. J. O Shaughnessy to A. Buchanan; *SR* 16 June, 14 July 1853; *CUM* 20 July, 16 November 1853. The two were named as Jane Walsh and M. Carey *CUM* 24 May 1854.

arrived at Quebec on 24 June. The Canadian authorities were not impressed when they discovered that they had not been furnished with personal details or even a complete list of the girls, ten of whom were suffering from ophthalmia and had to be hospitalised immediately. Most of the new arrivals remained in Quebec or Montreal, a handful were persuaded to go to western Canada, and a few went to friends in the U.S. It later emerged that some of the girls became involved in prostitution.[25] This did not surprise Mr Butcher, acting chairman of the Cork guardians, who believed that they had contributed to the women's downfall: 'we provided them with showy dresses, with flowers and ribbons; so that when they got into the streets in those large towns, they immediately entered into a career of profligacy. This, I understand happened also with those we sent out previously'.[26]

The ease with which pauper inmates were assisted to emigrate annoyed some observers. In a letter to the *Cork Constitution,* a correspondent, writing over the name 'Ratepayer', complained that many of the women should never have been allowed to enter the workhouse, as they were strong enough to fend for themselves. In the Cork workhouse the women

> are received and domiciled for two or three years, and thereby "qualified" as fit candidates for expatriation, at an enormous and outrageous expense to industrious and hardworking citizens. In the course of my occasional visits to the workhouse, on business, I have been struck with astonishment, and even with indignation, at the number of hale and hearty females perambulating the walks and corridors of the institution, with satisfaction at their comparative comforts and enjoyments.[27]

The newspaper itself believed that there was a scarcity of workers in some sections of Cork industry and it too questioned the justification and expense involved in sending able-bodied women to Canada.[28]

As it then cost about £4 per annum to feed, clothe and support each woman in the workhouse, the benefits of emigration were obvious. Some guardians would have gladly helped all long-term inmates to emigrate,

---

25 *CUM* 4 May 1853; *SR* 12 May, 17 May 1853; 14 July 1853.
26 *CC* 14 July 1853; see also *CUM* 26 October, 23 November, 30 November 1853; *SR* 24 November 1853. During 1853, correspondence from the Poor Law Commissioners indicates that workhouse inmates were assisted to emigrate to Panama, and the *Cork Constitution* reported that over 100 men were provided with such assistance. *CUL* 29 November, 1 December, 3 December 1853; *CC* 1 December 1853; *CE* 13 September 1854. A large number of these emigrants contracted yellow fever and perished in Panama. *CE* 5 May 1858, 27 June 1859.
27 *CC* 19 May 1853.
28 *CC* 17 May 1853.

and they endeavoured to get the assistance of the emigration commissioners to finance the passage of able-bodied women to Canada and Australia.[29] On 25 May 1854 T. W. Murdock, commissioner for emigration, Captain de Coursey, RN, government emigration officer in Cork, and John Besnard visited the workhouse to inspect able-bodied females. About 1,100 women were assembled in an upper floor of the industrial department and, following a detailed examination, 200 healthy, well behaved females of good character were selected for emigration. Widows were rejected at the initial selection and those chosen to travel were mainly aged between 18 and 25 years. Tenders were sought and that of Gregory O Neill, at £5. 5s. to transport each adult to Quebec, was accepted.[30] The guardians agreed to give each girl 20s. on landing and arrangements were made for bibles, prayer books and beads to be supplied to the girls by their respective chaplains.[31] On 30 June 106 females from Cork and 60 from Clonmel workhouses left Cork on the *Satellite*. Contemporary reports indicate that they were in high spirits as the ship departed and, after a good passage, all arrived safe and well at Quebec on 11 August. Some of the girls got jobs immediately and others decided to travel to various parts of Canada.[32]

Because of a commercial decline, emigration to North America and Canada declined in the mid 1850s.[33] When the economy improved the guardians selected 100 girls for a new scheme in May 1862.[34] Because most of the girls were 'not accustomed to the world, and were in fact nothing better than overgrown children', the appointment of a supervisor was agreed. Incredibly, Mrs Mary Mulqueeny, a workhouse staff member under investigation for drunkenness, was selected as a suitable matron. She was given £20 and a free passage for herself and her husband as payment for supervising the girls on their westward voyage.[35] On 14 June 1862 the girls left for Canada on the *St Andrew*. Of the 100 girls aged between 17 and 25 years, all but one were Catholics. Most had undergone training in the workhouse industrial department and each

29 *CUM* 10 May, 24 May 1854; *CUL* 30 May, 20 June, 11 July 1854; *SR* 11 May, 23 May, 25 May 1854.
30 *CUM* 31 May, 7 June 1854; *SR* 25 May, 8 June, 15 June, 22 June 1854; *CC* 27 April, 1854.
31 *CUM* 28 June, 5 July 1854.
32 *CUM* 30 August, 15 November 1854; *CUL* 19 October 1854; *SR* 1 July, 31 August 1854; *CC* 1 July 1854.
33 Helen I. Cowan, *British Emigration to North America*, pp. 200-201, 289, 293; *CC* 5 September, 7 September 1854.
34 *CE* 7 May, 21 May, 22 May 1862; *CUM* 14 May, 21 May 1862; *CUL* 21 May 1862.
35 *CE* 29 May, 4 June, 12 June 1862. On the evening prior to sailing Mrs Mulqueeny and her husband were seen in a 'drunken and incapable condition' in Queenstown. *CUL* 28 January 1868.

had a certificate confirming her ability at sewing, washing, ironing and garment making. The expense of sending the girls to Canada amounted to just over £8 each, which included £5 for the passage, £2.11s. for clothing and a gratuity of 10s. to each on arrival. The *St Andrew* arrived in Quebec on 29 June and, with the exception of one girl who was injured in a fall, all were in good health. One girl remained on board to work as a stewardess. Some of the others were employed in Quebec at $3 per month and 22 others were sent to work in Ottawa.[36]

Despite assurances that local employment was available, thirty of the girls headed for Montreal in search of work and adventure; fifteen others, including Mrs Mulqueeny and her husband, followed, and within days forty were in employment. In a letter to the guardians, the local emigrant agent, Alexander C. Buchanan complained that 'some of the party appeared to be nice, quiet girls, but a few of them were most refractory characters, and were unruly in their conduct, so much so as to prevent people from employing them'. He advised the guardians that in future not more than 25 girls should be sent at any one time.[37]

Assisted emigration from Cork workhouse – 1849-59

YEAR	15 YRS OR OLDER		UNDER 15 YRS	TOTAL	DESTINATION
	Males	Female			
1849-50		61		61	
1850-51	55	157	41	253	Quebec
	45	31	4	80	New Brunswick
1851-2		2	1	3	America
1852-3	1	11	3	15	America
		1		1	Australia
1853-4	133	7	7	147	America
1854-5	1	170	1	172	Australia
	1	309	50	360	Canada
1855-6		6	10	16	America
	1			1	Australia
1856-7	2	2	5	9	America
	2		3	5	Australia
		4	6	10	Canada
1857-8	1	5	4	10	America
	1			1	Australia
	1			1	Canada
		3		3	Cape

---

36 *CE* 14 June, 30 July 1862; *CUM* 11 June, 18 June 1862; *CUL* 19 June 1862; See also 23rd *Emigration report*, 1863, p. 35.

37 Mrs Mulqueeny returned to Cork and in 1868 she was refused an appointment as assistant nurse in the workhouse hospital. *CE* 17 July, 23 July, 1 October 1862; *CUM* 1 October 1862; *CUL* 28 January 1868.

1858-9	4	5	3	12	America
	1			1	Australia
		1	2	3	Canada
Total	249	775	140	1164	

(*Source: Poor Law Commissioners Annual Reports*: (1850), p. 133; (1851), p. 192; (1852), p. 204; (1853), p. 147; (1854), p. 94; (1855), p. 190; (1856), p. 123; (1857), p. 127; (1858), p. 255; (1859), p. 217.

Girls from the Cork workhouse were included in further emigration schemes to the Southern Hemisphere. At the end of August 1854 a large group of girls from the workhouse emigrated to Australia. They went by steamer to Plymouth and were transferred to the emigrant ship. On their arrival at Sydney on 8 December 1854, the emigrant agent reported that the girls 'appeared to have been carefully selected, as, when compared with those who have lately been received from that part of the United Kingdom, they were unquestionably superior, not only in personal cleanliness, but also in the qualifications calculated to fit them for service'.[38] Women were undoubtedly attracted into the workhouse by the prospect of a free passage to America or Australia. Though this annoyed some guardians it did have benefits. Many of those who were assisted to leave the house sent money back to help friends or relations make the journey after them. During the next couple of years the level of assisted emigration decreased.[39] Between March 1855 and April 1856 just 16 inmates were assisted to emigrate to America and one was provided with a passage to Australia. In the twelve months ending April 1857 a total of 19 inmates were sent to America or Canada and five went to Australia.[40]

During the summer of 1857 an emigration scheme involving the transfer of Irish females to East London in the Cape of Good Hope, where the British army's German Legion was stationed, was being concluded by the authorities. An emigration agent arrived in Cork and selected 50 girls whom he deemed suitable for the scheme – 40 girls had already been selected at Limerick workhouse. The Cork Union would have to pay the passage to Plymouth and provide a wardrobe of clothing, at a total cost of about £3.15s for each girl. Of the 50 girls, one had been

---

38 *CUM* 9 August, 30 August, 6 September, 18 October 1854; *CUL* 15 July, 18 July 1854; *SR* 13 July, 20 July, 10 August 1854; *CE* 26 September 1856; Robert F. Clokey, 'Irish emigration . . .' *Journal of Statistical . . . society* (July, 1863), Part, XXIV, p. 425.

39 See 'Pity the poor immigrant: Assisted single female migration to Colonial Australia', in Eric Richards (ed.), *Poor Australian Immigrants in the nineteenth century: Visible Immigrants: Two.* (Canberra, 1991), pp. 100-101; *Poor Law Commissioners Annual Report* (1855), p. 190.

40 *Poor Law Commissioners Annual Report* (1856), p. 123; *Poor Law Commissioners Annual Report* (1857), p. 127.

in the workhouse for 12 years, three for 8 years, eight for 10 years and six others for up to 6 years; only two had been in the house for 1 year or less. It was estimated that the total cost of maintaining the 50 girls in the workhouse would be about £200 per annum.[41] Initially, the girls were enthusiastic about the scheme and the opportunity to be 'taken under the protection of government and transferred to a new country, a new position, and a new place in society'. The emigration agent, Mr Chant, explained that there were plenty of jobs for servants in the Cape and that the resettlement scheme had the full support of government.

The real reason for seeking female emigrants emerged when he said that the authorities at the Cape would ensure that the girls were well treated, and that they were making 'special arrangements for their protection, with a view to giving the Germans an opportunity of taking them as their wives if they choose'. Once the discussion opened up, it became clear that many guardians had reservations about the scheme, and the girls' future. Though there was good will and enthusiasm, it was decided to get more information before the girls were allowed leave the house. The Poor Law Commissioners were also uneasy about the project, and they sought an assurance from the guardians that the girls were fully aware of their destination, and their prospects on arrival at the Cape.[42]

The implications for the girls became more complicated as the discussion developed. Of the 50 girls selected, 47 were Catholics and 3 were Protestants. It was not known if religious facilities would be available to the girls when they reached the Cape. Although some guardians were willing to send the girls, regardless of the consequences, others wished to investigate the religious issues before a final commitment was made. The girls were brought to the boardroom one by one. On being informed that the religious arrangements at the Cape were not known, each of them declined to accept the offer of emigration until they spoke to the workhouse chaplain. Fr. O Connell, the chaplain, admitted that he had advised the girls of the paucity of provisions for Catholics at the Cape. This feature was confirmed in correspondence from the Emigration Office, which said that 'there is probably no Roman Catholic clergyman in the neighbourhood of the German settlement'.[43]

The proposed scheme did not materialise. The *Cork Examiner* praised the girls for their stance on the religious issue, and blamed the authorities

---

41 *CUM* 12 August 1857; *CUL* 11 August, 14 August, 17 August 1857; *CC* 11 August, 13 August 1857; *CE* 14 August 1857.
42 *CUM* 19 August 1857; *CUL* 18 August, 20 August 1857; *CC* 20 August 1857; *CE* 14 August, 21 August 1857.
43 *CUM* 26 August 1857; *CC* 27 August, 3 September 1857; *CE* 28 August, 31 August 1857.

for attempting to organise a hasty emigration scheme without making all the information available.[44] The *Northern Whig* criticised the authorities for not selecting English or Scottish girls. It praised the Cork girls who, by refusing to go to 'a settlement in which religious freedom is an impossibility, exhibited a spirit of truth and independence most honouring to their character'. Some of the guardians were disgusted at the way the matter had concluded and they felt that the girls should have been forced to accept the offer of emigration.[45] The three Protestant girls did leave for the Cape with a large group of fellow Irish girls on the *Lady Kennaway*.[46]

The Cork board of guardians were involved in one further large-scale emigration scheme. During 1873 the board decided to participate in a government project to give female inmates a free passage to New Zealand where employment was available to servants and farm workers. Following an inspection by Mrs Caroline C. Howard, emigration agent, the embarkation of the first 37 girls took place on the *Asia* on 6 February 1874. A further 71 inmates, including some boys, were sent from Queenstown on the *Carrick Castle* at the end of April.[47]

Families and individuals continued to receive financial and material assistance to enable them emigrate to America and elsewhere.[48] In 1880 a small-scale emigration scheme in conjunction with the Convent of Mercy in Rochdale, New York, was implemented. A number of girls were sent to America from the Cork workhouse and on arrival in New York, they stayed at the convent until the nuns put them into suitable employment. Among the first girls selected for the venture were: Mary Neal,

---

44 *CE* 28 August 1857. For the background to this scheme and the subsequent careers of the participants see: K.P.T. Tankard, 'Drama and disappointment: The *Lady Kennaway* Girls', in *South African-Irish Studies*, 2, 1992, pp.278-86. See also Donal P. McCracken, 'Odd Man Out: The South African Experience', in Andy Bielenberg (ed.), *The Irish Diaspora* (Essex, 2000), p. 255.

45 *CE* 4 September, 18 September 1857; see also *CUL* 3 October 1857.

46 *CE* 19 February 1858; *Poor Law Commissioners Annual Report* (1858), Emigration, p. 251. This Commissioners' report records that a further ten inmates were assisted to emigrate to America or Australia. Between April 1858 and March 1859 assistance to emigrate to American ports was provided to 15 inmates of the workhouse and one man was sent to Australia. *Poor Law Commissioners Annual Report* (1859), p. 217.

47 *CE* 23 May, 30 May 1873, 30 January, 6 February, 7 February, 13 February, 17 February, 20 February, 17 April, 28 April, 1 May 1874; *CUM* 29 January, 12 March, 23 April, 30 April, 7 May 1874; also *CE* 8 June 1877, 12 August 1881. See *CUM* 23 April, 30 April, 7 May, 28 May 1874; *CUL* 19 October, 22 October, 1874 for details of girls selected for the initial shipment to New Zealand. See also *CE* 12 August 1881 for details of one emigrant who returned to the Cork workhouse because he was unable to find work in New Zealand.

48 See for instance: *CE* 2 December 1881, 17 November 1882, 16 March, 18 May 1883; *CUM* 14, 28 August, 18, 25 September, 2 October 1873, 14 October 1880, 18 October 1883, 29 March, 12, 26 April, 3, 17, 24 May, 9 August 1888.

Ellen O Brien, Hanora Ring, Margaret Ring, Margaret Riordan and B. West.[49] The innovation was a success and during the following year another group of girls went to New York.[50]

The assisted emigration of workhouse inmates, although intended principally for 'healthy young people in the prime of life . . . unburdened by dependants and suitable for immediate induction into the . . . workforce',[51] had benefits both for those who transmitted and received the emigrants, and for the settlers themselves. The former workhouse inmates were liberated from the confines and restrictions of their institutional upbringing. Free from the stigma of the poor law and their former identities, a variety of personal and career options was available. The recipient settlement benefited from the availability of new workers and partners for existing settlers. The transmitting poor law union was relieved from the continuing expense of supporting their often-discontented inmates.

Children at nurse

In his evidence to the select committee on Irish poor relief in 1861, Alfred Power, the chief commissioner of the poor law in Ireland, acknowledged that young children did not always receive adequate attention in workhouses. He outlined some of the changes which would occur when contemplated legislation came into force.[52] The subsequent Poor Relief Amendment Act of June 1862 empowered boards of guardians to place abandoned or orphaned children under five years of age with nurses outside the workhouse 'in order to secure for them the best substitute for that maternal care and solicitude of which the loss of their mothers has deprived them, and for which it is difficult if not impossible to provide a substitute in the workhouse'. Although a plea by the Dublin College of Physicians to have the children nursed out until 'as late an age as practicability will permit' – possibly 15 years – was not immediately successful, the age limit was increased in later

---

49 *CUM* 22 April, 29 April, 17 June, 8 July 1880; *CE* 5 March, 23, 30 April, 21 May, 18 June 1880, 29 April 1881.

50 *CUM* 17 February, 28 October, 25 November 1881.

51 Eric Richards, 'How did poor people emigrate from the British Isles to Australia in the nineteenth century?', *Journal of British Studies*, 32 (July, 1993), p. 263.

52 PP 1861, Vol. X, [408], *Report from Select Committee on Poor Relief*, pp. 37-9, 45-6. The Poor Law Commissioners had previously expressed support for boarding out workhouse children – NAI, CSORP 1859 5550, letter of 7 June 1859. For a contemporary opinion on boarding out workhouse children see: W. Neilson Hancock, 'On the importance of substituting the Family . . '. *Journal of Dublin Statistical Society* (March, 1859), Part, XIV, pp. 317-331.

years.[53] The children had to be placed with families of their own religion and in cases where a child was sick or delicate the nursing relief could be extended until the age of eight years.[54] Some guardians were opposed to the nursing out scheme, as they believed that it would encourage illegitimacy. The *Cork Constitution* was also against its introduction and warned: 'only let it be known that there are free rations and free lodgings, with a country air and its douche accompaniments, for free babes, and the rate-payers will be amazed at the rapidity with which they multiply'.[55]

Nonetheless, common sense prevailed and the Cork guardians voted for the introduction of the scheme. Thirteen children were eligible and in September 1862 the guardians sought applications from families willing to act as nurses. All applicants were required to submit a reference from a clergyman. To give the children the benefit of fresh country air, it was decided to place them with households at least two miles from the perceived contamination in the city's lanes.[56] On departure from the workhouse each child was provided with appropriate clothing, and the nurses received an annual fee of £5. This was paid only after an inspection to ensure that the child's health and wellbeing were maintained. In addition, the relieving officers were detailed to visit the children in their homes every two weeks and submit written reports to the guardians.[57]

The change from total immersion and reliance on the workhouse relief system was made necessary because of the high death rate among the young inmates. Women caring for the children in the Cork nursery were generally insensitive. One observer caustically remarked that compared to them the able-bodied women were angels and the prostitutes in the house were 'models'. Although the Poor Law Commissioners were among those who believed that a period away from the workhouse would benefit the

53 PP 1862, Vol. XLIX, [348], *Copy of Letter to Chief Secretary for Ireland . . . from Dublin College of Physicians* p.1; *Poor Law Commissioners Annual Report* (1863), pp. 5-6; *Poor Law Commissioners Annual Report* (1873), p. 63; *Poor Law Commissioners Annual Report* (1877), p. 49.

54 25 and 26 Victoriae, Cap. 83, Sec.9 (7th August 1862), *An Act to amend the Laws in force for the relief of the destitute poor in Ireland, and to continue the Powers of the Commissioners.*

55 *CC* 16 May, 30 May 1861.

56 See notice in *CE* 18 September 1862.

57 *CE* 10 September, 17 September, 16 October 1861, 28 August 1862; see also: – *General Order relating to the relief of orphans and deserted children out of the workhouse,* in *Poor Law Commissioners Annual Report* (1863), pp. 27-9. Many of these reports are to be found in the minute books of the Cork board of guardians, see, for instance: *CUM* 3 June, 30 September, 7 October, 14 October, 11 November, 18 November, 25 November, 9 December, 23 December, 27 April 1864, 5 January 1871, 15 January, 30 April 1874, 21 June, 5 July, 12 July, 30 August, 6 September, 8 November 1877.

young children, there was an ulterior motive in the scheme: 'the probability is, that the poor little creatures will become so endeared to their warm-hearted nurses that when the period of five years . . . expires, they will be retained by their new-found mothers, and not given up – or, at least, that the nurses will in most cases be reluctant to part with their little fledglings'.[58] The interest in nursing out workhouse children was greater than anticipated and, to cater for the demand, a few older children were also selected, thereby bringing the available number up to twenty-three. The selected nurses were given one child each, but in two instances, two Protestant applicants were each given charge of two children.[59]

Initial reports on the wellbeing of the children were satisfactory but before the end of 1862, some problems emerged. Rev. Charles Webster complained that two Protestant children had been given to a Catholic nurse named Harrington. The matter was investigated and it was established that her husband was a Protestant and that the children were to be instructed in the Protestant faith. Undaunted, Webster later complained that other Protestant children were given out to Catholic mothers and raised as Catholics. What annoyed him most was that on their return to the workhouse the children were registered as Catholics.[60] When one foster mother refused to return a child in her charge the Poor Law Commissioners admitted that, other than stopping her allowance, there was no other penalty open to the guardians. Relieving Officer Cornelius O Callaghan complained that another nurse frequently left her children unattended at her house. On one occasion he had found the orphan child playing in front of an open fire. The woman was warned that further carelessness would precipitate the removal of the child.[61]

Within months the plight of two boarded out children was being investigated. One of the children, Mary Walsh, had been sent to nurse with Bridget Mahony and her family at Berrings on 28 April 1863. The child was accidentally suffocated and returned as a corpse to the workhouse just four days later. At an inquest into the death, Bridget Mahony explained that the farmhouse had only one bedroom, with two beds. A servant and two of the Mahony children slept in one bed. The other, larger, bed measured six feet by four feet and accommodated seven sleepers. Mrs Mahony, one of her children, her brother and Mary Walsh slept at one end of the bed and her husband and two of their

---

58 *CC* 11 September, 1862; *CE* 11 September, 1862, 18 February 1862; PP 1861, Vol. X, [408], *Report on Poor Relief*, p. 90. See Joseph Robins, *The Lost Children. A study of charity children in Ireland 1700 – 1900* (Dublin, 1981), p. 272.
59 *CE* 16 October, 22 October 1862; *CUM* 8 October, 15 October 1862.
60 *CE* 22 October 1863; see also *CUM* 10 June 1863, also 24 June 1868.
61 *CE* 3 December 1862, 1 January 1863; *CC* 4 December 1862 see also *CUL* 6 January, 24 February 1863 for other evidence of ill-treatment.

children occupied the other end. During the night Mrs Mahony rolled on top of young Walsh and the unfortunate child was found dead on the following morning. A verdict of accidental death was returned.[62]

The other inquiry was of a more serious nature and involved the death of five-year-old Julia Fitzgerald, who had been placed at nurse with Julia Healy, her husband and five children in October 1862. During his monthly visits to the family, relieving officer Cornelius O Callaghan did not notice any problems and the child seemed to be in good health. By March 1863, the girl began to suffer from diarrhoea and was visited by Robert C. Madras, the local dispensary doctor, who prescribed medicine and gave advice on improving the child's diet. After four visits young Julia was convalescent and Dr Madras did not see her after 23 March. When O Callaghan visited the family at the start of April, the girl was again suffering from diarrhoea. He paid regular visits during the next couple of weeks but when the child's condition continued to deteriorate, she was returned to the workhouse 'in a fearful state of emaciation and disease' and she died on 15 May. An inquest was held and evidence from various witnesses showed that the child had been fed on a poor diet of Indian meal and sour milk. In an attempt to nourish the child, the Healys began feeding her on goat's milk before she returned to the workhouse. Even while she was sick, the girl was frequently beaten with a strap and a whip. She was also slapped in a manner, which, said a neighbour, 'I would not like to see my own child beaten the way the deceased was'. A verdict that the child had died from natural causes was returned. The jury also recorded that 'there was considerable neglect and want of proper attention to the said child by the nurse, her husband and the officers connected with the union examined [during] the inquiry before us, who, we find were very negligent in the discharge of their duties'.[63]

The Poor Law Commissioners were annoyed about the deaths of the two children. They said that Mary Walsh should not have been given to a family which clearly lacked adequate bedding for its own members. They were severely critical of Cornelius O Callaghan, whose delay in notifying the guardians about the condition of Julia Fitzgerald probably hastened the child's death. The relieving officer was severely reprimanded for the incident and the Commissioners 'reluctantly' agreed to his continued

---

62 *CE* 14 May, 20 May 1863; *CUM* 13 May, 20 May, 27 May 1863; *CUL* 2 June 1863; It is interesting to note that the evidence indicates that crowded beds were a common feature in the houses of Irish labourers and farmers. It is probable that the prospect of having to share a bed with one or two strangers in an overcrowded workhouse ward was a matter of little concern to most poor Irish people during the nineteenth century.

63 *CE* 18 May, 19 May, 22 May 1863; *CUM* 6 May 1863; *CUL* 23 May, 15 December 1863.

employment. In reality, the guardians themselves were partly responsible for these tragedies. Some members of the board used their influence to ensure that certain applications were not refused. As a result, proper inspections were not carried out on the residences of all applicants, and shortcomings were ignored.[64] During the summer of 1870 a girl who was nursed out with a woman at Matehy was burned to death when she accidentally set fire to her dress while playing with a carelessly hidden box of matches.[65] A few years later, nine-year-old Patrick Looney, who was at nurse with his aunt near Blarney, was killed by a train as he went to visit his sister at a nearby farm.[66]

Despite these setbacks, the nursing out programme continued, and it was not uncommon for nurses to adopt the children instead of sending them back to the workhouse, when they reached five years of age.[67] To keep in contact with nurses and children, the relieving officers were directed to ensure that the women applied in person for their monthly allowance.[68] Towards the end of 1866 there were about 70 children at nurse in the Cork Union. Close monitoring and inspections of their foster-homes convinced the medical officers that improvements were being made to their care and wellbeing and a further group of children was sent out to nurse before the year's end.[69] Although some of the young nursed out children were poorly treated, many enjoyed the comforts of a loving family; consequently they had a greater survival rate than their workhouse peers. Abandoned or orphaned infants who were deposited in the workhouse had a poor survival rate and Dr Townsend lamented that their high mortality resulted from 'the careless manner in which they were treated and knocked about by the nurses'. As the greatest chance of survival lay outside the workhouse, the guardians agreed to compile a register of wet nurses who could be contacted immediately a healthy infant arrived at the house. When seriously ill children were boarded out their chances of survival were of course considerably reduced.[70]

---

64 *CE* 4 June, 10 June 1863.
65 *CE* 16 June 1870. In July 1868 a child named as Anne Fitzpatrick was brought back to the workhouse as she was 'in a very bad condition covered with itch'. *CUM* 22, 29 July 1868.
66 *CE* 23 March, 6 April 1877; *CC* 23 March, 6 April 1877; *CUM* 5 April 1877, also *CUM* 3 November, 17 November 1881.
67 *CE* 1 June 1865; see also *CUL* 15 May, 29 May 1866; *CUM* 20 September 1868, 16 November 1871.
68 *CE* 22 September 1865.
69 *CE* 22 October 1866; *CUM* 12 December 1866, 27 February 1867.
70 This was probably the reason for a high death rate of boarded out children in 1882. PP 1884, Vol. [70], *Return of inmates of workhouses in Ireland on 24th February 1883*; *CC* 9 August, 4 December 1866; *CE* 9 August, 4 December 1866; See also William D'Esterre Parker, The Irish *Poor Law is a national grievance, with suggestions for its amendment* (Cork, 1868), pp. 29-30.

Although the nursing out allowance was increased to £6 per annum, it was still not very attractive and consequently younger children were sometimes sent to unsuitable homes where they were poorly fed.[71] During August 1874 William D'Esterre Parker suggested that the allowance for rearing children under 12 months of age should be increased to £8 per annum. In support of his motion, he produced figures to show that during the previous year 12 deserted or orphan infants had been received at the workhouse. Nurses or homes had been located for five of the children; one formerly healthy infant, for whom a nurse could not be located, was seriously ill in hospital and six others had died. Compassion was rare in the workhouse nursing system. In the institution, abandoned infants 'are kept in a room for two years, under the care of unpaid and irresponsible pauper women, who have neither love nor affection for the poor baby'. The infants were cared for by different paupers each day and were rarely, if ever, taken beyond the yard for exercise or fresh air.[72] Although Parker was supported by Dr Charles Croker King, who was in favour of paying up to £10 per annum to nurses of infant children, the guardians rejected the motion.[73] In an analysis of the guardians' decision, the *Cork Examiner* lamented that an opportunity to increase the allowance had been lost. Outside the workhouse, competition for the services of wet nurses was common and 'persons of station are constantly on the look out for healthy women who can act as foster mothers, and considerable pay, ranging from ten to twenty pounds a year, with the diet of a prize fighter, are the temptations usually offered'. Many of the external nurses had a preference for workhouse infants because, in contrast to private wet-nursing, they would not have to leave their own homes to take care of their charge. Increasing the rate for wet nurses would have cost about £50 per annum, so by voting against the extra expenditure, the guardians had endangered the lives of many infants for an insignificant sum. From a cold commercial point of view, the decision could perhaps have been justified, but, said *the Cork Examiner*, an 'economy which denies to deserted infants the substance proper for their age is an economy that we do not at all acquiesce in or admire'.[74]

---

71 *CE* 31 January, 11 August, 21 August 1874; *CUM* 10 October 1872. When it was found that some nurses were unable to provide footwear for boarded out children, the guardians granted a special allowance of 10s. to assist them. *CUM* 22 October, 5 November 1874.

72 *CE* 3 September 1874, see also *CE* 26 September 1863.

73 *CE* 14 August 1874.

74 *CE* 15 August, 4 September 1874; *Poor Law Commissioners Annual Report* (1873), p. 64; see also V. Fildes, *Wet Nursing A history from antiquity to the present* (London, 1988), pp. 194-6; Leonore Davidorr, Megan Doolittle, Janet Fink and Katherine Holden, *The family story: Blood, contract and intimacy 1830-1960* (London, 1999), p. 175.

For a variety of reasons, whether financial, personal or emotional, some of the nursed out children were returned to the workhouse on reaching five years of age. The official age limit was increased to ten years in 1869 and a large number of children re-qualified for nursing out. Nurses were again sought, and on 4 October 1869 a selection and matching session took place when some 100 children and prospective nurses met in the workhouse:

> Several of the children who had been out at nurse under the operation of the Act of Parliament which has been abolished, recognised their several nurses and rushed to meet them indifferent to the austere presence of the Board. The guardians selected those whose kindness to those placed under their care had been so demonstratively displayed as the fittest guardians of the children.

Many matches were made and before that day's session ended over 50 children were sent out to nurse. The remaining children were assigned to other nurses during the next couple of days.[75]

Natural mothers sometimes sent a child into the workhouse with the intention of nursing their own offspring and receiving payment.[76] On a few occasions deserted children who had been nursed out by the workhouse authorities were located by the natural mother and forcibly seized from the foster nurse. Sometimes children were taken from the workhouse under questionable circumstances. Towards the end of 1866 a woman named Sally Bartrett took two schoolgirls, named Cherry, from the workhouse as she claimed they were her nieces. At a subsequent meeting of the guardians her motive was questioned by Rev. James O Mahony, the workhouse chaplain. He knew that the woman kept a house 'not only of ill-fame, but the very worst of its sort in town'. She had been an inmate of the Lock hospital on two occasions and once, when it was feared that death was imminent, she had 'promised God and man to renounce her wicked vocation'. As the parents of the young girls were in India, the guardians initiated legal proceedings to resolve the matter and the children were taken by another relative. They also decided that in future, children under 15 years of age would not be handed over to relations, unless it had been discussed with the relevant chaplain and then sanctioned at a meeting of the board.[77]

---

75 *CE* 5 October 1869; 32 & 33 Victoriae, Chap. 25 of 12 July 1869. *An Act to amend the Act of the Twenty-fifth and twenty-sixth years of Victoria, chapter eighty-three, section nine, by extending the age at which orphan and deserted children may be kept out at nurse.* See also *Irish Times* 16 April, 19 April 1869.

76 *CE* 20 December 1872; 10 January, 17 January 1873.

77 *CE* 18 October, 1 November, 8 November 1866; *CUM* 17, 24, 31 October, 7 November 1866.

For many poor families the allowance received for nursing a child was a great attraction. Although many of the foster parents did adopt children, others were returned to the workhouse when they matured and the nursing allowance ceased.[78] This was rarely the case when infants and young children were placed with nurses who developed a bond with their charges. Between 1872 and 1874 just six infants under 12 months of age were placed with nurses, and all were reported to be in good health some time later.[79] 'Nothing so unquestionably successful in its results has yet been tried in connection with the Poor Law administration', said the editor of the *Cork Examiner*, for 'the children, reared in cottage homes, and with genuine home influences about them, are physically, morally, and mentally more healthy than those trained in the large institution, no matter how well managed the latter might be'.[80] Children sent to the country 'would most likely be kindly treated; would share the family life, have air and liberty, and learn practically the humours of babies, the ways of men and women, pigs and chickens, and if a girl how to knit'.[81] The scheme was generally successful and many children were adopted in the period before their foster parents were legally obliged to return them to the workhouse.

Formal inspections of the nursed out children were inaugurated in the mid 1870s when the children and their nurses, or foster parents, were brought into the workhouse. The guardians wished to establish that the children were being treated well and, more importantly, to the ratepayers' satisfaction, to check if any who had reached 10 years of age were in receipt of an allowance. At the inspection in May 1875 a total of 174 children were present. One observer found that it was easy to distinguish children who had been sent out as babies from those who had previously spent some years in the workhouse. The former 'showed a bright, courageous eye, a clear, rosy cheek, and a lithe form that was redolent of the green hillside, the open field and the free air of the country'. The latter children had a 'furtive restlessness that might be indicative of distrust or suspicion'.[82] They were separated into groups under the relieving officer of their district and the workhouse medical officers examined each child. The nurses adopted many of the children

---

78 *32 & 33 Victoriae, Chap. 25 of 12 July 1869. An Act to amend the previous Act of the Twenty-fifth and Twenty-sixth years of Victoria, chapter eighty-three, section nine, by extending the age at which orphan and deserted children may be kept out at nurse.* See also *Irish Times* 16 April and 19 April 1869.

79 PP 1879, Vol. LVI, [316], *Infants in Workhouses*, p. 114.

80 *CE* 18 December 1874.

81 Mrs. M. J. O Connell, Poor Law Administration in workhouses, in: *Journal of Statistical and Social Science*, part LVI, April 1880, p. 24.

82 *CE* 14 May 1875; *CC* 23 April 1875; see also *CUM* 29 July 1868.

who had passed their tenth year, but a few were left in the institution, or were returned when their allowance was terminated.[83]

The system had its successes. Between 1862 and 1876, of the 466 children placed with nurses, 118 were adopted, 88 were claimed by friends or relations and 12 died. One hundred and twelve children were called back to the workhouse at ten years of age but many of these managed to leave again. In the autumn of 1876, almost 140 children were still out with nurses. During the next three years another 84 children were nursed out and in mid-1879 almost 200 were living with their nurses and families. Many others succeeded in obtaining employment and had left the workhouse system.[84] A campaign to have the age for returning children to the workhouse increased from 10 to 13 years was successful in 1876, and a comprehensive set of regulations was issued to ensure that they were well cared for and educated.[85] The 1888 boarding out report showed that of the 284 children boarded out that year, eighteen were adopted. Since the commencement of the scheme in 1862, 1,073 children were boarded out and 392 were adopted; relations claimed 135, 215 returned to the workhouse and were subsequently placed in employment, 284 were still at nurse, forty-four had died and there had been just three unsuccessful placements.[86]

The district medical officers regularly monitored the health of the boarded out children while the relieving officers checked issues such as school attendance and general well-being. Because of the interest in the boarding out system, a ready supply of good homes was available. Foster

83 CE 14 May, 21 May 1875; also CE 25 May 1877.

84 CE 28 January, 25 August 1876; 11 May 1877; 12 September 1879; CC 11 May 1877; CUM 3 October, 10 October, 24 October 1878, 19 June, 17 July, 24 July, 18 September 1879. See also: CE 28 May 1879, 28 June, 6 August 1880; CC 23 April 1875; PP 1875, Vol. LXIII, [155], Copy of letter . . . by Mrs N. Senior . . . on workhouse schools, p. 12.

85 CE 5 May 1876; Poor Law Commissioners Annual Report (1877), pp. 42-5, 49-52; 39 & 40 Victoriae, Chap. 38, 11th August 1876. An Act to extend the Limits of Age up to which, with the assent of Boards of Guardians, orphan and deserted pauper children may be supported out of workhouses in Ireland; See also John K. Ingram, 'Additional facts on . . . boarding-out', in Journal of Statistical and Social Society, Feb 1876, part XLIX, pp. 503-523. In spite of its success at integrating children into families, the nursing out system did have critics. Following an inspection tour of the Cork workhouse in April 1878, Rev. B. E.Warren was fulsome in his praise of the young inmates but he questioned the lifestyles of their boarded out peers. Before signing the visitors' book he asked: 'how is it possible that children living with a low class, in houses devoid of cleanliness and decency, shared by fowls and pigs – can compete in language, habits and usefulness with children as carefully looked after and trained as those in this house'.

86 CE 17 August 1888; Twenty-sixth annual report of the Boarding-out committee, adopted by the Cork Board of Guardians on 4th August 1888 (Cork, 1888), p. 4; NAI, CSORP 1892 2547; CUM 2 August 1888.

parents had to be recommended by parties such as the clergy, medical officers, relieving officers and poor law guardians. There was some suspicion that, contrary to regulations, children whose parents were still alive were boarded out. In the workhouse, parents or guardians were able to make contact with their offspring but when the children were selected for boarding out, the parents were frequently forced to reveal their true identity and claim them before they disappeared into the country.[87] To prevent this a more rigid inspection and interview system was implemented in 1881.[88] Nonetheless, some cases of careless or poor treatment were recorded and the boarding out system was reviewed in 1884 following the death of a boy named Mathew Newton at Douglas. As a result, it was decided that when children were not receiving proper treatment, they would be returned to the workhouse.[89]

To add a new dimension to the monitoring and management of boarded out children, the Cork guardians agreed to the appointment of a ladies committee in 1884. An existing ladies committee, which helped train the workhouse girls at cooking and domestic skills, was given the additional responsibility of visiting and inspecting the boarded out children. The committee members were Mrs Allman, Mrs L. A. Beamish, Mrs Colthurst, Mrs Gillman, Mrs M. B. Leslie, Mrs N. Mahony, Mrs T. Mahony, Mrs J. Murphy and Mrs Penrose.[90] At the start of March 1885 a boy named Stephen Mc Donnell was ordered back to the workhouse following a visit to his home at Douglas by Mrs Leslie. The nominated nurse was in the process of marrying and moving house. Her father, who had taken charge of the boy, was frequently drunk. The house was filthy and had one bed, which was shared by the boy, the old man and three girls. When Mrs Leslie filed her report, the boy was immediately brought back to the workhouse and relieving officer Denis O Connor was severely reprimanded for failing to alert the guardians to the prevailing circumstances.[91] Sometime later a boy named Michael Murphy was brought back to the workhouse because his nurse, a Mrs. Carey, was ill-treating the infant. Another child named John Steadman was returned early in 1889. The boy had always been unhealthy and sickly; he died shortly after his return to the house and an inquiry established that death was the result of natural causes. An infant named Lizzie Branagan was returned to the house by her nurse when an allowance ceased. The allowance of 5s. per

---

87 *CE* 29 September 1885.

88 *CE* 25 February 1881; 12 October 1883; 11 September, 25 September, 2 October, 9 October 1885.

89 *CE* 29 November, 5 December, 12 December 1884, 9 January, 16 January, 20 January, 30 January, 13 February 1885.

90 *CE* 19 December 1884; *CC* 9 January 1885.

91 *CE* 6 March, 13 March, 27 March 1885.

week, which was being provided by Canon Harley, was discontinued when the girl's 15 year old mother emigrated to America.[92]

The ladies' committee took a genuine interest in the children, and homes of boarding out applicants were thoroughly inspected. Also, the nurses had to take the children to their local dispensary for regular health checks.[93] Sometimes arrangements for placing children in particular households were cancelled if the ladies submitted a critical report about conditions. Their judgement produced satisfactory results and at the annual area inspections children were rarely found to be in bad health or suffering from ill treatment.[94] This was the case at Blarney in June 1887 when many of the foster parents applied to adopt their charges.[95] The annual boarding out report for 1887 highlighted the success of the scheme when it indicated that many of the 251 children on that year's list had been adopted or had found employment. This report cited the case of a girl named Margaret Fitzgerald who had been boarded out with John Doyle at Carrignavar. When she left the household, she went to work as a servant, saved her earnings and emigrated to America. Again, she accumulated her earnings and after a few years sent £20 home to her foster family to enable one of the children join her in America.[96]

In spite of the ladies' vigilance, children were placed in homes that had not been inspected. On occasions they were given to families, even though clergy, guardians or the visitors had not signed the authorisation forms. The ladies committee complained that this had happened on four occasions between October 1887 and April 1888. In one instance a woman with four children of her own was given three others to board out, whilst in other areas, women with suitable qualifications and properly completed documentation were bypassed. A member of the boarding out committee explained that whenever a woman adopted a child, she had an automatic right to board out another in its place.[97] This facility had been introduced so as to encourage the adoption of children and thus save payment of the boarding out allowance. In many cases families waited until the child reached 13 years of age, thus ensuring that the maximum allowances were received.[98]

---

92 *CE* 22 March, 21 June, 28 June, 15 November, 22 November, 29 November 1889; *CUM* 28 March, 25 April, 20 June 1889.
93 *CE* 7 August, 11 September, 4 December 1885.
94 *CE* 12 March, 18 June, 1 July 1886, 4 February 1887; *CC* 1 July, 20 August 1886; *Twenty-fourth annual report of the Boarding-out Committee of the Cork Board of Guardians on the management of orphans and deserted children who are boarded out in the rural districts of the Cork Union* (Cork, 1886), p. 8; NAI, CSORP 1892 2547.
95 *CE* 9 June 1887; *CC* 9 June 1887.
96 *CE* 1 July 1887; *CC* 1 July 1887.
97 *CE* 20 April, 14 December 1888, 4 January 1889; *CUM* 19 April 1888; *CC* 14 December 1888.
98 See *CUM* 10 July 1890.

The boarding out system had numerous benefits. It removed children from adverse and negative influences and provided them with a base and identity outside the workhouse. Foster parents benefited both from the companionship of the children and the allowance paid by the poor law union.[99] The ratepayers were saved the expense of maintaining the children in the workhouse and when they were adopted, greater savings resulted. Helen Mac Donald's conclusion that the Scottish boarding out system sought 'to imbue poor law children with ethical principles, and to sever them from all links with pauperism'[100] is equally true when applied to the operation of the system in the Cork Union.

Outdoor Relief

In their annual report for 1860, the Poor Law Commissioners expressed their preference for indoor, as opposed to outdoor, relief. The principal advantages of workhouse relief were 'the certainty that sufficient relief is afforded in each individual case, and that the whole cost of what may be called personal relief is directly applied to its object'. Workhouse relief was rarely refused by hard-pressed applicants and most endeavoured to leave the institution when circumstances changed which ensured that the assistance was discontinued.[101] Conversely, when outdoor relief was granted, the authorities could never be sure that the relief was used solely by the recipient. Furthermore, most outdoor recipients never resigned voluntarily from the relief list.[102]

In Cork a majority of the board of guardians were totally opposed to the concept of outdoor relief. For many years these guardians successfully avoided its introduction by saying that unscrupulous applicants would exploit the relief and that, in time, it would escalate out of control. They choose to ignore evidence which showed that workhouse relief with its inherent costs and overheads was extremely expensive, and that for the same expenditure a greater number of people could be assisted if

---

99   Details of nursed out children were recorded in the board of guardians' minutes; see for instance: *CUM* 29 March, 5, 26 April, 3, 17, 31 May, 7, 28 June, 5 July, 2 August, 6, 13 September 1888, 4, 25 April, 2, 23 May, 5, 20, 27 June, 4 July 1889; see also *CE* 5 September 1879, 7 September 1888.

100 Helen J. Mac Donald, 'Boarding-out and the Scottish Poor Law, 1845-1914', *Scottish Historical Review*, Volume LXXV, 2, No. 200 (October 1996), p. 205.

101 *Poor Law Commissioners Annual Report* (1860), pp 6-8; *Poor Law Commissioners Annual Report* (1862), p.8; see also, *10th. Victoriae, c 31, An Act to make further provision for the relief of the destitute poor in Ireland.*

102 *Poor Law Commissioners Annual Report* (1862), pp. 7-8. At that time just less than 8 per cent of all relief granted by Irish boards of guardians was in the form of outdoor relief.

outdoor relief was widely available. They ignored the argument that the denial of outdoor relief was an unfair method of administering the 1847 Relief Act which included provision for such assistance. During a House of Commons debate in July 1860, Sir John Arnott criticised numerous aspects of Irish poor law administration. He said that protracted stays in a workhouse frequently rendered inmates unfit for work outside. Many destitute people would not enter its portals, and, lamented Arnott, 'the only class which will take refuge in such establishments is that which will suffer in silence, wanting the courage or ashamed to beg'.[103] He called for the general introduction of outdoor relief which would be more economical, and would assist more applicants than workhouse relief. Some weeks later, another attempt to introduce outdoor relief in the Cork Union failed, and the guardians opposing it were smugly confident that 'the relief of the poor in this union is, and has been, adequate and satisfactory'. Again, the reason for rejecting outdoor relief, as articulated by Mr Wiseman, was that its introduction would probably 'herald a huge increase in the number of applicants for relief'.[104]

The Cork board was not unique in its anxiety to avoid introducing outdoor relief – during the year ending September 1859 only 24 Irish unions were providing such relief to 4,945 applicants.[105] The Cork Union did provide token relief of food or lodgings to four applicants in that period; two years later the privilege was granted to another two applicants.[106] The subject of outdoor relief was mentioned with increasing frequency during the early 1860s and among its advocates was John Francis Maguire. When the guardians passed another vote against its introduction in May 1861, a special meeting was called to discuss the matter.[107] The topic attracted many speakers and in his address against the motion, an overly dramatic William D'Esterre Parker warned that its introduction would encourage deception and fraud and 'paralyse industry, and put down amongst the poor all stimulus to self-exertion'. Although some guardians were willing to grant outdoor relief to widows with families, or to families where the breadwinner was dead, in hospital or otherwise incapacitated, the board voted against introducing outdoor relief in the Cork Union.[108]

There was a noticeable increase in the number of guardians favouring

---

103 *CE* 27 July 1860; For background to the outdoor relief system, see: Seamus Ó Cinneide, 'The development of the Home Assistance service', *Administration* (Autumn 1969), Vol. 17, No. 3, pp. 291-97.

104 *CE* 31 August 1860; see also evidence of Alfred Power in PP 1861, Vol. X, [408], *Report on Poor Relief*, pp. 12-13, also evidence of Thomas R. Sarsfield p. 219.

105 *CE* 31 December 1860.

106 PP 1867, Vol. LX, [427], *Out door Relief*, pp. 4, 8.

107 *CE* 25 February, 8 May, 15 May 1861.

108 *CE* 17 May 1861; *CC* 16 May 1861; *CUM* 15 May 1861.

outdoor relief when the demand for workhouse accommodation increased steadily at the end of 1861 because of a downturn in trade. The first indication of a change in attitude occurred when an old man in the Monkstown division was granted relief without entering the workhouse.[109] The *Cork Examiner* devoted a number of editorials to the issue of outdoor relief and pointed out that it cost at least 4s. per week to maintain old and infirm inmates in the workhouse but that many had relatives and friends who would look after them for half that sum. Pointing out that the workhouse test of breaking up families and surrendering one's freedom, although necessary to discourage false claims for relief, had little relevance for aged and incapacitated applicants, the *Examiner* said that this class should certainly be given outdoor relief. The same criteria could be applied to claims from persons disabled by accidents or disease or to widows with young children. Because of a growing demand for assistance, the provision of outdoor relief would have taken pressure off the limited accommodation in the workhouse.[110]

Some guardians continued to campaign for the introduction of outdoor relief and at the guardians meeting on 30 January 1862, Thomas Lyons made a long and impassioned speech outlining its benefits, both to ratepayers and to certain categories of the poor. He based his argument on the financial benefit to the union. As it cost about 5s.6d. per week to maintain an adult woman and child in the workhouse, he showed that a large sum could be saved if, instead, they were given outdoor relief at 2s. and 1s. respectively. Other guardians said that the availability of outdoor relief would merely encourage people to come into the workhouse 'in order to be pensioned off'.[111] The medical officers were also in favour of some intervention. Most of the hospital beds were shared by two patients but, because of increased admissions, it was becoming more common to put a third person in the beds. Mr Lyons's proposal to appoint a committee to select outdoor relief candidates from infirm males and females and widows with children was not successful. Instead, a committee which reported on the general state of the workhouse suggested that the accommodation could be increased to 3,574 by constructing a shed and removing some patients to the North Infirmary. The guardians were satisfied that this would remove the necessity for introducing outdoor relief in the Cork Union. [112]

A gradual softening of the Cork board of guardians' abhorrence of outdoor relief emerged during subsequent months, and, although such

---

109 *CE* 7 August, 4 December 1861.
110 *CE* 23 January, 28 January, 30 January, 6 February 1862.
111 *CC* 23 January 1862; *CUM* 22 January 1862.
112 *CC* 30 January, 6 February 1862; *CE* 30 January, 31 January, 5 February 1862; *CUM* 22 January, 5 February 1862.

relief was granted to nine applicants during the winter of 1861-2, it seems that the resolution against initiating outdoor relief in the union was not rescinded.[113] During the following summer, the guardians agreed to grant outdoor relief of 5s. per week to a woman named Mahony who was seriously ill at Passage. The relief was objected to as unnecessary by some guardians and it was discontinued a week later.[114] At around the same time one week's relief of 3s. was given to a 90 year old man who was too ill to be removed to the workhouse.[115] A few other applicants were granted outdoor relief during the remainder of 1862, and in January 1863, a sick man named Callaghan was granted a small sum to save the necessity of removing him and his family to the workhouse.[116] When a woman named Bridget Cremin applied for outdoor relief for herself and her three children, because her husband was in the work-house hospital with a broken leg, she was granted an interim allowance of 4s. per week.[117] The granting of outdoor relief gradually increased – by May 1863 it had reached £6 per week and a month later 86 applicants were sharing over £7 in assistance.[118]

Although outdoor relief was only granted when the head of the family was in hospital, such relief was not automatically distributed. For instance, the wife of a man injured in an industrial accident was refused outdoor relief for herself and their children while he was in hospital, but a month later, a widow whose son was the family's breadwinner, was granted 2s.6d. per week to keep herself and the children out of the workhouse during his illness.[119] In November 1863 a widow with six children, three of whom had fever, applied for outdoor relief but her request was also refused. At that stage the cost of outdoor relief had increased to £12.4s.8d. per week. The workhouse clerk advised that careful controls would have to be introduced because the poor were aware that outdoor relief was available and many applied for assistance just as soon as a family breadwinner went to hospital.[120] Many guardians were unimpressed with the increasing expenditure on outdoor relief, which was not working out as cheaply as predicted. They advocated that when relief was granted, it should be kept as low as possible because

---

113 *CC* 5 September, 3 December 1862.
114 *CE* 4 June, 12 June 1862; *CC* 5 June, 12 June 1862.
115 *CC* 26 February 1862.
116 *CE* 19 November 1862, 7 January 1863.
117 *CE* 2 January 1863; see also PP 1867, Vol. LX, [427], Out-*door Relief*, op. cit, pp. 12-20.
118 *CE* 14 May, 10 June, 13 August 1863.
119 *CE* 16 July, 13 August, 20 August 1863; the regulations relating to the granting of outdoor relief to the families of hospital patients are explained in *Poor Law Commissioners Annual Report* (1864), pp. 21-2.
120 *CE* 5 November 1863; *CC* 5 November 1863.

workhouse relief was still available as an alternative.[121] The full board of guardians was not in favour of this interpretation. Thomas Lyons said that the board had introduced outdoor relief principally to save families from entering the workhouse while the breadwinner was in hospital, and a medical certificate was necessary to substantiate this. He produced figures to show that in the half-year ending 25 March 1863 outdoor relief had been granted in 157 instances at a total cost of £95.3s.10d., and, of the 157 cases, 35 were orphans sent out to nurse at a cost of £65.2s.11d for 26 weeks. The total cost of the other 122 recipients was £30, or just 6d. each per week. If the latter had been admitted to the workhouse, the cost of union relief would have been 2s.8¾d. each per week, or £577 for the 26 weeks. In the following half-year to 29 September 1863, outdoor relief had cost £170.10s.5d. for 357 recipients. Orphans at nurse accounted for £87, thus, the remaining 312 cases had been relieved for six months at a cost of £83.10s. Indoor relief for the latter group would have amounted to £1,785.[122]

Some guardians were opposed to giving outdoor relief to tradesmen who should have put away a percentage of their earnings for emergencies. Alternatively, they could have joined a benefit society, to ensure that their families had some income during periods of sickness or idleness. The *Cork Constitution* concurred with this argument and in an editorial observed that as tradesmen had no problem buying alcohol they should certainly be able to save a percentage of their wages.[123] A correspondent to that newspaper had sympathy for the plight of tradesmen and their families, and said that perhaps they did need assistance more than labourers because 'people in better circumstances before [prior to entering the workhouse], have more of a home to be broken up if they go to the workhouse than the lowest class of labourers, and it is harder to have their families obliged to associate with paupers'.[124] Regardless of whether they were labourers or tradesmen, the trauma of entering the workhouse, even for a short period, resulted in disruption and upset to the family and its social life. The board of guardians agreed to reject outdoor relief applications from families of tradesmen who had been in a position to join benefit societies. This resolve was embodied in a motion passed by the board early in 1864. At the same meeting the board decided that in future all outdoor relief payments to clients would be issued in small instalments.[125]

121 *CE* 5 November 1863.
122 *CE* 11 November 1863, 11 February 1864; *CC* 12 November, 24 December 1863; *CUM* 18 November 1863.
123 *CC* 6 November 1863; *CE* 12 November 1863.
124 *CC* 9 November 1863; *CC* 11 November 1863.
125 *CE* 11 February 1864; *CC* 11 February 1864.

In mid-April 1864 there were 80 recipients, representing 180 people, on the Cork Union relief list. Nationally, an increase in outdoor relief recipients was noted each year, which indicated 'a progressive change of opinion at the Boards of Guardians'.[126] In an attempt to discourage applicants in the Cork Union, the guardians instructed relieving officers to display a list of the previous six months' recipients on dispensary doors.[127] The hope that this would embarrass potential applicants was not realised and, in line with the national trend, the number of recipients gradually increased during the next few years. The *Cork Constitution* was concerned about the growth of outdoor relief and warned that it should be strictly controlled and monitored so as not to encourage a section of the population to abuse the facility. After all, said the newspaper, 'pauperism is propagated by it, for, if food could be obtained without labour, there are only too many who would be happy to live on those who were willing to support them'.[128]

At the start of October 1864 there were 2,209 inmates in the Cork workhouse and just 172 cases in receipt of outdoor relief. Of the latter, 40 were orphans at nurse, 118 were persons temporarily disabled by illness or accident; the remaining 14 were permanently disabled by old age or some physical or mental defect.[129] Although 585 adults with similar disabilities were being maintained at a greater cost in the workhouse, many of the guardians were still reluctant to sanction any increase in the level of outdoor relief. Instead, they voted to bring families into the workhouse even though it would have been less expensive to maintain them outside.[130] Relieving officers were intimidated by a section of the guardians who closely monitored and frequently disagreed with the amount of outdoor relief granted; some officers were frightened into believing that deductions would be made from their salaries if discrepancies were detected. In December 1866, when one of the city relieving officers recommended a sum of 4s. per week for a family of three persons, the guardians reviewed the case. The amount granted was deemed extravagant and on a vote, the relief was reduced to 3s. The case was discussed again on the following week and, even though it was shown that the head of the household was dying, that his bed clothes

---

126 *Poor Law Commissioners Annual Report* (1864), pp. 4-5; *Poor Law Commissioners Annual Report* (1866), p. 10; *Poor Law Commissioners Annual Report* (1867), p. 13; *Poor Law Commissioners Annual Report* (1868), p. 13; *Poor Law Commissioners Annual Report* (1869), p. 12; *Poor Law Commissioners Annual Report* (1870), p. 12; *Poor Law Commissioners Annual Report* (1871), p. 12.
127 *CE* 21 April 1864, *CC* 21 April 1864; *CUM* 20 April 1864.
128 *CC* 11 July 1864, also 9 April 1864, 13 October 1866.
129 *CE* 26 October 1864; PP 1867, Vol. LX, [572], *Number receiving outdoor relief,* p. 3.
130 *CE* 15 February, 22 February 1865; *CUM* 8 February, 15 February 1865.

consisted of one old sack and that the family lived in extremely squalid conditions, the majority of the guardians could not be dissuaded and the sum of 3s. was not increased.[131]

Details of Annual Relief in Cork Union – 1858-1871

Year ending: 29th Sept.	Total No. relieved in workhouse during year	Average daily No. in workhouse	Cost of indoor relief	No. receiving outdoor relief	Cost of outdoor relief
1858	8,968	2,061	£11,989. 9s. 6d.	0	0
1859	8,268	1,812	£11,681.16s.6d.	0	0
1860	10,008	2,034	£17,222.13s.11d	0	0
1861	11,938	2,321	£20,192.17s.1d.	8	£3.1s.0d.
1862	13,141	2,640	£20,341.12s.2d.	39	£13.7s.3d.
1863	12,425	2,513	£17,485.19s.8d.	472	£265.14s.3d.
1864	13,875	2,440	£17,286.5s.7d.	1,710	£597.3s.10d.
1865	11,341	2,133	£18,392.3s.4d.	2,511	£1,075.12s.0d
1866	12,603	2,341	£19,869.19s.5d.	2,971	£1,177.6s.1d
1867	14,086	2,571	£23,981.15s.2d.	2,775	£1,131.9s.3d.
1868	14,444	2,619	£24,126.6s.11d.	2,859	£1,117.19s.11d.
1869	11,836	2,606	£21,975.2s.8d.	2,437	£908.4s.2d.
1870	10,594	2,311	£18,984.15s.10d.	2,372	£1,425.9s.2d.
1871	9,650	2,106	£18,951.8s.3d.	2,558	£1,751.3s.5d.

(Source: *Poor Law Commissioners Annual Reports*). The average number of inmates in the Cork workhouse usually numbered around 2,000. A sharp increase during 1862 was blamed on a drop in trade resulting from the American civil war. (*Poor Law Commissioners Report*, 1862, p. 9) Bad weather and poor harvests contributed to the demand for workhouse relief during the next couple of years. (*Poor Law Commissioners Report*, 1864, p. 4, 1865, pp. 5-6) Increases in fever and other contagious diseases in the mid-1860s resulted in additional patients seeking relief in workhouse hospitals. (*Poor Law Commissioners Report* 1865, p. 5, 1866, p. 10, 1867, p. 12) The sharp increase in the 1868 and 1869 figures can be ascribed to unfavourable manufacturing conditions and particularly bad weather during the winter of 1866-7. (*Poor Law Commissioners Report*, 1867, p. 12) The Poor Law Commissioners credited 'a change in opinion' by the guardians' for the gradual increase in the outdoor relief figures. (*Poor Law Commissioners Report*, 1865, p. 5, 1866, p. 10, 1867, p. 13)

The responsibility for assessing outdoor relief applications rested with the relieving officers who were required to investigate all cases at

---

131 *CE* 7 December, 13 December 1866.

the initial stages; thereafter, they were expected to note any improvements with a view to removing undeserving cases from their relief lists. The dispensary medical officers also played a part and provided medical certificates as proof of illness or inability to work. Although it was the relieving officers who made the final recommendations on relief entitlement, the balance gradually altered and eventually the doctor's opinion carried more weight in the Cork Union. This emerged during an investigation into allegations that some outdoor relief recipients were capable of working for a living. In one case, a farm labourer named John Kenneally, who had been injured in a fall, was granted 3s. per week. This allowance was withdrawn when relieving officer Rowland saw the man forking manure on his potato beds.[132] Another recipient, a farm labourer named Daniel Sullivan, had spent time in hospital because of recurring eye problems. He had a wife and six children, three of whom were dependent on his earnings. During his incapacitation, the family received 2s. a week from one of his children and 5s. in outdoor relief. The relieving officer did not visit Sullivan after he left hospital because he was satisfied that the medical certificate from Dr Townsend was adequate proof of the man's inability to work. The doctor issued four medical certificates for Sullivan between mid-December 1868 and the following January. Certificates were necessary to confirm the state of a patient's health, but relieving officers in turn were expected to ascertain the necessity for assistance by 'personal inspection'.

By neglecting to visit recipients, relieving officers were effectively transferring decisions on the granting of outdoor relief to the dispensary medical officers. The Poor Law Commissioners were horrified to learn that the relieving officer had not visited Sullivan and Kenneally and that their relief allowance was based solely on Dr Townsend's medical certificates. Because relieving officer Rowland had acted on the medical certificates instead of on his own observations, he was deemed to have neglected his duty. Perhaps most damning was the discovery that the Cork board of guardians had introduced their own outdoor relief forms in place of the official documentation. The structure of the Cork Union document was somewhat confusing as 'it is framed in language which must convey to the medical officer that he is a responsible officer in the administration of outdoor relief; and to the relieving officer, that he is bound to carry out the medical officer's recommendations'. To avoid further confusion, the unofficial form was immediately withdrawn. Subsequently relieving officer Rowland was brought before the board of guardians and 'admonished' for neglecting

---

132 *CE* 26 January 1869.

his duty but the Commissioners were dissatisfied that he was not dismissed from his position.[133]

Sometimes, the guardians questioned decisions on medical treatment granted to patients by dispensary doctors. Such was the case when Dr McCarthy was asked to explain why he had prescribed a loaf of bread, a pound of beef, ¼ lb. of sugar and four glasses of whiskey per day to a patient named William Dorney. The guardians were of the opinion that a pint of milk would have been of more value to the patient than the whiskey, which was merely 'inculcating intemperance'. Dr McCarthy explained that he had been summoned to Dorney's house on a red ticket, which indicated a home visit was required.[134] In the house he found the 105-year-old man who was being cared for by his 80-year-old son. Both men were unwell and had neither food nor fuel for a fire. In preference to moving them to the workhouse, which would probably have resulted in Dorney senior's death, the doctor had issued the prescription. Although some guardians were dissatisfied with the explanation, the matter was allowed to drop.[135]

To prevent the duplication of assistance to the needy poor, officials from the Cork Union met regularly with members of the Society of St. Vincent de Paul. Each week the board sent a list of current outdoor relief recipients to the society to ensure that assistance was not given to undeserving cases; the Sick Poor Society also provided details of their assistance to relieving officers. A number of guardians were convinced that some of the recipients of financial or material assistance were in casual employment. Although the cost of outdoor relief was less than workhouse relief, these guardians resented the fact that widows with a number of children were supported outside instead of being forced to enter the workhouse. The doubters believed that the older children were working and that if relief was discontinued, few of the families would enter the workhouse. Following a discussion on the savings that could be realised if outdoor relief was granted to widows who were in the workhouse with their children, the Local Government Board intervened to oppose such a scheme, on the grounds that every widow in the country

133 *CE* 21 January, 29 January, 30 January, 11 February, 16 February, 18 February 1869; *CUL* 16 February 1869. For details of outdoor relief granted in Cork Union in year ending 29th September 1869, see PP 1870, Vol. LVIII, [299], *Expenditure on out door relief*, pp. 33, 106-7, and for year ending 29th September 1870, see PP 1872, Vol. LI, [43], Return *showing . . . relief for each Poor Law Union . . . for year ending 29*th *of September 1870*, pp.33, 106-7. See also, PP 1866, Vol. LXII, [377], *Return . . . of number of persons receiving relief . . .*, PP 1868-9, Vol. LIII, [136], *Return showing . . . relief for each Poor Law Union . . . for the year ending 29*th *September 1868*.

134 *Poor Law Commissioners Annual Report* (1867), p. 180; see also PP 1867, Vol. LX, [17], *Medical relief*, pp. 2-3.

135 *CE* 1 February, 5 February 1875; *CUM* 28 January and 4 February 1875.

would apply for workhouse relief if the plan was introduced.[136] During 1880 the guardians agreed to grant 3s. per week outdoor relief to blind inmates who could locate accommodation with friends or relations. It was also hoped that the initiative would make badly needed workhouse accommodation available. The idea had limited success but an attempt to increase the relief to 4s. indicates that a larger allowance was required to make the scheme attractive.[137]

Some relieving officers were accused of conducting the outdoor relief business in an unprofessional manner. One was accused of providing relief in the form of written orders for flour and meal at a shop in Carrigaline, which was owned by a poor law guardian. As well as being irregular, this was inconvenient for recipients who were forced to travel long distances. In reality, recipients should have been given cash to purchase supplies at a shop of their own choice.[138] Outdoor relief in the form of food and fuel was available to evicted families for a period of four weeks until they located alternative accommodation. Many families availed of this facility during the period of widespread evictions in the early 1880s.[139] The families of imprisoned politial 'suspects' were also given a limited amount of outdoor relief and one such beneficiary was the family of the Fenian, labour and land activist, C.P. O Sullivan. Generally, this emergency relief was limited to four weeks but in O Sullivan's case, the assistance continued for four months while he was in gaol and hospital.[140]

In time, the distribution of outdoor relief became a routine matter and cases were rarely reviewed and names were added to the relief lists without any real discussion. Some guardians were unhappy with this casual approach to business and Isaac Julian sarcastically suggested that 'it would be just as well to hand over the money to the relieving officers, and let them divide it out as they choose'.[141] The danger of not properly monitoring the business was confirmed in March 1882 when it was reported that a family named Tobin was living in appalling conditions in a cabin belonging to a farmer named Cogan. Because the relieving officer had not visited, the deterioration in the family's living conditions had gone unnoticed and unreported. As an emergency intervention, their relief was increased from 4s. to 9s. per week. On a number of occasions

---

136 *CE* 17 December 1880; *CUM* 16 December 1880; *CC* 18 February 1881.
137 *CE* 20 August, 17 September, 3 December 1880; *CUM* 24 October 1878, 6 May, 3 June, 19 August, 16 September 1880.
138 *CE* 19 August, 26 August, 16 September 1881; *CUM* 15 September 1881.
139 *CE* 9 December 1881.
140 *CE* 9 December, 16 December 1881, 27 January, 10 February, 31 March, 18 April, 5 May 1882; *CUM* 8 December, 15 December 1881, 26 January, 30 March 1882.
141 *CE* 3 February 1882; *CUM* 2 February 1882; *CC* 3 February 1882.

excessive outdoor relief was paid as a result of irregular monitoring. Such was the case with Kate Murphy of Glasheen who received 6s. per week for a number of years. When she married a man earning 14s. per week, she didn't alert the relieving officer to her changed circumstances. When the situation was uncovered after some months, relieving officer O Donovan was severely criticised for neglecting to visit his clients.[142] In October 1882, relieving officer John Creedon resigned when it was discovered that he was not distributing relief as directed. On occasions he failed to deliver the money on time and in a number of instances he underpaid the clients.[143]

Because the number of people receiving outdoor relief showed little sign of decreasing in the autumn of 1885, the guardians decided to review the entire list and cut off as many names as possible. All the city recipients were instructed to attend at the Liberty Street dispensary so that their current circumstances could be checked and evaluated. Because failure to appear in person would result in immediate removal from the list, 'a miserable crowd of squalid and poverty-stricken individuals, of all ages and sexes' turned up to stake their claim on 14 and 16 September 1885. Many people were interviewed but only a few were removed from the outdoor relief list. A small minority had their allowances reduced but these were renewed in a short time and the others were gradually returned to the list. The number of recipients continued to grow and a year later the Local Government Inspector complained that there were 640 more cases than when the revision had taken place. A downturn in the local economy with consequent hardship and distress was the principal cause.[144]

The Local Government Board also monitored the situation and when the national expenditure on outdoor relief continued to grow, it attributed the increase principally to a 'lax and unsound' system of administration by boards of guardians. It reminded guardians that many outdoor relief recipients would not accept workhouse relief, and in directing boards to reduce the number, it observed that 'no test of destitution had ever been found so thoroughly effectual as the workhouse test'. In calling for a more clinical approach to deciding on the type of relief granted, it asked guardians to remember that 'persons who are unwilling to procure for themselves the necessaries of life [are not] entitled to determine the form and manner in which assistance . . . is

---

142 *CE* 14 July 1882.
143 *CE* 27 October, 3 November, 10 November 1882; *CC* 28 November 1882.
144 *CE* 18 June, 19 June, 17 September 1885, 8 October, 14 October, 15 October, 28 October, 29 October 1886; *CC* 29, 30 October, 1, 5, 8, 15 November 1886. *CUM* 18 October 1885.

granted'.[145] A reading of the Local Government Board's letter precipitated another emotional discussion in the Cork board room, during which some guardians lauded outdoor relief, for keeping families out of the workhouse and because it was a cheaper form of relief.[146] Other guardians did everything in their power to restrict the amount of outdoor relief granted by the board. They protested about almost every applicant, regardless of the circumstances. Personal vendettas were no doubt involved in some of the attempts to remove or exclude recipients from the relief list. It was not unusual that small amounts of relief to old people, or indeed to widows with up to eight young children, were argued over by bitter and mean-spirited guardians of the poor. Common sense usually prevailed and in general, relief was granted, although sometimes allocations were reduced after a discussion.[147]

During the spring of 1889, the Local Government Board inspector again complained about the increasing cost of outdoor relief. At that time the list was comprised of 2,078 recipients representing 4,592 individuals and cost almost £300 per week. The practice of checking details with the Society of St. Vincent de Paul was still undertaken and in an attempt to make inclusion on the relief list even more difficult, the guardians decided that, whenever possible, future applicants would have to appear at full board meetings.[148] A new committee with power to visit and inspect clients was also appointed. During subsequent reviews, numerous cases were either struck off the lists or forced to enter the workhouse. The *Cork Examiner* described the increase in outdoor relief as 'alarming' and suggested that the publication of relief lists would help control the situation. The *Cork Constitution* was also horrified by the growing outdoor relief list which it described as an 'enormous leak' of public funds, and it too called for an 'entire reform of the outdoor relief system'.[149] The board of guardians decided to reduce allowances by up to 25% unless recipients were able to put forward a convincing argument.[150] A committee was appointed to investigate the distribution of relief and it concluded that the system was irregular and unbusinesslike and had no checks to establish if allowances were paid by relieving officers. The distribution of allowances at the Liberty Street dispensary was chaotic. The waiting room was overcrowded and 'the weaker are knocked about

145 *CE* 4 August 1887; *Poor Law Commissioners Annual Report* (1888), pp. 62-4.
146 *CE* 5 August, 19 August 1887; *CC* 16 August, 18 August, 19 August 1887; *CC* 11, 12, 20, 22 August 1887.
147 *CE* 4 May, 18 May, 25 May, 1 June, 6 July, 20 July 1888; *CUM* 3, 24 May 1888.
148 *CE* 1 March, 15 March, 29 March 1889; *CC* 15 March, 29 March 1889.
149 *CC* 24 May 1889; see also *CC* 22 September 1888.
150 *CE* 5 April, 24 May, 31 May, 7 June, 14 June, 17 June, 21 June 1889; *CC* 24 May, 25 May, 31 May, 6-8 June 1889; *CUM* 23 May, 30 May, 13 June, 20 June, 27 June 1889.

and crushed so shamefully by the stronger in the scramble for the money'.[151]

Following some disagreeable discussions, the Local Government Board decided to hold an investigation into the distribution of relief in the Cork Union. At the inquiry, during the autumn of 1889, the inspector found that many allowances were incorrectly recorded. In some cases, officials were making payments to people who had not been sanctioned by the full board. Names were added to lists at the whim of individual guardians because some were 'too prone to befriend their dependent and poorer neighbours by recommending them to the favourable consideration of the Relieving Officers'. Almost every week relieving officers were forced to change and revise the allowances so as to ensure that everyone received payment. As a result of the inquiry the inspector concluded that many relief cases were not properly investigated. Frequently, clients who had been officially removed, were returned to the list by relieving officers. The entire system was permeated by 'great laxity and irregularity'.[152]

In an attempt to regularise the system, the board of guardians introduced a number of safeguards. It was decided to examine the relief books each week and, in order to facilitate proper investigation, all relief applications would have to be made at the dispensary during business hours. The necessity of establishing a second relief office in the city's northern district and formulating a new ticket system was also discussed.[153] Subsequently, some recipients were removed from the relief lists and when the vice guardians were appointed in 1890, a tougher line was taken and allowances were reduced. Despite protests, the new scale of allowances was retained.[154] During the first week of May 1890, outdoor relief totalling £206 was granted to 1,826 cases, representing 4,226 individuals; this compared with nearly £283 for the same period during 1889.[155] This trend continued and by October 1890 the allowance of £186.10s. provided relief to 1,768 cases or 3,841 individuals – this compared with £256 for 4,363 persons on the previous year.[156]

---

151 *CE* 28 June 1889; *CC* 14 June, 15 June, 28 June 1889.
152 *CE* 5 July, 12 July, 19 July, 6 August, 7 August, 8 August, 13 August, 6 September 1889; *CC* 6 – 8 August, 13 August, 14 August, 4 September, 6 September, 29 November 1889.
153 *CE* 16 September 1889; *CC* 16 September 1889.
154 *CE* 25 October, 1 November 1889, 14 February, 21 February, 22 February, 28 February, 1 March, 3 March, 11 April, 25 April 1890; *CC* 1 March, 3 March, 4 March 1889.
155 *CE* 9 May 1890.
156 *CE* 31 October 1890.

Conclusion

Each of the interventions discussed above was successful either in relocating workhouse inmates to a new life outside, or in ensuring that applicants did not enter the workhouse. By assisting inmates to emigrate and by boarding out infants and young children, the guardians were presenting the parties involved with the opportunity to change their lives and permanently divorce themselves from the workhouse and its institutional limitations. The necessity for seeking admission to the workhouse was frequently eliminated by the granting of outdoor relief when an initial application was being processed. The decision to provide this external relief ensured that cases of genuine hardship were not initiated into the workhouse relief system.

These were laudatory achievements for which the guardians deserve praise. Unfortunately, improving the lot of hapless workhouse inmates or saving poor families from a period of separation in the institution was not a priority with all guardians. On too many issues, guardians' decisions were based on a financial comparison between two evils. Regardless of the resulting hardship, the least expensive option was generally chosen. Thus, the introduction and continued success of these interventions was often due to perseverance by individual guardians and officials rather than to a conscious resolve to improve the position of the unluckier members of society.

10 Ideology

Although the business of the Cork workhouse and its board of guardians was generally of a routine and predictable nature involving the control of paupers and staff, the purchase and distribution of food, medical and other supplies and the provision of sanitary, catering and domestic services, conflicting demands and priorities sometimes interfered with the successful delivery of these minimum requirements. Abuses of power and position also contributed to disharmony in the workhouse and its boardroom. Distrust emanating from disputes about perceived restrictions or interference in the free practice of religion caused many disagreements in the workhouse and in the boardroom. Conflicting interpretations of the various official rules and guidelines accounted for many bad-tempered arguments. The intransigence of the religious zealots was equalled, or sometimes excelled, by the narrow-mindedness of the political factions which occasionally manifested itself in the workhouse boardroom. Although it was sometimes entertaining, the conflict often brought business to a standstill. Many hours were squandered on arguments which had no bearing on the workhouse, were of no benefit to its inmates and only engendered bad-will, suspicion and distrust.

Religion

An undercurrent of religious intolerance, which was latent in many areas of Irish life, sometimes came to the surface in the workhouse.[1] This was not unique to Cork and Anne M. Lanigan has noted incidences of religious tension and intolerance in her history of Tipperary workhouses, as also has Helen Burke in her history of the South Dublin Union.[2] In April 1851 Thomas R. Sarsfield, chairman of the Cork board of guardians, refused to allow a discussion on transferring a foundling child from the workhouse to the care of a woman named Mary Kelly who lived outside

---

1 *CUM* 12 February, 26 February, 9 April 1851; *CC 21* February, 28 February 1854.
2 Anne M. Lanigan, *The Poor Law children of county Tipperary and their education 1840-1880* (M. Ed. thesis, UCC, 1988), pp. 217, 226-9, 266-70; Helen Burke, *The people and the Poor Law* (West Sussex, 1987), pp. 87-93.

the institution. Sarsfield was suspicious of the request because some time previously a Protestant registered child had been taken out of the work-house, re-baptised, and returned as a Catholic.[3] It was not unusual for paupers to voluntarily change religion while they were inmates of the workhouse.[4] In August 1851 a 14-year-old hospital inmate named William Scales applied, through his mother, to have the register of his religion changed from Protestant to Catholic. That same month four other inmates – Anne Berwick, Mary Cogan, Catherine Donovan and Henry Lester – also applied to have their registration details changed from Protestant to Catholic. Prior to this request, the Catholic curate had visited the four applicants and when his Protestant counterpart suggested that people were 'tampering' with the religious opinions of his flock it was decided to investigate and ascertain if pressure had been exerted on the inmates.[5] Nothing irregular seems to have been detected, but some months later a faction of the guardians was annoyed when a 42-year-old inmate changed his religion from Protestant to Catholic.[6] Again, in April 1852, when Bridget Reilly, a Protestant hospital patient, applied to change her religion, a delegation of three guardians visited the woman in her ward. Following an interview with the woman, they concluded that no pressure or influence had been exerted, so she was free to change her religion if she pleased.[7]

Disputes about religious freedom were sometimes initiated by trivial incidents. Some guardians were outraged when the workhouse tailors absented themselves from work on 1 February 1852, and they accused the men of taking it 'into their heads that it was a holiday'. The offended guardians were not satisfied when it was explained that the day was a Catholic Church holiday. They retorted by saying that, as the board was non-sectarian, the religious holidays of any inmates should not be acknowledged in the workhouse.[8]

In May 1854 an allegation that a workhouse laundress had maliciously destroyed a catechism belonging to a Protestant inmate named Mary Anne Shearman led to an investigation under Poor Law Inspector Hall. Under examination, Ellen Mullane explained that she had been minding the catechism for Miss Shearman. She went to the laundry and when the

---

3 *CUM* 29 March, 9 April, 24 April 1851; *CUL* 16 April 1851; *SR* 17 April 1851.
4 *SR* 24 April 1851; *CUM* 26 May, 2 June 1852; *CUL* 19 April 1851; Helen Burke, *The people and the Poor Law* (1987), pp. 87-93.
5 *CUM* 20 August 1851.
6 *CUM* 4 February 1852.
7 *CUM* 21 April 1852; *CUL* 15 April 1852; *SR* 22 April 1852. For other requests to change the register of religion see, for instance: *CUM* 26 May, 2 June 1852, 8, 22 November 1854, 10 August 1853, 6 September 1854, 25 March, 4 November 1857, 28 April 1858; *CUL* 30 March, 6 April 1852.
8 *CUM* 4 February 1852; *SR* 5 February 1852.

book fell out of her pocket, she read some of its contents, much to the amusement of the laundry girls. When the laundress, Mary Anne O Neill, entered the department she seized the book and tore it apart. Evidence from other witnesses produced a slightly different record of events. The laundry girls were permitted to sing while working, but sometimes, if the songs were of an improper nature, the privilege was withdrawn. When O Neill entered the laundry and saw the girls laughing, she assumed that the catechism was a songbook, so she grabbed it, and tore it apart without looking at its contents.[9] The hearing lasted a number of days and on being presented with the evidence, the Poor Law Commissioners were satisfied that the catechism had been destroyed accidentally, and that no insult was intended.[10]

Serious charges by a Catholic woman named Ellen Donovan that she had been forced to change the religion of her children in the workhouse led to an investigation into the allegations. During a six-day hearing in January 1856 the woman stated that, as she had been beaten by other inmates on a number of occasions, and because her children were persecuted, she had asked the master to change the register of the children's religion from Protestant to Catholic. George Larrymore, a clerk in the master's office, produced the workhouse ledger which showed that when Mrs Donovan first entered the institution in January 1855, her four children were registered as Protestants.[11] She left the workhouse and when readmitted in July, the mother was registered as Catholic and the four children were again registered as Protestants. Mrs Donovan was questioned at length on 4 January 1856. She and her husband John were from Rosscarbery and had married 14 years previously. At the time of their marriage, John had been a Catholic, but during the mid-1840s he became a Protestant and opened a school in his house. The school was later dissolved and John Donovan went to America about twelve months before his wife applied for workhouse relief. She claimed that during her time in the institution, she had been assaulted on a number of occasions, called a 'turncoat' by other inmates and her children had also been subjected to abuse.

A number of witnesses, including some Protestant inmates, gave evidence to show that they had never been victimised because of their religion. They agreed that Donovan had indeed been subjected to some abuse. She was not popular with other inmates and on one occasion had been assaulted following a row about work duties. Ellen Donovan's daughter, Mary, was also questioned. She claimed to have been taunted by the other school children who called her names. The evidence was

---

9 *SR* 22 May, 27 May, 30 May 1854; *CUL* 23 May 1854.
10 *CUM* 21 June, 9 August 1854; *CUL* 17 June 1854; *SR* 22 June 1854.
11 *CC* 8 January, 10 January 1856; *CUM* 26 December 1855, 2 January 1856.

transmitted to the Poor Law Commissioners who concluded that Ellen Donovan was entitled to register her children as Protestants because their father was of that faith.[12] They believed that she and her family had been subjected to personal violence and annoyance from other inmates. They implicated the Catholic chaplain in this, and they criticised the workhouse officers for failing to prevent the disorderly conduct.[13]

Persecution of workhouse paupers was not restricted to those who resided in the institution. During January 1856 a 13-year old Catholic orphan named Catherine Corcoran applied to be readmitted to the workhouse. Some months previously a Protestant relation named Michael Holland had taken her from the house on the understanding that he would respect her religious beliefs.[14] Despite the undertaking, the girl was subjected to cruelty. She was also prevented from attending Mass and was taken to a Protestant service instead. The admission committee was divided on whether she should be allowed return to the workhouse. One faction was adamant that the girl was not destitute. The spokesman for that group said that she had been prevented from attending Mass on just two occasions, and that in any case Holland read the bible aloud every night. The spokesman had no sympathy for the girl, and had never seen 'any one more devoid of principle than she, or more bigoted'. Those in favour of admitting the girl pointed out that she was subjected to serious physical abuse, particularly by Holland's wife: 'when the girl came for admission in the usual way her shoulder and back were stripped, and were found black and blue from beating, while her arm was one mass of jelly. She said she was beaten by a fire shovel, and Mr Hall found them to be marks of a sharp instrument'. Mr Jameson dismissed this by saying that, as some men beat their wives, the girl ought to be able to take some reasonable punishment.[15] In an editorial, the *Cork Constitution* advised that 'to such severity the guardians should not knowingly subject her again. Let her, too, have no annoyance on account of her religion. There is positive cruelty in the petty persecution which a taunting tongue can inflict on one in the condition of the dependent'.[16] The *Cork Examiner* was also anxious that the girl should be protected. It questioned the attitude of some guardians and deviously suggested that if an investigation were held, it could also establish 'for the information of the public, the precise legal

---

12 *CE* 4 January, 7 January, 9 January, 11 January 1856.
13 *CUM* 31 January, 6, 13 February, 1856; *CUL* 29 January 1856; *CE* 30 January 1856.
14 Holland, who had been a Catholic up to 10 years previously, was married to the girl's stepsister. *CUM* 13 February 1856.
15 *CC* 29 January, 31 January 1856; *CUM* 30 January 1856; *CE* 30 January 1856.
16 *CC* 2 February 1856.

diameter of the stick, with which, according to the lawyers of the Board, a man may beat his wife'.[17]

Though the girl was not immediately admitted, her application was successful at the next committee meeting. Some guardians greeted the decision with outrage. In a veiled threat, they warned that the work of the board could suffer as a result of the decision: 'we regret that the harmony which has so long existed amongst the members of the Board is very likely to be disturbed by the attempts which are evidently working to introduce a sectarian spirit amongst them, which if not checked with a firm hand, must produce the worst results'. Michael Holland applied in person at the guardians' meeting for custody of the girl, but following a heated debate, it was decided to deny his request.[18] He attended again on the following week and, despite some support, his application was refused. He complained to the Poor Law Commissioners but they refused to become involved, saying that the Cork Board of Guardians had the ability and authority to assess the situation and make a fair decision.[19]

When nursed-out foundlings matured, the children were either returned to the workhouse, or adopted by the family. Problems sometimes occurred when Catholic families wished to adopt children who had been baptised as Protestants before they left the workhouse.[20] These matters were usually resolved without acrimony but occasionally disagreements ensued. In the mid 1850s James Sweeny, church warden of St. Peter's parish, arranged for a Protestant foundling named Anne Jackson to be nursed by a Murphy family in Millstreet. Mrs Mary Murphy had five young sons and the new arrival was well cared for and treated as a family member. A regular half-yearly nursing allowance was forwarded to Mrs Murphy. This ceased in October 1858 when the child was four years old, and Sweeny told the woman to return the child to the Cork workhouse. Sweeny agreed that the child could stay with the family until Christmas but when the Murphys failed to give the girl back, he sent a man to seize the child. Mary Murphy brought the child back to Cork and pleaded with Sweeny to allow her keep the 'fat, fair-haired, rosy-cheeked, little girl, with a strong country look'. He refused and she accompanied him to the workhouse where the matter was discussed with some guardians. When Sweeny pointed out that, according to official regulations, a Protestant child could not be given to a Catholic for

17 *CE* 1 February 1856.
18 *CE* 6 February, 13 February 1856; *CC* 2 February, 5 February, 7 February 1856; *CUM* 13 February 1856.
19 *CUM* 27 February 1856; *CUL* 26 February 1856; *CE* 29 February 1856.
20 *CUM* 4 May, 11 May 1859; *SR* 5 May, 9 May, 10 May, 14 May 1859; *CC* 12 May 1859; *CUL* 10 May 1859.

adoption, unless the appropriate chaplain sanctioned it, the girl was admitted to the workhouse on 4 May 1859.[21] The Poor Law Commissioners disagreed with this action which had no legal basis. They instructed the guardians to 'give up the child to the nurse from whom it was improperly taken, as it is not competent to them to delegate to any of the chaplains of the workhouse, a discretion which entirely belongs to themselves'.[22]

At around the same time another family had a similar experience. Their own child had died in a fire and they were given a foundling named John Condon to nurse by Sweeny. They gave the orphan the name of the dead child and treated him as their own son. Again, when the child reached four years of age Sweeny told the family to return the boy. In spite of all sorts of pleas – even a promise to bring the child up as a Protestant – they were forced to return the boy. Acting on the belief that these children were not destitute, and that force and threats had been used to have them returned to the workhouse, Nicholas Mahony, one of the Cork guardians, contacted the Commissioners regarding both incidents.[23]

William O Brien, the Poor Law Inspector, held an investigation into the incidents on 9 May 1859. He was instructed by the Commissioners that if force had been used to effect the return of the children, then they should be given back to their nurses. Nicholas Mahony presented his evidence to the inspector and he asked if the law could force nurses to return foundlings. He also asked if it was just to force the ratepayers to support children whose nurses were willing to adopt them. The child nursed by the Murphys had been well cared for and the tears shed by the foster mother and the girl, when they were torn apart 'was such as ought to make the most stringent stickler for the letter of the law pause, before perpetrating so evident an act of cruelty'. Sweeny was questioned on his reasons for separating the pair. He explained that as the child had been baptised a Protestant, he believed that it could not be given to a Catholic family for adoption. He was apprehensive also that the child might not be well cared for because the Murphys already had five children and the father worked as a labourer. The Poor Law Commissioners were unaware of any regulation which compelled nurses to return foundlings to the workhouse at four years of age. They advised the guardians to return the child to Mrs Murphy and following a disagreeable discussion, the board voted in favour of this action.[24]

The transfer of John Condon to his foster family was not achieved

---

21 CUM 4 May 1859; SR 5 May, 10 May 1859; CC 12 May 1859.
22 *CUL* 10 May 1859.
23 *SR* 9 May 1859.
24 *CUM* 1 May 1859; SR 14 May 1859.

with such smoothness.[25] On 25 May 1859 the guardians debated a resolution that the boy should be returned to his nurse. During the heated
discussion, two guardians 'put themselves into a fighting attitude across
the table, Mr. Sheehan with clenched fist, and Mr. Jameson with uplifted
stick'. When the matter was eventually voted on, it was decided by eleven
to ten votes to put the boy into Sweeny's charge.[26] Sweeny re-admitted
the boy to the workhouse and the decision was criticised by the Commissioners who would not issue any directive, but said that this was illegal
because the boy was not in fact destitute.[27]

Controversies of this nature were followed with interest by the general
public. In the wake of the John Condon incident a special meeting was
held in Drishane church on Sunday 22 May 1859 to discuss the 'illegal
conduct of Romish Poor-Law Guardians in giving up Protestant
foundlings to be reared by Romish nurses in their own faith, and as their
own children'. The motion was discussed for some time and eventually a
resolution was passed which condemned

> the insidious attempts to proselytise foundling children baptised into
> the Protestant Faith through the medium of nurses making applica-
> tion to the Poor Law Guardians to retain as their own the children
> placed at nurse with them, with the evident design of bringing them
> up in the Romish Religion.[28]

There was no word of appreciation for the services and commitment
of the nurses. That these women removed infant foundlings from the
dangers of infection, neglect, boredom and hardship in the workhouse
was neither recognised nor acknowledged by those attending the protest
meeting.

The zeal with which the majority of foundlings were registered as
Protestants did not have general approval. In one 12 months period, all
the foundlings delivered to the Cork workhouse were registered to that
faith. As the majority of the city's population was Catholic, some
observers argued that most of the children should be registered as such.
Conferring exclusive credit for the city's foundlings on the Protestant
population was 'casting a stigma' on that religion, it was argued.[29]
Nonetheless, the legislation dictated that if the religion of a foundling
was not known it should be raised 'in the religion of the state'.[30]

---

25 *CUM* 11 May 1859.
26 *CUM* 25 May 1859; *CC* 26 May 1859; *SR* 26 May 1859.
27 *CC* 9 May 1859; *SR* 9 May 1859.
28 *CC* 24 May 1859.
29 *SR* 22 September 1859.
30 *Poor Law Commissioners Annual Report* (1859), p 20; see also correspondence pp
153-9.

When the guardians were discussing the workhouse school in May 1857, Mr Jameson complained that a water font at the entrance to the building was offensive to non-Catholic pupils and officers.[31] Following a proposal that the font should be removed, the matter was investigated and it was discovered that the font had been unofficially erected about 12 months previously. An unemployed stonecutter named Thomas Barry who was an inmate of the house had been detailed to re-cut foot grips on the worn stairways in the institution. When this work was finished, Barry, a Protestant, and another inmate found a suitable stone and decided to replace an old tin dish with a proper water font. Barry worked the stone into shape and the men erected the new font without authorisation. At the investigation, the Catholic chaplain said that if he had been approached, he would not have given his permission, because the building was not a regular place of worship. On the instructions of the Commissioners, the font was removed and the matter ended amicably.[32]

During July 1857 when an infirm prostitute named Mary Anne Griffith applied to change her religion from Protestant to Catholic the matter generated little discussion. Some weeks later when another Protestant prostitute named Hanora Tehan, made a similar application, the Protestant chaplain alleged that 'souperism' was being practised in the workhouse. He said that when the girls changed their religion, they were rewarded with the superior hospital diet. He also complained that when girls left the workhouse to enter the Protestant refuge, some of them returned to the workhouse and re-registered as Catholics. As a reward, they were sent to the body of the house instead of to the penitentiary ward. The girl Tehan was brought to the boardroom and she stated that she had been admitted to the hospital with a chest complaint, but that it had long been her intention to change her religion.[33] Dr Popham confirmed that the girl had been in the penitentiary ward for almost two years, that she was an acute asthma sufferer and that she had been returned to the separation ward in the Lock hospital, not the general workhouse hospital, as had been alleged.[34]

A few weeks later a Presbyterian inmate, named Henrietta Miller, applied to change her religion to Catholic because she was 'lonesome'. The board questioned her and Mr Julian asked "was it since you came into the classic precincts of the workhouse this light came on you?" The girl was adamant that she had made the decision of her own free will. Having discussed the matter for some time, the board concluded that it

---

31 *CUM* 20 May 1857; *CE* 15 May, 22 May 1857.
32 *CUM* 10 June 1857; *CUL* 4 June 1857; *CE* 3 June, 12 June 1857.
33 *CE* 11 September 1857 The workhouse master described Tehan as 'always the most troublesome woman in the house'. *CC* 10 September 1857.
34 *CC* 17 September 1857; *CE* 18 September 1857.

had no power to prevent inmates from changing their religion if they so desired.[35] When a 64-year-old Protestant inmate named Anne Brodie applied to change her religion to Catholic in December 1859 the workhouse minutes recorded that 'the master thinks she is quite out of her mind'.[36] A similar judgement was made some years later when Eliza Riordan, an inmate of the lying-in ward, sought to change her religion and that of her unborn child to Catholic. Dr Wherland's prognosis was that 'when women were in this delicate state [i.e. pregnant] they sometimes went mentally astray; and perhaps it would be better to wait for a short time to see if she would come to her right mind'. The guardians decided to allow the woman change her religion as she wished.[37]

Religious tensions in the workhouse were exploited by some inmates. During 1877 a Catholic woman named Robinson created some controversy when she claimed that, with her three children, she had left the house on the understanding that they would be put on the outdoor relief list. She also claimed that she had been encouraged to send the children to an institution in Dublin where they would be raised as Protestants. The woman's allegations were the subject of a number of inquiries during the Autumn of 1877.[38] During the following year Rev. Webster claimed that a Protestant boy named Daniel Burchill had been discharged from the workhouse and re-admitted a couple of days later as a Catholic with the name John Joseph Burchill. Following a discussion it transpired that the change of registration had been sanctioned by the boy's mother who was an inmate of the Lock ward.[39]

The Protestant chaplain, Rev. Dr George Webster, was particularly vigilant about his flock. His concern often turned into suspicion and he frequently reacted or indeed over-reacted to any sign of interference. In 1873 he complained with justification that a five-year-old Protestant girl had been taught the following lines by a Catholic child:

> [Proddie, woddie, greenguts] never said her prayers,
> Catch her by the two legs and throw her down the stairs,
> The Minister he broke his back,
> The fairies cried out "Whack, Whack, Whack".[40]

The practice of accommodating Protestant men in general wards with Catholic inmates also annoyed the chaplain and in January 1879 he requested the guardians to provide a separate ward and to discontinue

---

35 *CUM* 24 August, 21 December 1859; *CE* 23 October 1857; *CC* 22 October 1857.
36 *CUM* 14 December 1859.
37 *CE* 7 December 1883.
38 *CE* 3, 4, 9, 10 August, 21 September 1877.
39 *CE* 12, 19, 25, 26 April, 3, 17 May 1878.
40 *CUM* 5 June 1873.

scattering them throughout the house.[41] Similar attempts were also made to keep sick Protestant ladies together. Their ward was occupied by a variety of patients. Because of its poor state, Dr Wall's suggestion that a nearby area should be modified for 'delirious patients, or those afflicted with maladies of an unavoidably offensive nature' was investigated by the hospital committee.[42] In one area of the ward, sick and dying women suffering from cancer and other diseases, had their torments accentuated by the 'crying and squealing of the young children', so it was decided to move the children and their mothers to the workhouse nursery. Almost immediately, some guardians objected because the mothers and their charges would have to fraternise with Catholics in an atmosphere of 'regular pandemonium'. Although the chairman of the board doubted that any 'harm would befall the Protestant children physically or morally, by their mixing with the Catholic children', the concerns were given cognisance.[43]

Rev. Webster was also against the suggestion of placing Protestant mothers and children in the general nursery ward where he feared they would come into contact with Catholic nurses or even Sisters of Mercy:

> I strongly object to giving a little Protestant child into the charge of a Roman Catholic nurse. Everyone knows that a little child in the first few years of its life may receive a religious prejudice under the influence of its nurse, of which it may never afterwards be able to divest itself. What I claim for myself and my own people I willingly concede to others.

Some of the Protestant guardians did not agree with Rev. Webster's inflexibility and they questioned the necessity and expense of providing a separate ward. Some of them doubted that the children's faith would suffer. 'I think', said Captain Sarsfield, 'they are not of an age to enter into theological or controversial discussions with other babies of seven or eight months old'.[44] Although the guardians were divided on the issue, speakers from both sides did concede that there was no valid reason for separating the children and that in fact it would be better to leave them together.

In the event, it was decided to put the Protestant infants in the general workhouse nursery. A number of infants and their mothers were moved into a section of the ward.[45] Rev. Webster did not agree with the decision

---

41 *CE* 17 January 1879.
42 *CUM* 8 May 1879; *CE* 2 May, 9 May 1879.
43 *CC* 16 May, 30 May 1879; *CE* 16 May, 30 May 1879.
44 *CUM* 5 June 1879; *CE* 6 June 1879.
45 *CUM* 12 June, 19 June 1879; *CC* 6 June, 13 June, 20 June 1879; *CE* 6 June, 13 June, 20 June 1879.

and he still wanted a separate location. In a letter to the board he declared: 'I am not satisfied with the order of the Guardians that *healthy* infant Protestants should be located in a Roman Catholic ward, which is the *hospital* for Roman Catholic children. I want a Protestant nursery for healthy Protestant children until they are three years of age under Protestant nurses'.[46] In this instance, no further changes were made and during subsequent years, just a few incidents of religious intolerance occurred in the workhouse boardroom and its wards. During 1885 the Catholic chaplain complained that when the Protestant sisters visited the lunatic wards, they frequently brought gifts of fruit, meat and biscuits to inmates. He was apprehensive that members of his flock would change their religion in order to receive gifts from the sisters. At the end of 1888 controversy erupted when it became clear that Sister Elizabeth Dunckley, a Protestant nurse, had played a part in removing a boy named William Pitt from the workhouse. The young lad was later found begging at Douglas and committed to the Protestant Marble Hall Industrial school in Cork.[47]

The Poor Law Commissioners investigated disputes about religious issues and allegations of proselytism in workhouses other than Cork. For instance, an investigation about baptising a foundling child as a Catholic was held in the Tulla workhouse in 1868,[48] and in 1842 a dispute occurred when two orphans were registered as Catholics in Dundalk workhouse.[49] A more serious situation developed in Dingle when it emerged that certain inmates were given money when they attended Protestant services in the workhouse. Inmates who changed their religion were permitted to keep their children in the house but for those who did not convert, the offspring were removed to another premises.[50] Allegations about interfering with the religious convictions of inmates were not uncommon and cases were investigated at Fermoy,[51] Bantry,[52] South

---

46 *CC* 20 June 1879; *CE* 20 June 1879; see also, Alfred G. Dann, *George Webster, D.D., A memoir* (Dublin, 1892), pp. 29-30. In 1888 the Protestant sisters again complained about infants being placed in the care of Catholic nurses; see *CE* 31 August 1888.

47 *CE* 3 July, 17 July 1885, 21 December 1888, 16 January 1889.

48 PP 1867-8, Vol. LXI, [275], *Copy of the correspondence between the Poor Law Commissioners and the guardians of the poor of the Tulla Union, respecting the religion of a foundling child in that Union.*

49 PP 1842, Vol. XXXVI, [545], *Copies of the Minutes of Proceedings of the Board of Guardians of Dundalk Union relative to two pauper children, Sarah and William Montgomery. . .*

50 PP 1851, Vol. XLIX, [427], *Copy of a report made by Captain Spark, relative to certain charges of proselytising in the workhouse of Dingle Union. . . .*

51 *CE* 9 January 1856.

52 *CE* 4 May, 14 May, 23 May, 28 May, 30 May 1860.

Dublin[53] and other workhouses in subsequent years. Other disputes about appointments or remunerations for workhouse chaplains also generated bad feelings amongst inmates, guardians and the general public.[54]

Politics

From around the late 1870s the Cork board of guardians' proceedings were disrupted with increasing frequency by political discussions. When the new board assembled on 14 April 1881, the business of electing the chairman, vice chairman and deputy vice chairman was dispatched rapidly when the three sitting officers were jointly proposed, seconded and re-elected in a routine manner. Anticipations that newly elected Land League representatives, or 'sans culottes guardians', as the *Cork Constitution* branded them, would disrupt that meeting did not materialise. Protestations by the incensed nationalists that the officers should have been selected and then voted on individually were to no avail, nor were the demands of the tenant farmer representatives for even a token position of deputy vice chairman.[55]

Within a few weeks the business of the board was disrupted when a motion of protest at the arrest of John Dillon, M.P. was put forward by the nationalist guardians. The chairman's refusal to accept this political motion was frowned upon by the nationalists, while the other guardians protested about time being wasted. A noisy and argumentative debate ensued as the protagonists and antagonists discussed the validity of tendering motions of a political nature. The nationalists made other attempts to have the resolution accepted during the next few weeks, but all their efforts were fruitless. Finally, in desperation,

---

53   *CE* 11 June 1860; PP 1862, Vol. XLIX, [492], *Copies of orders made by the Poor Law Commissioners in Ireland, sanctioning the payment of remuneration to Roman Catholic clergymen for occasional duties at the workhouses of Mitchelstown Union during the vacancy in the office of Roman Catholic chaplain; and of correspondence on the subject of such remuneration between the Commissioners and the Mitchelstown Board of Guardians, in 1858 and 1861; also, of correspondence, since 1st June last, between the Youghal Board of Guardians and the Commissioners, on the subject of similar remuneration as to the Youghal Workhouse*; PP 1862, Vol. XLIX, [472], *Copies of all correspondence adopted by the Youghal Board of Guardians, on the subject of filling up the vacancy in the Roman Catholic Chaplaincy to the Workhouse, caused by the resignation of Rev. John Twohig.*

54   *CE* 27 January, 30 January, 1 June, 4 June 1860, 17 May 1871, and 15 April 1862.

55   *CE* 18 March, 15 April 1881, see also *CE* 14 April, 15 April 1882. For an interesting study of nationalists' agitation in regard to poor law elections, see: William L. Feingold, 'Land League Power: The Tralee Poor-Law Election of 1881', in S. Clark and J. S. Donnelly, Jr. *Irish Peasants*. (Manchester, 1983), pp. 285-310.

when the chairman dissolved the board meeting, the nationalists put one of their members in the chair and proceeded to propose and second the motion. A meaningless charade followed, and the clerk refused to record the details as the official meeting had been dissolved. The dissatisfied nationalists sought an opinion on the affair from the Local Government Board. The board ruled that the chairman had the authority to close the meeting when the legitimate business had finished, and he was authorised to refuse any question he deemed 'not fit to be put as leading to or suggesting illegal conduct, or being wholly inconsistent with the duties of the guardians'.[56]

Further disruptions occurred in May 1881 when the nationalists unsuccessfully sought to have motions, criticising the arrest of Fr. Eugene Sheehy of Kilmallock, passed at the board meeting. Again in the autumn of 1881, valuable time was wasted on arguments about the relevance of a motion criticising the Coercion Acts.[57] The nationalists' desire to advance their cause was paramount at all times and frequently the guardians meetings were used as a platform for political rhetoric. This was unfair to workhouse inmates, ratepayers and fellow guardians who had nothing to benefit from the petty political point scoring. Repeated arguments about procedures and the etiquette of business also discouraged members from attending board meetings. Nonetheless, meeting time, which should have been spent discussing worthwhile matters, was squandered on issues which were unrelated to workhouse business.[58]

During one lengthy debate on the 1882 Crimes Act,[59] the nationalists sought to establish its relevance to the poor law by showing that the results of evictions were not merely political as they contributed greatly to destitution and poverty. The effort was wasted as the meeting's chairman refused to accept any political motion and when he adjourned the meeting none of that day's business relating to the workhouse had been discussed.[60] Such behaviour was repeated on many subsequent occasions and only rarely did the nationalists succeed in winning the day. For instance, in July 1882 they succeeded in having a vote of condolence passed on the death of Fanny Parnell and in February 1886 the board passed a resolution in support of Home Rule. In the following August a resolution condemning evictions was passed and

56 *CE* 13 May, 20 May, 27 May, 10 June, 17 June 1881; *CUM* 5 May, 12 May 1881.
57 *CE* 21 October, 28 October 1881.
58 *CE* 15 July 1881, 2 June, 23 June 1882; *CC* 24 February 1882; *CUM* 27 October 1881, 23 February 1882; see also *CE* 14, 15 April 1882.
59 *44&45 Victoriae, Ch. 25, Prevention of Crime (Ireland) Act, 1882.*
60 *CE* 7 July, 14 July, 21 July, 4 August, 11 August, 18 August, 25 August, 1 September 1882.

on 26 May 1887 a resolution condemning the government's Coercion Act was passed by thirteen votes to eight.[61]

Because of the superior voting power of the unionist guardians and their ex-officio colleagues, the nationalists were unable to secure the position of chairman, vice chairman or deputy vice chairman at the board meetings.[62] Despite determined efforts at the first meeting of a new board in April 1884 they failed to bring about a change and the previous year's officers retained the positions. The nationalists eventually succeeded in making a breakthrough when Michael Ahern was elected vice-chairman in April 1885 and again in 1886.[63] He retained this position in 1887 when the unionist/conservative faction, with some assistance from Catholic ex-officio guardians, had no trouble in taking the position of chairman and deputy vice chairman with Captain Sarsfield and Henry L. Young respectively. The appointment of Captain Sarsfield was viewed with disgust by the *Cork Examiner*, which remarked that he was

> a respectable gentleman in private life, but it is no exaggeration to say that in the South of Ireland, if searched, could not produce a more bitter partisan . . . He is Grand Master of the local Orange Lodge, and Chairman of the Property Defence Association. To put him forward is simply a declaration of war to the knife, not only against Nationalism, but against the merest Liberal policies.[64]

Following Sarsfield's appointment, arguments and disagreements were frequently heard in the boardroom. In June, when the nationalists sought the board's approval to present an address to William O Brien on his return from Canada, the conservatives, who were in the minority at the meeting, attempted to block a discussion. 'This little clique, including some perfect figureheads of flunkeyism, fell back on the usual pretence of the resolution having "nothing to do with the business of the board"'. Eventually, after a large part of the meeting had been wasted, it was agreed that a deputation would go to Queenstown to present the address to O Brien.[65] In September 1887, Captain Sarsfield refused to

---

61 *CE 28* July 1882, 27 May 1887; *CC* 12 February, 13 August 1886; NAI, CSORP 1887 9329.

62 For a discussion on the dominance of unionist factions in Irish poor law boards of guardians, see William L. Feingold, 'The Tenants' movement to capture the Irish Poor Law Boards, 1877-1886', in Alan O Day (ed.), *Reactions to Irish Nationalism* (Dublin, 1987), pp. 79-94. See also Virginia Crossman, The New Ross Workhouse Riot of 1887: Nationalism, Class and the Irish Poor Laws, *Past and Present*, No. 179, May 2003, pp. 135-58, for another perspective on politics and workhouse life.

63 *CE* 18 April, 19 April 1884, 10 April 1885, 16 April 1886.

64 *CE* 15 April 1887.

65 *CE* 17 June 1887.

take resolutions relating to the behaviour of the RIC at the Limerick workhouse and to the arrest of William O Brien. When Sarsfield and most of the unionist guardians eventually left the boardroom, vice-chairman Michael Ahern took the chair and the contentious motions were passed. Arguments about the strategy adopted and the legality of the process used in passing the resolutions dominated the next board meeting. The unionists, with more that a little justification, disputed the legality of the proceedings but, eventually, Sarsfield agreed to sign the minute book, even though he had not been convinced that the records were not tainted.[66]

Some weeks later the patience of the unionists was further tried when the nationalists succeeded in passing a resolution to withdraw advertisements and notices from the pro-landlord *Cork Constitution* newspaper. The motion was discussed again on 1 December 1887 when Dr Charles Tanner, M.P., proposed that because of its 'malignant attitude', the *Cork Constitution* should continue to be excluded as an advertising medium by the Cork Union. The meeting degenerated into a bad-tempered melee at which personal insults were freely traded between the factions. The resolution to withdraw the advertising was upheld by a six-vote majority. In disgust at the proceedings, Captain Sarsfield resigned as chairman and, accompanied by his supporters, stormed out of the boardroom.[67] By using a strategy of subterfuge two weeks later, the nationalists succeeded in postponing the election of a new chairman for almost five hours. When the unionist vice-guardians, many of whom were old and frail and did not have the staying power of their adversaries, had left the boardroom, Michael Ahern was elected chairman of the board.[68]

The methods used by the nationalists were at times opportunistic and underhand and led to calls to have the business of the board transferred to paid officials. The nationalists' own supporters were sometimes critical of their elected representatives. When a deputation of labourers applied to the board of guardians for assistance during a period of high unemployment and hardship, they were annoyed that the nationalist guardians were unable to secure any real help. Disillusioned by this failure, a spokesman for the labourers, many of whom were active in local politics, lamented that the guardians were 'the very national party, who we were aiding and assisting, breaking our melt, running down the streets cheering for'.[69] The unionist *Cork Constitution* did not let this opportunity pass, and in an editorial on the labourers' ire, the newspaper noted that they

---

66 *CE* 23 September, 30 September, 1 October 1887; see also *CC* 16 July, 7, 21 October, 4, 18 November, 2, 7, 10, 13 December 1887.
67 *CE* 7 October, 21 October, 18 November, 2 December, 30 December 1887.
68 *CE* 16 December 1887.
69 *CC* 1 October 1886.

were 'plainly as dissatisfied with the support given them by the nationalist party as Oliver Twist was with his supply of workhouse porridge, and
they have had, in the estimation of the Parnellite faction, the "outrageous" presumption to ask for "more"'.[70]

Although it was contrary to official regulations, discussions on political issues were conducted with increasing frequency at the Cork
guardians' meetings. The Local Government Board was forced to inter-
vene and it formally alerted the guardians to the illegality of their
action.[71] The Board pointed out that it was contrary to regulations to
discuss political issues before the regular business was completed. The
Board warned the guardians that 'if they desire to retain the management
of the affairs of the union in their hands, they must not continue to
conduct the proceedings at their meetings in the irregular and illegal
manner' shown at recent meetings.[72] Tempers flared again in February
1888 when the subject of advertising in the *Constitution* was discussed.
Following some provocative displays, the unionists succeeded by 28
votes to 26 in rescinding the resolution to withdraw advertisements from
the newspaper.[73]

At the first meeting of the new board of guardians on 12 April 1888,
Michael Ahern was re-elected chairman by 44 votes to 42. As the votes
were being counted, two more ex-officio guardians entered the room.
Two candidates, Thomas Gallwey (unionist) and the nationalist P.F.
Dunn were proposed for the position of vice-chairman. When the votes
were counted, each candidate had 43 votes although there were 87
guardians entitled to vote in the room! When the count was analysed it
was discovered that one of the unionist votes had not been recorded.
Various allegations were made and the unionists concluded that one of
their members – Mr. Pike – had been locked outside the door until after
his name had been called. A second vote did not take place and the
disputed appointment was postponed for a week. In the meantime, the
unionists contacted the Local Government Board which initiated an
inquiry, thus deferring the appointment. Without proper notice, the
nationalists went ahead with the election. In spite of protests from a few
unionists present on 26 April, they confirmed the appointment of Dunn
as vice-chairman by 35 votes to 10. A week later the Local Government
Board ruled that Mr. Pike's vote should have been counted and they
ruled that Thomas Gallwey was the legitimate vice-chairman. Bad feelings again erupted when the nationalists refused to comply with the

---

70 *CC* 2 October 1886; see also 4 and 15 October 1886.
71 *CE* 28 October, 4 November, 23 December, 24 December 1887; *CC* 4 November
    1887.
72 *CE* 20 January 1888; *CC* 21 January, 24 February 1888.
73 *CC* 24 February 1888.

ruling and referred the matter back to the Board. When the guardians trooped into the boardroom for their meeting on 10 May, Thomas Gallwey was in situ at the head of the table. Michael Ahern was not present but when Henry L. Young, the deputy-vice-chairman, arrived, Gallwey offered him the chair. The unionist guardians told him to remain where he was, but the nationalists demanded that he vacate the chair. Uproar ensued, with each side shouting at the other, but when things calmed down, Gallwey remained in the chair and conducted the business. The Local Government Board insisted that Gallwey was the legitimate vice-chairman, so the nationalists were left with no choice but to cancel Dunn's appointment and accept this ruling.[74] Such an incompetent and dishonest attempt to commandeer the vice-chairmanship of the Cork Union did not deserve success, but it must certainly have damaged the reputation and standing of the nationalists.

In October 1888, Dr Tanner gave notice of a motion about the hardships resulting from evictions. He pointed out that many evicted tenants and their families entered the workhouse or received outdoor relief for a number of weeks while they came to terms with their changed circumstances. Some guardians agreed with this and they said that increases in the urban rates could be traced to demands for relief by country people who had been forced by eviction to come to the city. Tanner was unable to attend when the motion came up for discussion, so he sought to have the matter postponed for a week. This was permissible but the unionists, who had assembled in force, to defeat the motion, demanded that the rules should be strictly enforced, and that the motion be discharged from the books. The chairman refused to take a resolution to remove Dr Tanner's motion from the books. This precipitated another long and bad-tempered meeting, which was eventually adjourned without a vote on the matter and before the regular business had been concluded. Colonel Spaight, the Poor Law Inspector, wrote to the Local Government Board and alerted it to the 'disorderly practice at the weekly meetings of the [Cork] Board, by which the transaction of business was impeded', and by which the printed rules of the board were being ignored. When some guardians criticised Spaight for contacting the Local Government Board, he pointed out that all sides of the boardroom were contributing to the disorder, so he was not singling out any individuals or faction for criticism.[75]

The Local Government Board did not let the matter rest and, in response to its inspector and to a critical communication from the unionist guardians, it informed the Cork board, and particularly its

---

74 *CE* 13 April, 20 April, 27 April, 15 May, 18 May 1888; *CC* 12 April, 13 April, 20 April, 27 April 1888; *CUM* 12 April 1888.
75 *CE* 14 September, 21 September, 5 October, 19 October, 26 October 1888; *CC* 16 October, 19 October 1888; *CUM* 6 September 1888; NAI, CSORP1888 21816.

chairman, that he had breached regulations by his refusal to take a vote on discharging Dr Tanner's motion. Even though the Local Government Board's letter arrived prior to the guardians' meeting on 25 October, Michael Ahern made no reference to it, so a number of hours were again wasted on a virtual re-run of the previous week's debacle. This attempt to conceal the Board's ire earned more criticism for Ahern, and further damaged the credibility of the nationalists as a fair and honest force. Undaunted, when the melee had subsided and with just one unionist remaining in the chamber, the nationalists took the time to pass a motion condemning the imprisonment of Tom Moroney of Herbertstown! The Local Government Board was not impressed with the attitude of the nationalists and it sent another warning about the manner of conducting business. It called attention to the earlier warning and advised the board that this second lapse had been noted. Again, it repeated the warning about the consequences of repeating 'such an irregular course of proceedings'.[76]

The behaviour of the nationalist guardians at this period was certainly underhand. They, on occasions, gave notice of a controversial motion to which the unionists responded by mustering their forces and assembling at the given time. In an attempt to avoid a fruitless conflict, the nationalists then sought some pretence to postpone or delay the matter. This succeeded on a number of occasions but sometimes they dragged proceedings out until an adequate number of unionists had been forced to leave and then a snap decision was made to take the vote. An empty victory was thus achieved when the motion was passed under such circumstances.

Political issues continued to appear before the board of guardians even after the Local Government Board's warning. On 17 January 1889 a motion condemning rent increases by the Land Commission was passed and two weeks later the board was forced to adjourn because of a discussion on the prison treatment being meted out to William O Brien.[77] At the first meeting of the newly elected board on 11 April, the 47 unionist guardians outvoted their opponents, thus ensuring that none of the 37 nationalists got any of the officer posts.[78] This set the scene for future hostilities and during the next few months arguments, disruption and adjournments resulted when nationalist raised such matters as the jailing of Dr Tanner in May, the contents of a National League circular in June, and evictions at the Ponsonby estate in July.[79] Following another

---

76 *CE* 2 November, 16 November 1888; *CC* 19 October, 26 October, 2 November, 16 November 1888.
77 *CE* 18 January, 8 February 1889
78 *CUM* 11 April 1889; *CE* 11 April, 12 April 1889.
79 *CE* 20 April, 24 May, 5 July, 12 July 1889; *CUM* 4 July 1889; *CC* 28 June 1889.

disruption on 1 August when the nationalists again raised the matter of Dr Tanner's imprisonment, the meeting was adjourned before the business was completed. The Local Government Board issued another warning about the possibility of dissolving the board of guardians. The nationalists took little notice of the 'mild little threat' and promised to continue with their tactics for 'we will not be cowed down by a letter of that sort, and will continue to act in the same way when the occasion arises'. The *Cork Examiner* blamed the unionist majority for their intransigence towards the nationalists.[80]

Another major row ensued when the nationalists again raised the matter of the Ponsonby estate on 19 September, and the meeting was abandoned in uproar.[81] The Local Government Board again complained that business relating to 'the welfare of the destitute poor' was neglected. It issued a final warning to the Cork board of guardians that 'if without sufficient reason they continue to leave undischarged the important functions entrusted to them, the Local Government Board will feel compelled to relieve them of duties which they appear unable or unwilling to continue to fulfil'. Again, the *Cork Examiner* blamed the unionists for the turn in events because that party had turned out in full force to ensure that their candidate, Dominick Philip Sarsfield, would be elected to a position as a rate-collector. 'This transaction', said the *Cork Examiner*, 'will remain as one of the blackest and most scandalous proceedings of a Unionist Administration in Cork'.[82] In an editorial, the *Cork Constitution* said that many efficient guardians had ceased attending meetings because of the time wasted on political arguments. Why, said the newspaper, should 'gentlemen of education and position, whose time is presumably of some value to them. . . sit quietly by whilst some yokel, anxious for a parish reputation, assails them in language calculated to provoke a breach of the peace'.[83] The paper concluded that 'there is no use in having rules for regulating the proceedings of the Board unless they are carried out, and there is no use in appointing chairmen to conduct the business unless their ruling is obeyed'.[84]

The year 1890 opened with further disruption when the unionists refused to accept a motion relating to Charles S. Parnell. Arguments and insults were freely traded before the meeting was adjourned without its business concluded.[85] The performance was repeated on the following

---

80 *CE* 19 July, 2 August, 9 August 1889.
81 *CE* 20 September, 27 September 1889; *CC* 20 September, 27 September 1889.
82 *CE* 4 October 1889.
83 *CC* 24 September 1889.
84 *CC* 20 September 1889.
85 *CE* 10 January, 17 January, 18 January 1890; *CC* 10 January 1890.

week and 'more ruffianly behaviour has, we venture to say, rarely taken place at a public board. The Chairman's ruling was openly defied from start to finish – defied too, with every accompaniment of insult unprovoked and unmerited'.[86] Although it lamented that 'in the end brute force predominated', the *Cork Constitution* was pleased that 'out of evil sometimes cometh good, and as a result of yesterday's performance, we shall be very much surprised, indeed, if the Local Government Board any longer permit their authority to be flouted, and the interests of the ratepayers and the poor to be sacrificed to those of a political faction'.[87] The Local Government Board implemented its threat, and a sealed order dissolving the Cork Union board of guardians was issued on 22 January.[88] This action was criticised or celebrated by many individuals and observers.[89] A satisfied *Cork Constitution* asked 'if there be any amongst them who really and truly regard their dismissal in the light of a grievance, they must at all events confess that their political leaders and the Board laboured hard and unceasingly to bring about such a climax, and if they do happen to indulge in any lamentations, it is to be hoped they will place the responsibility in the proper quarter'.[90] In an editorial, the *Cork Examiner* analysed the sequence of events which led to the dissolution; it concluded that 'the nationalists walked into the hands of the enemy, fell victims to the plotters with their eyes open, and supplied the Local Government Board with the much-desired excuse for dissolving the Board'.[91] Vice guardians were appointed to run the affairs of the Cork Union and they assumed duty on 30 January 1890.[92]

Conclusion

For a time, an unsavoury undercurrent of religious intolerance and one-upmanship contaminated life in the Cork workhouse. This intolerance permeated all levels of society and workhouse inmates were not immune to contamination. Consequently, issues, which should not have intruded into the boardroom or the wards, were allowed to cause misery and

---

86 *CC* 17 January 1890.
87 *CC* 17 January 1890; see also 18-23 January 1890.
88 *CE* 24 January 1890; *CC* 24 January 1890; *Local Government Board Annual Report* (1890), pp. 13, 59-60.
89 *CE* 24 January, 25 January, 31 January, 4 February, 5 February, 7 February 1890; *CC* 25 January, 27 January, 31 January, 7 February, 12 February, 21 February 1890.
90 *CC* 24 January, also 25 January 1890.
91 *CE* 27 January 1890. As a result of the disorder at the meeting on 16 January, the nationalist guardian, Dr Tanner, M.P., was bound to the peace for 12 months because of his behaviour towards Smith Barry, M.P. *CC* 24-30 January 1890.
92 *CE* 31 January 1890; *CC* 31 January 1890.

distress to inmates and staff. Because of their limited numbers, Protestant inmates must have been subjected to intimidation and to avoid isolation and exclusion, some of them changed their religion. Political issues played a similarly divisive role and on many occasions legitimate workhouse business was abandoned in favour of petty party politics. Valuable time was squandered on discussions and arguments about issues which had no relevance to conditions in the workhouse. This was indicative of a selfish disregard for the plight and vulnerability of the hapless workhouse inmates and a disregard for the time allocated to workhouse business. Although little was achieved by the misdirected squabbling, disorder and disagreement temporarily reigned in the boardroom. Following the dissolution of the Cork board of guardians, its business was conducted by paid vice-guardians until this responsibility was returned to elected guardians in April 1891.[93]

---

93 C. O Mahony, *In the Shadows: Life in Cork 1750–1930* (Cork, 1997), pp.291-4; *Local Government Board Annual Report* (1891), pp. 18-19.

Conclusion

In the period covered by this study, the Cork workhouse functioned as a refuge for long-term paupers, temporarily distressed people, orphans and abandoned children, and famine victims seeking a refuge from starvation and disease. Also seeking refuge were short-term lodgers who sought a bed and a roof over their heads during their journey to employment or while searching for seasonal work. The institution also provided hospital accommodation for a variety of patients, including expectant mothers, infants, accident victims, and senile, aged and infirm people. It also catered for victims of epidemics such as cholera and smallpox, and, occasionally, special provisions were introduced to isolate and accommodate sufferers.

The majority of those who entered the workhouse were forced to do so because of poverty, sickness, old age or some misfortune. The motivation was rarely of great interest to the guardians, workhouse staff or officials and in the institution no special treatment was reserved for victims of trauma or distress. Many of the workhouse guardians had little compassion for the hapless applicants or inmates, and they frequently behaved in a mean, insensitive and uncaring manner. One guardian's belief that 'paupers should get pauper diet, just enough to keep them alive and no more',[1] is not untypical of that class. They did not trust the poor and were convinced that all relief applicants were lazy, intent on defrauding the system and not interested in earning a living outside the institution. Their principal reason for attending meetings and joining committees was to ensure that expenditure was controlled and kept to the lowest possible level. The interest of the ratepayers was the dominating motive for the behaviour of these guardians. Their task, in the words of the *Cork Constitution*, was 'to scrutinise every case, to steel their hearts against affecting tales of fictitious sorrow'.[2] Other guardians tended to be generous and were anxious to improve conditions for the unfortunate poor. They were determined to provide a better workhouse diet and easier access to outdoor relief. They were also in favour of boarding out

---

1 *SR*, 25 May 1847.
2 *CC*, 8 December 1855.

young inmates and improving the standard of workhouse education. Reducing poor rate expenditure was not a priority with these guardians.

The conflicting aspirations of the two factions, coupled with a high degree of inflexibility, frequently resulted in bad feelings, distrust and intransigence. The effectiveness of a reasonable argument by one party was sometimes undermined by the other side's blind adherence to an impractical and unfair stance. Sometimes an undercurrent of political or religious intolerance surfaced and the business of the day was abandoned in favour of trivial point scoring. A balance was of course essential to save the union from bankruptcy and to preserve workhouse inmates from persecution and hardship, but, although the Cork Union was never declared bankrupt, on occasions its workhouse inmates subsisted on inadequate food allowances in overcrowded and uncomfortable conditions.

In general, the opportunity to provide a solid and worthwhile, if basic, education for workhouse children was neglected, or indeed squandered. Teachers' remuneration was small and during the 1860s and 1870s salaries offered by some unions were blamed for discouraging good quality candidates for the post of workhouse teacher.[3] Poor teachers and scarce resources limited educational activities, and attempts to augment the curriculum with stimulating subjects were frequently opposed by guardians. In preference to providing an interesting and useful programme, which would have benefited the children, guardians opted for a curriculum which was little better than a gesture. It has been observed that most Irish workhouses 'failed to provide any real education for the child inmates'. [4]

The sheer monotony of workhouse life with its predictable routines, lack of stimulation, overcrowded and impersonal wards and a repetitive diet of plain and unimaginative food must have had a depressing effect on many inmates. Because of the nature of the workhouse and its threat to individuality, inmates who lacked strong will-power must have fallen prey to its mindless routine. Nonetheless, all inmates were not equal. Some were given special treatment, such as extra food or drink, because of participation in different duties in the workhouse. This, of course, created a hierarchical system among the inmates.[5] As well as this exploitation of pauper inmates, workers from outside the house were deprived of a chance to earn some money by fulfilling the workhouse tasks.[6]

---

3 *CE*, 16 March 1869, 24 February 1871.

4 J. Robins, *The lost children A study of charity children in Ireland 1700-1900* (Dublin, 1981), p. 224.

5 M.A. Crowther, *The Workhouse system 1834-1929: A history of an English Social Institution* (London, 1981), p. 197.

6 *CC*, 25 October 1861.

The total immersion in the workhouse environment did not encourage creative traits and latent talents in workhouse children. Nursing out and boarding out young children presented a positive opportunity to sever the connection with the workhouse and establish an independent life outside. Also, it saved money by cutting down on workhouse expenditure. Nonetheless, ever-suspicious guardians in Cork and elsewhere, who feared that the poor would abuse and exploit the system, resisted the implementation of an efficient boarding out programme. Outdoor relief was also a less expensive method of assisting poor people who were in need of help. As it did not have the many overheads associated with workhouse relief, it was cheaper to administer, and cost the ratepayers less than indoor relief. Again, its implementation in the Cork Union was resisted and postponed by suspicious representatives, many of whom had little interest in the welfare of the poor but were really 'Guardians of their own pockets'.[7]

Privation and humiliation were not unique to the Cork institution and inmates of other Irish workhouses were frequently subjected to primitive and inhumane conditions, mainly as a consequence of the attitudes and actions of guardians.[8] On occasions, the diet in the workhouse was brought down to a level little above that of subsistence and it was not unknown for food or milk to be adulterated.[9] Inmates were expected to sleep in overcrowded wards and beds, and were often deprived of proper clothing, footwear or washing facilities.[10] Strenuous physical activities, such as stone breaking and laundry work, were routinely meted out to inmates of the Cork workhouse. Inmates in most Irish workhouses were treated in a manner similar to that experienced by the occupants of the Cork institution.[11] In his study of children in Irish charitable institutions, Joseph Robins found that high death rates, overcrowding, poor sanitation, and inadequate training and education initiatives were endemic in many workhouses.[12]

In Irish folk-memory, the workhouse will forever be inextricably connected with the tragedy of the Great Famine. During those years of extreme destitution and hardship workhouses became the only refuge for many of the Irish poor. Many of those who found succour within their walls would not otherwise have survived that period of dearth and

---

7 *SR,* 4 February 1847; *CC,* 24 October 1861, 17 January 1863.
8 On a few occasions death resulted from ill treatment as was the case when Patrick Connelly died in the black hole at Youghal workhouse in May 1849, *Province of Munster,* 5 May, 19 May 1849.
9 *CE,* 8 June 1849, 29 June 1860.
10 *CE,* 7 January 1847, 27 April, 5 May 1865.
11 See for instance Jack Johnson (ed.), *Workhouses of the north west* (1996), p. 14.
12 Joseph Robins, *The lost children,* pp. 189-92, 228, 232, 238, 240-1.

disease. The high mortality rate in Cork and other workhouse, which was mainly caused by disease and overcrowding, formed a lasting impression and memory of the workhouse.

It cannot be denied that a certain amount of unintentional, and sometimes deliberate, cruelty or deprivation took place within workhouses at other periods also. During its lifetime the Cork workhouse did of course offer a refuge to those who fell on hard times, or who became ill or incapacitated. For some, it was a consolation to realise that such a haven was available. For others, the workhouse was a constant reminder of the fate that awaited all but the diligent. These saw it as a refuge for the helpless, the hapless and the hopeless, and admission was sought only when all other avenues had been exhausted. As a reputation for hardship discouraged applications for relief and reduced expenditure, most of the guardians were unconcerned about the public's poor perception of the house. In time, the repressive reputation, so carefully fostered and justifiably earned by the guardians, came to dominate all other memories of the workhouse.

Although the Cork workhouse is but a memory and some of its older buildings have been demolished, a large part of the structure still survives. The site of the former workhouse is now the location of St. Finbarr's hospital on the Douglas Road. Modern structures have been erected on the grounds and services provided at St. Finbarr's include geriatiric and psychiatric departments, a children's unit and a maternity unit.

Biographical Notes

SIR JOHN ARNOTT came to Cork from Scotland in the late 1830s and became involved in the retail business. He was a gifted businessman and was associated with many local and national companies. As Mayor of Cork he was knighted in 1859 when the Lord Lieutenant officially opened the new Patrick's Bridge. He was a poor law guardian on a number of occasions. He is remembered for his damning report on the state of children in the Cork workhouse, which initiated many badly needed reforms. He died on 29 March 1898.

NICHOLAS DUNSCOMBE of Mount Desert, a sitting chairman of the board of guardians, died on 25 April 1876. An obituary recorded that 'he was sincerely anxious for the welfare of the poor, though to some his views seemed to incline rather too much to the economical side of administration . . '.

ISAAC JULIAN, a sometimes-controversial member of the Cork board of guardians, died at his residence Montpellier Terrace, on 3 February 1887 aged 72 years.

JOHN FRANCIS MAGUIRE founded the *Cork Examiner* in August 1841. He was a Nationalist MP for Dungarvan from 1852 to 1865 and for Cork from 1865 to 1872. He served as Mayor of Cork in 1853, 1862, 1863 and 1864. His numerous books include one on Irish Industry, and a study of the Irish in America. He lived at Ardmanagh, Passage West and died in Dublin on 1 November 1872.

NICHOLAS MAHONY was a partner in the Blarney woollen firm of Martin Mahony Brothers. He was brother of Rev. Francis Mahony (Fr. Prout) and of Mrs Ellen Woodlock, the campaigner for educating and training poor girls. He died aged 85 on 6 December 1891.

DOCTOR DENIS C. O CONNOR was medical officer of the Cork workhouse for 17 years. In his resignation letter at the end of 1856, he recalled that 'during much of the time the performance of my duties was beset with difficulties seldom, if ever, surpassed. That they were accomplished without discredit, I owe to the kindness and forbearance of the poor people entrusted to my care, who were ever ready to accept kind intentions in lieu of the perfect performance of duty, which, under the circumstances it was impossible to bestow'. On his departure from the workhouse, he took up duties at the newly established Mercy Hospital. He held the chair of medicine at Queen's College Cork for 39 years. He died at his residence, 2, Camden Place on 22 November 1888, aged 80 years.

William D'Esterre Parker served as a Poor Law guardian for many years. He actively and ceaselessly campaigned for improved conditions for workhouse inmates. As a result of his interventions, outdoor relief was introduced in the Cork Union. He had a great interest in education, public health and the advancement of his native Passage West. He died on 20 July 1899.

Dr JOHN POPHAM died, following an accident at his son's residence in Ealing, on 26 August 1884. He had served as physician at Cork's North Infirmary for many years.

DOMINICK RONAYNE SARSFIELD, son of Thomas R. Sarsfield, served as chairman of Cork board of guardians for a short period. He was sheriff of Cork in 1878 and stood as an unsuccessful Unionist candidate in the Cork Parliamentary election of 6 November 1891. He served as Deputy Grand Master of the Orange Society of Ireland and as Grand Master for Cork. He died in Cork on 4 February 1892.

THOMAS RONAYNE SARSFIELD was chairman of the Cork Board of Guardians on a number of occasions. He died at his residence, Doughcloyne on 7 October 1865.

REV. GEORGE SHEEHAN was the first Catholic chaplain in the workhouse. He resigned to take up duty as parish priest of Bantry in June 1853. He died on 27 June 1887.

Dr C. D. TANNER had been a Unionist but changed allegiances and served as Nationalist MP for mid-Cork from the 1880s. He was a gifted orator but his behaviour was sometimes disruptive. As an MP and guardian, he was noted for his interest in the advancement of the less well off members of society. He had been a Protestant but became a Catholic a few years before his death on 21 April 1901.

Dr WILLIAM C. TOWNSEND was a medical officer at the workhouse. He worked tirelessly to improve conditions for the inmates. He died at his residence, Oakhurst, Queenstown, on 13 February 1899, aged 81 years.

Dr JOHN WALL a medical officer at the Cork workhouse, died on 4 December 1883 from typhus fever contracted in the pursuit of his duties. He specialised in diseases of the eye. He also acted as consulting sanitary officer for Cork Corporation. His father, Dr Thomas Wall, a former Cork Union guardian, died on 4 December 1878 aged 81 years.

REV. GEORGE WEBSTER was Protestant chaplain of the workhouse for a number of years. His interventions were sometimes controversial. He died on 17 December 1890.

EDWARD WALSH was headmaster at the workhouse in the late 1840s. He was a noted Gaelic scholar and also wrote and translated Irish poetry. He died aged 45 on 6 August 1850.

HENRY LINDSAY YOUNG was a member of numerous boards of guardians and occupied the chairmanship of the Cork board on a number of occasions. He was involved in the corn and milling business. He served as a Justice of the Peace and as County High Sheriff. He died at Leemount, Carrigrohane on 8 March 1901.

Appendix 1

1. Workhouse dietaries

Cork Union: Dietary of able-bodied inmates.
Classes 1 and 2, July 1861

		WEEKLY COST
Breakfast	8 oz. Indian meal ¾ pint sweet skimmed milk	5¼ d.
Dinner	1 lb. Brown bread, 1½ pints farinaceous soup, composed of 8 oz. Oatmeal, and 3 oz. Rice, to a gallon of water, with vegetables, pepper and salt	10¼ d.
	COST OF FOOD PER WEEK	1s.3 ½d.

(*Source*: PP 1861, Vol. LV, [533], p. 1)

Cork Union: Scale for healthy inmates.
March 1864

Diet 1 – Class: Able-bodied males

BREAKFAST	8 oz. Indian meal and ¾ pint milk
DINNER	1 lb. Brown bread; 1½ pints of porridge
SUPPER	8 oz. White bread, 1 pint of new milk

Diet 2 – Class: Able-bodied females not acting as hospital nurses and school assistants

BREAKFAST	8 oz. Indian meal and ¾ pint milk
DINNER	1 lb. Brown bread; 1½ pints of porridge
SUPPER	8 oz. White bread, 1 pint of new milk

Diet 3 – Class: Aged and infirm males and females, and able bodied females acting as hospital nurses and school assistants

BREAKFAST	8 oz. White bread, 1 pint tea
DINNER	8 oz. White bread, 1 pint soup (made with meat on 3 days)
SUPPER	N.B. – The inmates of this class who act as assistants in hospital and school get the same diet as class 3 (sic) [class 2?]

Diet 4 – Class: Boys and girls aged 9 to 15 years

BREAKFAST	3 oz. Indian meal, 3 oz. Oatmeal, 1 pint of milk
DINNER	¾ lb. White bread; *Sun and Thur*, a pint of porridge, with 8 oz. Meat added; *Mon, Wed and Fri*, 1 pint of porridge; *Tues and Sat*, 1 pint milk
SUPPER	¼ lb. White bread, ½ pint milk

Diet 5 – Class: Children aged 5 to 9 years

BREAKFAST	½ lb. White bread, ¾ pint new milk
DINNER	½ lb. White bread, ¾ pint new milk; on *Sun and Thur*, a pint of porridge with 6 oz. Meat added
SUPPER	¼ lb. White bread, ½ pint new milk

Diet 6 – Class: Children aged 2 to 5 years

BREAKFAST	½ lb. White bread, ½ pint new milk
DINNER	¾ lb. White bread, 1 pint new milk
SUPPER	¾ lb. White bread, ½ pint new milk

Diet 7 – Class: Infants under 2 years

BREAKFAST	4 oz. White bread (first quality), ½ pint new milk
DINNER	4 oz. White bread (first quality), ¼ pint new milk
SUPPER	4 oz. White bread (first quality), 1 pint new milk

Note: Delicate children, 9 to 15 years (class 4) get a special diet of 1½ lbs. White bread and 2 pints of new milk daily; and on two days each week, meat soup, with 8 oz. Meat, instead of 1 pint of milk.

Porridge or Soup:
Eight oz. Oatmeal and three oz. Rice to each gallon of porridge, with vegetables, pepper, salt etc. Vegetables, pepper, salt etc., to be added to the meat soup.

Tea:
Two oz. Tea, five oz. Sugar and 1 pint new milk to each gallon. (*Mem.* The general scale prescribed by the Commissioners only requires 1 oz. Tea, 4 oz. Sugar and ½ pint new milk.)

Milk:
The term milk implies what is sufficiently sweet to stand the test of boiling, without cracking; and new milk means what is delivered as it comes from the cow.

Meat:
The meat given to classes 4 and 5 is not ordinary 'soup meat', but consists of the best parts of the carcass.

30 March 1864.   R. J. O Shaughnessy, Clerk of the Union.

(*Source*: PP 1864, Vol. LII [260], *Dietaries in use in certain workhouses in Ireland*. p. 7)

Cork Union: Dietary for healthy inmates.
March 1887

Diet 1 – Class: Able-bodied working men

BREAKFAST	8 oz. Indian meal and ¾ pint of boiling milk
DINNER	¾ lb. Brown bread and 1½ pint porridge
SUPPER	½ lb. Brown bread and 1 pint cocoa
DAILY ALLOWANCE	8 oz. Indian meal, 1¼ lbs. Brown bread, ¾ pint boiling milk, 1 pint cocoa, and 1½ pints porridge

Diet 2 – Class: Able-bodied working females

BREAKFAST	8 oz. Indian meal and ¾ pint of boiling milk
DINNER	¾ lb. Brown bread and 1½ pint porridge
SUPPER	½ lb. Brown bread and 1 pint cocoa
DAILY ALLOWANCE	8 oz. Indian meal, 1¼ lbs. Brown bread, ¾ pint boiling milk, 1 pint cocoa, and 1½ pints porridge

Diet 3 – Class: Wet-nurses

BREAKFAST	2 oz. Oatmeal, 8 oz. Indian meal, ¾ pints boiling milk
DINNER	2½ lbs. Potatoes and 1 pint boiling milk, or ½ lb. Household bread and 1½ pints of porridge
SUPPER	½ lb. Household bread and 1 pint of tea
DAILY ALLOWANCE	½ lb. Household bread, 2½ lb. Potatoes, 1 pint of tea, ½ lb. Indian meal, 2 oz. Oatmeal, 1¾ pints Boiling milk or ½ lb. Household bread and 1½ pint porridge, in lieu of potatoes and milk

Diet 4 – Class: Women in care of children in hospital

BREAKFAST	½ lb. Household bread and 1 pint tea
DINNER	½ lb. Household bread and ½ pint new milk
SUPPER	½ lb. Household bread and 1 pint of tea
DAILY ALLOWANCE	1½ lbs. Household bread, 2 pints of tea and ½ pint new milk

Diet 5 – Class: Special diet for laundresses and cooks

BREAKFAST	½ lb. Household bread and 1 pint tea
DINNER	½ lb. Household bread, 1 pint porridge, ½ lb. Raw mutton with bone, on *Sundays*; 2½ lbs. Potatoes, 1 pint boiling milk on *Tuesday and Thursday*, instead of bread and porridge
SUPPER	½ lb. Household bread and 1 pint of tea
DAILY ALLOWANCE	1½ lbs. household bread, 2 pints of tea, 1 pint porridge, ½ lb. mutton on *Sunday* ; 2½ lbs. Potatoes. 1 pint boiling milk, on Tuesday and Thursday, instead of bread and porridge

Diet 6 – Class: Male and female hospital, school and probationary assistants and Infirmary assistant nurses

BREAKFAST	½ lb. Household bread and 2 pints tea
DINNER	½ lb. Household bread and 8 oz. Soup beef on *Sunday* and *Thursday*
SUPPER	½ lb. Household bread, 1 pint new milk and 2 pints of tea
DAILY ALLOWANCE	1½ lbs. Household bread, 4 pints of tea, 1 pint of new milk, 8 oz. Soup beef on *Sunday* and *Thursday*

Diet 7 – Class: Fever hospital assistants

BREAKFAST	½ lb. Household bread and 2 pints tea
DINNER	½ lb. Household bread and ½ lb. Mutton
SUPPER	½ lb. Household bread, 2 pints tea and ½ pint new milk
DAILY ALLOWANCE	1½ lbs. Household bread, 8 oz. Mutton, 4 pints of tea, ½ pint new milk, ½ lb. Butter and 7 lbs. Potatoes weekly

Diet 8 – Class: Aged and infirm men and women

BREAKFAST	½ lb. Household bread and 1 pint tea
DINNER	½ lb. Household bread and 1 pint boiling milk on 4 days; 1 pint meat soup on three days instead of milk
SUPPER	½ lb. Household bread and 1 pint tea
DAILY ALLOWANCE	1¼ lbs. Household bread, 2 pints tea, 1 pint boiling milk on 4 days: *Mon*, *Wed*, *Fri* and *Sat*; 1 pint meat soup on *Sun*, *Tue* and *Thur*

Diet 9 – Class: Boys and girls 9 to 15 years

BREAKFAST	½ lb. Household bread and ½ pint new milk
DINNER	2½ lbs. Potatoes, ½ pint new milk and ½ lb. Household bread; 1 pint meat soup on *Sunday* in lieu of potatoes and milk
SUPPER	3 oz. Indian meal, 3 oz. Oatmeal and ½ pint new milk
DAILY ALLOWANCE	3 oz. Indian meal, 3 oz. Oatmeal, ½ lbs. household bread, 2½ lbs. potatoes, 1½ pints new milk, ½ lbs. Household bread and 8 oz. Soup beef on *Sunday* in lieu of potatoes and milk

Diet 10 – Class: Boys and girls 5 to 9 years

BREAKFAST	½ lb. Household bread and ¾ pints new milk
DINNER	2 lbs. Potatoes, ¾ pint new milk, except *Sunday*, when they get ½ lbs. Household bread and 1 pint of meat soup, in lieu of potatoes and milk

SUPPER	¼ lbs. Household bread and ½ pint new milk
DAILY ALLOWANCE	¾ lbs. Household bread, 2 lbs. Potatoes, 2 pints new milk, except *Sunday* when they get ½ lb. Household bread and 1 pint meat soup in lieu of potatoes and milk

Diet 11 – Class: Children 2 to 5 years

BREAKFAST	¼ lb. Household bread and ½ pint new milk
DINNER	½ lb. Household bread and 1 pint new milk
SUPPER	¼ lb. Household bread and ½ pint new milk
DAILY ALLOWANCE	1¼ lbs. Household bread and 2 pints new milk

Diet 12 – Class: Infants under 2 years

BREAKFAST	4 oz. Household bread and ½ pint new milk
DINNER	4 oz. Household bread and ½ pint new milk
SUPPER	4 oz. Household bread and ½ pint new milk
DAILY ALLOWANCE	¾ lb. Household bread and 1 ½ pints of new milk

Cesspool cleaners:

1 ¼ lbs. Household bread, 1 pint cocoa, and ½ lb. Mutton daily in addition to able-bodied diet, except for meat on *Friday*.

Bakers:

¾ lb. Household bread, 2 pints cocoa daily, and ¾ lb. Mutton on *Tuesday, Thursday* and *Saturday* in addition to No. 1 diet, porridge excepted, 4 oz. Shell cocoa, 6 oz. Sugar, 1 ½ pints new milk to each gallon of cocoa.

(*Source*: PP 1888, Vol. LXXXVII, [83], *Return of the scale of dietary in force in each Union workhouse in Ireland on the 25th day of March 1887*. p. 71)

2. Hospital diets

Cork Union: Hospital Dietary
March 1864

Diet 1 – Class: Fever diet

Four oz. Bread and three pints of milk daily

Diet 2 – Class: Children aged 2 to 5 years

BREAKFAST	4 oz. Best bread, 1 pint new milk
DINNER	4 oz. Best bread, ½ pint new milk
SUPPER	4 oz. Best bread, ½ pint new milk

Diet 3

BREAKFAST	4 oz. Oatmeal, 2 oz. Rice ½ pint milk
DINNER	12 oz. Brown bread, 1 pint soup
SUPPER	4 oz. Brown bread, ½ pint milk

Diet 4

BREAKFAST	4 oz. Bread 1 pint tea
DINNER	8 oz. Bread, 1 pint soup
SUPPER	4 oz. Bread, 1 pint milk

Diet 5

BREAKFAST	8 oz. Bread, 1 pint milk
DINNER	10 oz. Bread, 1 pint soup
SUPPER	6 oz. Bread, ½ pint milk

Diet 6

BREAKFAST	6 oz. Bread, 1 pint tea
DINNER	6 oz. Bread, 1 pint soup, 6 oz. meat
SUPPER	4 oz. Bread, 1 pint milk

Infants under two

12 oz. Best white bread, and 1 pint new milk daily

30 March 1864.   R.J. O Shaughnessy, Clerk of the Union.

(*Source*: PP 1864, Vol. LII [260], *Copies of the dietaries of the following workhouses in Ireland*, p. 8)

Cork Union: Hospital Dietary
March 1887

Diet 1

BREAKFAST	4 oz. Household bread, ½ pint new milk
DINNER	4 oz. Bread, ½ pint new milk
SUPPER	4 oz. Household bread, ½ pint new milk
DAILY ALLOWANCE	12 oz. Household bread, 1 ½ pints new milk

Diet 2 – Admission diet, General hospital

BREAKFAST	4 oz. Household bread, 1 pint tea
DINNER	8 oz. Household bread, ½ pint new milk
SUPPER	4 oz. Household bread, 1 pint tea
DAILY ALLOWANCE	1 lb. Household bread, 2 pints tea, ½ pint new milk

Diet 3

BREAKFAST	4 oz. Household bread, 1 pint tea
DINNER	8 oz. Household bread, 1 pint beef tea, 1 pint new milk
SUPPER	4 oz. Household bread, 1 pint tea
DAILY ALLOWANCE	1 lb. Household bread, 2 pints tea, 1 pint beef tea, 1 pint new milk

Diet 4

BREAKFAST	2 oz. Household bread, 1 pint tea
DINNER	4 oz. Household bread, 1 pint beef tea, 1 pint new milk
SUPPER	2 oz. Household bread, 1 pint tea, 1 pint new milk
DAILY ALLOWANCE	8 oz. Household bread, 2 pints tea, 1 pint beef tea, 2 pints new milk

Diet 5

BREAKFAST	4 oz. Household bread, 1 pint tea
DINNER	8 oz. Household bread, 1 pint rice, 1 pint new milk
SUPPER	4 oz. Household bread, 1 pint tea
DAILY ALLOWANCE	1 lb. Household bread, 2 pints tea, 1 pint rice, 1 pint new milk

Diet 6

BREAKFAST	6 oz. Household bread, 1 pint tea
DINNER	6 oz. Household bread, or 1 lb. Potatoes, 6 oz. Meat, 1 pint new milk
SUPPER	4 oz. Household bread, 1 pint tea, 1 pint new milk
DAILY ALLOWANCE	1 lb. Household bread, 6 oz. Raw mutton, except *Tue* and *Fri*, 2 pints new milk, 2 pints tea, 1 pint beef soup on *Tues*

Diet 7

BREAKFAST	½ lb. Bread, 1 pint tea
DINNER	½ lb. Bread, 8 oz. Mutton, 1 lb. Potatoes, 1 pint new milk
SUPPER	½ lb. Bread, 1 pint tea
DAILY ALLOWANCE	1½ lbs. Bread, 2 pints tea, 1 pint new milk, 8 oz. Mutton, 5 days a week except *Tues* and *Fri*, 1 lb. Potatoes

Fever Hospital Dietary

Diet 1 – Fever diet for children

4 oz. Bread, 3 pints new milk, 1 pint beef tea

Diet 2 – Convalescent diet for children

8 oz. Bread, 2 pints new milk, ½ pint beef tea, 4 oz. Mutton, 1 egg, rice pudding, 1 oz. Rice, ¼ pint milk, ½ oz. Sugar, 1 egg for three puddings

Diet 3 – Fever diet for women and boys

8 oz. Bread, 1 pint coffee, 3 pints new milk, 2 pints beef tea, 1 egg

Diet 4 – Convalescent diet for women and boys

12 oz. Bread, 2 pints new milk, 2 pints tea, 8 oz. Mutton, 1 lb. Potatoes, 1 egg

Diet 5 – Fever diet for men

8 oz. Bread, 1 pint coffee, 4 pints new milk, 2 pints beef tea, 1 egg

Diet 6 – Convalescent diet for men

1½ lbs. Bread, 2 pints new milk, 2 pints tea, 10 oz. Mutton, 1 egg, 1 lb. Potatoes, beef tea: 1 lb. Beef to the pint

Diet 7 – Skeleton diet

8 oz. Bread, 2 ½ pints milk

4 oz. Coffee, 8 oz. Sugar and 1 pint new milk to the gallon

(*Source*: PP 1888, Vol. LXXXVII, [83], *Return of the scale of dietary in force in each Union workhouse in Ireland on the 25th day of March 1887*, p. 72)

Appendix 2

Cork Mayors 1837-1891

Year	Mayor	Year	Mayor
1837	John Saunders	1865	Charles F. Cantillon
1838	John Bagnell	1866	Francis Lyons
1839	Lionel J. Westropp	1867	Francis Lyons
1840	James Lane	1868	Francis Lyons
1841	Julias Besnard	1869	Daniel O Sullivan
1842	Thomas Lyons	1870	William Hegarty
1843	Francis B. Beamish	1871	John Daly
1844	William Fagan	1872	John Daly
1845	Richard Dowden (Richard)	1873	John Daly
1846	Andrew Roche	1874	Daniel A. Nagle
1847	Edward Hackett (Died April)	1875	Daniel A. Nagle
1847	Andrew Roche	1876	Sir George Penrose
1848	William Hackett	1877	Barry J. Sheehan
1849	Sir William Lyons	1878	William V. Gregg
1850	Sir William Lyons	1879	Patrick Kennedy
1851	James Lambkin	1880	Patrick Kennedy
1852	John Shea	1881	Sir Daniel V. O Sullivan
1853	John Francis Maguire	1882	Daniel J. Galvin
1854	John N. Murphy	1883	Daniel J. Galvin
1855	Sir John Gordon	1884	Daniel J. Galvin (to June)
1856	William Fitzgibbon	1884	Barry J. Sheehan
1857	William Fitzgibbon	1885	Paul J. Madden
1858	Daniel Donegan	1886	Paul J. Madden
1859	Sir John Arnott	1887	John O Brien
1860	Sir John Arnott	1888	John O Brien
1861	Sir John Arnott	1889	Daniel Ryan
1862	John Francis Maguire	1890	Daniel Horgan
1863	John Francis Maguire	1891	Daniel Horgan
1864	John Francis Maguire		

Appendix 3

John Arnott's entry in Cork workhouse visitors' book — 6 April 1859

I have this day minutely inspected the various divisions of this workhouse . . .

The inmates are all comfortably housed, and well clothed, and I now intend to make a few remarks about their diet. I am aware that the food of a workhouse must necessarily not alone be considered as affording sustenance, but also as a test of destitution, so that the lazy and vicious may not prey upon the industrious and sometimes hardly pressed ratepayers. This test can however only be used with reference to those who have bodily strength to labour, if justice and humanity be consulted, therefore, three out of four of the classes in the house should be from their physical state, entirely exempted from this trial; these are the sick, the aged and infirm, and the children. To drive them out of doors would be to destroy them; they have no option but remain in the house, whatever be their treatment; and not alone kindness, but the highest obligation binds those who are their guardians to provide for their health and sustenance. I have said that the sick are properly provided with good food, and the infirm have sufficient; although in my opinion it might be varied, and somewhat bettered at a slight expense; but I have been shocked – I may say appalled – from my observation of the state of the children; and the result of my inquiries have led me to the deliberate conclusion that it would be a mercy to close the gates of the union house against them, and let them attain the mercy of death, rather than be reared deformed, maimed and diseased objects, through the system of feeding to which I have reason to believe their terrible state is attributable. For want of proper nutriment and change of diet, scrofula has so infected these young creatures, that there was scarcely one of them whom I examined that did not bear plain and frightful tokens that their blood had been wasted to that degree that the current which should have borne vigour and health to their frames, was only a medium of disseminating debility and disease, not to speak of some 50 children sent from this institution to the Blind Asylum, for ever lost to the first blessings which God poured upon creation, from this disease, engendered by the diet here; not to dwell on the cruel spectacle of the infirmary, where in every phase this shocking infliction may be seen in its most revolting forms.   I will only point attention to the children who are still able to attend school, as I have said, there is scarcely one of these not diseased; but besides 115 that can move about, and are not perfectly ruined, there are in an upper school-room 48 young creatures so stunted in growth and intellect, and awfully affected, that no humane man could look upon them without the deepest compassion.   In the female school the same general remarks apply; but there are 92 girls still presentable, and 84 in the infant class; but there is another lazar department of 64, as fearful objects as those I have just described.   There is no separate register of the deaths of children kept in the house, but I have been told, and can well believe it from what I have witnessed and detailed, that four out of every five die before they are adults, and that the survivor is, in the majority of instances, destroyed in constitution.

Against the system which produces such results, I desire at once to make my warmest protest.   I believe it could be remedied with little cost, or taking into account the increased hospital charges thus swelled, perhaps with a saving to the ratepayers.   But into such a question I would not enter, where an issue of life and death is in the balance.   I am certain that I need only call the attention of the humane gentlemen of the Board to these facts, and that they will liberally concur with me, and provide against the continuance of this disastrous and terrible condition, in which I have found these destitute and unfriended children.

Bibliography

Manuscript Material

Cork Archives Institute (South Main St., Cork)

Cork Board of Guardians Records:

Minute Books of Cork Union Board of Guardians (Series BG69)
    1838 to 1890

Letter Books of Cork Union Board of Guardians (Series BC)
    Incoming letters: 1844 to 1873
    Outgoing letters:
    Vol. No. B1 –19 June 1839 to 6 April 1854
    Vol. No. B4 – 6 June 1879 to 22 February 1886

Visiting Committee Report Book
    No. BG69 FM1 8 November 1847 to 19 July 1865

Workhouse Indoor Register
    Selected entries

National Archives (Bishop St., Dublin)

Chief Secretary's Office Registered Papers

Poor Law Commissioners, Letters to James Burke Jan-Dec. 1844
                              Jan-Dec 1845
                              Jan-Dec 1846
                              Jan-Dec 1847
                              Jan-Dec 1848
                              Jan-Dec 1849
                              Jan-Dec 1850
                              Jan-Dec 1851

Official Publications

Parliamentary Papers

Bill for amending the laws with respect to the removal of Irish Poor from England to Ireland. PP 1820, Vol. 1, [259]
Copies of the Correspondence between the Chief Secretary of Ireland, the Sovereign of

Belfast, and others, respecting Paupers sent from England to Ireland. PP 1820, Vol. IX, [212]

Report from the Select Committee on the existing laws relating to vagrants. PP 1821, Vol. IV, [543]

Report from the Select Committee on the laws relating to Irish and Scottish Vagrants. PP 1828, Vol. IX, [513]

Report from the Select Committee on Irish vagrants; with the minutes of evidence taken before them. PP 1833, Vol. XVI, [394]

Second Report from Select Committee on the Poor Law Amendment Act; with the minutes of evidence. PP 1838, Vol. XVIII, [138]

Return, specifying the number, name and local situation of each union in Ireland, which has not within itself any supply of spring water also specifying those from which there is none, or insufficient sewerage. PP 1843, Vol. XLVI, [227]

Copies of the Estimates for erecting each of the Poorhouses now open in Ireland . . . and the Number of Paupers in each Poorhouse, in the first week of every Month since the opening of each Poorhouse . . . and stating the Number that received Instruction . . . and the Number that may have been in the Hospital or Infirmary in each Month.

Copies of any Instructions, relating to the Education of Paupers . . and Copies of any Correspondence upon that Subject . . . Return of the Paid Officers belonging to each Poorhouse, and . . . of the whole Expenditure of each Poorhouse up to the present Time.

Copies of any Resolutions by a Board of Guardians for a Rate to be levied . . . PP 1843, Vol. XLVI, [616]

Copies of the estimates for erecting each of the Poor-Houses now open in Ireland, approved of by the Poor Law Commissioners. . . stating, also, the present Condition of each Poor-house, and whether any further Outlay is required for the Completion, Alteration or Repair of such House . . . PP 1843, Vol. XLVI, [275]

Report from the Select Committee on Union Workhouses (Ireland). PP 1844, Vol. XIV, [441]

Report of the Commissioners for inquiring into the execution of the contracts for certain Union Workhouses in Ireland; with Appendix, Map, etc. PP 1844, Vol. XXX, [562]

Appendix to the Report of the Commissioners on Union Workhouses in Ireland, with Plans. PP 1844, Vol. XXX, [568]

A Return 'in Provinces' of the number of children sent out to service from the Union workhouses in Ireland in the years 1842, 1843 and 1844 . . . PP 1845, Vol. XXXVIII, [351]

Report from the Select Committee of the House of Lords on the Laws relating to the Relief of the Destitute Poor, and into the Operation of the Medical Charities in Ireland; together with the Minutes of Evidence taken before the said Committee. PP 1846, Vol. XI – part I, [694 – I]; part II, [694 – II]

Report of the Commissioners of Inquiry into matters connected with the failure of the potato crop, 6 February 1846, PP 1846, Vol. XXXVII, [33]

Copy of the Report of Dr *Playfair and Mr. Lindley on the present state of the Irish potato crop and on the prospect of the approaching scarcity, dated 15 November 1845.* PP 1846, Vol. XXXVII, [28]

Abstracts of the most serious representations made by the several Medical Superinten-

dents of Public Institutions (Fever Hospitals, Infirmaries, Dispensaries, etc.) in the provinces of Ulster, Munster, Leinster and Connaught. PP 1846, Vol. XXXVII, [120]

Scarcity Commission – the weekly reports of the Scarcity Commission, showing the progress of disease in potatoes, the complaints which have been made, and the applications for relief, in the course of the month of March 1846. PP 1846, Vol. XXXVII, [201]

Scarcity Commission – Further returns. showing the progress of disease in potatoes. . . PP 1846, Vol. XXXVII, [213]

Report of the Select Committee of the House of Lords on colonization from Ireland together with minutes of evidence. PP 1847, Vol. VI, [737]

First Report from the Select Committee on Settlement and Poor Removal . . . PP 1847, Vol. XI, [82]

Second and third Reports from the Select Committee on Settlement and Poor Removal . . . PP 1847, Vol. XI, [135]

Seventh and Eight Reports from the Select Committee on Settlement and Poor Removal . . . PP 1847, Vol. XI, [518]

Correspondence from July 1846 to January 1847, relating to the measures adopted for the relief of the Distress in Ireland; with maps, plans and appendices (Board of Works Series). PP 1847, Vol., L, [764]

Correspondence from January to March 1847, relating to the Measures adopted for the relief of the Distress in Ireland. Commissariat Series, [Second part]. PP 1847, Vol. LII, [797]

Papers relating to the proceedings for the relief of the distress and state of the Unions and Workhouses in Ireland. (Fourth series) – PP 1847 Vol. LIV

A copy of the report made to the Board of Health in Dublin, by the Medical Officer, sent to inquire into the state of the workhouses in Cork, Bantry and Lurgan. PP 1847, Vol. LV, [257]

First Report from the Select Committee of the House of Lords on Colonization from Ireland. . . (Session 1848), Vol. VI (2). PP 1847-8, Vol. XVII, [415]

First Report from the Select Committee on Poor Laws (Ireland), 1849. Containing 1st, 2nd, and part of 3rd, report. Minutes of Evidence. PP 1849, Vol. XV, [9]

Tenth Report from the Select Committee on Poor Laws (Ireland). PP 1849, Vol. XV. (part 2), [356]

Fourteenth Report from the Select Committee on Poor Laws (Ireland). PP 1849, Vol. XV, [572]

Reports made to the Poor Law Board by their Inspectors, Mr. Doyle, Mr. Furness and Sir John Walsham on the education and training of pauper children in their respective districts, in the year 1850. PP 1851, Vol. XLIX [646]

Return "of the Amount of the Salaries and Remuneration of Officers of Unions in Ireland who are employed in the Secular Instruction or Industrial Training of the Children who are relieved in Workhouses, on the 1st day of July, 1851". PP 1851, Vol. XLIX, [591]

Return from each of the Poor Law Unions in England, Wales and Ireland, showing what kinds of employment are carried on in the workhouses, or on land attached; the number of adult able-bodied persons on the books as recipients of relief on 1 July

1852, and the proportion engaged in handcraft and agricultural industry, etc . . . PP 1852-3, Vol. LXXXIV, [513].

Return from each Union in Ireland, showing the extent of Land under Crops or Garden Cultivation, [and] . . . Return from each Union in Ireland of the Expenses incurred in Manufacture and Trades . . . stating the Number of Persons Employed, distinguishing those under Fifteen Years of Age from those above Fifteen, and showing the Profit or Loss, for the Year ending the 29th day of September 1852. PP1853, Vol., LXXXIV, [904]

Report from the Select Committee appointed to inquire into the operation of the Act 8 & 9 Vict., c. 117, relating the Removal from England of chargeable Poor Persons . . . PP 1854, Vol. XVII, [396]

A Return "of the Industrial Employment of the Juvenile Inmates of the Workhouse in each Union in Ireland, to the latest date in 1853 to which the information may have been made up . . . and the Number of Hours daily devoted to the Industrial Training of the Boys; also, the Number of Boys employed at each Trade taught in the Workhouse; also, the nature of the Industrial Training or Employment of the Girls in the Workhouse, the Number of Girls receiving an Industrial Education . . . also, the Number of Children under Fifteen Years of Age, known to have obtained Employment outside the Workhouse in the Year 1852 . . . PP 1854, Vol. LV, [77].

The Census of Ireland for the year 1851. Part III. Report on the status of Disease. (Dublin, 1854). PP Vol. LVIII, [1765]

Report from the Select Committee on Poor Removal; together with the proceedings of the committee, minutes of evidence, Appendix and Index, PP 1854-55, Vol. XIII, [308]

Returns from each Union in Ireland, showing the extent of land under crops or garden cultivation, the number of persons employed on the farm, distinguishing the number under fifteen years of age, and the number above fifteen years of age . . . (in continuation of Parliamentary Paper, No. 904, of Session 1853). PP 1855, Vol. XLVII, [345]

Census of Ireland for the year 1851, Part V, Table of Deaths, Vol. 1, Containing the reports, tables of pestilence and analysis of the tables of deaths (Dublin, 1856). PP 1856, Vol. XXIV, [2087-1]

Report from the Select Committee on Irremovable Poor; together with the proceedings of the Committee, Minutes of Evidence and Appendix. PP 1857-58, Vol. XIII, [374]

Report from the Select Committee on Irremovable Poor; together with the proceedings of the committee, minutes of evidence, appendix and index. PP 1860, Vol. XVII, [520]

Returns showing the number of paupers who became chargeable to the twelve under mentioned unions in Ireland, during the year ending the 25th day of March 1859, on being removed from England or Scotland . . . Name of Union: Belfast, Cork Drogheda, North Dublin, South Dublin, Dundalk, Limerick, Londonderry, Newry, Sligo Waterford, and Wexford (similar to return up to the 25th day of March 1854). . . PP 1860, Vol. LVIII, [331]

Second Report from the Select Committee on Poor Relief (England), together with the minutes of evidence and appendix. PP 1861, Vol. IX, [323]

Copy 'of the Report of the Inspector appointed to hold an investigation into the state of the Cork Union Workhouse, in the Months of April and May, 1859, and of the Evidence taken before such Inspector, and of any Correspondence relating thereto'. PP 1861, Vol. LV, [184]

Return 'of what is strictly called the able-bodied Dietary, and the Cost of the same per Week, now in use in the Cork, Limerick, Tralee, Clonmel, Waterford, Newry, North Dublin, Belfast and Lisburn Union Workhouses'. PP 1861, Vol. LV, [533]

Report from the Select Committee on Poor Relief (Ireland); together with the proceedings of the committee, Minutes of Evidence, and appendix. PP 1861, Vol., X.1, [408]

Copy of a letter addressed to the Chief Secretary for Ireland, and other Members of the Government, by the Dublin College of Physicians, on the Physical Effects of Rearing Children in Workhouses. PP 1862, Vol. XLIX, [348]

Twenty-third general report of the Emigration Commissioners, 1863. PP 1863, Vol. XV

Census of Ireland for the year 1861, Part III, Vital Statistics, Vol. 1, Report and Tables relating to the status of diseases, [and] *Report and Tables relating to deaths.* PP 1863, Vol. LVIII

Return 'by counties and parishes, of the names of all schools in connection with the Board of National Education in Ireland . . . in operation on the 31st day of December 1862. . '. PP 1864 Vol. XLVII [481 –I]

Copies of the Dietaries in the following Workhouses in Ireland:- North Dublin, Ballinasloe, Belfast, Colraine, Cork, South Dublin, Dunfanaghey, Gorey, Westport, Youghal . . . PP 1864, Vol., LII, [260]

Return showing the name of each Poor Law Union in Ireland; the number of paupers for which accommodation is made in the workhouse or workhouses of each Union; the number of patients for which the infirmary of each has accommodation. . . PP 1866 Vol. LXII [309]

Copy of Report of John Lambert, Esq., Poor Law Inspector. . . on the System of Medical Relief to the Out-Door Poor in Ireland under the Dispensaries Act, 1851. PP 1867, Vol., LX, [17]

Return of the number of Able-Bodied Persons who have received Provisional Out-Door Relief in cases of sudden and urgent necessity (Stating whether in Food, Lodging, Medicine, or Medical Attendance), from Relieving Officers in every Poor Law Union in Ireland, under the Power vested in them as defined in the 7th section of the 10th Vict., c. 31, from the year 1858 to the present time. PP 1867, Vol., LX, [427]

Return of the number of persons relieved in each Workhouse in Ireland during the quarter ended the 31st of March 1867; Of the number of persons who received out-door relief in each Poor Law Union in Ireland in the same quarter; and of the total cost of the outdoor relief that was given in each Poor Law Union. PP 1867, Vol., LX, [572]

Unions in Ireland in which a third meal is not yet allowed daily in the several classes of healthy inmates of the workhouses, specifying in each case the classes not so provided. PP 1867-8, Vol. LXI, [322]

Copies of Circulars issued by the Poor Law Commissioners in Ireland to the Clerks of Unions, dated the 6th day of February 1868, and the 7th day of March 1868, relating the diminution of Small Pox in Ireland, And of Correspondence relating to

the Five Unions in which it appeared that Small Pox was still existing at the time of Inquiry. PP 1867-8, Vol., LXI, [196]

Report from the Select Committee on Law of Rating (Ireland); together with the proceedings of the Committee, minutes of evidence and Appendix. PP 1871, Vol. X, [423]. pp. 220.

Return of all Poor Persons removed from England and Wales, to Ireland, and a similar return of those removed from Scotland to Ireland, from the 1st day of January 1867 to the 31st day of December 1869. PP 1871, Vol., LIX, [8],

Return of the number and names of all Workhouses in Ireland in which Nuns are engaged as Nurse . . . PP 1873, Vol. LV, [246]

Return with Christian and Surname of each, of Infants Born in Irish Workhouses, or Admitted thereto when Healthy under Twelve Months Old, and attempted to be reared therein during the year 1872, showing what has since become of them, . . . Similar Return of Healthy Infants under Twelve Months Old who were sent out to Nurse in 1872 by Boards of Guardians in Ireland, and attempted to be reared in the Homes of Foster Parents . . . PP 1879, Vol., LVI, [316]

Return of Poor Persons who have been removed from England and Scotland to any Union in Ireland, under the authority of Removal Warrants, between the 1st day of July, 1878 and the 1st day of January, 1880. PP 1880, Vol. LXII, [358]

Return giving the amount and volume of alcoholic stimulants used in the several workhouses in Ireland during the year 1880, number of sick persons treated, and death rate in each workhouse. PP 1881, Vol. LXXIX, [352]

Return of the mortality of children in Irish workhouses from infancy up to twelve years of age, for the year 1881. PP 1882, Vol. LIX, [277]

Return of the scale of dietary in force in each Union workhouse in Ireland on the 25th day of March 1887. PP 1888, Vol. LXXXVII, [83]

Acts

An Act to amend the Laws respecting the Settlement of the Poor, so far as regards renting Tenements. 59 George III, Cap. 50, 2 July 1819.

An Act to repeal certain Acts, relating to the Removal of poor Persons born in Scotland and Ireland, and chargeable to Parishes in England, and to make other Provisions in lieu thereof, until the First Day of May One Thousand eight hundred and thirty-six, and to the End of the then next Session of Parliament. 3 &3 George IV, Cap. 40. 14 August 1833.

An Act for the Amendment and better Administration of the Laws relating to the Poor in England and Wales. 4 & 5 George IV, Cap. 76, 14 August 1834.

An Act for the more effectual Relief of the destitute Poor in Ireland. 1 & 2 Victoriae, Cap. 56, 31 July 1838.

An Act for the further Amendment of an Act for the more effectual Relief of the destitute Poor in Ireland. 6 & 7 Victoriae, Cap. 92, 24 August 1843.

An Act to amend the Laws relating to the Removal of Poor. 9 & 10 Victoriae, Cap. 66, 26 August 1846.

An Act for the temporary Relief of destitute Persons in Ireland. 10 Victoriae, Cap. 7, 26 February 1847.

An Act to amend, and continue until the First Day of November One Thousand eight

hundred and forty-seven, and to the End of the then next Session of Parliament, an Act for making Provision for the Treatment of poor Persons afflicted with Fever in Ireland. 10 Victoriae, Cap. 22, 27 April 1847.

An Act to make further Provision for the Relief of the destitute Poor in Ireland. 10 Victoriae, Cap. 31, 8 June 1847.

An Act to amend the Laws relating to the Removal of poor Persons from England and Scotland. 10 & 11 Victoriae, Cap. 33, 21 June 1847.

An Act to provide for the Execution of the Laws for Relief of the Poor in Ireland. 10 & 11 Victoriae, Cap. 90, 22 July 1847.

An Act to amend the Laws relating to the Removal of the Poor, until the First Day of October One thousand eight hundred and forty-eight. 10 & 11 Victoriae, Cap, 110, 23 July 1847.

An Act to amend the Laws regarding the removal of the Poor and the Contribution of Parishes to the Common Fund in Unions. 24 and 25 Victoriae, Cap. 55, 1 August 1861.

An Act to amend the Law relating to the Removal of Poor Persons to Ireland. 24 and 25 Victoriae, Cap. 76, 6 August 1861.

An Act to amend the Law relating to the Removal of poor persons from England to Scotland, and from Scotland to England and Ireland. 25 & 26 Victoriae. Cap. 113, 7 August 1862.

An Act for the further amendment of the law relating to the removal of Poor persons, natives of Ireland, from England. 26 and 27 Victoriae, Cap. 89, 28 July 1863.

An Act to amend the Act of the twenty-fifth and twenty-sixth years of Victoria, chapter eighty-three, section nine, by extending the age at which orphan and deserted children may be kept out at nurse. 32 & 33 Victoriae, Chapter 25, 12 July 1869.

An Act to extend the limits of Age up to which, with the assent of Boards of Guardians, orphan and deserted pauper children may be supported out of workhouses in Ireland. 39&40 Victoriae, 1876, Chapter 38, 11 August 1876.

National Education Reports

Eight Report of the Commissioners of National Education in Ireland, 1841 (Dublin, 1842) to *Fifty sixth Report of the Commissioners of National Education in Ireland, 1889* (Dublin, 1890)

Poor Law Commissioners Annual Reports

*Second Annual Report of the Poor Law Commissioner (*1836)

First Report of the Commissioners for Administrating Laws for the Relief of the Poor in Ireland (Dublin, 1847-48) to *Twenty-fifth Annual Report of the Poor Law Commissioners (*Dublin, 1872)

Local Government Board Annual Reports

First Annual Report of the Local Government Board for Ireland (Dublin, 1873) to *Eighteenth Annual Report of the Local Government Board of Ireland* (Dublin, 1890)

Reports

Annual report of the Cork Fever Hospital and House of Recovery for the year 1847 (Cork, 1848)

Annual Report of the North Charitable Infirmary of the city of Cork . . . from 5th January 1848 to 5th January 1849 (Cork, 1849)

20th Annual Report of Strand Road Dispensary, for year ending 30 June 1851 (Cork, 1851)

General Valuation of Rateable Property in Ireland. County of Cork, Barony of Cork. Valuation of the several tenements comprising such portion of the Union of Cork as is situated at the Barony above named. [Richard Griffith] (Dublin, 1852)

Amended Report of the Committee appointed to inquire into the internal management of the Cork Workhouse; together with a comparative summary of analysis of medicines, instruments, appliances, etc, included in the list of the Local Government Board. Also, a comparative summary of analysis of medicines, instruments, appliances, etc., not included in the list of the Local Government Board. (Cork, 1884)

Twenty-fourth annual report of the Boarding-out committee of the Cork Board of Guardians on the management of the orphan and deserted children who are boarded out in the rural districts of the Cork Union (Cork, 1886)

Twenty-sixth annual report of the Boarding-out committee, adopted by the Cork Board of Guardians on 4th August 1888 (Cork, 1888)

Newspapers

Cork Constitution
January 1838 to December 1890

Cork Examiner
August 1841 to December 1890

Freeman's Journal
Selected issues

Irish Times
Selected issues

Province of Munster
January to December 1849

Southern Reporter
January 1838 to December 1854
January to December 1859

Contemporary Works

John Arnott, *The investigation into the condition of the children in the Cork Workhouse, with an analysis of the evidence* (Cork, 1859)

B. Banks, *Compendium of the Irish Poor Law: Containing the Acts for the relief of the destitute poor in Ireland, and various statutes connected thereto* (Dublin, 1872)

Terence Brodie, *The Report of Terence Brodie, Esq., M.D., Poor Law Inspector, to the Commissioners for Administering the Laws for the relief of the poor in Ireland, upon an investigation held into the condition of the children in the Cork Workhouse, and the sanitary state of that institution, together with the minutes of evidence taken during said investigation* (Cork, 1859)

Robert F. Clokey, 'Irish emigration from workhouses', in *Journal of the Statistical and Social Inquiry Society of Ireland*, Part XXIV, July 1863, pp. 416-434

Alfred G. Dann, *George Webster, DD, A memoir* (Dublin, 1892)

Susanna R. Day, 'The workhouse child', in *Irish Review*, June 1912, Vol. II, No. 16, pp. 169-79

John Forbes, *Memorandums made in Ireland in the autumn of 1852* (London, 1853)

Rev. C. B. Gibson, *History of the County and City of Cork* (Cork, 1861, 1974 reprint)

W. Neilson Hancock, 'Should Boards of Guardians endeavour to make Pauper labour self-supporting, or should they investigate the causes of pauperism? A paper read before the Statistical section of the British Association, at Ipswich, July 7th, 1851', in *The Transactions of the Dublin Statistical Society*, Vol. 2 (1849-51)

W. Neilson Hancock, 'On the importance of substituting the family system of rearing orphan children for the system now pursued in our workhouses', in, *Journal of the Dublin Statistical Society*, Part XIV (March, 1859), pp. 317-331

John K. Ingram, 'Additional facts and arguments on the Boarding-out of pauper children', in *Journal of the Statistical and Social Inquiry Society of Ireland*, Part XLIX (February, 1876), pp. 503-523

Thomas Aiskew Mooney, Compendium *of the Irish Poor Law (*Dublin, 1887).

Sir George Nicholls, *A history of the Irish Poor Law* (London, 1856, New York, 1967 reprint)

Denis Charles O Connor, *Seventeen years experience of Workhouse life: with suggestions for reforming the Poor Law and its Administration* (Dublin, 1861)

Rev. John O Rourke, *The History of the Great Irish Famine of 1847, with notices of earlier Irish famines* (Dublin, 1875)

William D'Esterre Parker, *The Irish poor law is a national grievance, with suggestions for its amendment* (Cork, 1868)

A.G. Stark, *The south of Ireland in 1850; being the journal of a tour in Leinster and Munster* (Dublin, 1850)

Transactions of the Central Relief Committee of the Society of Friends during the Famine in Ireland in 1846 and 1847 (Dublin, 1852)

J. Windele, *Historical and descriptive notices of the city of Cork and its vicinity; Gougaun-Barra, Glengariff, and Killarney* (Cork, 1846, edition)

Modern Works

Donald H. Akenson, *The Irish Education Experiment, The National system of education in the nineteenth century* (London, 1970)

Ian Anstruther, *The scandal of the Andover workhouse* (Gloucester, 1984 edition)

Sarah Barber, 'Irish migrant agricultural labourers in nineteenth century Lincolnshire', in *Saothar*, Vol.8, 1982, pp.10-23

Jane Barnes, *Irish industrial schools, 1868-1908 origins and developments* (Dublin, 1989)

Andy Bielenberg (ed.), *The Irish Diaspora* (Essex, 2000)

George R. Boyer, *An economic history of the English Poor Law, 1750-1850* (New York, 1990)

Helen Burke, *The People and the Poor Law in nineteenth century Ireland* (West Sussex, 1987)

S. Clark and J. S. Donnelly, Jr., *Irish Peasants* (Manchester, 1983)

L.A. Clarkson and E. Margaret Crawford, *Feast and Famine: Food and Nutrition in Ireland, 1500-1920* (Oxford, 2001)

K. Codell Carter, 'Puerperal Fever', in K.F. Kipple, *Cambridge World History of Human Disease* (Cambridge, 1993), pp. 955-957

John Coolahan, *Irish Education: Its history and structure* (Dublin, 1981)

S. H. Cousens, 'Regional death rates in Ireland during the Great Famine, from 1846-1851', in, *Population Studies*, Vol. XIV, no.1, July 1960, pp. 55-74

Helen I. Cowan, *British Emigration to North America The first hundred years* (Toronto, 1961)

Ross Cranston, *Legal foundations of the welfare state* (London, 1985)

E. Margaret Crawford (ed.), *Famine: The Irish Experience 900-1900; Subsistence Crisis and Famines in Ireland (*Edinburgh, 1989)

E. Margaret Crawford, 'Indian Meal and Pellagra in nineteenth century Ireland', in J.M. Goldstrom and L.A. Clarkson, *Irish Population, Economy and Society. Essays in honour of the late K.H. Connell* (London, 1981), pp. 113-133

E. Margaret Crawford, 'Dearth, Diet and Disease in Ireland 1850; A case study of Nutritional deficiency'; *Medical History*, Vol. 28, No 2. (1984), pp. 151-161

E. Margaret Crawford, 'Scurvy in Ireland during the Great Famine', in *Social History of Medicine*, Vol. 1, No. 3., December 1988 (pp. 281-300)

E. Margaret Crawford, 'Subsistence Crises and Famines in Ireland: A Nutritionist's view', in E Margaret Crawford (ed.), *Famine: The Irish Experience 900-1900; Subsistence Crises and Famines in Ireland* (Edinburgh, 1989) pp. 189-219

E. Margaret Crawford, 'Food and Famine', in Cathal Póirtéir (ed.), *The Great Irish Famine* (Cork, 1995)

E. Margaret Crawford (ed.), *The Hungry Stream, Essays on Emigration and Famine* (Belfast, 1997)

E. Margaret Crawford, 'Migrant Maladies: Unseen Lethal Baggage', in E. Margaret Crawford (ed.), *The Hungry Stream, Essays on Emigration and Famine* (Belfast, 1997) pp. 137-150

E. Margaret Crawford, 'Typhus in nineteenth century Ireland', in E. Malcolm and G. Jones (eds.), *Medicine, Disease and the state in Ireland, 1650-1940* (Cork, 1999), pp. 121-137

Frank Crompton, *Workhouse children* (Gloucestershire, 1997)

Virginia Crossman, The New Ross Workhouse Riot of 1887: Nationalism, Class and the Irish Poor Laws, *Past and Present*, No. 179, May 2003, pp. 135-58

M. A. Crowther, *The Workhouse system 1834-1929: A history of an English Social Institution* (London, 1981)

M. A. Crowther, 'The Tramp', in Roy Porter (ed.), *Myths of the English* (London, 1992), pp. 91-113

Leonore Davidoff, et al, The *family story: Blood, Contract and Intimacy 1830-1960* (London, 1999)

Graham Davis, 'The historiography of the Irish Famine', in P. O Sullivan (ed.), *The meaning of the Famine* (London, 2000), pp. 15-39

Robert Dirks, 'Famine and Disease', in K. F. Kipple (ed.), *The Cambridge World History of Human Disease* (Cambridge, 1993), pp. 157-163

James S. Donnelly, Jr., *The Land and the People of nineteenth century Cork. The rural economy and the land question* (London, 1975)

James S. Donnelly, Jr., 'Famine and government response, 1845-6', in W.E. Vaughan, *A new history of Ireland, Vol. V, Ireland under the Union, I, 1801-70* (Oxford, 1989), pp. 272-285,

James S. Donnelly, Jr., *The Great Irish Potato Famine* (Gloucestershire, 2001)

Francis Duke, 'Pauper education', in D. Fraser (ed.), *The New Poor Law in the nineteenth century* (London, 1976), pp. 67-86

R. Dudley Edwards and T. Desmond Williams, *The Great Famine – Studies in Irish history 1845-52* (New York, 1957, edition).

David Englander, *Poverty and Poor Law Reform in Britain: From Chadwick to Booth, 1834-1914* (Essex, 1998)

William J. Feingold, 'Land League Power: The Tralee Poor Law Election of 1881', in S. Clark and J.S. Donnelly, Jr. (eds.), *Irish Peasants* (Manchester, 1983), pp. 285-310

William L. Feingold, 'The Tenants' movement to capture the Irish Poor Law Boards. 1877-1886', in Alan O Day (ed.), *Reactions to Irish Nationalism* (Dublin, 1987), pp. 79-94.

Valerie Fildes, *Wet Nursing: A History from antiquity to the present* (London, 1988)

Valerie Fildes, Lara Marks and Hilary Marland, *Women and children first* (London, 1992)

Frances Finnegan, *Poverty and prejudice – A study of Irish immigrants in York, 1840 -75* (Cork, 1992)

David Fitzpatrick, 'The settlers: Immigration from Ireland in the nineteenth century', in Colm Kiernan (ed.), *Ireland and Australia* (Cork, 1984), pp. 23-33.

David Fitzpatrick, "A peculiar tramping people': The Irish in Britain, 1801-70', in W. E. Vaughan, *A New history of Ireland, Vol. V. Ireland under the Union, I, 1801-70* (Oxford, 1989), pp. 623-660.

Derek Fraser (ed.), *The New Poor Law in the nineteenth century* (London, 1976)

Roger K. French, 'Scrofula (Scrophula)', in K.F. Kipple, *The Cambridge World History of Human Disease* (Cambridge, 1993), pp. 998-1000

Edward Garner, *To die by inches; the Famine in North East Cork* (Fermoy, 1986)

Laurence M. Geary, 'Famine, Fever and the Bloody Flux', in C. Póirtéir (ed.), *The Great Irish Famine* (Cork, 1995), pp. 74-85

Laurence M. Geary, "The late Disastrous Epidemic'; Medical Relief and the Great Famine', in C. Morash and R. Hayes, *'Fearful Realities': New Perspectives on the Famine* (Dublin, 1996), pp. 49-59

Laurence M. Geary, 'What people died of during the Famine', in Cormac Ó Gráda (ed.), *Famine 150, Commemorative Lecture Series* (Dublin, 1997), pp 95-112

Laurence M. Geary, '"The whole country was in motion": Mendicancy and vagrancy in pre-Famine Ireland', in Jacqueline Hill and Colm Lennon (eds.), *Luxury and Austerity: Historical Studies XXI* (Dublin, 1999), pp. 121-136

Laurence M. Geary, *Medicine and Charity in Ireland 1718-1851* (Dublin, 2004).

J. M. Goldstrom and L. A. Clarkson, *Irish population, Economy and Society. Essays in honour of the late K. H. Connell* (London, 1981)

Janice Gothard, "Pity the poor immigrant': Assisted single female migration to Colonial Australia', in E. Richards (Ed.), *Poor Australian immigrants in the nineteenth century: Visible Immigrants: Two* (Canberra, 1991), pp.97-116

Peter Gray, *Famine, Land and Politics. British Government and Irish Society 1843-50* (Dublin, 1999)

Pauline Gregg, *A social and economic history of Britain; 1760-1972* (London, 1973)

Robin Haines, 'Indigent Misfits or shrewd operators? Government-assisted emigrants from the United Kingdom to Australia, 1831-1860', in *Population Studies*, Vol. XLVIII (1994), pp. 223-247

A. James Hammerton, *Emigrant Gentlewomen – Genteel poverty and female emigration 1830-1914* (London, 1979)

Victoria A.. Harden, 'Typhus, Epidemic', in K. F. Kipple (ed.), *The Cambridge World History of Human Disease* (Cambridge, 1993), pp. 1080-84

Daniel Hegarty and Brian Hickey, 'The Famine Graveyard on Carr's Hill near Cork', in *Journal of the Cork Historical and Archaeological Society*, Vol. 101 (1996), pp.9-14

Ursula R. Q. Henriques, *Before the Welfare State: Social administration in early industrial Britain* (London, 1978)

Jacqueline Hill and Colm Lennon (Eds.) *Luxury and Austerity, Historical Studies XXI* (Dublin, 1999)

Cecil J. Houston and William J. Smyth, *Irish Emigration and Canadian settlement: Patterns, links and letters* (Toronto, 1990).

Felicity Hunt (ed.), *Lessons for life: The schooling of girls and women, 1850-1950* (Oxford, 1987)

John Archer Jackson, *The Irish in Britain* (London, 1963)

Jack Johnson (ed.), *Workhouses of the North West* (1996)

Stanley C. Johnson, *A history of emigration from the United Kingdom to North America 1763-1912* (1913, London; 1966, edition)

Mary C. Karasch, 'Ophthalmia (Conjunctivitis and Trachoma)', in K.F. Kipple (ed.), *Cambridge World History of Human Disease* (Cambridge, 1993), pp. 897-906

Liam Kennedy, et al, *Mapping the Great Irish Famine: A survey of the Famine Decades* (Dublin, 1999)

Christine Kinealy, *This Great Calamity – The Irish Famine 1845-52* (Dublin, 1994)

Christine Kinealy, 'The role of the Poor Law during the Famine', in C. Póirtéir (ed.), *The Great Irish Famine* (Cork, 1995), pp. 104-122

Christine Kinealy, *Death Dealing Famine: The Great Hunger in Ireland* (Chicago, 1997)

Norma Landau, 'The Laws of Settlement and the surveillance of immigration in Eighteenth-century Kent', *Continuity and Change*, 3 (3) (1988), pp.391-420

Norma Landau, 'The eighteenth-century context of the laws of settlement', *Continuity and Change*, 6 (3) (1991), pp. 417-439

Keith Laybourn, *The evolution of the British Social Policy and the Welfare State* (Staffordshire, 1995)

Lynn Hollen Lees, *The Solidarities of strangers – The English Poor Laws and the People 1700-1948* (London, 1998)

Norman Longmate, *The Workhouse* (London, 1974)

Irvine Loudon, 'Some international features of maternal mortality, 1800-1950', in Valerie Fildes, Lara Marks and Hilary Marland, *Women and children first* (London, 1992), pp. 5-28

Maria Luddy, '"Angels of Mercy": nuns as workhouse nurses, 1861-1898', in Elizabeth Malcolm and Greta Jones, *Medicine, Disease and the state in Ireland, 1650-1940* (Cork, 1999), pp. 102-117.

Sir William P. MacArthur, M.D., DSC, FRCP, 'Medical history of the Famine', in R. Dudley Edwards and T. Desmond Williams (eds.), *The Great Famine – Studies in Irish History 1845-52* (New York), 1957, pp. 261-315

C.J.F. MacCarthy, "The Angelic Doctor", Denis Charles O Connor, M.D., L.L,D., 1807-1888, in *Bandon Historical Journal*, No. 9, 1993, pp. 24-28

Oliver MacDonagh, Early Victorian Government 1830-1870 (London, 1977)

Trevor McClaughlin, *Barefoot and Pregnant? Irish famine orphans in Australia* (Melbourne, 1991)

Donal P. McCracken, 'Odd Man Out: The South African Experience', in Andy Bielenberg (ed.), *The Irish Diaspora* (Essex, 2000), pp. 251-271

Helen J. MacDonald, 'Boarding-out and the Scottish Poor Law, 1845 –1914', in *Scottish Historical Review*, Volume LXXV, 2; No. 200, October 1996, pp. 197 -220

Dympna McLoughlin, 'Superfluous and unwanted deadweight: the emigration of nineteenth-century Irish pauper women', in P. O Sullivan (ed.), *Irish women and Irish migration* (London, 1995), pp. 66-88

Elizabeth Malcolm and Greta Jones (eds.), *Medicine, Disease and the state in Ireland, 1650-1940* (Cork, 1999)

Lara Marks, 'Medical care for pauper mothers and their infants: Poor Law provision and local demand in East London, 1870-1929', in, *Economic History Review*, XLVI, 3 (1993), pp. 518-542

Joel Mokyr and Cormac Ó Gráda, 'What do people die of during famines: The Great Irish Famine in comparative perspective', in *European Review of Economic History*, Vol. 6 (2002), pp. 339-363.

W.J. Mommsen (ed.), *The emergence of the Welfare State in Britain and Germany* (London, 1981)

Gerard Moran, "Shovelling out the poor': assisted emigration from Ireland from the great Famine to the fall of Parnell', in Patrick J. Duffy (ed.), *To and from Ireland: Planned Migration Schemes c. 1600-2000* (Dublin, 2004), pp. 137-54.

Chris Morash and Richard Hayes (eds.), *'Fearful Realities': New Perspectives on the Famine* (Dublin, 1996)

Kathryn Morrison, *The Workhouse: A study of Poor-Law Buildings in England* (Swindon, 1999)

John A. Murphy, *A history of Queen's College / University College Cork, 1845-1995* (Cork, 1995)

Frank Neal, 'Lancashire, the Famine Irish and the poor laws: A study in crisis management', in *Irish Historical Studies* (1995), Vol. XXII, pp. 26-48

Frank Neal, *Black '47: Britain and the Famine Irish* (London, 1998)

John O Brien and Pauric Travers (eds.), The *Irish Emigrant experience in Australia* (Dublin, 1991)

Gerard O Brien, 'The Establishment of Poor Law Unions in Ireland, 1838-43', in *Irish Historical Studies*, Vol., XXIII, No. 90 (November, 1982), pp. 97-120

Gerard O Brien, 'The new poor law in pre-Famine Ireland: A Case study', in *Irish Economic and Social History*, Vol. XII (1985), pp. 33-49

Gerard O Brien, Workhouse Management in pre-famine Ireland, *Proceedings of the Royal Irish Academy*, Vol. 86c. (1986), pp. 113-134

Seamus Ô Cinneide, 'The development of the Home Assistance Service', in *Administration*, Autumn 1969, Vol. 17, No. 3, pp. 284-308

Alan O Day, Reactions *to Irish Nationalism*, (Dublin, 1987)

Cormac Ó Gráda, *Black '47 and beyond, The Great Irish Famine in history, economy and memory* (New Jersey, 1999)

Colman O Mahony, *In the shadows: life in Cork 1750-1930* (Cork, 1997)

Michelle O Mahony, *Famine in Cork city* (Cork, 2005)

Thomas P. O Neill, 'The organisation and Administration of Relief – 1845-1852', in R. Dudley Edwards and T. Desmond Williams (Ed.), *The Great Famine – Studies in Irish History 1845-52* (New York, 1957), pp. 207-260

Patrick O Sullivan (ed.), *The Irish world wide: History, Heritage, Identity (Volume 2), The Irish in the new communities* (London, 1992)

Patrick O Sullivan (ed.), *The Irish world wide: History, Heritage, Identity (Volume 4), Irish women and Irish migration* (London, 1995)

Patrick O Sullivan (ed.), *The Irish world wide: History, Heritage, Identity (Volume 6), The meaning of the Famine* (London, 2000)

Katherine Ott, *Fevered Lives: Tuberculosis in American culture since 1870* (London, 1996)

Cathal Póirtéir (ed.), *The Great Irish Famine* (Cork, 1995)

Roy Porter (ed.), *Myths of the English* (London, 1992)

Margaret H. Preston, 'Lay women and philanthropy in Dublin, 1860-1880', in *Éire-Ireland*, XXVIII: 4, Winter, 1993, pp. 74-85

Eric Richards (Ed.), *Poor Australian immigrants in the nineteenth century: Visible Immigrants: Two* (Canberra, 1991)

Eric Richards, 'The importance of being Irish in Colonial South Australia', in John O Brien and Pauric Travers (eds.), *The Irish Emigrant Experience in Australia* (Dublin, 1991), pp. 62-105.

Eric Richards, 'How did poor people emigrate from the British Isles to Australia in the nineteenth century', in *Journal of British Studies*, 33 (July, 1993), pp. 250-279

Joseph Robins, *The Lost children A study of charity children in Ireland 1700-1900* (Dublin, 1981)

Joseph Robins, 'The emigration of Irish workhouse children to Australia in the 19th century', in John O Brien and Pauric Travers (eds.), The *Irish Emigrant experience in Australia* (Dublin, 1991), pp. 29-45

David Roberts, 'How cruel was the Victorian Poor Law?', in *Historical Journal*, 1963, pp. 97-107

Michael E. Rose, 'Settlement, Removal and the New Poor Law', in D. Fraser (ed.), *The New Poor Law in the nineteenth century* (London, 1976), pp. 25-44

M. E. Rose, 'The crisis of Poor Relief in England, 1860-1890', in W. J. Mommsen (ed.), *The emergence of the Welfare State in Britain and Germany* (London, 1981)

F. B. Smith, *The retreat of tuberculosis 1850-1950* (London, 1988)

K.D.M. Snell, 'Pauper settlement and the rights of poor relief in England and Wales', in *Continuity and Change*, 6 (3), 1991, pp. 375-415

K.D.M. Snell, 'Settlement, Poor Law and the Rural Historian: New Approaches and Opportunities', in *Rural History*, 3 (2), 1992, pp. 145-172

Roger Swift and Sheridan Gilley, *The Irish in Britain 1815-1939* (London, 1989)

Roger Swift, 'The historiography of the Irish in nineteenth century Britain', in P. O Sullivan, Ed., *The Irish world wide History, Heritage, Identity, Volume 2, The Irish in the new communities* (London, 1992), pp. 52-81

K.P.T. Tankard, '*Drama and Disappointment: The Lady Kennaway Girls*', in *South African-Irish Studies*, No. 2 (1992), pp. 278-86

James Stephen Taylor, 'A different kind of Speenhamland: non resident Relief in the Industrial Revolution', in *Journal of British Studies*, Volume, 30, No. 1 (April, 1991), pp. 183-208

James Stephen Taylor, 'The impact of pauper settlement 1691-1834', in *Past and Present*, No. 73 (November, 1976), pp. 42-74

Annmarie Turnbull, 'Learning Her Womanly Work: the Elementary School Curriculum, 1870-1914', in Felicity Hunt (ed.), *Lessons for Life The schooling of girls and women, 1850-1950* (Oxford, 1987), pp. 83-100

E.S. Turner, *What the butler saw, Two hundred and fifty years of the servant problem* (London, 2001 edition)

W.E. Vaughan (Ed.), *A New history of Ireland. (Vol. 5), Ireland under the Union, I. 1801-70* (London, 1989)

David Wardle, *English popular education, 1780-1975* (London, 1976)

Jeffrey G. Williamson, 'The impact of the Irish on British labour markets during the industrial revolution', in R. Swift and S. Gilley, *The Irish in Britain 1815 -1939* (London, 1989), pp. 134-162

Cecil Woodham Smith, *The Great Hunger: Ireland 1845-9* (London, 1962)

Works of Reference

Kenneth F. Kipple (ed.), *The Cambridge World History of Human Disease* (Cambridge, 1993)

Melloni's Illustrated Medical Dictionary, 3rd, Edition (New York, 1994)

New Encyclopaedia Britannica, 15th. Edition (Chicago, 1989)

Theses

Catherine Mary (Kate) Cotter, *'From Pauperism to Prosperity': the Poor Law Union of Midleton during the Great Famine* (M.Phil., thesis, N.U.I. Cork, May,1999)

Patricia Kelly, *From workhouse to hospital – The role of the Irish workhouse in medical relief to 1921.* (M.A. thesis, An Coláiste Ollscoile, Gaillimh, Autumn, 1972)

Anne M. Lanigan, *The Poor Law children of county Tipperary and their education 1840-1880* (M. Ed. thesis, UCC, 1988)

Gerard O Brien, *The Administration of the Poor Law in Ireland* (MA thesis, UCC, 1980)

Colman O Mahony, *Workhouse relief in Cork 1838-1888* (PhD. Thesis, UCC, 2003)

Michelle O Mahony, *The impact of the Great Famine on Cork Union Workhouse* (M. Phil., thesis, N.U.I., Cork, 2000)

Index

Admissions xv, 5, 7, 8, 35, 38, 39, 56, 60, 126, 166, 167, 183, 210

M. Ahern 285, 286, 287, 288, 289

Alcohol 199, 222, 223, 224, 225, 226, 227, 228, 229, 230

Apprentices 110, 112, 130-35

Sir J. Arnott 137, 185, 186, 188, 189, 190, 259, 297, 308

Attitude of guardians 293-4

E. Bailey 17

Bakery 22, 40-1, 58, 147, 149, 156

Bandon 41, 53, 60fn, 80

Bankwood 130

Barrack Street hospital 42, 53, 59, 61, 62, 63, 66

D. Barry 4

T. Barry 279

S. Bartrett 253

Basement 170, 211, 219-20

W. Beamish 59

Bed linen 152, 153-4

Beds 5-6, 11, 12, 31, 42, 42, 55, 175, 198, 212, 213, 219, 220, 226, 249, 260, 295

Beggars 7, 42fn,

Belfast 75, 90, 223

Benevolent Apprentices Society 133-4, 144

W. Berwick 105

J. Besnard 242

Birmingham 88, 89

Blind Asylum 31-2, 61 212

Boarding out, see nursing out

Bodies of deceased 8, 216

L. Branigan 256

Bread 22, 40, 43, 46, 50, 58, 64, 156, 174, 175-6

Breakfast for non-inmates 35-6, 37

Bristol 75, 76, 89

Captain Brandling 102

A. Brodie 280

Dr Brodie 188, 189, 190

Captain Broughton 69

Dr D.B. Bullen 3, 59

D. Burchill 280

Burials 9, 66, 67-71, 72

Asst. Comm. J. Burke 28, 32, 55, 56, 68

Col. J. Burke 2

J. Byrne 163

D. Cagney 2

Dr R. Callaghan 201fn

Dr A. Callanan 186, 187

J. Cantillon 3

Capstan mill 145, 146, 148, 149, 154, 156-60

C. Carr 78

G. Carr 13, 60, 68, 70, 71, 85, 86, 146

Carr's Hill 69, 70, 71, 216, 218fn

C. Castles 14

Catechism 273-4

Catalepsy 218-9

Cat Fort 61, 62

Cherry children 253

Children and work 150-1, 157, 158, 159

Cholera 63, 64-7, 202fn

Christmas dinner 20, 41fn

Classification 3, 6, 10, 13, 14, 175

Rev. H. Clifford 100

Conditions 18, 20, 21, 231

J. Condon 277, 278

Corn Exchange 60, 65fn

Corporal punishment 99

Costs 18, 19, 22, 29, 41, 44, 45, 50, 226

W. Cottress 2

W. Coughlan 111

Country paupers 61-2, 64

County gaol 156, 159

J. Crawford 2

W. Crawford 2, 3

A. Crean 112

Dr P.J. Cremen 218, 228, 231

J. Crofts 14

Dr Cronin 213

B. Cross 129

M. Crowley 15
Dr Cummins 215
Cutlery 184

Deaths 54, 56, 62, 64, 65, 66, 67-71, 196
Diet 17-18, 19, 20, 21, 22, 23, 28, 30, 41,
    44-51, 158, 174, 175, 176, 178,
    184-5, 186-7, 188, 189, 190, 224,
    295
B. Dillon 91
Domestic service 115
J. Donaghy 107, 111
E. Donovan 274-5
R. Dowden 32, 60, 154, 239, 240
Douglas Street store 65, 66
Drawing classes, 114, 120, 121
– Drew 123, 128
Drunk patients 225, 226
Dublin 75, 78, 83, 89, 90
P.F. Dunn 287, 288
N. Dunscombe 141, 228, 297
J. Duross 85, 86, 87
Dysentery 62, 63

Education, 98-121, 294
M. Egan 161-3
Eggs 224, 225, 226
Elections 2, 22-3, 25, 283, 285, 289
Elizabeth Fort 53
Emigration XII, 121, 236-47, 257
Expelling paupers 38, 39

W. Fagan 2, 23, 32, 56, 57
Farm work 100, 107, 108, 112, 121, 123,
    125, 126, 127, 128-9, 132
Fever 51, 52, 53, 55, 59, 60, 61, 62 63,
    196
Fever hospital 31, 33, 34, 43, 53, 59, 61,
    198-9, 200-1, 226, 229
G. Fitzgerald 164-5
W. Fitzgerald 90, 92
Flogging 111
Dr J. Forbes 178fn
J.S Foster 146fn, 147, 148, 174
Footwear 154, 179-80, 189
J. Frost 83, 84, 89, 90, 91, 92

T. Gallwey 287, 288
W.S. Gardiner 4
M. Gates 164-5
Sr. M.A. Goodwin 203
Graveyard 68-71, 72
Greer 14, 46, 69

Inspector Hall 108, 183

Harvest workers 76, 77
F. Hennis 123, 128, 180, 183
M. Holland 275, 276
House of Industry 3, 5, 7, 18, 31, 39
Hospital XIII, 41, 45, 174, 175, 176, 177,
    183, 187, 192, 193, 195, 196,
    197-202, 205, 206, 207, 208, 210,
    211, 212-15, 218, 282
C. Horgan 4, 13
Hospital uniform 197

Industrial training 100, 107, 145
Industry 12, 145, 146, 147-52, 154-6
Inspection of workhouse 185, 186
Irremovability 82, 86, 88, 89, 93, 94, 95,
    96

A. Jackson 276-7
Dr A. Jacob 176
R.L. Jameson 85, 275, 279
T. Jennings 39, 60
I. Julian 137, 138, 223, 224, 225, 226,
    227, 228, 267, 279, 297
Sr. C.A. Jump 203
Jupiter 79, 80

J. Kavenagh 102, 103, 105
Kindergarten 121
Dr C. King 252
Kinsale 41

Ladies Visiting Committee 135, 138,
    139, 140, 141, 142, 144
S. Lane 2, 3
G. Laurance 43, 59
Leeches 215, 223fn
Local Government Board 266, 268,
    269, 270, 284, 287, 288, 289,
    290, 291
Lock Ward 16, 202, 203, 214, 228, 253,
    279
London 76, 77, 78, 79, 80, 81, 82, 83, 84,
    85, 87, 89, 90, 91, 92, 135
Lunatics 31, 211, 231-5
Lying-in ward 280
M. Lynch 162-3
T. Lyons 2, 62, 138, 260, 262

J. Mac Manus 91
Sir W. P. McArthur 52
Dr McCabe 116
F.McCormack 111
J.E. McCarthy 2
Rev. McSweeney 30
P. McSwiney 2, 102

Dr R.C. Madras 250
Fr. A Maguire 52, 60
J.F. Maguire 85, 128, 139, 199, 259, 297
N. Mahony 129, 136, 137, 138, 227, 229, 277, 297
Manchester 77, 130
Marriages 14-15
Captain. W. Martin 124, 174
Marquis of Downshire, 10, 11, 23
Mary Street 140, 141, 142, 143
Fr T. Mathew 9, 41, 53, 61, 68
Dr H. Maunsell 42fn, 58fn
Mayor of Cork 10, 23, 33, 57, 65, 83
Measles 178, 202
Medical students 217, 218
Middlesex 76, 78, 83, 89
Migration 73, 74, 126
Morgan family 215
T. Moore 161-4
M. Mulqueeny 242, 243
Music classes 120, 121

Nailers 150
Naval training 123, 124
Navy 123-5, 132
Net making 105
M. Newton 256
North Infirmary 59, 61, 62, 198, 260
Nuns 203, 204, 231
Nursery 55, 65, 190-1, 193, 194, 212, 231, 232, 251, 281
Nurses 11, 32, 46, 49, 66, 174, 175, 193, 194, 196-7, 199, 203-4, 206, 208, 214, 215, 230, 232, 233, 247, 248, 249, 251, 252, 278, 282
Nursing out 193-4, 247-58, 262, 276
Nursing out committee 256, 257, 295

Operating theatre 214-5
J. O Connell 212-3
C. O Connor 249, 250
Dr D.C. O Connor XV, 4, 8, 13, 19, 28, 31, 33, 38, 43, 45, 51fn, 53, 54, 5, 56, 57, 59, 64, 133, 135, 159, 174, 178, 188, 297-8
Dr G.P. O Farrell 221-2
G. O Neill 238, 240, 242
Ophthalmia 176, 177, 178fn, 196, 221-2
R.J. O Shaughnessy 60, 85, 86, 91, 92
C.P. O Sullivan 267
J.O Sullivan 218-9
Outdoor relief, 35, 36, 37, 65, 71, 72, 212, 258-71, 295
Overcrowding 31, 32, 38, 42, 43, 44, 51, 52, 55, 58, 175, 183, 195, 198, 202-3, 211, 213, 214, 219-20, 231, 232, 233, 234, 235, 250fn

Panama 241fn
Wm. D'Esterre Parker 120, 193, 194, 235, 252, 259, 298
Dr D. Phelan 42fn, 65
J. Phillips 91, 92
Phrenology 130
Wm. Pitt 282
Politics 23-4, 272-5, 283-92
Poor Law Commissioners XII, 1, 3, 12, 13fn, 21, 31, 32, 36, 38, 39, 40, 47, 51, 65, 70, 78, 81, 93, 102, 105, 105, 107, 108, 110, 115, 120, 126, 127, 132, 140, 237, 238, 239, 245, 248, 249, 250, 265, 274, 275, 276, 277, 282
Dr J. Popham 32, 45, 54, 55, 66, 188, 201, 279, 298
Puerperal fever 190
Porridge 19, 22, 23, 45, 46, 48
Post mortems 217
Potatoes 27-8, 29, 30
Prostitutes 6-7, 8, 10, 13, 16, 48, 161, 214, 241, 248, 279
Punishment 15, 16, 17, 104, 111, 112, 158-9, 181-2

Queen's College 217

J. Rankley 87, 88
Ratepayers 19, 20, 36, 44, 113, 120, 152, 154, 171, 226, 227, 228
Recruiting 169
Relief depots 41
Relieving officers 248, 263, 264, 265, 267, 268, 270
Religion 14, 98, 249, 272-83
Removal XIII, 73, 74, 75, 76, 77, 78, 79, 80, 81, 82, 83, 85, 86, 87, 88, 90, 91, 92, 93, 94, 95, 96, 97
Results fees 118, 119
Ringworm 196
Riot 9, 16, 17, 20, 47
Robinson family 280

St. Finbarr's Hospital 296
St. John's graveyard 68
St. Joseph's graveyard 9
St. Patrick's Orphan Asylum 61
Salaries 99, 101
Dr A. Sandford 221
Captain Sarsfield 281, 285, 286, 298

T.R. Sarsfield 29, 35, 44, 45, 51, 60, 128, 223, 240, 272, 273, 298
Scarlatina 198, 202, 206
School 43, 98-121, 170, 232, 233
School conditions 102, 103, 104, 105, 106, 107, 108, 109, 113, 115, 116
School monitors 103, 104, 107, 110
Scrofula 186, 187, 188, 196
Settlement 73, 74, 75, 77, 78, 81, 82, 86, 88, 95, 97
Sewage 4, 10, 58, 170, 180-1, 211
W.J. Shaw 137, 138
Sheds 40, 43, 51, 53, 61, 71, 206, 207
Rev. G. Sheehan 4, 6, 13, 14, 100, 298
Shoemaking 146, 151, 152
Sick Poor Society 266
Sisters of Mercy 202, 203, 208, 281
Smallpox 63, 95, 191-2, 198, 205-10
Society of St. Vincent de Paul 266, 269
Solitary confinement 15, 16
Soup kitchens 57
Soup recipe 41
South Dublin Union 130, 229fn
South Infirmary 3, 199
'Spike' ward 220
Spinning 147, 148, 151
R. Star 153
R. Steele 163
Dr R. Stephens 54, 55, 56
Stone breaking 34, 102, 146, 152, 167, 168, 170
W.K. Sullivan 218
Surgery 215
J. Sweeny 276, 277

Dr C. Tanner 286, 288, 289, 290, 298
Tea 227, 228
Teachers 98, 99, 100, 101, 102, 128
Teachers duties 99, 101, 102, 104, 106
Tipperary 83, 100, 101, 125, 157, 176
Toilets 211, 214
Surgeon Townsend 63, 66
Dr Wm. Townsend 188, 217, 298
Training 12, 13, 100, 101, 111, 114-5, 116, 117, 118, 119, 120, 121, 132, 134, 135, 136, 137, 151, 155fn, 156

Training Home 139-43
Tramps 167-8, 169, 220
Transferring paupers 39-40
Transporting 75, 78

– Uniacke 51

Vaccination 207
Vagrants 75, 76
Venereal disease 184
Ventilation 56
Wm. Voules 18, 19, 21, 22

Dr J. Wall 215, 227, 281, 299
Dr T. Wall 217, 227, 299
E. Walsh 102, 103, 299
M. Walsh 249, 250
Washing 177, 182
Washing clothing 52, 62
Water font 279
Water pumping 181-2
Water supply 4, 177, 181, 214, 230, 231
Weaving 146, 147, 152, 160fn
Rev. W. Webster 215, 216, 249, 280, 281, 299
Wet nurses 193-4, 251, 252
Dr J.R. Wherland 224, 225, 226
Sir Wm. Wilde 176
Wine 44, 49, 57
R. Wiseman 166-7, 259
T. Wiseman 128, 129, 239, 240
E. Woodlock, 137fn
Wool production 146, 147-8
Work activities XIV, 10, 11, 12, 13, 136, 167, 168, 169, 170
Workhouse, as threat to trades 149-50
Workhouse closure 53, 72
Workhouse clothing 5
Workhouse rules 15, 98, 99, 164, 175
Workhouse site 3, 4
Workhouse test 36, 150, 160, 167, 260
Workhouse Visiting Society 135
Dr Wycherly 66

Xerophthalmia 177, 196

H.L. Young 285, 288, 299

THE CORK HOUSE OF INDUSTRY IN THE EARLY YEARS OF
THE NINETEENTH CENTURY
From: Will West, *Cork Directory* (Cork, 1810), p. 62

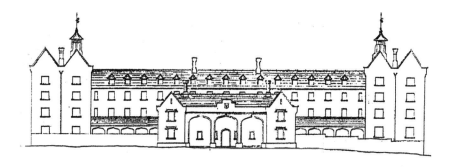

ARCHITECT GEORGE WILKINSON'S DRAWING OF
CORK WORKHOUSE IN 1844
From: PP 1844, Vol. XXX [568], *Appendix to the report of the Commission appointed to
inquire into the execution of the contracts for certain Union workhouses in Ireland,*
facing page 53.

THE CAPSTAN MILL IN THE CORK WORKHOUSE IN THE LATE 1840s

From: NAI, Poor Law Commissioners, Letters to James Burke, 1848 – Letter from the Hive Iron Works, Cork, of 22 December 1848 enclosing an illustration entitled 'Registered Capstan Mill, Hive Iron Works, Cork'.

STREET BEGGARS IN CORK IN THE EARLY 1840s
From: Mr and Mrs S.C. Hall, *Ireland, its scenery and character*
(London, 1841), Vol. 1, p. 7

DISTRIBUTION OF INDIAN CORN AT THE GOVERNMENT'S
CORK STORE IN APRIL 1846
From: *Illustrated London News* 4 April 1846

'INTERIOR OF A PEASANT'S HUT' AT THE TIME OF THE FAMINE
From: Robert Wilson, *The life and times of Queen Victoria* (London, 1887),
Vol. 1, p. 276

JACK MURPHY, A LUNATIC PAUPER IN THE
CORK WORKHOUSE IN 1850

'Jack is clad in the garb of the house – viz., grey frieze, with a white stripe that proclaims its origin, should it be presented for sale at the shops of the pawnbrokers. Cracked as he is, he has a hale and hearty look, and is not a little proud evidently of the iron-grey ringlets that adorn each cheek, and which have been spared to him by the usually merciless shears of Denis Driscoll, the barber . . '.

From: A.G. Stark *The stranger in Ireland in 1850, being a journal of a tour in Leinster and Munster* (Dublin, 1850), p. 103

JEREMIAH SULLIVAN, A PATIENT SUFFERING FROM 'MORBID
SOMNOLENCE', IN THE CORK WORKHOUSE HOSPITAL DURING 1885

Various tests and experiments were conducted on the unfortunate man. In this illustration he is
positioned between two chairs 'the tip of the shoulder resting on one chair, the heel of the left foot on
the other, and the right limb bent at a right angle to the trunk, a weight of forty pounds was supported on
the rigid chest, without causing the slightest yielding or movement from the position described until
muscular relaxation took place. He remained in this cataleptic state often for four or five days at a
time, sometimes even for a longer period; and the only method which would effectually arouse him to
consciousness was a strong current from a magnetic-electric machine, which made him start up, crying
out lustily; but, if this were not kept up for a time, he often sank back again into the somnolent state'.

From: Case of 'Morbid Somnolence', by Dr P.J. Cremen, in *British Medical Journal*, 12 December 1885,
P. 1105

Dr CHARLES TANNER MP THE CORK
UNION POOR LAW GUARDIAN
From:, *Cork Examiner* 23 April 1901

REV. GEORGE WEBSTER,
PROTESTANT CHAPLAIN OF
CORK WORKHOUSE
From: Alfred G. Dann, *George Webster,
D.D. A memoir* (Dublin, 1892),
frontispiece

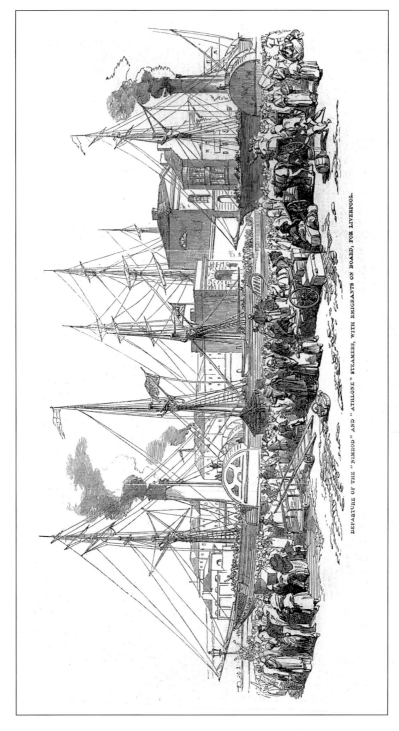

DEPARTURE OF THE "NIMROD" AND "ATHLONE" STEAMERS, WITH EMIGRANTS ON BOARD, FOR LIVERPOOL.

EMIGRANT STEAMERS AT CORK IN 1851
From: *Illustrated London News*, 10 May 1851

CONDITIONS IN A BEDROOM OF A CORK TENEMENT IN THE EARLY
YEARS OF THE TWENTIETH CENTURY (From: Author's collection)

SIR JOHN ARNOTT
From: M.J.F. McCarthy, *Five years
in Ireland, 1895–1900* (London,
1901), facing page 113

OLD ENTRANCE GATE TO CARR'S HILL
GRAVEYARD (From: Author's collection)

LANES IN CORK CITY AT THE BEGINNING OF THE TWENTIETH CENTURY
These were typical of the areas from which many inmates came to the workhouse.
(From: Author's collection)